Fr. Patrick J. Turohy, S.J.
St. Michael Mission
Including, WA 99138

The Writer and
the Shaman

———◆◆———

*A Morphology of
the American Indian*

The Writer and the Shaman

———•❖•———

A Morphology of the American Indian

———•❖•———

ELÉMIRE ZOLLA

Translated by Raymond Rosenthal

A Helen and Kurt Wolff Book

Harcourt Brace Jovanovich, Inc.

New York

Permission to reprint poetry excerpts has been obtained from the follow-
ing. E. P. Dutton & Co., Inc: from *Dawn Boy* by Eda Lou Walton,
Copyright 1926 by E. P. Dutton & Co., Inc. Liveright Publishing Corp-
oration: from "The Bridge" and "The Dance" by Hart Crane in *The
Collected Poems and Selected Letters and Prose of Hart Crane*, Copyright
© 1933, 1958, 1966 by Liveright Publishing Corporation. Doubleday &
Company, Inc.: "I see a star" and "To the East" by Alonzo Lopez, from
The Whispering Wind, edited by Terry Allen, Copyright © 1972 by The
Institute of American Indian Arts. Allen Katzman: "Comanche Cantos,"
from *The Immaculate*, published by Doubleday & Company, Inc., 1970.
The Smithsonian Institution Bureau of American Ethnology: poems used
and translated by Frances Densmore in her collection of Indian poems
and songs. The Institute of American Indian Arts, Bureau of Indian
Affairs, Santa Fe, N. M., and the following authors, whose poems were
written there as students: Phil George, "Old Man, the Sweat Lodge";
Agnes Pratt, "Ebullient sun" and "Rebel"; Marie Jacob, "Rival of Voices";
Julie Wilson, "I traveled to the west."

Library of Congress Cataloging in Publication Data

Zolla, Elémire.
    The writer and the shaman.

    Translation of I letterati e lo sciamano.
    "A Helen and Kurt Wolff book."
    Includes bibliographical references.
    1.   American literature—History and criticism.
2. Indians in literature.   I. Title.
PS173.I6Z613   810'.9'352   73–6632
ISBN 0–15–199560–5

First edition
B C D E

Contents

IV The Enlightenment and the Indians   61

The New Progressivism · William Robertson, Baron de
Lahontan and Lafitau · George Berkeley · John Arch-
dale, William Byrd, John Lawson · Robert Beverley,
John and William Bartram · Benjamin Franklin · Cad-
wallader Colden, Hugh Henry Brackenridge, James Madi-
son, Philip Freneau · Thomas Jefferson · John Adams
· William Gilmore Simms and the Enlightenment of the
South.

V Enlightenment Zealots and Romantics   86

Sarah Wentworth Morton, James Fenimore Cooper ·
James Wallis Eastburn and Robert Charles Sands, George
Catlin, William Cullen Bryant · Washington Irving ·
Captain Bonneville · The Idea of a Half-Breed Nation
· Joaquin Miller.

VI The Tradition of Benevolence from the
Seventeenth to the Nineteenth Century   105

The Extremists of the Reformation · Roger Williams ·
William Penn, Francis Daniel Pastorius, John Heckewelder,
John Woolman, Jonathan Dickinson · James Kirke Paulding, Thomas C. Battey · George Bancroft · John Greenleaf Whittier · Henry Wadsworth Longfellow · Henry
Thoreau · Herman Melville · Henry Adams · Hamlin Garland.

VII The Tradition of Progressivist Hatred
in the Nineteenth Century   134

Charles Brockden Brown · Robert Bird, Edgar Allan Poe
· Henry Marie Brackenridge, Pierre-Jean de Smet, John
James Audubon · Ralph Waldo Emerson · Francis
Parkman · Henry James · Mark Twain · Elizabeth
Madox Roberts · The Western.

Leggings and John Joseph Mathews · Don C. Talayesva
· John G. Neihardt · Black Elk · Joseph Epes Brown
and Black Elk, Hosteen Klah, N. Scott Momaday.

The Writer and the Shaman

A Morphology of
the American Indian

Introduction

————————•••————————

The history of the many images of the Indian that appear in the course of American literature sets a whole series of works and authors in an unusual, revelatory perspective. It is also extremely instructive, for it shows us the (quite simple) stylistic means by which a program of genocide can be facilitated. It also shows us that the chief culprit, the actual agent of the slaughter, was the idea of progress, which by its very nature demands the elimination of everything that it decrees old, obsolete, out-of-date and nostalgic, while at the same time it represses the love, so congenial to man, of that delicate, wise patina that time deposits on the things of this world.

After having successfully completed his obligatory instruction, the votary of progress gains access to a sacramental communion, identifies himself with his deity by a process of incorporation, and the sacrament of progress consists in cutting down, like a god, all those who might stand in its way—were it not unimaginable and blasphemous to attempt to halt the irresistible March of Time (another name for the god). Of course, each member of the communion lives through this bloody sacrament in keeping with his nature, that is, either with a fierce grimace or a look of compassion for those who are being immolated.

Thus the idea of progress has not only justified and promoted the slaughter—at times physical, at times spiritual, depending on the circumstances—but it has even removed it from consciousness. Indeed, when it was opportune, the idea of progress also remolded, revised the Indian's image, and even made it invisible.

But the history of the Indian, as it appears in these pages, proves to be not so much a history as a morphology, since the works and times are linked more in accordance with (almost) permanent forms than with the

3

strict demands of chronology. The material involved changes and varies with the times, yet the basic forms or entelechies persist, frequently disappearing only to re-emerge at some later date. For example, the stamp that the ideology of philosophical Libertinism puts on both men and events—I refer, of course, to that current of thought which had its beginnings in the early sixteenth century in France and other European countries and which, with its antinomian attitudes to religion and religious authority, was the principal fountainhead of the Enlightenment—is today clearly predominant. Yet the same ideology was undoubtedly instrumental in shaping certain specific seventeenth-century views of the aboriginal world. In the same way, the tradition of hypocritical Enlightenment benevolence, which poses the Indian in certain set attitudes, is quite old and well established; and one could provide other examples of this recurrence of fundamental morphologies.

On the other hand, the *intelletto d'amore*—that "intellect of love" which to Dante and his school meant the higher understanding that comes from "the divine love that moves the Sun and the other stars" and sheds its light from above on every aspect of the sublunar world—also proves to be a form of thought that not only casts a great light on the Indians as a whole but also constitutes the extraordinary discovery of most recent times. Almost as if in compensation for truculent, progressivist Libertinism, many examples of intelligence and charity have made possible true portraits of the Indians, filling the skies of our world with a kind of stellar light. And another great novelty—these portraits are often self-portraits: the oppressed speak out for themselves, though often through mediators. An Indian literature is coming into existence.

Chapter I

———◦•◦———

America, Projection of Renaissance England

In Renaissance England, at the time it set out to colonize America, at least two opposing ideas of history—the progressive and the retrograde—identical to those that were dominant in ancient thought, shaped the historians' imaginations in the classic image.

In his novel *The Sot-Weed Factor,* John Barth features Ebenezer, a seventeenth-century Libertine, who with amiable buffoonery lists

sundry theories of history—the retrogressive, held by Dante and Hesiod; the dramatic, held by the Hebrews and the Christian fathers; the progressive, held by Virgil; the cyclical, held by Plato and Ecclesiasticus; the undulatory, and even the vortical hypothesis entertained . . . by a gloomy neo-Platonist of Christ's College, who believed that the cyclic periods of history were growing ever shorter and thus that at some not-unpredictable moment in the future the universe would go rigid and explode, just as the legendary bird called *Ouida* . . . reputed to fly in ever-diminishing circles until at the end he disappeared into his own fundament.[1]

The progressivism "held by Virgil" was cultivated in Rome at the time of the declining Republic and the first Principate, when Cicero asked whether there were men so perverse that they would feed on acorns after grain had been discovered, and Dionysius of Halicarnassus declared that all honor must be paid to so progressive an age, while Lucretius' Epicurean doctrine taught that mankind, savage since the dawn of time, had at last advanced step by step to civilization:

> Practice and the experience of men's diligent mind
> Have gradually taught them as they progressed step by step;
> Thus time draws forward each and every thing little by little.

This ancient theory was summed up by Francis Bacon in the infamous aphorism: *Veritas filia temporis* ("Truth, the daughter of time"). Young peoples are barbarians, and therefore the ruler of Bacon's New Atlantis explains: ". . . marvel you not at the thin population of America, nor at the rudeness and ignorance of the people; for you must account your inhabitants of America as a young people, younger a thousand years at the least than the rest of the world."[2]

Bacon thought that progress followed historic norms and is continual. "In the youth of a State, arms do flourish; in the middle age of a State, learning; and the both of them together for a time; and in the declining age of a State, mechanical arts and merchandise."[3] Since time always advances, it is forever necessary to innovate, even without seeming to do so, in order not to arouse resistance, remembering that "a froward retention of custom is as turbulent a thing . . . and they that reverence too much old times are but a scorn to the new."[4] The ideal is the indefinite progress of the New Atlantis: "the enlarging of the bounds of human empire, to the effecting of all things possible."[5] America could not help being a land of conquest.

In contrast, also deriving from classical antiquity, is the Hesiodian and Platonic doctrine,* which taught the constant regression from the golden age, or in Plato's *Laws* from Egypt (or in Plato's *Timaeus* from Atlantis), to a secular civil life and a humanity corrupted by luxuries. In the autumn of the Middle Ages, this was the theme of the prologue to John Gower's *Confessio Amantis*, as it had been Chaucer's:

> A blisful lyf, a paisible and a swete
> Ledden the people in the former age:
> They helde hem payed of fruites that they ete,
> With that the feldes gave them by usage.[6]

During the Elizabethan age, Spenser continued the eulogy of the ancient world, which had been inimical to dishonesty and pride, so widespread in his own time. In *The Faerie Queene* (1. 12.14) he points out that ". . . th'antique world excesse and pride did hate;/ Such proud luxurious pompe is swollen up but late." He also extolled the retrograde theory of history:

> So oft as I with state of present time,
> The image of the antique world compare,
> When as mans age was in its freshest prime,

---

* In "The Debate on Primitivism in Ancient Rhetoric" E. H. Gombrich notes that "the first great philosophical opponent of the Greek faith in progress pointed to Egypt as the model, the civilization where art and ritual were one and neither was allowed to change." (*Journal of the Warburg and Courtauld Institute*, XIX, 1966.)

And the first blossome of faire vertue bare,
Such oddes I finde twixt those and these which are,
As that, through long continuance of his course,
Me seemes the world is runne quite out of square,
From the first point of his appointed sourse,
And being once amisse growes daily wourse and wourse.

[5, Proem, 1-9]

Sannazaro's poems* nourished the Arcadian sensibility, which merged harmoniously with Montaigne's reflections. Even an aversion for arts and letters was flaunted by Montaigne and by important figures of the Italian Renaissance. In his poem *Virgidemiarum*, Joseph Hall used the Arcadian dream to berate his century, which had declined since the time in which

The king's pavilion, was the grassy greene,
Under safe shelter of the shadie treene,

and men

Not wishing any ease, not fearing wrong:
Clad with their owne, as they were made of olde,
Not fearing shame, not feeling any cold?

[3. vv. 28 ff]

The decline, according to Hall, could be traced to pride, which had destroyed communion with the animal.

But America, unlike Europe, probably was still immersed in an Arcadian state. Such was the hope kindled by Montaigne's essays *Des Cannibales* and *Des Coches*, which were famous in England even before Florio's 1603 translation. Does the new continent seem barbarous? But that is true of anything *"ce qui n'est pas de son usage"*; certainly the Europeans, torturers under a mantle of piety, could not afford to censure the natives of the new continent.

But no matter how far apart, the opposed versions of progress or retrogression both led in England in the sixteenth and seventeenth centuries to an identical feeling: history must be a continuous *reformation* (the word is thematic even outside the religious sphere, together with the word *project*). The progressive must progress, but even he who dreams of a past golden age, instead of praising the civilization in which he lives, implies that this civilization must be reformed.

For Cotton Mather, for example, as for the Puritans in general, *reformation* signified reaction. "The first Age was the *golden* Age: to return to

---

* Jacopo Sannazaro (1456–1530) imitated the idyllic poetry of the classics; his major work, *Arcadia*, presents a utopian vision of bucolic life.

that, will make a man a Protestant, and I may add, a Puritan," Mather says in the general introduction to *Magnalia Christi Americana,* referring to the golden age of early Christianity.

The Oxford dictionary states that in the fifteenth and sixteenth centuries *reformation* meant rehabilitation or cure and reconstruction, correction or control. In 1523 Henry VIII ordered that all foreigners plying a trade, *mistery* or *handy craft* be put under surveillance—*Serche and Reformacion*—by the guilds. Precisely because of this semantic latitude, the term lent itself to being made into an ideological slogan that the masses could identify with. It seemed to cover a vast gamut of confused yearnings, and in responding to it, each person deluded himself that he was pursuing his own aims, when in fact he was being rallied in the name of "reform," either civil or religious. The clandestine heretical body of Lollards, at that time in decline, did not have clear-cut aims or a precise theology but simply a violent, extremely vague desire to change religious customs, so much so that they did not even imagine what turn the desired "reform" might take. Once a rallying cry is launched, the will of the few can be imposed in whatever specific direction it desires; a stroke of the thumb gives the fermenting mass its shape. James Gairdner observes that before Henry VIII took action one could not find a trace of schismatic and nationalistic aims among the Lollards: "I fail to see any evidence of such a feeling in the copious correspondence of the twenty years preceding. I fail to find it even in the prosecutions of heretics."[7] Nor did the *concilium de emendanda Ecclesia,* instituted in 1538, have clear aims, though it expressed a generic zealousness.

In the 1548 edition of Elyot's dictionary a *reformer* is defined as "he that bringeth a better facion." But Ben Jonson derides this delirium in his play *Bartholomew Fair;* Rabbi Zeal-of-the-Land Busy grants a bigot the right to eat roast pork, provided she swallows it "with a reformed mouth." Moreover, King James says of the young Laud, who is restless, loves tumults, and is blind to the general welfare because of his anxious desire to tune everything to the diapason of an imagined reform: "He hath a restless spirit, and cannot see when things are well, but loves to toss and change and bring things to a pitch of reformation floating in his own brain."[8] The word *project* is almost equally polyvalent, for it can mean plan, conception, proposal, forecast, or projection. For example, Ben Jonson writes in *Every Man in His Humour:* "Oh, Beauty is a Project of some power."

On these shifting sands was built the reigning ideology of the century, whose harbinger was a procession of emblems through the streets of

Florence in 1513. To symbolize the new century Pontano had suggested these images: over a dead warrior rises a naked, gilded infant, the golden age.[9] And Thomas Elyot would draw inspiration from Pontano for his *Governour.*

Renovatio had been the thematic word, the "reformation" of the Italian humanists stripped of its Joachimist religious coloration. The word that would be counterposed to the perturbing psychic forces evoked by *reformation* was *establishment,* which, in John Bridges' work of 1587, *The Defence of the Government Established in the Church of England,* rings out in defense of pacification.

Against this general tendency, and within the new Anglo-Catholic order, Edmund Spenser saved as many forms of the past as he could and proclaimed that "all change is perillous and all chance unsound." Yet the mild, gentle Spenser, who argued against Giordano Bruno, for whom God was a perpetual becoming, still personifies Evil in the fascinating *Titaness Mutabilitie,* born of blood and earth, a perpetual snare threatening the sense of the eternal and of spiritual bliss.[10] And although he praises knighthood and remote, Arcadian antiquity—the golden age, Eden, the garden of Adonis, Fairyland, of which Guyon reads in Alma's house—and contrasts these with the civilization of luxury, Spenser nevertheless proves himself a product of the times by calling in his *View of the Present State of Ireland* for a terrifying form of progress for that country. Having examined the islanders' ancient customs one by one and though admiring the courage of their warriors and the inspiration of their bards, he nonetheless brands all these things as "evil usages," which is tantamount to saying that a *reformation* is necessary. To achieve this, it will be necessary to compel the native population to choose between carrying out the reform or being thoroughly, systematically exterminated.

On the other hand, it is not surprising that Bacon did all he could to persuade the sovereign to entrust him with the task of a *reformation* of English law through codification, for it was he who suggested in *New Atlantis* what the evil angel put into the head of Marlowe's Faust:

> Go forward, Faustus, in that famous art
> Wherein all nature's treasury is contained:
> Be thou on earth as Jove is in the sky,
> Lord and commander of these elements.

The desire for change so pervades the English collective spirit that when Dr. John Dee, Queen Elizabeth's adviser and the promoter of exploratory expeditions to America, dedicates himself to spiritualistic evocations, his "entities" prescribe and prophesy a "General Reformation." (This is described by Mericus Casaubonus in his *True and Faithfull Relation of What Passed for many yeares between Dr. John Dee and some spirits. Tending [had it Succeeded] To a General Alteration of Most States and Kingdomes in the World,* printed in London in 1659.)

Libertine thought would exalt the image of primordial Arcadian innocence not as a reflection of the divine giving direction to fallen man but rather as a pretext for revolt against the existing order. In the name of the "first laws," which the new ones contradict, Malefort in Massinger's play, *The Unnatural Combat,* grants himself every liberty, including incest.

This restless will for "reform" had its roots in the study and imitation of antiquity, as an extraneous body of thought injected into the *ordo catholicus.* Hobbes denounces that outcome in *Leviathan:*

By reading of these Greek and Latin authors men from their childhood have gotten a habitude (under a false show of liberty) of favouring tumults and of licentious controlling the actions of their sovereigne and again of controlling those controllers, with the effusion of so much blood, as I think I may truly say that never was anything so dearly bought as these Western parts have bought the learning of the Greek and Latin tongues. [2. 21]

Despite his piety, Thomas More's *Utopia,* considered objectively, belongs to the Libertine tendency: it called forth fantasies that inevitably favored the destructive spirit of change. When brought to trial, Sir Thomas refused to serve a king who, in the ways sanctioned by history and his own rapacious instincts, destroyed the monastic orders and so cleared the road, and not just metaphorically, for that new culture that he and his friend Erasmus had helped bring about and supported.

Campanella stated explicitly the consequences that would follow from his teacher's text. "Thomas More, recently martyred, who described an imaginary Utopian republic, after whose example we have founded the institutions of our republic," he says in *Questioni sull'Ottima Repubblica.* He even went so far as to affirm that the egalitarian Utopia was evoked whenever one wished that the divine will be done on earth as it is in heaven. Thus Christian sensibility, which the Libertine spirit could not eradicate, was put at the service of progress toward a Utopia in which every religion would be tolerated (as Thomas More had already prescribed).

The Libertines, followers of the new philosophy that ascribed every suggestion of the supernatural to empiric and human causes (as Lafeu complains in *All's Well That Ends Well*), were divided among themselves. Some were atheists, some pantheists—as, for example, some of the friends who welcomed Bruno in London—and some adherents of still other philosophies, yet all had in common the belief that progressive changes were possible or necessary. So far as aims go, More's Utopia and Bacon's Atlantis stand at opposite poles (and so, at the height of the Enlightenment, would the state of nature without art or science yearned for by Rousseau contrast with Condorcet's fantasy of a perfected and scientific civilization). Nonetheless, the effect of each of the opposing fantasies was identical: the present must be changed, if need be, apart from, and even in spite of, any and all immediate, tangible goals. The Libertine and cynical spirit of the age and the cult of passion that pervades much of Elizabethan drama unite, either out of truculent vital exuberance or melancholy splenetic humor, to spur on this eagerness to discover abuses and bring about changes. Iago says: "I confess, it is my nature's plague to spy into abuses" (*Othello*, Act 3, Scene 3, 146–47).

Just as in the succeeding centuries the proponents of the Enlightenment violently imposed their civil rule in the name of tolerance, so Thomas More, despite his great show of humanistic feeling, was an ideologue of colonialism. The inhabitants of his Utopia invade without restraint other people's sparsely populated lands, benevolently inviting the dispossessed to remain under the aegis of Utopian laws, which they consider far superior. When, however, these people prove insensitive to so much benevolence, they are expelled, if necessary by means of the cruelest warfare.

More's ideal people considered this the most just cause of war: "When any people holdeth a piece of ground void and vacant to no good or profitable use: keeping others from the use and possession of it, which, notwithstanding, by the law of nature, ought thereof to be nourished and relieved."[11]

To these forces were added, as a consequence of the new scientific discoveries, the release of a fantasy no longer confined by an unimaginable cosmology corresponding to our sense perception. This subversion was apparent to the more sensitive poets: John Donne in "First Anniversarie" or Drummond of Hawthornden in "A Cypress Grove," where he meditates on the new science in this fashion:

Is it knowledge? But we have not yet attained to a perfect understanding of the smallest flower, and why the grass should rather be green than red. The Element of Fire (it would now seem by our latest Science) is quite put out; the Air is but Water rarified; the Earth is found to move, and is no more the centre of the Universe; Stars are not fixed, but swim in the celestial spaces. . . .

Thus Sciences, by the diverse motions of this globe of the brain of man, are become opinions, nay errors, and leave the imagination in a thousand labyrinths. . . . We have not yet agreed about the chief good and felicity. It is, perhaps, all artificial cunning.[12]

This is the backdrop for the new fantastic dreams against which the Indians of America were to be projected. To some they would appear, in keeping with the dominant humanistic studies of the time, archaic Greeks and Romans called up from the dead. To those who lived immersed in dreams of a lascivious Arcadia and feasted on Vespucci's highly stimulating bits of information they seemed natural beings close to a communitarian, innocent Utopia. But to the more cynical, "impassioned" adventurers, who were such perfect models for the murky, sanguinary heroes of the Elizabethan stage, they were seen as a straightforward opportunity for piratical trade.

The diffusion of the Christian religion was the avowed purpose of traders and usurpers, yet despite repeated statements writ large in the royal patents, very rarely was this the real aim. The navigator John Davys wrote to Walsingham that if the indigenous population were converted, it would certainly become more civilized and so could be sold the coarser products of the woolen mills.

The Renaissance reawakened not only a taste for Ciceronian prose, the cult of the civic and purely human virtues (as in Roger Ascham's *Toxophilus* and even more in Thomas Elyot's *Governour*), the cult of eroticism (as in Marlowe's *Hero and Leander* and Helen's scene in *Doctor Faustus*), pleasure in mythological ornamentation, the cult of fame bestowed by men of letters, and contempt for pedants but also, inevitably, the idea of Empire. This concept of Empire was not the transmission of ecumenical authority sanctioned by the Church but a form of civilization to which the barbarians must submit, a national renown that would increase through conquests, following the pagan Roman conception. The propagation of the faith was simply another of the various rhetorical devices employed to extol the idea of the civilization that must be spread.

So not only did the Indian become part of two opposing erudite fantasies, appearing now as an Arcadian, now as a savage; he was also forced to become a supernumerary on the stage of Empire. Occasionally, during the seventeenth century, a Mennonite or Quaker, an eccentric and isolated cultivator of the outmoded virtues of humility and meekness, treated the Indian with true benevolence, but almost never was his complex ceremonial life, evolved under the spell of the supernatural, understood in and of itself.

The first account of America in English was written by an anonymous author. The Indians in it make one's flesh crawl. They resemble the primitive men Cicero mentioned: "When men in the fields wandered aimlessly like beasts." They have no king, master, or God, the anonymous author noted. They own everything in common and go about covered with feathers, like beasts without reason. They subsist by eating one another: "The man etethe his wyfe, his chylderne as we also have seen and they hange also the bodyes of persons fleeshe in the smoke as men do with swynes fleshe."[13]

William Cunningham, writing in 1559, was just as extreme: "There is no law or order observed of wedlocke; for it is lawful to have so many women as they affect, and to put them away without any daunger. They be filthy at meate, and in all secrete acts of nature, comparable to brute beasts."[14]

In 1582 Sir George Peckham drew up a manifesto of imperialism (included in the third volume of Richard Hakluyt's voyages), in which the ideologies of the period are given free rein. First of all, it is a Christian duty to increase the flock of the faithful, but it will also benefit the Crown if its territories are enlarged (justly ratifying the ancient titles of America acquired by the Welsh kings, according to certain chronicles); hateful laziness must be banished from the kingdom (that is, a remedy must be found for the consequences of suppressing the monasteries); decayed cities are to be repaired and the wretched given solace. The idolaters must learn to know Christ, innocent peoples must be protected from their bloodthirsty, tyrannical neighbors, and, lastly, the diabolical custom of human sacrifice must be abolished.

The right to trade with anyone was vouchsafed by the right of "mutuall societie and fellowshippe betweene man and man."[15] If human brotherhood obliged the savages to consent to the trading, the wars among the natives also from time to time provided the opportunity to protect the side under attack and especially to intervene against cannibals. Some of these points were feudal, some already modern, such as the rhetoric about civilization veiled by Christian and missionary pretexts, the theme of a dutiful increase of material well-being. They were also modern because they exhumed pre-Christian political rhetoric, the apologetics for Roman imperialism. The pretext of doing away with nefarious sacrifices was characteristic of the Romans, who enjoyed the spectacle of the massacres in the arenas. In book XXX, chapter XXIII of his *Natural History*, Pliny lauded "the great providence of our Romans, who have abolished these monstrous and abominable arts, which, under the show of religion, murdered men for sacrifice to please the gods; and under the color of physic, prescribed the flesh to be eaten as wholesome meat." The fierce imperialists, religious persecutors, and torturers of the Renaissance harked back to this reasoning and used it to their advantage.

Richard Hakluyt submitted to the Queen a *project* to channel into America the energies released by the country's seditious unrest. The desperate, the debtors, the sons of begging vagrants, "valiant youths rusting and hurtful by lack of employment," should all be sent across the seas. As for the Puritan ministers guilty of indiscreet and subversive zeal, let them expend this emotion in missionary work. This program of social channeling, which was supposed to purge the country of the most belli-cose, agitated products of the reform atmosphere, was transformed into a martial ode by Drayton, the poetic recruiting officer:

> You brave heroic minds
> Worthy your country's name,
> 　That honour still pursue,
> 　Go, and subdue,
> Whilst loit'ring hinds
> Lurk here at home, with shame.

Here honor is abstracted from its real roots, that is, loyalty to the feudal lord and fidelity to one's social ties* and becomes, precisely like *reformation*, a mere suggestive word. And just as *reformation* conjures up an indeterminate good, so in nationalistic poetry the word *honor* re-echoes in its mere abstractness the theme of the knight-errant, while favoring adventures in which the medieval chivalrous spirit plays not the slightest part.

America was also colored with erotic associations. "Come boys, Virginia longs till we share the rest of her maidenhead," shouts the captain in *Eastward Hoe*, the play written by Marston, Chapman, and Jonson, while John Donne in his licentious youthful poetry cries to his disrobing mis-tress: "O my America!"

Purchas, Hakluyt's continuator, believed that the New World was at once an Eden and a place for legitimate exploitation. Was it not right for King Solomon to trade with Ophir? And was not the constant dancing of

---

* Leo Spitzer described the essence of real and aristocratic honor in his examination of the motto *Yo soy quien soy.*

the Indians a sign of barbarism? And yet those Indian cries Purchas
mentions, which sound like a mimicry of wild beasts, were most likely the
source of Ariel's first song, a mark of the complicated art with which
Shakespeare embraces both the thesis of despicable barbarity and that of
a surviving golden age.

In fact, Prospero speaks like a colonist without illusions:

> Abhorred slave,
> Which any print of goodness wilt not take,
> Being capable of all ill, I pitied thee,
> Took pains to make thee speak. . . .

Just like the Virginians, Caliban must obey because the devil, god of
his mother Sycorax, is inferior to Prospero:

> I must obey: his art is of such pow'r
> It would control my dam's god, Setebos. . . .

This echoes Purchas's rhetorical question: "Can a Leopard change his
spots? Can a Savage remayning a Savage be civil? . . . And were not
Caesars Britaines as brutish as Virginians?" The Britons were as the
Virginians are: progress establishes the quality of peoples. Yet in the
figure of Ariel there also resounds the idea of the uncorrupted child of
nature.

Many travelers had seen a Virginia populated with Ariels. The discovery of a Hesiodian golden age in "Virginia earth's own paradise"
("Like Adam's time before he ate," John Donne would later write) could
be as impressive in a mild and delectable way as the vision of the aborigines as fierce monsters, abhorred for Epicurean and Ciceronian reasons.
The Edenic mirage became a good business deal for investors in companies engaged in colonial exploitation. Speaking to the young louts of
London, the ship's captain in *Eastward Hoe* praises to the skies the
wonders of Virginia; and in *The Tempest* (act 2, scene 1) Shakespeare
puts the dream of the golden age on Gonzalo's lips:

> I' the commonwealth I would by contraries
> Execute all things; for no kind of traffic
> Would I admit, no name of magistrate.
> Letters should not be known; riches, poverty,
> And use of service, none. . . .

Arthur Barlowe, who with Philip Amadas, led the 1584 expedition to
Virginia, left a report, included in Hakluyt's third volume, in which he
exclaims that "we found the people most gentle, louing, and faithfull,

voide of all guile and treason, and such as live after the manner of the golden age." They cooked tasty foods, adored an idol "of whom they aske counsel, as the Romans were wont of the Oracle of Apollo," marched into battle not to the roll of drums and the sounds of trumpets but singing.

As for their origin, starting with Lumnius in *De Extremo Dei Judicio et Indorum Vocatione,* published in Venice in 1569, some said the natives were the remnants of the lost tribes of Israel. Others, like Stephen Batman, believed them to be Chaldeans; or Welshmen, as did the magician Dr. Dee, Queen Elizabeth's adviser, and David Powell; or Asians, as did Gregorio Garcia; or Canaanites, as did Jean de Lery; or descendants of Noah, as did Marc Lescarbot.

The thesis that saw them as Jews was the one most widely accepted; in time to come Cotton Mather, John Eliot, William Penn, and Samuel Sewall would all consider it valid. Thomas Thorowgood listed fifty customs common to the Indians of America and the Jews, from tearing one's clothes when in mourning to jubilees. The differences were supposedly due to the Indians' hard craniums, which had caused the tribes to degenerate. Converting them would mean the fulfillment of the Scripture's precepts. Yet, whether savages or people of the golden age, Welshmen or Jews, the natives must be colonized and converted, for the good of all.

The charter for the colonization of Virginia in 1606 put forth as one of its aims the conversion of the savages "to human Civility, and to a settled and quiet Government." The colonists were convinced that they could peacefully bring the natives all that is good, and indeed some of them spoke like the fervent inhabitants of a Utopia.[16] The charter of the Massachusetts Bay Colony set conversion as its highest goal: "[To] wynn and incite the Natives of [this] Country, to the Knowledg and Obedience of the onlie true God and Sauior of Mankinde, and the Christian Fayth, which in our Royal intencion, and the Adventurers free Profession, is the principall Ende of this Plantacion." The wealth of the New World, Purchas proclaims, was no more than the reward for Christian and civic zeal.

At the beginning of the century Richard Johnson declared that the natives were like the deer in the forest but quite loving, and that benevolence would conquer them more effectively than cold steel, though one must still labor to save them from Satan.

Alexander Whitaker observed that the Virginians recognized a supreme and good God but feared the devil more and worshiped him. Among them lived honored hermits, as among the Catholics, from whom rain, lost objects, and the cure of the sick were obtained. Their priests were witches ("No other but such as our English witches are"). The same view was held by William Wood and Henry Spelman.

The first to assert that they worshiped the devil, as the Romans did Vediovis, was William Strachey, secretary and annalist of Virginia, in *The Historie of Travaile into Virginia Britannia* (1612). "Their chief god they worship is no other indeed than the devill, whome they make presentements of and shadow vnder the forme of an Idoll which they entitle *Okeus* and whome they worship as the Romaynes did their hurtfull god Veiouis more for feare of harme than of hope of any good."[17] They honor priests versed in the mysteries as the ancient Ephesians honored the priests of Diana—"the best grave luckye well instructed in their misteryes . . . no less honoured then was Dianaes priests at Ephesus." The entrance to their temples faces the east, black figures stand on pillars and look down upon the faithful, and in a secret vault covered with mats is hidden their god, "all black . . . with chaynes of Pearle . . . which doth them all the harme they suffer." It is not the good god who imposes duties but the evil one, Okeus, who measures every deed on the "severe Scale of Justice." But how could the colonists, since they lacked philological knowledge, know how much this theology coincided with the double aspect of God's justice and mercy in the monotheistic religions?

The aboriginal temple was filled with images of kings and devils, scattered with tombs, and "In this—as the Grecian nigromancers psychomantie did use to call up spirits—eyther the priests have conference, or consult; indeed with the devill, and receive verbal answers." Indian reality was transposed into Greco-Latin terms, and judgments common to Christian polemicists of the early centuries were revived. As a consequence, understanding of the native religious reality and theology was carefully precluded.

Strachey wrote after the first English colony in Virginia, founded in 1585, had disappeared, having been destroyed by the natives. King Powhatan had been warned by prophets that he would be overwhelmed by an enemy coming from Chesapeake Bay, so he exterminated the people of that region. Later English colonists were thus able to land there without meeting any resistance. The promptness with which the Indians had followed the oracles (what's more, true to the facts) horrified Strachey, who did not hesitate to see in this the mark of the devil, when in fact Biblical stories of the patriarchs could have offered him parallel instances of precisely the same behavior. The only person who showed some caution in accepting the thesis of Indian Satanism was a Catholic,

Father Andrew White. In his report on Maryland he does not advance an opinion, alleging his lack of knowledge of the language and the little trust he puts in his Protestant interpreters.[18]

And yet the view, so widespread among travelers, that the natives worshiped the devil was wholly imaginary, as is proven by the Algonquin mythology that Leland gathered at the close of the nineteenth century. Brinton also observed that *Kiehtan* does not mean, as seventeenth-century travelers thought, "God Almighty," for the word *Kiehta* simply means "great." According to the travelers, the other divinity, Hobbamock or Okeus, was the devil, but *oke* means the divinity or tutelary genius that appears in visions, gives the hunter his prey, and cures illnesses.[19]

∴

The only man capable of describing with any depth and complexity the first encounter with the Indians was John Smith. Born in 1580, the son of a Lincolnshire farmer, he was, in his restless openness to experience, a perfect reflection of the times. At fifteen, he says, he was just about to run away from home to go to sea—"his mind being even set upon brave adventures, he sold his satchel, bookes, and all he had"—when his father's death stopped him.

In 1596, an orphan and rich, he became the apprentice of a great merchant. The following year he was wandering about France. Having spent his money, he enlisted in the French army. When the war ended, he served with the Dutch. He stayed for a while in Scotland. Returning home, he meditated upon Machiavelli and Marcus Aurelius during a rural retreat. He lived with an Italian, Teodoro Polaloga. Then he traveled across France and embarked on a ship full of pilgrims to Rome who, infuriated by his heresy, abandoned him on a tiny island. He was picked up by a ship bound for Alexandria, and the captain grew fond of him. Smith landed in the south of France after an adventurous voyage through the Levant. In Rome he witnessed a Papal Mass. He enlisted in the imperial army, killed three Turks in single combat, was wounded on the field of battle in Transylvania in 1602, and then was captured. He was imprisoned at Constantinople, where a young girl took a fancy to him. Her brother, the Pasha of Tartary, to whom she recommended and entrusted Smith, tortured him out of spite and threw him, with a chain around his neck, among the lowest slaves. Taking his persecutor by surprise and killing him, Smith fled to Christian Muscovy. In Leipzig

Prince Sigismund gave him a reward. He sailed from Morocco and after many mishaps and excitements at sea reached London in 1605. He invested his earnings as a sailor in an expedition of the Virginia Company, quarreled with the royal authorities who sold the colonial patents, and, finally, in December 1606, left for America with one hundred and forty other colonists. Aboard ship he was accused of plotting, and a gallows was erected to hang him. In 1607 the party landed at Jamestown; he won a trial and was cleared of all charges.

The same year he went off with a few companions to trade with the Indians. Of the group, he was the only one to survive in captivity. One of the men was flayed alive with sharpened seashells.

Emperor Powhatan received Smith seated on a pile of rugs; he questioned him, surrounded by his women and his warriors. Smith made himself invaluable, especially by teaching the capricious Indians how to use a compass:

> But when he demonstrated by that Globelike Iewel the roundnesse of the earth, and skies, the spheare of the Sunne, Moone and Starres, and how the Sunne did chase the night round about the world continually; the greatness of the Land and Sea, the diuersitie of Nations, uarietie of complexions, and how we were to them Antipodes, and many other such like matters, they all stood as amazed with admiration.
>
> Notwithstanding, within an houre after they tyed him to a tree, and as many as could stand about him prepared to shoot him, but the King holding vp the Compass in his hand, they all laid downe their Bowes and Arrowes, and in a triumphant manner led him to *Orapaks*, where he was after their manner kindly feasted, and well vsed.[20]

In order to penetrate and uncover Captain Smith's true feelings and intentions, the Indians mounted a special ceremony. They made him sit on a mat in a hut. The priest entered anointed with blackish oil, his head adorned with stuffed snakes and weasels, feathers dangling over his face. He howled, frenziedly shaking a rattle.

> With most strange gestures and passions he began his invocation, and environed the fire with a circle of meale; which done, three more such like devils came rushing in with the like antique tricks, painted halfe blacke, halfe red; but all their eyes were painted white, and some red stroakes like Mutchato's, along their cheeks.

The three men painted red and black danced and were joined by three more similarly adorned; then all sat down and sang. At certain intervals they stopped singing and placed kernels of corn on the ground. Finally, they laid some sticks on the ground. They repeated the ceremony for three days, fasting all the while. "The circle of meale signified their Country, the circles of corne the bounds of the Sea." The ceremony proved, quite realistically, to be a testimony against the captain, who was forthwith led to the torture; but the king's daughter, Pocahontas, threw herself on him to save him from the blows. The king decided to free him.

In 1608 Smith was elected president of the colony; he guaranteed its peace with a few military campaigns. But new tumultuous colonists who landed in 1609 stirred up the conflict again, revolted against him, and wounded him severely. In 1609 he was once more in London, while the majority of the colonists, deprived of his guidance, died of hunger. In the succeeding years he explored the coastline—"always in mutinies, wants, miserie, in the midst of wars, pestilence, and famine"—and gave it the name of New England.

In his last years John Smith petitioned in vain to enter Francis Bacon's service and guide the Puritan pilgrims. Before dying, in 1631, he gave proof of being a great, bizarre, disorderly but captivating writer of prose. And in 1616 he had the opportunity to recommend to the Queen the beautiful Pocahontas, his rescuer in Virginia, now converted and come to England with her young English husband, Rolfe, where she was feted as the symbol of a conciliation with the converted natives.

"He who does not believe in God fears the most." "That which seems to be hardship is a remedy." These two Latin aphorisms dear to Smith sum up the lesson learned from so many dangerous situations and fateful escapes. "It was not Ariadne's thread, but the direct line of God's providence," he says of someone else's adventure, but the sentence describes perfectly the connecting link that binds together all the extraordinary events of his own life.

His political intelligence was that of an astute, reflective man endowed with religiosity of a Shakespearean stamp, who, while contemplating the terrible mutability of fate, detached himself from its vicissitudes. With the farsighted clarity of the Machiavelli he had meditated upon during his adolescent retreats he identified the dynamic that propels the march of Empire. The state of feverish imaginativeness that had driven him into the most fearful adventures was in some sense shared by everyone of his time, and only the overseas exploits could pacify people so greatly in turmoil. Thus, after having explored the coast of the northern part of

America, Smith addressed himself to those with a zest for the new, for personal conquest: "Who can desire more content, than hath small meanes, or but only his merit to advance his fortunes then to tread and plant that ground he hath purchased by the hazard of his life?" To these worldly, proud incentives Smith added the pleasure of converting—"seek to convert those poore Salvages to know Christ, and humanitie." What is the value of a tranquil, domestic life? "Who would live at home idly (or thinke in himself any worth to live) onely to ease, drink and sleepe, and so die?"

All the commonplaces of classical oratory are put to use: the theme of the opposition between cowardice and audacity, of Hercules at the cross-roads, the argument of fame with posterity, of love of country (did not the ancient cities acquire power and glory by sending their colonists overseas?). What fate awaits a people who live quietly instead of expanding? Does not Byzantium, wiped out by the Turks, hold a lesson for us? After all, is not America an ideal place in which to siphon off the pernicious "humors" of the social body? And is not this an excellent occasion for the rich to invest their money so that it will yield a profit, compelling the populace to get busy instead of loafing?

In Rome the plebs were reduced to idleness because "the meere covetousness and extortion of a few . . . so moved the rest, that not having any imployment but contemplation, their great judgements grew to so great malice, as themselves were sufficient to destroy themselves by faction." Smith alludes perhaps to the reform of the Gracchi and later to the plebeian party: the colonies, besides enriching investors, would forestall similar upheavals in England.

Smith was not given the time to describe the Indian world in greater depth. In his succinct sketches it appears austere, chivalrous, inclined to the exacerbation of the awesomely frightful. One scene recalls the frenetic style of the Japanese theater: orators welcome guests, expressing their love for them with such vehemence that they break into a sweat and fall gasping to the ground.

Smith, as a follower of Machiavelli, was drawn to examining aboriginal institutions, which seemed to him wise though barbarous (he *was* educated by the classics). They were, he claims, tiny monarchies subject to an emperor, where unwritten law and fear upheld the political machinery. Like most builders of the British Empire, Captain Smith takes note of even the slightest variations in that impalpable and decisive element, prestige, liable to so many fluctuations among the natives.

The episode with Pocahontas, which Smith had neglected in the first versions of his book, was glorified by him as soon as he realized its value as a political symbol. The ideology of an imperial half-breedism was implicit in the girl's gesture, which for her was so fateful that, when grown up, she converted and married a white man. Smith was quick to see its implications. In 1610 he circulated a letter, transcribed by Ralph Hamor, of Pocahontas' husband to the governor,* in which Rolfe protests that he is not moved by carnal feelings but rather by a love of country and a sense of apostleship. This commitment transcends his state as a man enchanted, "intangled, and inthralled in so intricate a laborinth" which Pocahontas' fascination had led him into "that I was even awearied to unwinde myself thereout." Had not Euphues been the model for the Elizabethan nationalist? His incarnation in Virginia was able to combine a labyrinthine rhetoric with the practical aims of imperialism.

The entire Pocahontas episode provided first-rate material for the making of a myth. The Tudors had refurbished as the "myth of their origins" the Britannic tales of Geoffrey of Monmouth and the glories of King Arthur (and John Dee had claimed the "northern lands" for the Elizabethan empire as Arthurian colonies), while the unlucky Stuarts were almost devoid of a myth, although Laud had evoked David's Old Testament monarchy, Caesar, and Frederick II. Much later, however, the democrats, by glorifying "Saxon democracy," managed to devise a workable one. In any event, the foundation of the American empire created a mythological vacuum that Pocahontas' amorous experience could well have filled. It had everything: the element of chivalry, the missionary, the savage, not to mention, given the protagonist's rank of princess, the continuity of royal rule. In it the Libertine could find an ennobling background for his exotic amours (Rolfe's letter could be read as an unsolicited defense), the Christian an incentive to baptism, and the

---

* "Let therefore this my well advised protestation, which here I make betweene God and my owne conscience, be a sufficient witnesse, at the dreadfull day of judgement (when the secret of all mens harts shall be opened) to condemne me herein, if my chiefest intent and purpose be not, to strive with all my power of body and minde, in the undertaking of so mightie a matter, no way led (so farre forth as mans weaknesse may permit) with the unbridled desire of carnall affection: but for the good of this plantation, for the honour of our countrie, for the glory of God, for my owne salvation, and for the converting to the true knowledge of God and Jesus Christ, an unbeleeving creature, namely Pokahuntas. To whom my hartie and best thoughts are, and have a long time bin so intangled, and inthralled in so intricate a laborinth, that I was even awearied to unwinde myself thereout." See *A True Discourse of the Present Estate of Virginia* (in *Narratives of Early Virginia, 1606–1625*, ed. L. G. Tyler, New York, 1907).

pioneer the blessings of authority transmitted "through matrimonial law." Not by chance the myth of Pocahontas would generate endless poems and plays during the Romantic period. Yet politically it was ineffective: the Libertine spirit was in a minority, and most people felt an instinctive revulsion for the half-breed.*

Smith noted the magical ceremonies, observing them with quick but profound attention. He also described the initiation rituals: each year there is a sacrifice of young boys—

fifteene of the properest young boyes, between ten and fifteen yeares of age they painted white. Having brought them forth, the people spent the forenoone in dancing and singing about them with rattles. In the afternoone they put those children to the roote of a tree. By them all the men stood in a guard, every one having a bastinado in his hand. . . .

The mothers weep over the boys as if they were dead, while the men gather under a tree and guard the boys, waving their clubs; later, the boys disappear. Have they been decimated? Have they been killed only in appearance? Some certainly return initiated, priests; perhaps the others, after undergoing an ordeal, have been sacrificed.

What else was done with the children [Smith writes] was not seene, but they were all cast on a heape, in a valley as dead, where they made a great feast for all the company.

The Werowance being demanded the meaning of this sacrifice, answered that the children were not all dead, but that the Okee or Divell did sucke the bloud from their left breast, who chanced to be his by lot, till they were dead; but the rest were kept in the wildernesse by the young men till nine moneths were expired, during which time they must not converse with any; and of these were made their priests and conjurers.

To Captain Smith the characteristically theological background remains impenetrable: he accepts the general view that the Indians worship the devil. Nor does he delve more deeply into their unquestionably symbolic customs, which he describes with Roman brevity:

In each ear commonly they have three great holes, whereat they hang chaines, bracelets, or copper. Some of their men weare in those holes, a small green and yellow coloured snake, near halfe a yard in length, which crawling and lapping

---

* Leslie Fiedler in the chapter titled "Love in the Woods," in *The Return of the Vanishing American* (New York, 1968), with the intention of making Pocahontas into a *pucelle d'Orléans* among the American Voltaires, recounts the mockeries and obscenities to which her myth has given birth.

herself about his necke oftentimes familiarly would kisse his lips. Others weare a dead rat tyed by the taile.

∴

The Relation of Maryland in 1635 opposed the idea of permanent warfare advocated by Captain Smith. On the contrary, the anonymous author praised the noble savage for the observance of natural laws which led him to offer the first fruits of his farming, hunting, and fishing to God and to believe in the immortality of the soul.

The same Maryland inspired a diametrically different prose in George Alsop, horrified by the Indians' tattoos ("hieroglyphics and representations of the furies"), which seemed to him not simply emblems of bears, tigers, and panthers but of demons. He did not share Captain Smith's admiration for the Indians' political structures, but at least he ·realized that they were of a labyrinthine complexity. Centuries had to pass before structural anthropology proved that Alsop's words were not metaphorical games but the plain truth:

Their Government is wrapt up in so various and intricate a Laborynth, that the speculativ'st Artist in the whole World, with his artificial and natural Opticks, cannot see into the rule or sway of these *Indians,* to distinguish what name of Government to call them by.[21]

Libertine thought was present from the very beginning of colonization, and in the heart of the Puritan colony it was represented by Thomas Morton, a lawyer, who had settled at Merry Mount, the present Quincy, near Boston. He immediately set about his subversive activities. He took in the Puritans' runaway servants and made friends with the natives, to whom, Bradford claimed, he began selling arms. Enormous developments might well have been born from this modest germ of subversion. A coalition of Indians and Libertines would have transformed America not only into the refuge of "God's saints" but also of all those in Europe who fondly cherished at one and the same time the memory of ancient paganism and the noble savage of the new land. The Puritans did not hesitate to resort to repressive measures.

To vilify them and absolve himself, Morton wrote the *New English Canaan,* published in 1632 in London and in 1637 in one of the Amsterdam printshops that hoped to form a Libertine current of opinion in the new Europe. Naturally, Morton assumed a disguise, protesting that he was a follower of the Church of England persecuted by new iniquitious

Pharisees furiously intent on extorting tithes on mint and cumin. In reality, he had celebrated May Day, a festival of pagan origin hated by the Puritans, erecting a flower-bedecked pine Maypole, the same pole that the eighteenth-century heirs of Libertine thought would raise in Europe's squares as "the tree of liberty." Around this pole adorned with a ram's horns, the festival began with the roll of drums, rifle shots, and the distribution of beer. A song was then sung in chorus and a round dance performed with Indian women invited for the occasion. On the pole Morton had affixed a depressing piece of limping verse laced with obscene allusions:

> Rise Oedisseus, and if thou canst unfould,
> What means Caribdis underneath the mould,
> When Scilla solitary on the ground,
> (Sitting in forme of Niobe) was found
> Till Amphitrites darling did acquaint
> Grim Neptune with the tenor of her plaint
> And caused him send forth Triton with the sound,
> Of Trumpet lowd, at which the seas were found,
> So full of Protean formes, that the bold shore,
> Presenteth Scilla a new parramore,
> So strong as Sampson and so patient,
> As for himselfe, directed thus, by fate,
> To comfort Scilla so unfortunate,
> I doe professe by Cupids beauteous mother,
> Heres Seogans choise for Scilla, and no other;
> Though Scilla's sick with griefe because no sign
> Can there be found of vertue masculine.

The Puritan Bradford commented that Morton and his followers, like pagans at the feasts of Flora, "also set up a may-poll, drinking and dancing about it many days together, inviting the Indian women for their consorts, dancing and frisking together like so many faries, or furies, rather; and worse practices." The orgy with the Indian women was the central ritual of the Libertine counterreligion, the sale of arms its most threatening political move. Morton, faultless organizer of the Atlantic Cytherea, even composed songs in which he extolled Hymen, nectar, garlands of leaves, and the wantonness of nymphs:

> Lasses in beaver coats, come away;
> Ye shall be welcome to us, night and day.

The classic antiquity cherished by Renaissance Libertinism was on the point of becoming the fulcrum of a new society. The protracted, crude, and obscene abasements of drunken English servants under the witchlike sign of ram's horns would soon be ennobled by a whole literature (as would also happen later on for the "enlightened" Libertines of the eighteenth century), and ties of fraternity were established with the Indians, a "league of brotherhood."

Just as the Indian women took on the aspect of wood nymphs, so the New England landscape described by Morton answered to all the canons of the *locus amoenus* of classic rhetoric—the murmur of brooks, flowering meadows, fertile dales, dense clumps of luxuriant trees crossed by flights of little turtledoves—in precise opposition to the huge, dreadful forest that rose before the eyes of the Puritans. One might well ask whether there is such a thing as a pure sensation, separate from ideology and its aura of attendant images?

For Morton, following Montaigne's footsteps, the poverty of the Indians was a sign of bucolic purity.

Now since it is but foode and rayment that men that live needeth (though not all alike) why should not the natives of New England be sayd to live richly having no want of either: cloaths are the badge of sinne, and the more variety of fashions is but the greater abuse of the Creature. . . . According to humane reason guided onely by the light of nature, these people leades the more happy and freer life, being voyde of care, which torments the minds of many Christians.

Their regime is communist, as in Utopia, for "they are so loving also that they make use of those things they enjoy—the wife onely excepted—as common goods." And the sarcastic conclusion of *New English Canaan* is a prelude to the eulogy of the Lucifer of modern Libertines:

They may be rather accompted to live richly wanting nothing that is needful; and to be commended for leading a contented life, the younger being ruled by the Elder, ruled by the Powahs, and the Powahs are ruled by the Devill, and then you may imagine what good rule is like to be amongest them.[22]

Morton's hatred for the Puritans gives us a glimpse of the truth, and the sacrilegious outrage inflicted by the invaders on the Indians' holy places appears in its natural light. "The planters of Plymouth . . .," he writes, "having defaced the monument of the dead at Pasonayessit by taking away the hearse-cloth, which was two great bears' skins sewed together at full length, and propped up over the grave . . ." He also throws into relief the desperate defense of the insulted Indians after their chief had had a holy vision.

The other Libertine, John Josselyn, in *New England Rarities Dis-*

covered, published in 1672, looked at the bodies of the Indian women, "generally as plump as partridges," with the eyes of a Dutch painter of drunken revelry. He dedicated a poem to them, a study in the contrast between light and dark skin, which was simply an excuse to insinuate a Satanic hint among the praises of a dark, smooth epidermis:

> Maugre then all that can be said
> In flattery of White and Red;
> Those flatterers themselves must say
> That darkness was before the Day.

Chapter II

---◆◆◆---

The Warrior Theocracy

At its inception the Puritan theocracy of Massachusetts pursued inner perfection as the highest goal of a civilized society ruled wholly by the idea of a special pact with God. Not events so much as a decadence of men's spirits undermined Puritan society, which at the beginning of the eighteenth century still survived but was virtually prostrate. A weakening of ideas and faith was the intangible cause of the collapse, although the material cause was the much more active and secular economic life that changing customs brought about and which were the despair of the last, sarcastic Puritan moralists. Even James Fenimore Cooper, a Deist with little love for Puritanism, could not refrain from a moving threnody to that world in which for a certain period disorder, misery, and blasphemy had been unknown—a world, he confessed, that was an example of peace and rectitude and was certainly hated by the father of all iniquity.

Long before Max Weber advanced his theory of a rapacious, precapitalistic Puritanism, Cooper claimed more lofty ideals for the Puritans in his book *The Wept of Wish-ton-Wish*.[1]

The Puritan . . . was frugal from habit and principle more than from an undue longing after worldly wealth. He contented himself, therefore, with acquiring an estate that should be valuable, rather from its quality and beauty, than from its extent. . . . Long use and much training had accustomed them to a blending of religious exercises with most of the employments of life. . . . Devotion to the one great cause of their existence, austere habits, and unrelaxed industry in keeping alive a flame of zeal had been kindled in the other hemisphere, to burn longest and brightest in this, had interwoven the practice mentioned with most of the opinions and pleasures of these metaphysical though simple-minded people.

To a witness to the decline, the Cotton Mather of *Magnalia Christi Americana*, it seemed that it was not even doctrinal dissension that destroyed the theocracy.

Some little *controversies* [Mather writes] likewise have now and then arisen among them in the administration of their *discipline;* but Synods then regularly called, have usually and presently put into *joint* all that was apprehended *out.* Their chief *hazard* and symptom of degeneracy, is in the verification of that old observation, *Religio peperit Divitias, et filia devoravit matrem* [Religion brought forth Prosperity, and the *daughter* destroyed the *mother*]. . . . The one would expect, that as they grew in their *estates,* they would grow in the payment of their *quit-rents* unto the God who *gives them power to get wealth,* by more liberally supporting his ministers and ordinances among them; the most likely way to save them from the most miserable apostasy . . . nevertheless, there is danger lest the *enchantments* of the world make them to forget their errand into the wilderness.

For two generations the quest for perfection and thus for inner felicity had maintained a primacy over secular concerns, and the Puritan, pure pilgrim on the face of the earth, dead to the world, had with a firm hand established his theocratic government, remaining inflexible and industrious to the extent that he transcended the very world he was shaping. He felt as if already dead. "Place yourself in the *Circumstances* of a *Dying Person,*" Mather writes in *Manuductio ad Ministerium,* "your *Breath* failing, your *Throat* rattling, your *Eyes* with a dim Cloud, and your *Heads* with a damp Sweat upon them: And then entertain such Sentiments of this *World,* and of the *Work* to be done in this World, that such a *View* must needs inspire you withal."[2] He was overwhelmed with bliss and in a mood of constant wonderment and discovery. He based his life on beatitude, and in order to attain it he employed the hammer blows of sin, the terror of hell, banishing all diversions. His countenance was austere because he was rapt in his happiness as one of the elect.

∴

He came into contact with the Indians but without the slightest feeling of fraternity: not in spiritual joy, since the Indians seemed to him completely carnal, and not in faith, since their Dionysian dances and the practices of their shamans were repugnant to Puritan reserve and seemed a clear case of Satanism. In the *Records of the Colony of New Plymouth in New England* for 1653 it is affirmed:

That the Indians whoe know not god but worshipp and walke after the prince of the power of the aire serving their lusts hatefull and hating one another should grow Insolent and sundrey wayes Injurius to strangers of contrary Judgment and practise can not seem strange to any whoe duly consider what proportion and agreement there is ordenaryly betwixt the fruit and the tree.

Thus, since spiritual contact was barred, there could only prevail attitudes of an instinctive feeling of disgust toward a different race, combined with rapacity and scorn for people who seemed to lack all civilized customs.

All these Puritan contradictions exploded in Cotton Mather's biography of John Eliot, a missionary among the Indians. Eliot is shown leveling a long list of accusations against these "tawney serpents," the "veriest ruines of mankinde." When one sees them, he said, one learns what a hard master the devil is to his vassals. Living in a land filled with iron and copper deposits, these abject creatures still use simple stone tools and for money make do with sea shells strung like beads on a necklace! Their houses are made of mats stretched on poles over the bare earth, and instead of wrapping themselves in blankets they warm themselves at a fire; and finally, for clothes they cover themselves with the skins of animals!

The native delicacy is a spoonful of roasted meal, which, together with a drink of water, is enough for them to face an entire day's march. They do not have salt and have never heard of it. As for their medicine, except for certain specifics, it is reduced to a steam bath or a session of witchcraft. Their baths are caves into which, after having produced an intense heat, they enter in bands and sit for an hour sweating and smoking, and then rush out and leap into an icy stream. The witchcraft session is, however, their major resource and for this they summon a powwow, that is, "a priest who has more familiarity with Satan than his neighbours." This priest roars and howls, performing magical acts on the sick. Furthermore, what should be said of these Indians who, despite the abundance of wood, do not know how to exploit it to construct a fleet of ships? Or of their laziness, which allows the women to build their huts? They excel at hunting but have no artisans. They are also mechanically skillful, more or less like beavers.

This list of accusations, dictated by a pride in mechanical and technical conquests, stands completely apart from the Puritan afflatus that pervades Mather's unalloyed praise of John Eliot's saintliness, in a book that is studded with delicate, theologically perceptive observations. (For example, "A Man's Carriage in his own House is a part, or at least a sign, of his due Deportment in the House of God." Here, the qualifying phrase is pregnant with meaning: obedience and at the same time superiority to these same rules were typical traits of the Puritan, to whom the rules are signs and tests rather than the aims of devout life.) In this indictment of the Indians, however, the bitter man bursts forth, arrogantly straining toward an ideal of technical development and indifferent to or contemptuous of the inner life of those who do not possess the practical comforts of civilization.

And yet, perhaps, defenseless and lacking in technique as they are, the Indians do have some sort of spiritual tradition? Yes, he answers, they do.

They have somewhat observed the motions of the *Stars;* among which it has been surprising unto me to find that they have always called "Charles's Wain" by the name of *Paukunnawaw,* or *the Bear,* which is the name whereby Europeans also have distinguished it. Moreover, they have little, if any, traditions among them worthy of our notice. . . .

They believe everything to be divine that produces singular effects, and they attribute every event to divine ire or favor. "As in a time of calamity, they keep a *dance,* or a day of extravagant ridiculous devotions to their god; so in a time of prosperity they likewise have a *feast,* wherein they also make presents one unto another." The Indians relate that their greatest god extracted man and woman from a stone, but, dissatisfied, broke them up and then drew them from a tree.

"And when they have any weighty undertaking before them, it is an usual thing for them to have their assemblies, wherein, after the usage of some diabolical rites, a devil appears unto them. . . ." Then, advised by the devils they have called up, they act. During the wars, since the colonists' dogs barked at their furtive approach and endangered them, they sacrificed a dog to the devil, after which "no English dog would bark at an Indian for divers months ensuing."

Although suffused with the Puritan spirit, Cotton Mather concealed a positive feeling for the Enlightenment. He could not hide a contradiction common among Puritans between the cult of spiritual wealth and support of the ideals formulated by Francis Bacon and embodied in the Royal Society and the doctrine of civil progress.

In Mather's argument against the Indians, a people incapable of creating a factory civilization, and in John Eliot's remarks on the connection between conversion and economic progress, one finds in embryo the spirit that in 1855 would lead Lyman Whiting to proclaim: "Like the pillars of Hercules, Education and Religion define and defend the path of Trade."[3]

Contact with the Indians had a traumatic effect on the Puritan, revealing to him what he was in spite of himself: bound more to the ideology of progress than to the evangelical virtues and, moreover, the victim of instinctive racial furies. A confused, tormented, and therefore weak man like Cotton Mather represented the majority, which was completely hostile to the Indians, much more effectively than solid and mature persons with solid, mature characters.

Their traumatic reaction is revealed in a stylistic peculiarity character-istic of all the popular Puritan descriptions of the Indians: the compul-sion to use the automatic denigratory epithet. The trauma became petrified and reinforced by repetition.

William Byrd, a Libertine and monarchist hostile to the Puritans, insinuated that their aversion to the Indians was in fact a sensual attrac-tion so excessive that it terrified them, making them fear the loss of the very basis of their existence should they ever yield to it.

These Saints [he writes] conceived the same Aversion to the Copper Com-plexion of the Natives, with that of the first Adventurers in Virginia, who would, on no Terms, contract alliances with them, afraid perhaps, like the Jews of Old, lest they might be drawn into Idolatry by those Strange women.[4]

The most renowned Puritan theologians were blind to the humanity of the Indians. In Thomas Hooker's sermons, for instance, that humanity appears only to inspire this usually seraphic thinker with a few cruelly warlike metaphors.[5] The Puritan poets scarcely mention them. Yet some verses that prove to be an exception can be found—for example, those of the Reverend William Morell, who was, however, an Anglican. Having arrived with a small group at Wessagusset in 1623, he soon returned to England, where in 1625 he published his poem in Latin hexameters, "Nova Anglia."[6] He praises the fertile land:

> A land rich in fruitful plowed furrows and covered with plains;
> Abounding in beasts of many kinds and laced by rivers,
> Warm enough in climate, and sheltered from biting cold.

By what right, he asks, are these lands occupied by these "wondrous cruell, strangely base and vile" natives, living in "houses like to sties"? Here and there one sees something lovely in the ornaments woven by the women—"rare stories, princes, people, kingdomes, towers"—but their music is primitive:

> Even though all writing is unknown to them, they do have some songs,
> And make flutes from reeds of various lengths; they also
> Play a rustic music in their villages, unpleasant, lugubrious,
> With noisy and blunt sounds that charm their hearts, their feelings,
> And their ears, which lack all refinement.

However, an effort must be made to redeem this depressing barbarism; Morell exhorts the English to provide an example of devotion that will enthrall and convert:

> If my efforts can help this barbarous people,
> If my artless poetry can please the Anglican,
> And easily give back strong rulers to these people
> And persuade hard-working and pious settlers to come;
> If it can teach the life and customs of our forefathers,
> If the English will give the Indians examples of a happy life,
> By which they can attain the uppermost bounds of heaven:
> Then all will come true according to my prayers, and I hope
>   that these verses
> Of mine will have been the forecast of an exalted kingdom.

The Puritan Michael Wigglesworth, toward the end of the century, did not repeat Morell's reaction of Anglican repugnance and condescension, yet there are distinct signs of horror and impatience in his poem "God's Controversy with New England," where the shores of Massachusetts before the arrival of the pilgrims were

> A waste and howling wilderness,
>   Where none inhabited
> But hellish fiends, and brutish men
>   That devils worshipped.

In other words, the island of Sycorax and Caliban before the arrival of Prospero, where England's dregs had their first contact with the Indians. In 1621, Sir Ferdinando Gorges' speech to the House of Commons already deplored the wicked fishermen and traders:

first in their manners and behaviour they are worse than the very Savages, impudently and openly lying with their Women, teaching their Men to drinke drunke, to sweare and blaspheme the name of God, and in their drunken humour to fall together by the eares . . . besides, they cozen and abuse the Savages in trading and trafficking.[7]

The Puritans left Holland convinced that they would encounter "Salvage and brutish men which range up and down, little otherwise than the wild beasts." William Bradford[8] noted the natives' zest for "flaying some alive with the shells of fishes, cutting off the members and joints of others by piecemeal and broiling on the coals, eat the collops of their flesh in their sight whilst they live." In fact, the tortures employed in England, like those in Spain, were no less terrible, with the result that, rather than run the risk of incurring them, the Puritan community preferred to confront the hazards of America.

For the Puritan, in contrast to a John Smith or a Morton, New England was a desolate, bleak country peopled by brutes, according to what Bradford tells us. And yet in their first explorations of the dreadful waste, in the dense forest of trees denuded by the severe cold, the newly disembarked colonists had come upon indications of compassion. From far off they saw Indians sharing fish among themselves, tried to reach them, and, following tracks in the sand, came to the border of the forest where first they saw a path, then a graveyard, encircled by a palisade fence and containing graves more ornate than those left behind in England. Clearings in the forest were proof that the Indians had cultivated this land in the past. So hunting, fishing, and sporadic agriculture constituted the basis for their simple economy, and an elaborate cult of the dead their peculiar piety.

A plague had depopulated Massachusetts just before the Puritans landed. Cotton Mather remarked that this was why "the woods were almost cleared of those pernicious creatures, to make room for a better growth."[9] However, an Indian, Squanto, saved the pilgrims threatened by famine. In this episode, which later came to be celebrated each year as Thanksgiving Day, Bradford saw the hand of God, but he did not feel the slightest gratitude toward the Indian, who "was a spetiall instrument sent by God for their good beyond their expectation. He directed them how to set their corne, where to take fish and to procure other commodities, and was also their pilott in bringing them to unknowne places for their profitt."

Squanto was kidnaped by an English ship, managed to escape, and returned to his native region; perhaps his sorrow over the plague that decimated his people persuaded him to join the English.[10] Later he resorted to all sorts of intrigues to remain the sole mediator between his people and the colonists; the English let him and another Indian collaborator compete jealously. Bradford observed that at his death Squanto's English friends, who inherited his belongings, were saddened by his loss.

Revulsion was Bradford's reaction to the Indian. Cotton Mather was equally cold, even icy. In the *Magnalia*, besides exulting over the epidemics among the Indians, he describes the colonists' first horrifying encounters: "The very *looks* and *shouts* of those *grim salvages*, had not muche less of terrour in them, than if they had been so many devils." He also writes of the "special providence" that would help the Puritans in their contacts with the sparse, sorely tried natives:

It seems that this unlucky Squanto having told his countrymen how easie it was for so great a monarch as K. James to destroy them all, if they should hurt any of his people, he went on to terrifie them with a ridiculous *rhodomantado*, which they believed, that this people kept the *plague* in a cellar (where they kept their powder), and could at their pleasure let it loose to make such havock among them, as the distemper had already made among them a few years before. Thus was the *tongue* of a dog made useful to a feeble and sickly Lazarus!

"Divine providence" helps them again when an Indian plot is averted.

Massasoit, the southern Sachim [Mather writes], falling sick, the Governour of Plymouth desired a couple of gentlemen, whereof one was that good man, Mr Winslow, to visit this poor Sachim; whom after their long journey they found lying at the point of death with a crue of hellish Powaws, using their ineffectual spells and howls, about him to recover him. Upon the taking of some English phisick, he presently revived; and thus regaining his lost health, the fees he paid his English doctors were, *a confession of the plot among several nations of the Indians to destroy the English.*

Ridiculous when friends, detestable when enemies, the Indians could not expect any sort of favor. Rare were the cases in which this Puritan wall of ice gave way and permitted some natural amiability.

∴

To forestall an Indian plot against the advanced outposts of Wessagusset, Myles Standish slaughtered the native warriors in 1623, and after this the Plymouth Colony had peace. This gave rise to a complaint; from Leiden the minister of the Plymouth church wrote to Bradford:

How happy a thing had it been, if you have converted some before you had killed any. . . . You will say they deserved it. I grant it; but upon what provocations and invitements by those heathenish Christians? . . . It is also a thing more glorious in men's eyes, than pleasing in God's, or convenient for Christians, to be a terror to poor, barbarous people; and indeed I am afraid lest, by these occasions, others should be drawn to affect a kind of ruffling course in the world.

The same rare, unferocious sentiment is expressed by the religious leaders in 1640, as John Winthrop recorded in his diary: "We received a letter from the magistrates at Connecticut declaring their dislike of such as would have the Indians rooted out as being of the cursed race of Ham, and their desire of our mutual accord in seeking to gain them by justice and kindness."[11] A spirit of true benevolence also lights up *A Memorial Relating to the Kennebeck Indians,* in which in 1721 Samuel Sewall attempted to oppose the dominant inhumanity of the time.

The literature produced by the war against Philip, the Indian king, reveals the hatred for the Indian in its basest crudity, with squalid, repetitious, stylistic clauses made up of denigratory epithets—"barbarous," "cruel," "savage." William Hubbard rings the changes on "faithless and ungrateful," "bloudy and deceitful monsters," "perfidious, cruel and hellish monsters."

Nobody thought for even a moment that King Philip might be reacting to injustices he had suffered; if anything, the presence of Quakers or the lack of faith was considered to be responsible for God's wrath. Peter Folger prescribed:

> If we then truly turn to God,
> He will remove his Ire,
> And will forthwith take his Rod,
> And cast it into Fire.
> Let us then search what is the Sin
> That God doth punish for;
> And when found out cast it away,
> And ever it abhor.

Captain Winthrop wrote equally graceless verses:

> Repent therefore, and do no more advance thyself so high,
> But humbled be, and thou shalt see these Indians soon wyll dy.
> A swarm of flies, they may arise, a Nation to annoy,
> Yes Rats and Mice, or Swarms of Lice a Nation may destroy.[12]

Increase Mather established a perfect harmony between historic destiny and Puritan spirituality. He claimed that the Pequots were beaten in 1637 because of "a mighty Spirit of Prayer and faith then stirring"; the faith of the first generation of Puritans preserved the peace, but the second generation sinned, hence the struggles and misfortunes.[13]

When a Quaker from Salem, Thomas Maule, dared to defend the Indians led by King Philip,[14] Cotton Mather in *Decennium Luctuosum* criticized his theological views by means of legal quibbles, and was shocked by the Quaker's assertion that whoever has in himself a "body of sin" is a witch, or that the devil, sin, and death are not substantial. Then Mather flung at him a pure and simple string of curses, as though overcome with horror because the Quaker dared to write: "God hath well rewarded the inhabitants of New-England for their unrighteous dealings towards the native Indians, whom now the Lord hath suffered to reward the inhabitants with a double measure of blood, by fire and sword."

Maule recalled the massacres of Indians carried out at the beginning of the colonization. Cotton Mather had no other recourse than to scream at him and to employ base emotional blackmail: "Thus are the Ashes of our *Fathers* vilely *staled* upon by one who perhaps would not stick at the Villainy of doing as much upon their *Baptism* itself."[15]

Increase and Cotton Mather projected the Puritan struggle with the Indians against the background of the Old Testament, identifying the Puritans with the Jews fighting in Canaan (without noticing the obvious contradiction, given their theory that the Indians were part of the lost tribes of Israel). In the second book of the *Magnalia,* Cotton Mather transforms the whole affair into a clear-cut Biblical episode: King Philip has a dream in which he sees himself the prisoner, like the man in the Midianite army, of the English. Immediately after, this Agag is attacked and killed in the very place where he plotted and perpetrated his evil deeds. Then he is drawn and quartered, and his hands are borne in triumph through Boston, his head through Plymouth: God sends "the head of a *leviathan* for a *thanksgiving-feast.*"

In the same vein Increase Mather described how all the Indian chiefs who rose in struggle against "Israel in the desert" were punished by God. But one case stands out from among the host of examples, the description of the death of Squanto, who, so Mather relates, had a vision of the English God in the shape of a minister, who told him to stop drinking rum, to observe the Sabbath rest, and to deal justly with his neighbors; if he obeyed, he would go to heaven.

But this pretended God said nothing to him about Jesus Christ. However, this apparition so wrought upon Squanto as that he left his drunkenness, and became a strict observer of the Sabbath day: yea, so that he always kept it as a day of fast, and would hear the English ministers preach, and was very just in his dealing.[16]

Later the same ghost reappeared and told Squanto to commit suicide, giving him the guarantee that this would be followed by his resurrection and eternal life. At first his wife and friends succeeded in dissuading him, but afterward he gave way and hanged himself.

∴

In his *Narrative of the Troubles with the Indians in New-England,* published in Boston in 1677, the minister William Hubbard tells the story of the wars against King Philip with the customary coldness. The netops—Indian friends of the colonists—are admired for their dexterity and cunning in war but detested for barbarous acts that put them in the same category as their fellow Indians.

The tortures that they inflict on their prisoners provoke English tears. However, the sight of a rebellious Indian tortured and forced to dance as the fingers of his hands and the toes of his feet are being torn off, yet able to endure all this with great indifference, calls forth from Hubbard not admiration but the usual epithets—"this unsensible and hardened monster." Whereas Increase Mather stands aloof from all passion and becomes insensitive in order to be able to discern a wholly divine design in this history, a design in which the English and the Indians are mere pawns and external events are linked with the inner state of souls, Hubbard's insensitivity is a humanly base partisanship. He informs us that the English let their Indian auxiliaries torture prisoners "lest by a denial they might disoblige their Indian friends."

In his description of the war against the Pequots in *Newes from America* (1638), John Underhill, a professional soldier who emigrated to America in 1630, faces up to a question that was perhaps not infrequent: Why are the Puritans so enraged? Should not Christians show mercy and pity? He replies that the Indians are ferocious, that the Scriptures sometimes ordered the killing of even women and children. On other occasions, perhaps, Scripture advises us to act differently: "We will not dispute it now. We have sufficient light from the word of God for our proceedings."

This "light from the word" that guides the Puritan warriors casts a sumptuous, sinister glitter over the cruel description of King Philip's death, which forms the baroque, rhetorical climax of Increase Mather's *History of King Philip's War.*

The seraphic surrender urged in Puritan sermons can degenerate into the justification of every form of dishonesty and cruelty. The Puritan army and Parliament were accustomed to justify every one of their acts as the fruit of divine inspiration, and so Samuel Butler could write in *Hudibras:*

> . . . For breaking of a faith and lying,
> Is but a kind of self-denying,
> A saint-like virtue . . .
>
> [II, vv. 33–35]

In any event, an indignant critic was observing the Puritans from within their own ranks. Edward Randolph, agent of the King of England, wrote that according to some persons the war was due to the imprudent zeal of magistrates who wanted to convert the natives before civilizing them, imposing the strict observance of Puritan laws on licentious people who were encouraged to drink and intoxication by a money-greedy rabble. There was a fine for drunkenness, but the natives preferred the floggings, so the punishment was commuted to forced labor—hence the widespread anger and the war.

Others attributed the sudden sedition to maneuvers of the Jesuits, still others to the injustices suffered by King Philip, from whom land had been extorted.

Randolph, an enemy of the Puritans, adds that instead of attributing their misfortunes to these causes, they impute them to extravagant fashions, to the neglect of religious functions, or to the presence of the Quakers. God would appear to have used the Indians in order to punish these outrages.

The main cause of the war should rather be traced, he says, to the imprudent granting of arms to the Indians and the formation of a militia composed of converted natives, who afterward proved to be the most barbarous enemies. Because of the war, the King's informant suggests, the men most loyal to the crown are dead, while the members of the Puritan church took their ease at home.[17]

.·.

A century later America's first epic poem, *The Destruction of the Pequods* (1794), was written by a late follower of Puritanism, in the totally antagonistic climate of the Enlightenment. Timothy Dwight, Jonathan Edwards's grandson, retells the first war of his ancestors. Just as his verse reverberates with the ancient horror of the devil's progeny challenging the new Israel, so in his treatises Calvinist theology makes a final sortie against the dominant philosophy of Deism. Yet the setting of diabolical horror is closer to the Gothic fashion of the period than to Puritanical austerity; the Indian village resembles one of those grim fortresses in the Catholic Apennines conjured up by the truculent imagination of Enlightenment narrators:

> Far in the wildering wood's impervious gloom
> A lonely castle, brown with twilight dread,
> Where oft the embowelled captive met his doom,
> And frequent heaved, around the hollow tomb,
> Scalps hung in rows, and whitening bones were strew'd;
> Where, round the broiling babe, fresh from the womb,
> With howls the Powaw fill'd the dark abode,
> And screams and midnight prayers invoked the evil god.
> But now no awful rites, nor potent spell,
> To silence charmed the peals of coming war.

Chapter III

———— ✦ ————

Missionaries, Demonologists, and Puritan Captives

In Puritan literature three names in particular are associated with the Indians—the missionaries John Eliot, Experience Mayhew, and David Brainerd.

John Eliot emigrated to Boston in 1631. Though as a youth he had the privilege of living close to Thomas Hooker, the great mystical theoretician of the struggle against fantasizing and the concomitant attainment of perfect felicity, Eliot's spirituality was orderly rather than fervent, painstaking but mediocre. The external severity of the masters of Puritanism often hid a burning spirit, straining single-mindedly to heed the subtle voices of divine inspiration; but in Eliot that austere coldness had penetrated to his very core, and his emotions were that of a diligent but simple person. Deep down he was essentially a good family man. As one of those who had sentenced Anne Hutchinson to banishment, he found her claim that she had received revelations from God particularly reprehensible.

Of the fervor with which the Puritans flung themselves at the kingdom of heaven he had preserved only a relic: the conviction that since the Indians were of Hebrew extraction, once they were converted the prophecy of the Second Coming would perforce be fulfilled. This was a special obsession of the Puritans. One of them, William Gouge, in 1621 published *The Calling of the Jewes,* in which he announced a world-wide Hebrew empire following that people's conversion. This work provoked the ire of King James, to whom it seemed a crime of *lèse-majesté.*

Eliot had no doubts about the descent of the Indians from the Hebrew tribes dispersed at the time of Ezra. The belief was so widespread that John White, one of the founders of the Massachusetts Bay Colony, regretted that the name of Salem had been given to the port on that large bay, since the indigenous name Naumkeag was already Hebraic: *Nahum Keike,* or "consolation cove."[1]

There is no record, however, of the many systematic attempts to square the Puritans' persuasion that they themselves were the true Israel (or the remains of Israel), in flight from Anglican Egypt, with their other conviction of the Hebraic character of the Indians. It is true that the epigraph in Thomas Thorowgood's book, a passage from St. Jerome's comments on Isaiah, worked it all out: "The Ethiopians are turned into the sons of God, if they have repented, and the sons of God are turned into Ethiopians if they have fallen into the abyss of sin."

Eliot prepared to convert the Indians with the prudent cautiousness of a good family man, first compiling a grammar of the Algonquin dialects of Massachusetts and only then, in 1646, beginning to preach to them. In his first sermon in the native language, based on a passage from Ezekiel (XXXVII, 9, 10), Eliot set forth the Ten Commandments. The Indians asked: How was it possible to know Christ? Could Christ understand speeches in the native tongue? Had the English been as ignorant of holy matters in the past as they, the Indians, were now? How could there be an image of God, given the prohibition of idolatry? In line with the second commandment, would the good son of an evil father be offensive to God? Why, despite the flood, is the world so full of people?

In his turn Eliot asked if they would like to see God, and they replied that He was to be seen "with the spirit that lives inside one." That first dialogue concluded with the unanimous decision to build a town in which they could live according to the rules that had been revealed to them.

At the second meeting the Indians asked why it was that since there was a common heavenly Father there were such great divergences in the religious knowledge of the English and the Indians. Eliot replied with a short compendium of universal history. They then asked how one was to serve God, and Eliot taught them the Puritan method as explained by his teacher, Hooker: first, one had to have a full awareness of one's own unworthiness, then implore the undeserved and undeservable mercy, and finally discern the will of God in the same way that a child tries to understand what his father wants of him. Fourth question: Why is water in the sea salty and water on land sweet? Eliot fell back on God's inscrutable decree, but nevertheless added a few scientific explanations. Thus, in reply to a question about the distribution of water on the earth (the theme of one of Dante's Latin writings), he endeavored to teach them the spherical shape of the earth. At the end of the meeting, at the moment of prayer, one of the Indians burst into tears.

At the third meeting Eliot spoke of the devil, and the questions were: Is it right to pray to him? What is meant by humiliation? What is a spirit? And, finally, should one pay attention to signs?

Cultivated preachers were needed to reply to such questions as: Who was created first, man or the devil? Does the devil live in us as in a house? What was the devil's first sin? In view of His omnipotence, why doesn't God kill the devil, who makes all men so evil? The Puritan missionaries were greatly comforted by such signs "of the working of the Spirit by the word on them."

As a result, a literature of pamphlets on missionary work sprang up in England, filled with the confessions, sermons, and deathbed statements of converted Indians;[2] the character of Friday, in Defoe's novel *Robinson Crusoe*, is a literary descendant of the Indians in this genre.

Thanks to his pupils' questions, Eliot began delving further into the Indian world. The man who had asked him whether it was right to pray to the devil was a leader of medicine men, who were persuaded to change their lives. Eliot observed that a man was called to "witchcraft" through a dream or the vision of a serpent and that for two days his tribe celebrated his vocation with dances.[3]

Eliot was convinced that only when the Indians became more civilized could one convert them. (In his funeral eulogy of Eliot, John Danforth declared that Eliot had vainly hoped for the tree of grace to flourish "in forests where civility can't live."[4]) In their new village Eliot's converted Indians became industrious and engaged in trade, giving up games of chance (the Puritan theologians considered gambling a prostitution of divine providence) and the shamanistic treatment of illness. When the pagan Indians mocked them because in spite of their conversion they were as poor as before, Eliot explained that divine gifts are of two kinds: the minor and visible, and the major, the skilled knowledge of heavenly matters. Because of the latter, one obtains the former. In fact, to the extent that they became wiser and better Christians, they would be more industrious, more orderly, and, as a consequence, would have better clothes, more comfortable homes, and other things besides.

The Indian women, who had become weavers, dared to ask such questions as: If my husband prays and I do not say anything, yet my heart experiences what he says, do I pray?

It is Thomas Shepard, friend of Eliot and New England divine, who jots down the most thoughtful questions: How does one recognize the iniquitous? If a body is shut up in an iron box that is thrown into the fire, how does the soul get out? Why did not God give everyone a good heart? How can one discern when faith is good and prayer is good?

A strange doctrine circulated: the truths announced by Eliot were known in past times but had been lost, the Indians having been, as it were, asleep. At a later date Francis Parkman would explain that mysterious theory as a teaching of the Catholic missionaries; others would trace it back to a group of French survivors of a shipwreck, though it could quite simply have been accepted as an actual Indian tradition.

∴

One of the catechumens' questions had been: Why had the colonists waited so long before converting them? Eliot replied that only now were they prepared to listen to the Word. Actually, the Puritan undertaking had by now failed, and Eliot wanted to revive Utopia with the new converts.

As to the English in the colonies, Eliot looked forward hopefully to the blessed day when the Word of God would be their "Magna Charta and chief lawbook," and all men of law would have to study the Scriptures.*
But he hoped to make that dream an actuality first of all through the Indians. The programmatic text of the new theocratic Utopia was *The Christian Commonwealth,* which was published in London in 1659.[5]

But how could one bring this theocracy to birth if people preferred the stellar light of their own beliefs to the sun of the Scriptures? Only the theologically uncorrupt and passive Indians would follow all the divine commands. Eliot's modest prose waxes almost rhetorical: they will be guided entirely by the Scriptures in all things, both in ecclesiastical and civil matters: "The Lord shall be their lawgiver, the Lord shall be their judge, the Lord shall be their King, and unto that frame the Lord will bring all the world ere he hath done."

The example of an absolutist theocratic community will be, Eliot predicts, irresistible. In the meanwhile, inspired by Mosaic norms, he starts in 1651 with the foundation of Natick, the new village of "praying

---

* In one of the letters appended to Henry Whitfield's *The Light appearing more and more Towards a Perfect Day. Or, a Farther Discovery of the Present State of the Indians in New England, Concerning the Progress of the Gospel among them. Manifested by Letters from Such as Preacht to them there,* published in London in 1651.

Indians," and believes that he is seeing the scattered bones uniting to form a skeleton.

Under his spiritual guidance the Indians were approaching the heart of Calvinist theology; they were already asking if God knew who would repent. One can imagine Eliot's Puritan exultation when he asked his community what demonstrated the divine origin of the Scriptures and received the reply that they transformed hearts, infusing them with wisdom and humility. The interpreters were consulted time and again to ascertain the exactness of their translations. Then Eliot asked what sin is, and the Indians replied that there is radical sin that originates in an iniquitous heart and actual sin that is the violation of God's law.

These enthusiasms were soon crushed by King Philip's War, which divided the Indians into opposing groups. The chroniclers of King Philip's War have only words of scorn for the "praying Indians," even though the native preacher Sassamon was King Philip's first victim.

Another of the apostles to the Indians, Daniel Gookin, a soldier who emigrated from Virginia in 1644, discerned the hand of God in the extermination of the pagans, the divinity's wrath having been aroused by their rejection of the Gospel. Had not one of the peace clauses proposed by the Narragansetts asked for the prohibition of missionary activities? The converted Indians, "subtle and wily" by nature, were faithful allies of the Puritans, but the peoples' hostile clamor increased not only against them but against the English who treated them charitably, especially Eliot. The Puritans asked: Isn't this cruel spirit promoted by Satan to prevent conversions?[6]

With Gookin begins the tradition that divides Indians into good ones (at the time, the converts to Puritanism, later, with Cooper, those of Deist tendencies) and bad ones—people "greatly addicted to war, spoil, and rapine," who sing all the time, even in prison.

Some Quakers at Martha's Vineyard tried to convert the Puritan Indians, teaching them that "they had a light within them, that was sufficient guide to happiness." But an Indian countered with: "You tell us of a light within us, that will guide us to salvation; but our experience tells us that we are darkness and corruption, and all manner of evil within our hearts."

∴

When he was about twenty, David Brainerd experienced the dark night of the soul. Bereft of all comfort, he felt damned until the revelation of a sudden happiness came to him, everything looked different, and time ceased to flow.

At twenty-five he began to preach in a community of converted Indians at Kent, and in 1743 a missionary society of New York put him in charge of the church of Kaanaumeek. He was sick and assailed by doubts concerning the efficacy of his apostolate. "I longed for death beyond measure," he wrote in his diary.

The Indians listened to him with reverence, but the whites who frequented the place were sullen and vulgar: "Oh, I thought, what a hell it would be to live with such men to eternity!" And what a divine gift it was to be different from them! He also turned this salutary contempt against his own weaknesses, remarking:

I fell down before the Lord and groaned under my vileness, deadness, barrenness, and felt as if I was guilty of soul-murder, in speaking to immortal souls in such manner as I had then done. . . . At night I spent some time in instructing my poor people. Oh, that God would pity their souls! I thought, if God should say, "Cease making any provisions for this life, for you shall in a few days go out of time into eternity," my soul would leap for joy. . . . I always feel comfortably when God realizes death and the things of another world to my mind.

What Puritan skill in heightening his trouble and hammering his spirit to the point of utter exasperation! Brainerd knew how to stimulate divine revelations, as on this day in 1742:

Tuesday, December 21. Had a sense of my insufficiency for any public work and business, as well as to live to God. I rode over to Derby and preached there: it pleased God to afford me assistance and enlargement, and to enable me to speak with a soft, tender power and energy. We had afterwards a comfortable evening in singing and prayer. God enabled me to pray with as much spirituality and sweetness as I have done for some time: my mind seemed to be unloaded of sense and imagination and was in measure let into the immaterial world of spirits. This day and evening was, I trust, through infinite goodness, made very profitable to a number of us, to advance our souls in holiness and conformity to God: the glory be to Him for ever. Amen. *How blessed it is to grow more and more like God.*[7]

Brainerd managed to arouse the same reactions in the Indians. He recounts how his interpreter's mind seemed to be totally devoid of religiosity; one day he would appear to be touched by grace, only to return to his habitual impassivity. Then he became ill and asked what he should do to save himself. He saw a mountain rise up before him; it was riding up into the sky, it seemed to him, but the road was bordered by briars, so thickly grown that he could not advance an inch. Finally, Brainerd writes, he discovers that he cannot overcome the obstacles simply by his own power, begins to realize his sinfulness, and lo and behold, the Puritan dialectic functions: he has become another man. A childish old woman also has a vision, and suddenly she is conversant with spiritual matters; Brainerd whispers to himself that only a spirit, good or evil, could explain this triumph over nature.

No other figures, however, stand out in his diary, and from his book *Divine Grace Displayed* one gets the picture of people living in fetid huts filled with the noise of shrieking infants whom no one restrains, of people childishly reluctant to fix their attention, accustomed to live from day to day without concerning themselves with the hereafter. The questions asked by the Indians are often the same as those addressed to Eliot. For example: Why didn't God forgive His Son without also exacting His sacrifice? The idea that there could be sinners who had never done wrong was alien to the Indians.

But one day Brainerd met some Indians who greeted his sermons with rapture. So, in 1745, at Crossweeksung, his life underwent a radical change: from among fewer than forty Indians, three listeners to his sermon cried out and wept bitterly. "They all, as one, seemed in an agony of soul to obtain an interest in Christ. . . . Most were much affected, and many in great distress for their souls; some few could neither go nor stand, but lay flat on the ground, as if pierced at heart, crying incessantly for mercy."[8]

It was as though the vision of a God who calls longingly to men incapable of reaching Him had kindled the completely Dionysian religiosity of the Indians. During the baptism of these converted Indians, Brainerd finally realized their true nature; he describes their reciprocal affection in the new happiness in vivid, moving terms.

Thus the pagan Indians "living in the shadow of death," among whom Brainerd traveled for a long time along the Susquehanna, are sharply portrayed, particularly the medicine men, who try to capture the spirit of disease hovering over the region, shrieking and twisting their bodies, nervously passing their hands over their faces, and then extending their arms as though to ward something off, their fingers spread out, sitting on the ground and bowing down to it (exactly as was done by the converted at Crossweeksung, after they had sensed the appearance of a new invisible presence). Brainerd reacted with horror and dismay, yet made an effort to look at them with compassion. Soon after, however, he encountered a startling apparition: a horrendous, varicolored mask set on a bear's skin advancing toward him with the bounds of a frightful tree frog—an Indian priest wanting to restore the ancient faith and tradition lost after the whites introduced alcohol. It is as though Brainerd had met his double in Indian form; perhaps he knew in his heart that he, too, was a relic, a reactionary restorer of declining Puritanism.[9]

The two men engaged in a lengthy discussion, the Indian relating that, in revulsion from a corrupt world, he had withdrawn to a hermit's life, but that God had visited him in his solitude, exhorting him to devote himself to his people and to restore the ancient religion. Many Christian truths expounded by Brainerd were accepted by the priest as similar to his own revelations, but he denied the existence of Satan as contrary to the authentic tradition he was following. A serious and religious man, Brainerd said to himself as he left.

In the meantime, the converted Indians were acquiring Puritan calm and temperance, learned to pay their debts, gave up alcohol, and renounced divorce. Brainerd's experiences with the Indians were so absorbing that, for a time, they dispelled the sense of disconnection and of depression characteristic of the disease from which he suffered—tuberculosis. But soon his illness began to consume him with the typical rapidity of its final phase.

After the sacrament, [I] could scarcely get home. . . . I lay in pain till some time in the evening, and then was able to sit up and discourse with friends. O, how was this day spent in prayers and praises among my dear people! One might hear them all the morning before public worship, and in the evening till near midnight, praying and singing praises to God. . . . My soul was refreshed, though my body was weak.

Finally, he had to give up the mission. Comforted by the devoted love of Jonathan Edwards's eighteen-year-old daughter, a year of spiritual bliss was still granted to him. To her he said on the point of death: "Are you willing to part with me? I am willing to part with you. . . ."—an inimitably Puritan, wholly edifying deathbed scene, similar to the death of Cotton Mather's first wife, when the couple renounced the great comfort of holding hands to show their submission to the divine will.

An inspired sermon by Jonathan Edwards terminated Brainerd's funeral ceremony, concluding the drama of an austere spirit whose energies had been spent struggling against a body that generated a desire for death and a sense of desolation. Indians formed the chorus that intoned the funeral hymns.[10]

From the exalted mystic Edwards one would expect at least a trace of feeling equal, if not to the saintly Canadian Marie de l'Incarnation, at least to that of the upright Quaker John Woolman in his relations with the Indians. No abundance of sympathy, however, can be found in his writings. He tells us that Brainerd taught him compassion for the Indians, who had been brought to America by the devil to create a completely demonic realm withdrawn from Christian influence. In a letter he advises the teaching of English to the native children, but as he writes he is carried away by the idea of a pedagogy that would help the children to think about holy matters, gradually divesting them of their timidity; they must be educated at a very early age, above all in sacred music, which softens the heart, harmonizes the emotions, and gives one a taste for superior things. In this manner it will become possible to tear them away from the "coarseness, and filth, and degradation" of their savage life.[11] Perhaps the wretched, degenerate state of the native population of Stockbridge could inspire only an honest struggle against their exploiters, not a work that was pervaded by their actual existence.[12]

It would fall to Experience Mayhew to get to the heart of their humanity and delineate the life of the converted Indians in his biographies of Indians, but these already belong to literature of an Indian stamp.

In *Bonifacius, an Essay Upon the Good,* Cotton Mather, while announcing the final extermination of the last pagan natives in New England, mentions colonies of converted Indians for whom, in addition to the Bible, other books of devotion have been translated:

. . . the pertinent *prayers* and (*sine monitore, quia de pectore* [without guidance, but from the heart] the orthodox *sermons* (at the hearing whereof, the very children of a dozen years old will readily turn to the proofs), and the singing of *psalms,* with a melody outdoing many of the English, in their meetings, have been frequently observed with admiration.[13]

∴

New England's Prospect, the work of a man of acute intelligence by the name of William Wood, otherwise unknown, was published in London in 1634. It is the only glimpse we have of all that is noble and gentle in the character of the natives. They cannot tolerate violent or provocative disturbances and are dismayed when the English give way to them, "such is the mild temper of their spirits." Wood admits that it is difficult to penetrate the natives' religious world. However, he believes that according to their religion, the benevolent god, Ketan, like some sort of Ceres, bestows harvests on them and also dispenses clement weather, rain, and the cure of illnesses. But the most important cult is that of the necromancers or *powaws,* capable of making water burn, moving rocks, causing trees to dance, and transforming themselves into pure flames, even though it has been objected that these are simple optical illusions. But certainly the other ability of the witch doctor Visscannawa cannot be attributed to suggestion: in the winter, when there is not a trace of greenery, he burns an old leaf and, after immersing its ashes in water, produces a new, green leaf.

This is one of the common assertions made by the alchemists of Europe. Thomas Vaughan, brother of the poet Henry Vaughan, also made it in his book *Anthroposophia theomagica.* Sir Thomas Browne taught that nature is a phoenix that is able to rise from its ashes. The vision of living forms being reborn from the ashes is still alive in H. P. Lovecraft's imagination. He introduces *The Case of C. D. Ward* with an epigraph from Giovanni Borelli: "The essential Saltes of Animals may be so prepared and preserved, that an ingenious Man may have the whole ark of Noah in his own studie and raise the fine shape of an animal out of its ashes at his pleasure."[14] Wood's Indian was even capable of resurrecting a living serpent from a dead skin. So from the inception of the colony one feels that a close link existed between shamanistic practices and the alchemical methods of Europe. New England had a school of alchemy that counted among its teachers—as Hawthorne surprisingly guessed, though without proof—one of the art's most famous adepts, Ireneo Filalete.

Wood is almost always facetious, especially when he describes the fiercely awesome aspect of the Indian chiefs:

But a sagamore with a humbird in his ear for a pendant, a black hawk in his occiput for his plume, mowhackees for his gold chain, good store or wampompaege begirting his loins, his bow in his hand, his quiver at his back, with six naked Indian spatterlashes at his heels for his guard, thinks himself little inferior to the great Chan; he will not stick to say, he is all one with King Charles. He thinks he can blow down castles with his breath, and conquer kingdoms with his conceit.

He describes a shamanistic therapeutic session with the same verve: the *powaw* sits and

the rest of the Indians give attentive audience to his imprecations and invocations, and after the violent expression of many a hideous bellowing and groaning, he makes a stop, and then all the auditors with one voice utter a short canto; which done, the powaw still proceeds in his invocations, sometimes roaring like a bear, other times groaning like a dying horse, foaming at the mouth like a chased boar, smiting on his naked breast and thighs with such a violence as if he were mad. Thus will he continue sometimes half a day; spending his lungs, sweating out his fat, and tormenting his body in this diabolical worship.

But in this way the sick are often healed, and the authority of the priesthood is confirmed.

These ceremonies, Wood notes, are now almost abandoned, since the English are averse to them, yet do not seem to lack all good things. Indeed, since they have settled in the region, perhaps because of their orderly cultivations, the fury of the heavens has abated, there are far fewer thunderbolts, and long droughts have been averted. Confronted by such solid good fortune, the Indians have forsaken their priests and converted to the English God.

The same reassurance is given by Thomas Lechford, a leading Boston lawyer, in a book he published in London in 1642, *Plain Dealing: or, News from New-England*. The Indian priests—"Powahes, or Priests, which are Witches"—on certain holidays observe their religion, which they now call prayer: "The Powaw labours himself in his incantations, to extreme sweating and weariness, even to extasie."

The accounts are similar to those from Virginia. Yet one trait that distinguishes the New England environment from the Virginian is perhaps the insistence on the native magic's ineffectiveness with the English. The same preoccupation can be found in Edward Johnson. In a popular and therefore ornate style, as Perry Miller observes (only the clergy had acquired simplicity through study), he tells the story of American colonization in his book, *Wonder-Working Providence of Sions Saviour*, published in London in 1654.

Christ figures at the beginning of the book as a king who issues a proclamation to the Puritans to gather together. The style is a throwback to the folk tone of certain exhortations in *Piers Plowman*. On the other hand, the devil reigns over the Indians and keeps them subjugated by means of brute fear, except that he gives his ministers the ability of now and then curing the sick: "One of them was seen, as is reported, to cure a squaw that was dangerously sick by taking a snake's skin and winding it about her arm, the which soon became a living snake crawling round about her arms and body."[15] Other priests cure the sick by making them walk on burning coals.

Before the arrival of the English, the demon sometimes appeared as a monster who would drag his victims out of their huts and subsequently make them disappear; at other times he appeared in the shape of a white infant. The good demon Abbamocho granted the curing of illness. It seems incredible that Johnson did not notice that with the mention of a kind divinity symbolized by a holy child his exclusively demonological explanation of the Indians' faith collapses.

Johnson adds certain memorable cases of the ecstasies of warriors:

There were some of these Indians, as is reported, whose bodies were not to be pierced by their sharp rapiers or swords of [for] a long time, which made some of the soldiers think the Devil was in them, for there were some Powaws among them, which work strange things with the help of Satan. But this was very remarkable, one of them being wounded to death, and thrust through the neck with a halbert, yet after all, lying groaning upon the ground, he caught the halbert's spear in his hand and wound it quite round.[16]

∴

Cotton Mather was impressed by Indian rituals, which were remarkably similar to the Thessalian ceremonies described in Lucan's *Pharsalia* (vv. 680 ff):

> Then her voice, more powerful than any herb
> To charm the gods of Lethe, first spreads dissonant
> Murmurings altogether unlike human speech.
> Her voice contains the bark of a dog and a wolf's howl,
> The hoots of a restless horned owl and of a nocturnal screech owl,
> And a serpent's hiss; she also
> Imitates the crashing of a wave against the rocks,
> The murmur of forests and thunder bursting from a cloud.

In his play *Sophonisba,* Marston had imitated and exaggerated these horrors so alluring to the Elizabethan imagination.

Cotton Mather assures us that "the Powaws, by the infernal spirits, often killed persons, caused lameness and impotency, as well as shew'd their art in performing things beyond [the] humane, by diabolick skill; such who have conversed much among them have had no reason to question." To carry out their acts the witches call up a spirit or perform special rites with certain objects, a piece of leather shaped like an arrowhead, to which is tied a hair or a fishbone. "Such inchanted things have most certainly either entred the bodies of the intended to be by them wounded, or the devil hath form'd the like within their flesh, without any outward breach of the skin." At other times they captured part of the spirit of those they wanted to kill as it strayed during sleep—"something of the *spirit* (as the devil made them think) of such [as] they intended to torment or kill, while it wandred in their *sleep*"—and preserved it in the form of a fly; what was inflicted on the fly appeared on the body of the victim.

Mather tells of a witch doctor who was able to identify the place where stolen goods were hidden, but when an Englishman asked for his services, he answered: "If you can believe that my God will help you, I will try what I can do." This same witch doctor did not prevent his wife from observing Christian rites.

Cotton Mather also describes a cure of the shamanistic type performed by a Jesuit. An Indian wounded by a hostile tribe lay among his companions, who were weeping over his approaching death and, since they were Christians, singing: "May he live, O God! if it so please thee." The Jesuit arrived and recited the articles of faith to the dying Indian, urged him to repent his sins and received his confession. Then, lifting his heart up with hope and confidence in God, he recited the office for the dead and the Lauretian Litany, advising him to entrust himself to the intercession of the Holy Virgin, and ceaselessly invoking the sacred name of Jesus. Finally, the Jesuit placed the relics of the cross he carried with him on the wounds of the dying man, and left. The next day he met him rowing on the river, completely healed and surrounded by his exultant friends. The spear wound, which had gone straight through his chest, was now reduced to two small red marks, "nor from the hour at which the father had left yesterday had he ceased to invoke the most holy name of Jesus."

But were the new colonists really insensitive to Indian magic? Had not certain mysterious portents appeared during the war with King Philip? In the course of an eclipse of the moon an Indian scalp was seen at the center of the invisible celestial body, an Indian bow was outlined in the sky, the wind shrieked like the whistle of bullets, horses could be heard galloping in the sky, and the howls of the wolves were recognized as the prophecy of calamity that Cotton Mather had promised.

Perhaps some part in preparing the atmosphere of the great crisis of demonopathy in Puritan Salem was played by the Indians' claims of being able to cause misfortunes during the campaigns of 1675 when, as the anonymous author of *The Present State of New England with Respect to the Indian War* narrates:

On the 28th Day of August, happened here at eleven a Clock at Night, a most violent Storm of Wind and Rain, the like was never known before; it blew up many ships together. . . . The Indians afterwards reported that they had caused it by their Powaws (i.e. worshipping the Devil). They further say, that as many Englishmen shall die, as the Trees have by this Wind been blown down in the Woods: but these Heathenish Stories are consonant to their Barbarous Crueltie, and ought to be valued accordingly, by all who own any Thing superiour to it or them.[17]

Thus a group of Indians and Frenchmen attacked Gloucester in 1692. For half a month the Puritans fought with them but did not wound a single man; finally they claimed that these enemies were devils in disguise.[18]

It is quite probable that a Devil's Coven did exist near Salem. The considerable literature about Puritan devil fear—that is, scholarly works such as the *History of Salem Witchcraft* by Charles W. Upham and *Salem Witchcraft* by Caroline Upham, the poetry of Longfellow, the essays of Lowell, plays up to and including Arthur Miller's *The Crucible* —has woven an understandable veil of pity around the persons unjustly tortured and killed, and, except for Hawthorne, none have recognized the existence of a reality behind the aberrations, puerilities, illusions, and brutal injustices. Montague Summers believed that Deliverance Hobbs's testimony gives proof that she belonged to a Devil's Coven, and the proofs indicate that the Reverend George Burroughs, Bridget Bishop, and Martha Carrier were among its members. Mary Osgood, the wife of Captain Osgood, went to a pool where she said the devil or his representative immersed her face in the water, making her renounce baptism and ordering her to become forever his creature, body and soul. It is probable that the Reverend Mr. Burroughs acted on behalf of the devil, administering the satanic sacrament, that is, according to Abigail Williams, red bread with red wine, most likely raw flesh and blood.[19]

What is the link with indigenous witchcraft? The crisis of demonopathy started in the house of the Reverend Mr. Parrish, whose servant Tituba, a native of Barbados, was in the habit of entertaining the minister's daughters and their friends with stories of necromancy, divination, and human sacrifice. It may have been the suggestive power of the images evoked by the Indian woman that set off paroxysms in the young girls—"odd postures, antic gestures, loud outcries . . . ridiculous, incoherent and unintelligible expressions."

When they arrested her, Tituba confessed that the devil, sometimes in the form of a pig, sometimes in the guise of a black mongrel dog, had ordered her to torment the bewitched girls and on her refusal had changed into a man and by means of a yellow bird threatened her or promised her rewards. Two cats had also appeared before her, ordering her to pinch the bewitched girls and even to kill them. She saw horrible

shapes of beasts or men alongside the aforesaid witches. Having confessed and repented, she was let out of prison.

In Deodat Lawson's *True Narrative* one notes the intrusion of Indian
methods commonly employed to expose the invisible persecutors of the
bedeviled: Parrish's two Indian servants, man and wife, make a cake of
rye flour kneaded in the urine of young boys and give it to a dog to eat,
after which they can see the invisible tormentors.

Robert Calef, the merchant who, in *More Wonders of the Invisible
World* (published in London in 1700), exploited the witchcraft trials to
strike at the theocracy, proves to be a secret Libertine in the pages where
he speaks of the natives. He tells the story of a converted Indian, a sort of
leader of the proselytes, who in Puritan fashion had praised the will of
God at the death of his son, "though the Indians use upon the Death of
Relations, to be the most passionate and outragious Creatures in the
World."

Soon after, he had fallen ill and on his deathbed advised his relatives to
be sincere when praying and to shun drunkenness and idleness.

Just as the spirit of the English seventeenth century dictates to Calef
that special touch which couples "passionate" and "outragious," so it
leads him to make the following comment on the death of the virtuous
Indian: the English who were so concerned with maintaining a tone "of
good fashion" did not care to travel so great a distance to attend the
Indian's funeral.

A short time before his death this notable Indian, while working, saw a
black, horrible, gigantic man, who enjoined him not to preach any more
about Christ, and when he courageously refused, proffered him a book: if
he signed it, he would stop persecuting him. With a prayer the Indian
saved himself. He was the first victim of demonopathy in Massachusetts
and had given, Calef implies, a lesson on how to escape it, which the
Puritans were later incapable of following.

∴

Nathaniel Hawthorne, perfect heir of the Puritan fathers, discerned the
interweaving of occult, unavowed, yet tenacious, Indian influences in the
life of his forefathers. Thus in his story "Roger Malvin's Burial" their
funeral customs seemed to him marked by an Indian concept: "An almost
superstitious regard, arising perhaps from the customs of the Indians,
whose war was with the dead as well as with the living, was paid by the
frontier inhabitants to the rites of sepulture," and in "Young Goodman

Brown," where the acolytes of a band of devil worshipers gather together
with the Indians for a black mass in the heart of the forest: "Scattered
also among their pale-faced enemies were the Indian priests, or pow-
wows, who had often scared their native forest with more hideous
incantations than any known to English witchcraft." Other sinister figures
in his fiction have Indians as accomplices; the satanic alchemist and
betrayed husband in *The Scarlet Letter* has learned certain secrets from
the natives, while the old witch in *Septimius Felton* possesses both Indian
blood and lore.[20]

In Puritan writings in which the Indians are branded as cruel barbarians—hardened, insidious, "bloodthirsty"—we are never shown their
faces nor is a custom or a passion ever patiently observed: the stereotyped formula is the sign of spiritual blindness.

Yet sometimes a Puritan is taken prisoner: Will he then be forced to
"see" his captor? There are in fact cases of Puritans who were converted
to Indian life and even to Catholicism.[21] But there is no middle way
between this extreme and the usual coldness.

In a completely new literary genre, the "narrative of captivity," the sight
of the captor is, incredibly, avoided. The autobiography of Mary Rowlandson, *Captivity and Restoration of Mrs. Mary Rowlandson,* which
appeared in 1682, became famous. The dry, Biblical style is illuminated
by passages descriptive of the Puritan's sublime inner life; and yet whenever the Indian appears on the scene, there is not even a hint of curiosity.
He is a ferocious enemy, bloodthirsty and savage: the epithets are taken
for granted. As for the protagonist, her story opens with a confession:

I often before this said, that if the Indians should come, I should choose rather
to be killed by them than taken alive, but when it came to the trial, my mind
changed; their glittering weapons so daunted my spirit, that I chose rather to
go along with those (as I may say) ravenous bears, than at that moment to end
my days.

And here is the scene of violent *chiaroscuro* that will become canonical
in the new genre: on one side, "the roaring and singing, and dancing, and
yelling of those black creatures in the night" and, on the other, the
prisoners, many of them wounded, holding wailing infants in their arms,
hungry and utterly dejected.

In Mrs. Rowlandson's book acts of Indian gentleness or kindness are
barely mentioned, dismissed as negligible aspects of brute nature, while
acts of harshness are exaggerated. And yet do we not see an Indian
horseman place a wounded child on his mount in order to help the

mother on the long march? Do not others run charitably to bring her food when they see her cry? Did not their chief offer her a pipe to smoke, and did he not treat her gallantly? And did they not pay her honestly for the work as a seamstress which they commissioned her to do? And does not King Philip comfort her with the grace of a knight in a medieval poem? And do not all the warriors respect the prisoners and slaves?

In her story these acts become abstract, do not arouse gratitude, do not even appear to have come from human beings. The reiteration of abusive epithets has blunted not only all natural kindness but also any sort of curiosity about the Indians. The colonists wander about among them as though shut up in a transparent and impenetrable sphere, like figures in the paintings of Hieronymus Bosch.

Yet what intense spiritual wealth is hidden on either side of that sphere! For the Puritans the bare fact of having survived is sufficient in itself to give rise to endless praises to God, no matter how terrible their afflictions may be. Indeed, they then praise not only God's mercy but also His power. Mary Rowlandson says: "But the Lord renewed my strength still, and carried me along, that I might see more of His power, yea so much that I could never have thought of, had I not experienced it."

What joys are bestowed on the dejected and exhausted prisoner by the idea that God in his mercy did not unleash the waters of annihilation! What profit she gets from the clear vision of her own and the universal, innate iniquity that comes to the surface at every examination of conscience (how much time she has wasted, even in smoking) and that would both justify and demand the annihilating wrath of God.

And yet wholly taken up as she is in her sagacious paean of praise, which imparts to her the sense of a winged, heavenly succor, she does not feel the slightest gratitude toward the good Indian who offers her food. As she eats it, she thinks only of the passage in the Bible in which Jonathan exclaims: "See, I pray you, how mine eyes have been enlightened, because I tasted a little of this honey."

.·.

In drawing a picture of the "narrative of captivity," one must also listen to Cotton Mather's grim, violent, uncertain voice. "Truly the dark places of New England, where the Indians had their unapproachable kennels, were habitations of cruelty," he exclaims in the second book of the *Magnalia,* listing some cases of repulsive and ghoulish horror. Here, for example, is a child captured by the Indians:

It was not long before the child had a sore eye, which his master said proceeded from his weeping on the forbidden accounts; whereupon, laying hold on the head of the child with his left hand, with the thumb of his right he forced the ball of the eye quite out, therewithal telling him that when he heard him cry again he would serve th'other so too and leave him never an eye to weep with withal.

Other children were held under water and tortured in different ways. Mather concludes: if you, my reader, are not horrified, it means that you have been turned into stone, like that corpse in Rome which is on show at Villa Ludovisi.

In *The Return of the Vanishing American,* Leslie Fiedler has analyzed one of the most important narratives of captivity from the *Magnalia.* In 1697 a small group of Indians captured Hannah Duston, her infant, and her maid. Her husband had managed to escape, taking the other children with him. When taken prisoner, Hannah Duston, whose infant the Indians had slaughtered, persuaded a young companion to help her, and having got one of the Indians, who she knew was adept at scalping and conceited about it, to teach her how to do it, she applied her newly learned skill in the middle of the night, and returned home with the grim trophies. Later, Hawthorne remarked in an essay upon a detail that his forefathers had refused to see: among those she scalped were also Indian children. Fiedler adds that these Indians were devout Catholics, and so that episode becomes simply another of the many in the religious wars that the Reformation had fomented between northern and southern Europe.[22]

John Williams, a graduate of Harvard and minister at Deerfield, reports that one morning in 1704 "not long before break of day, the enemy came in like a flood on us, our watch being unfaithful." When the Indians burst into his room, he grabbed his pistol, at the same time calling out a short prayer and quoting a passage from Isaiah. The pistol misfired, and the Indians took him captive. His thoughts ran to his wife: "I begged of God to remember mercy in the midst of judgement." His prayer was heard, and the Indians permitted him and his wife to dress before leaving. During the journey they carried the small children in their arms— "God made the heathen to pity our children."

His beloved wife, the apple of his eye and the companion of so much happiness and affliction, who had not uttered a word of complaint in all their tribulations, was separated from Williams halfway through the march to Quebec. He soon heard that, having fallen in the water while wading across a stream, she was finished off with a blow from a tomahawk.

At Quebec, his Indian captor and master, a Catholic, tried to force him to make the sign of the cross and kiss the crucifix, and at his refusal he threatened him with an ax. Not succeeding even in this way in budging him, he told him that he would tear out his fingernails with his teeth and in fact bit one finger, but then immediately desisted, exclaiming: "No good minister, no love God, as bad as the devil," a crude caricature instead of a portrait.

.·.

The Memoirs of Odd Adventures and Signal Deliverances in the Captivity of John Gyles, Esq., published in Boston in 1736, opens with the usual simplicity of narratives of captivity: on August 2, 1689, the Gyles family, while at work in the fields, is surprised and captured. The father asks permission to pray with his children, and calling down on them the heavenly blessing, bids them farewell: "He parted with a cheerful voice, but looked very pale by reason of his great loss of blood, which boiled out of his shoes. The Indians led him aside. I heard the blows of the hatchet, but neither shriek nor groan." The chaste perfection of the style is such that its effect is at once that of wonderment and terrifying pity. Almost the entire story is kept at this intense and moving pitch.

The prisoners are tortured, but the narrator manages to survive. He then experiences a life of hardships and wanderings, of sudden beatings and maltreatment, until he is freed. From time to time he learns something of the intimate life of his captors: he dares to watch a hut from close by in which the medicine men immersed in a steam bath are shrieking in order to enter into contact with the spirits; he notices the frequently accurate responses they obtain, attributing them to the power of the devil. He learns some of their fantastic tales: a young girl is of such perfect beauty and such refined breeding that she cannot find an appropriate husband; she disappears, abandoning her relatives in her desperation, until one day they see her "diverting herself with a beautiful youth whose hair like hers flowed down below his waist, swimming, washing, et cetera, in the water, but the youths vanished on their approach." From then on they appealed to this son-in-law and aquatic spirit to obtain good fortune for the chase, applying to him for this or that animal, and no sooner had they expressed their wish from the riverbank than the desired creature came swimming toward them. Spirits preside over the sources of that river, and nobody has ever been able to get near them: they seem to pull back as the explorers push forward, and then the latter are overcome by a delirious vertigo.[23] In the native imagination the young prisoner discovered a world of "elementary spirits" similar to those described by Paracelsus and by the Parisian occultists of whom Gabalis gave an account and whom La Motte-Fouqué introduced in his stories.

.·.

Philip Freneau, a follower of the Enlightenment hostile to the Puritan idea, in 1793 reluctantly ₁ ¹blished in *The Freeman's Journal* "The Narrative of the Perils and Sufferings of Dr. Knight and John Slover," another captivity account, which had been procured for him by H. H. Brackenridge.[24]

John Slover was a simple, devout Virginian who refused to attend his captors' nightly war dances, considering them a diabolical practice. But even though his vision is distorted by hatred, he lets us see some of the many whites who had gone over to the Indian side.

Tribulations aroused in him the piety typical of this edifying literature of cruelty. His resignation to a possible death at the stake was worthy of a Puritan of the preceding century. He realized that although he observed his religion and many times repented of his sins, he had never experienced the confirmation in faith that people spoke of. And then, behold—

But early this day, instantaneously, by a change wrought upon me sudden and perceivable as lightning, an assurance of my peace made with God sprung up in my mind. The following words were the subject of my meditation: "In peace thou shalt see God. Fear not those who can kill the body. In peace shalt thou depart." I was on this occasion, by a confidence in mind not to be resisted, fully assured of my salvation. This being the case, I was willing, satisfied, and glad to die.

So for an instant the eighteenth-century Enlightenment atmosphere is pierced and illuminated by a return to Puritanism. In England, however, the genre became a vehicle for brutal social criticism, either based on the cult of the instincts, as in the truculent "narrative of Indian captivity" included in Smollett's *Expedition of Humphry Clinker* or in the apology for Indian life contained in the *Memoirs of a Captivity among the Indians of North America,* which John Hunter published in 1823.

———◦•◦———

Chapter IV

The Enlightenment
and the Indians

The atmosphere produced in England by Libertinism and the Enlightenment already dominated the stage with the plays of the young Dryden, Davenant, and Aphra Behn. Its influence was apparent even before the great, destructive eighteenth-century storm, when, through such magazines as the *Tatler* and the *Spectator,* a relativistic public opinion was formed and the savages of America were glorified, the better to criticize European certainties.

During the eighteenth century, Libertinism often shed its past reticence, and the theme of progress discarded the Christian embellishments and pretexts of the previous century (when Henry More presented the prophecies of the Apocalypse as allegorical, and so, having a free hand, passed off as Christian the idea of a divine plan for the world and history, as a result of which human nature would progress toward a final golden age). However, in the eighteenth century the vague and obsessive key word ceased to be *reformation;* too many people responded to it with the exasperation of Torrismondo in Dryden's *Spanish Friar:*

> That's a stale cheat,
> The primitive rebel, Lucifer, first us'd it,
> And was the first reformer of the skies.

Instead of *reform,* the word *progress* now was obsessively reiterated. The new term created an attendant aura of propitious associations: *progress* is also a procession, a series of successive titles to a royal right.

Dryden, like Spenser in the Elizabethan age, had vainly fought the cult of innovation, especially in his poem *Absalom and Achitophel,* asking in the prologue to *The Unhappy Favourite:*

Tell me, you powers, why should vain man pursue,
With endless toil, each object that is new
And for the seeming substance, leave the true?

In America the almost solitary opponent of the century's general tendency was Jonathan Edwards, who declared that the Enlightenment's error sprang from a mistaken notion of the will and its manner of functioning. The belief is that the will is the faculty by which one chooses what reason judges to be good, and by which one abhors and shuns what, on the contrary, it condemns. But experience teaches us that there does not exist a neutral lapse of time between judgment and act. The whole man, and not just a separate faculty, is involved in the choice and the action: "the very willing is the doing; when once he has willed, the thing is performed." There is no empty interval in which one deliberates; man does not transcend the concatenation of causes that form his nature. Just the opposite is true; he is tied to the inclinations and wishes of his heart.

"Edwards most infuriated the liberal," Perry Miller tells us in his biography of him,[1]

by placing upon him a responsibility, entirely within the order of causes, not for overcoming obstacles nor for constructing churches and factories, but for being the kind of person he is. . . . In 1752 Edwards remarked concerning the liberals of his day, the forerunners of those who for two centuries have told our civilization that man rises outside of nature, that their opinions are commonly attended, not only with a haughty contempt, but an inward malignant bitterness of heart, toward all the zealous professors and defenders of the contrary spiritual principles. These gentlemen, he noted, are advocates of freedom of thought, but they easily become persecutors under some good cloak.

In the American tradition, Edwards is the most formidable defiance yet leveled against the liberal spirit, against the cult of progress that starts with the denial of man's kinship with nature.

The usual ambivalence underlies the progressive ideology in the new century; at times the primitives appear querulous, savage, and bestial, at other times enlightened creatures of nature. The adherents of the first thesis are particularly fierce in their attacks on the American Indian, and with a good "scientific" conscience. This becomes possible the moment progressive European thought accepted the legend of the continent's youth and immaturity, which in turn is reflected in its aborigines. Francis Bacon had already proposed this idea in passing and was echoed by John Donne, who spoke of the "unripe side of the world," but the French naturalist Buffon develops it further, furnishing it with full scientific credentials. Is not the fauna in America altogether inferior? Is not the puma a diminished lion, the tapir a ridiculous elephant, the llama a measly camel, owing to the cold, humid, and putrid nature of its soil, so propitious for snakes? Thus, following this line of logic, the aborigine must inevitably be unfeeling, beardless, insensitive, dull, fearful, and spiritless. For Buffon, as one author comments, there is a "singular connection between the impotence of the savage and the absence of large ferocious beasts, the connection of a subtly scabrous eighteenth-century eroticism."[2]

Since, according to an Enlightenment dogma, eroticism is the major and central force of life, the imaginary frigidity of the Indian becomes a sign of inferiority, as his paganism was in the eyes of Christian society ("Abbé Guillaume" Raynal later pities their weakness in that "prime instinct, prime knot of society").

In the Dutchman Corneille de Pauw's *Recherches philosophiques sur les Americains*—imbued, as Antonello Gerbi notes, with the irreligiosity and impudence of the Enlightenment—society is transformed into the Prime Mover, progress has usurped the place of moral principle, and so, following in Buffon's footsteps, the aborigines are smitten by a radical zoological anathema. These denigratory legends, which later Kant and Hegel will accept (Hegel condemns the Indians in the name of the unfolding of the Spirit), become active elements in the thinking of William Robertson, the Scottish historian of America. For him, the American Indians' inferiority is as obvious as the darkness of the Middle Ages. His famous, influential historical interpretations are based on these two vague yet unshakable legends.

In the *History of America* he asserts that the natives' intellectual powers are confined to the satisfaction of their needs and that their actions never go beyond the boundaries of the passion which momentarily agitates them. True, long negotiations and protracted oratorical exhortations are frequent among them, all conducted with a great semblance of wisdom. But these manifestations cannot be attributed to any particular depth of emotion; they are simply due to the coldness of their temperament, which makes them slow to come to a decision.

Their intellects undeveloped, their hearts base, the Indians are crude, distrustful, immured in a hard reserve, capable of remaining silent for days on end. Since they have not sacrificed their freedom, as we have sacrificed ours, to the superior reason of society, they are suspicious and cunning. These savages, Robertson feels, living in situations of danger and misery, sunk in their wretched thoughts and projects, are nothing but grave and melancholy animals.

They have two virtues, strength and attachment to the community, yet, stupefied by events, they fling themselves into superstition, and their magicians dominate them, passing themselves off as the intermediaries of the heavenly powers. The native religion is not worth studying, for it "occupies no considerable place in the thoughts of a savage." The aborigine's essential flaw is his unwillingness to improve himself, an apathy due in fact to historical conditions, but by now incapable of being changed, a completely infantile state.

At the opposite pole, as in Elizabethan times and during the Restoration, there continued the glorification of the noble savage,[3] which Shaftesbury picked up again: the highest good lies in the free expression of impulses, therefore in the man of nature. Freed of all impediments, man's instinctive tendencies would be kind and gentle; only coercion deforms and perverts them. This apology for evil must obviously conceal itself behind a screen of humanitarian, if needs be tearful, sentimentality: in other words, eighteenth-century *sensiblerie*. In England this was the theme of Henry Mackenzie's *The Man of Feeling*, in which a young English soldier, punished for having helped an old Indian prisoner escape, in turn escapes and is succored by the same dignified old man. Kitsch is born as humanitarian propaganda.

The crude and the savage become the objects of Libertine yearnings: the glorification of the servant and the savage above their cultivated leaders results in class hatred and the desire for equality. The belief in a former golden age gives rise to a desire for its return.[4] But there is not a trace of *intelletto d'amore* in eighteenth-century descriptions of the Indian, except in William Blake's passing reference in *The Marriage of Heaven and Hell*, where Ezekiel explains what propels him to his ecstasies: "The desire of raising other men into a perception of the infinite: this the North American tribes practise." A very different thing from "simplicity of nature"!

Simplicity is a vague term that serves, as does *progress* (which has taken the place of *reform*), to gather into a single nexus a host of agitated, anxious, fluctuating, obscure, and extravagant emotions—the *discontent* later to be denounced by Edmund Burke. The desire is to return to *simplicity*. "Nature is pleased with simplicity," ordained Newton, whose merit, according to the poet James Thomson, was to have restored the sky to simplicity, that is, to the single law of gravitation:

> The Heavens are all his own, from the wide rule
> Of whirling vortices and circling spheres
> To their first great simplicity restored.[5]

From this accepted meaning of the term—"scientific hypothesis which explains the greatest number of phenomena"—one passes without any justification to another, the so-called "elegance of unfeigned passions"— for which the "simple" heroines of the sentimental novel, Pamela and Clarissa, were praised.

The instinct that is passed off as pristine, spontaneous, is actually filtered through the taste for Arcadian affectation, thus provoking the same favorable mental associations, the same flattering prestige that surrounds the law of universal gravitation. The simplicity of the ancients, of savages, and of English gardens is extolled. Enlightenment mediation is palmed off as immediacy. Its Libertine representation and falsification of the Indian is taken for a living, truthful portrait.

The basic text of Libertinism celebrating the noble savage is the *Dialogues curieux entre l'auteur et un sauvage de bon sens qui a voyagé*, issued in 1703 and the work of Baron de Lahontan.[6] The *Journal de Trévoux* recognized in it "the summary of all that Deists and Socinians bring forward against the submission which we owe to the faith"; we find in it the ideas that Montesquieu, Diderot, and Rousseau were going to spread in the years before the French Revolution. The *Spectator* and the *Tatler* were to take up Lahontan's ideas, and the English and Scottish philosophy of the Enlightenment era would be imbued with them. But Lahontan was not an inventive precursor; he "has done nothing but repeat opinions, protests, and criticisms, which, if not generally accepted, were current since the beginning of the century. He makes us legitimately suspect that from 1703 the 'philosophic' army had made deeper infiltrations than is usually thought."[7] Lahontan, like the advocates of Enlightenment later on, foresees a world in which property is unknown and anarchy rules. From his long residence in pious Quebec he had gathered fuel for his anger against State and Church, and from his familiarity with the Hurons an image of an uncoerced society and a form of primitive communism, which Swift was to use in his description of the Houyhnhnms. There is neither *mine* nor *yours;* each person helps his neighbor in accordance with his needs; money, "the serpent of the French," is scorned, and hierarchies are disparaged in favor of equality. The Hurons are "carefree people," their sex lives are free and without passion, marriages are dissolved at will. In case of illness, a rare occurrence, they turn to the "wizards" (Lahontan regards them as charlatans, asserting that everyone derides them, tolerating them only as diverting clowns). Chinard remarks that Lahontan is already putting into circulation formulas destined to become the catchwords of the 1789 Revolution.

An opposite view is exposed in *Moeurs de Sauvages Amériquains comparées aux moeurs des premiers temps,* by the Jesuit Lafitau, published in Paris in 1724. Lahontan made his savage Huron, Adario, the mouthpiece of a criticism of the Catholic religion's claim to uniqueness. Lafitau asserts the unity of a tradition derived from the one original revelation: all peoples unite in accepting certain religious and ethical principles. Adario's speeches are assailed as European Libertinism in unconvincing disguise—"one easily uncovers in them one of those Libertines who, confused by intractable truths, want others to have no more religion than themselves."

But Lahontan's reasoning, as often happens with bad money, was to gain the upper hand in the ideological struggle revolving around the savage. In England it permeated a good part of Jonathan Carver's *Travels Through the Interior Parts of North America* (1778–1779) and was presented with seductive grace by Lord Shaftesbury. Imbued with classical culture in the manner of a sixteenth-century humanist, Shaftesbury asserted that all instincts should be allowed to develop freely. What mattered was that none of them should be excessive, their intensity and duration to be regulated not by "pedantry" but by "taste" (in other words, by fashion and not by ethics).

And was this not the precept of "honest Iago," an early exponent of the antimoral ethic, which became not only Shaftesbury's but also that of the entire Enlightenment (all the way to Fourier and beyond)?

Virtue! A fig! 'Tis in ourselves that we are thus or thus. Our bodies are our gardens, to the which our will are gardeners. So that if we will plant nettles or sow lettuce, set hyssop and weed up thyme, supply it with one gender of herbs or distract it with many, either to have it sterile with idleness or manured with industry—why, the power and corrigible authority of this lies in our wills. If the balance of our lives had not one scale of reason to poise another of sensuality, the blood and baseness of our natures would conduct us to most preposterous conclusions; but we have reason to cool our raging motions, our carnal stings, our unbitted lusts. . . .[8]

Glorification of the simple children of nature and forcing them to submit to "progress" went hand in hand. On one side the entire gamut of the instincts was accepted; yet on the other they were pitilessly leveled. In his admirable biography of Thomas More, R. W. Chambers, a dean of twentieth-century historical critics, casts great light on a whole perspective of English progressivism: the same thread runs from the Reformation to the Enlightenment, from the destruction of the monasteries to the aristocratic mansions of the enlightened eighteenth century. The Duke of Bedford celebrated Jacobin victories in what had formerly been Woburn Abbey, beneath the shadow of an oak on which the last abbot had been hanged; and a few years later, Lord Byron, inheriting the house that had been Newstead Abbey, became the prophet of the Revolution. In this case, too, the proponents of progress admitted some unpleasantness: indeed, John Morley deplored the fact that Byron destroyed domestic ideals, but he approved the dissoluteness that set the poet in contrast to George III.

From the progessivism of the Oxford Reformers, of Grocyn, Linacre, and Colet, who attacked "the congeries of blatant errors spread by our predecessors," from the Machiavellian Libertinism of Thomas Cromwell (or the Shakespearean Iago), it is a natural step to Shaftesbury. And the ideological world of Shaftesbury leads in its turn to the Jacobinism of Godwin and the young literary men dreaming of a Utopia on the banks of the Susquehanna. But it would be a mistake to see in this ideal continuity of progressivism a narrowly political development, since its outcome could be determined as much by reformist or revolutionary tendencies as by conservative or reactionary trends. The Indian is exalted for his simplicity, but this is precisely because he is considered good material for a political Utopia of any kind (for moral architecture, as Shaftesbury put it), even for the reactionary dreams of the idealist George Berkeley, who excellently represents that "progressivism of the right" that was eighteenth-century Anglicanism. Both of the conflicting political doctrines, by virtue of the dialectic of the Enlightenment, are perfectly in agreement on the matter of reducing man to material.

On his return from a journey in Italy, the Anglican Berkeley proclaimed the coming ruin of England, where public opinion had supplanted public spirit, the frenzy for luxuries the ancient thrift, gambling and stock market speculations decent amusements, and atheism religious feeling. Therefore, he looked to America and planned a university in the Bermudas, where the natives would be educated alongside the sons of the plantation owners. This new society composed of the two races would be inculcated with the now shaky principles of the mother country, those "public-spirited principles and inclinations" that the Indian graduates would then spread among their racial brothers.[9]

In *A Proposal for a College in Bermuda* he remarks that the work of evangelism, despite the missionary organizations, makes no headway; one has to form a group of native Christian college graduates, recruiting students with flattery or rounding up boys less than ten years old before evil has taken root in them, though only after they are fully articulate in their native tongue.

So that they may not go astray, it is necessary, as the idealist Berkeley adds sternly in discussing this "delusive" human material, to educate them for an ecclesiastical career "without any other prospect or provision of employment,"[10] and to keep them on an island so that they cannot escape to the mainland. It is further necessary to inculcate in them the duty to lift their country out of barbarism, a duty "early and constantly instilled . . . by repeated lectures and admonitions."[11] Thus, with the help of this unconquerable missionary militia, the Catholic advance will be held in check.

To Berkeley the native seems to have a potential of inestimable value:

The savage Americans, if they are in a state purely natural, and unimproved by education, are also unencumbered with all that rubbish of superstition and prejudice, which is the effect of a wrong one. As they are less instructed, they are withal less conceited, and more teachable.[12]

The Turkish Sultan used young boys rounded up in their formative years to staff the fanatic corps of Janissaries; in Berkeley's mind a corps of native ministers would have guaranteed the victory of virtuous Protestantism.

An Enlightenment dream of Anglican virtue takes the place of the bankrupt Puritan ethic in Berkeley's poetic *envoi* to his project:

> In happy climes, the seat of Innocence,
>   Where Nature guides and Virtue rules,
> Where men shall not impose, for truth and sense,
>   The pedantry of courts and schools:
>
> There shall be sung another golden age,
>   The rise of empire and of arts,
> The good and great inspiring epic rage,
>   The wisest heads and noblest hearts.
>
> Not such as Europe breeds in her decay;
>   Such as she bred when fresh and young,
> When heavenly flame did animate her clay. . . .

The project was not realized, and after preaching in Rhode Island for a few years Berkeley returned to England, where in 1731 he reported, in a lecture at the Society for the Propagation of the Gospel, on what he had witnessed.

The wretched pioneers on the frontier were for the most part Libertines or indifferent to religion; like rich Englishmen, the colonists dreamed only of imitating the ways of life in the metropolitan centers. The Indians were reduced to a few servants of the English Puritans, who ruined them with alcohol and, motivated by an inveterate antipathy, believed that they could treat them as the ancient Hebrews treated the Canaanites and Amalekites—"as in certain other particulars affecting to imitate Jews rather than Christians."[13] In contrast, the French and Spaniards married native women, converted the subjected peoples, and established local governments. The guilt that should be properly assigned to the abstract and fantastic nature of this Utopia is shifted to Anglican England's usual scapegoat, the Puritan.

Vilified Puritanism had a reincarnation in the eighteenth century, at the very start of the Industrial Revolution, in the Methodist movement, which was faithful to Calvin's theology. But the Methodists declared themselves friends of the Indians. James Edward Oglethorpe, who advised the House of Commons to send insolvent debtors to America and in 1732 received a charter for a colony in Georgia as their haven, exhibited the Indian chief Tomo-Chichi in London's salons, to the delight of the enlightened lovers of the noble savage. In 1735 John Wesley, the founder of Methodism, joined with Oglethorpe and agreed to become the guide of the spiritual life in Savannah, the capital of Georgia; but he had to return to England without ever having come into contact with the natives. In a report on Georgia, Oglethorpe affirmed that the Indians were ready to accept Christianity, provided it was presented to them in a suitable manner. Already free from many vices, their harsh acts of vengeance were the understandable price they were paying to escape social coercion. The elders deliberated after a free debate, and their decisions were carried out by the younger men, who were convoked to hear their verdicts—an eighteenth-century political fable that is not even affected by the Calvinist vehemence of early Methodism.[14]

∴

Across the Atlantic Ocean the Libertine tradition was presented from the start in two antithetical versions that had a concordant effect. Progressivism in its hostile stance toward the backward native was proclaimed in *A New Description of Carolina* (1707) by Governor John Archdale. A so-called Quaker, Archdale secularized the millennarianism of Cromwellian times, which saw the world on the threshold of a new aeon, "the dawning Day for the Accomplishment of many Promises." This millennium or imminent reign of God, had been announced by "preparative Strokes": the invention of the printing press and gunpowder, the latter "a means to subjugate millions of people who exist in a barbarous and bestial state. And how can one not help seeing the hand of a Progressivist Providence in the decimation of the Indian population on the eve of the European landings, in the opportune havoc caused by wars and plagues? The colonists introduced "a Civilized State, good and stable Preparatory for the Gospel State."[15]

The Virginian William Byrd, a leading Libertine, dreamed of the fusion of races by means of eroticism. In his *History of the Dividing Line* he praises Governor Spotswood, who devoted himself to the conversion of Indian children, using the methods of the Enlightenment, which prefers to work on human beings uncontaminated by civilization:

> Long has the furious priest essayed in vain,
> With sword and faggot, infidels to gain,
> But now the milder soldier wisely tries
> By gentler methods to unveil their eyes. . . .
> The lion's whelp there, on the Libian shore,
> Is tamed and gentled by the artful Moor,
> Not the grim Sire, inured to blood before.

William Byrd considers the fearfulness of the warlike Indian with irony and dwells with amorous obsession on the Indian women, the alluring negligence of their native dress—the gleams of "their Mehogony Skins appear'd in Several Parts." Moreover, since the period's eroticism is fed by classical references, they remind him of "the Lacedemonian damsels of old." He notices the charm of their abundant hair gathered in braids that fall over their shoulders, and of their faces, rarely pretty but lit up by a look of innocence and modesty which, if they were not so dirty, might be attractive. They smear themselves with bear grease, which protects them from insects and softens the skin. Free in their love-making, they are, however, venal and rarely give themselves out of pure affection. Yet so much, he believed, could be gained through mixed marriages. Only circumstances create the differences between the races, and after two generations even the skin color would change. Byrd is one of many Libertines who celebrate the delights of a new, indigenous golden age.

In his *History of North Carolina*[16] John Lawson describes Charleston in 1700 as the perfect city of enlightened progress, which has been able to attract scientific talent to educate the young in the most modern fashion, and where complete freedom of worship exists. Leaving the city, Lawson ventured into the interior with some companions, all sharing the typical lustful eighteenth-century notions, excited by Indian women with "a tawny complexion, their eyes very brisk and amorous," who are happy to welcome them since "the Indian men are not so vigorous and impatient in their love as we are." Besides having acquiescent, venal women, the noble savage is majestic: "They never walk backward and forward as we do, nor contemplate on the affairs of loss and gain, the things which daily perplex us."

Lawson's curiosity was aroused by Indian therapy. He took note of a treatment that let a snake wind itself around the patient's body like a belt, but he was convinced that the elders and witch doctors were frauds and presented them as such, with mock admiration.

Lawson simply projected the Libertine fantasies of the Restoration theater on the forests of Virginia; his native women resemble London's prostitutes in the literature of the period.

∴

Robert Beverley, a Virginia plantation owner and slaveholder, wrote *The History and Present State of Virginia* in London in 1705; the work was also published in France and Holland and reissued in London in 1722.[17] He observed the Indians and their customs with the skepticism of an eighteenth-century aristocrat. As Philip Freneau was to do later, he endeavored to link them with the ideology of the Enlightenment. He was interested in their initiations, already fleetingly described by John Smith, and denied that they practiced human sacrifice. "For I take this story of Smith's to be only an example of huskanawing . . . an institution or discipline which all young men must pass before they can be admitted to be of the number of great men or cockarouses, of the nation." The young men are isolated in an enclosure, where they stay for months without seeing anyone, drinking a poison. Because of the harsh discipline they are subjected to, they turn raving mad and are kept in this state for about twenty days. They must forget everything, even their language: "They unlive their former lives and commence men by forgetting that they ever have been boys." But, Beverley wonders, perhaps they simply pretend to have forgotten everything. And he tries to explain the mystery. It must be a trick of the priests to seize the young men's property, since none of them ever seems to want to take possession of it again and all of them begin by earning a gratuity after their complete destitution. All that remains is to find an acceptable meaning for the ceremony, and since a follower of the Englightenment cannot imagine a higher goal than his own, persuaded that he is without prejudices since he has replaced metaphysical axioms with Enlightenment dogmas, he convinces himself that the initiation aims at making the Indians similar to himself:

The Indians . . . pretend that this violent method of taking away the memory is to release the youths from all their childish impressions, and from that strong partiality to persons and things which is contracted before reason comes to take its place. They hope by this proceeding to root out all the prepossessions and unreasonable prejudices which are fixed in the minds of children. So that, when the young men come to themselves again, their reason may act freely, without being biased by chains of custom and education. Thus also they become discharged from the remembrance of any ties by blood, and are established in a state of equality and perfect freedom, to order their actions and dispose of their persons as they think fit, without any other control than the law of nature.[18]

So the initiation of the Indians of Virginia appeared to be inspired by the egalitarian Utopia of the Illuminati of Bavaria, and the native priests were imagined to be replicas of the "hierophants" of the secret communist society founded by Weishaupt. Thus, in Abbé Jean Terrasson's novel *Séthos,* which inspired Mozart's opera *The Magic Flute,* Egyptian priests become replicas of eighteenth-century mystagogues. In much the same way, medieval poets sang of the exploits of Aeneas as though he were a feudal knight.

The Libertine spirit prompted Beverley to express a thought worthy of Diderot or the ethnographic Marquis de Sade: the Indians of Virginia offer the most distinguished guests three virgins who first undress, then lie down next to them, ready to please them in any fashion: "After this manner perhaps many of the Heroes were begotten in old time, who boasted themselves to be the sons of some way-faring God."

Beverley often looks on the Indians with a kindly eye, and his praise of their agility and speed anticipates James Fenimore Cooper, as he shows them able to discern a track by clues invisible to anyone else—the softness of the ground, the stiffness of the grass, or the stirring of the leaves.

Among the Libertines roaming the American forests but also lost in the maze of their "enlightened" fantasies, John and William Bartram are outstanding figures. John, a naturalist with a melodious style in which the Attic modes of the eighteenth century combine with seventeenth-century opulence, kept a journal of his joint expedition with Conrad Weiser, who was sent to make peace with the Iroquois in 1743. John Bartram describes a visit to a medicine man's hut built to resemble an oven and heated with red-hot stones. Inside, a priest cries and writhes:

The priest agitates his body after the most violent manner, till nature has almost lost all her faculties before the stubborn spirit will become visible to him, which they say is generally in the shape of some bird. There is usually a stake driven into the ground about four feet high, and painted. I suppose this they design for the *winged airy Being* to perch upon while he reveals to the invocant what he has taken so much pain to know. However, I find that different nations have different ways of obtaining the pretended informations. Some have a bowl of water into which they often look when their strength is almost exhausted and their senses failing, to see whether the bird is ready to answer their demands.[19]

With the same diligence, Bartram describes the cooking of eels, the topographical setting, and the various species of plants. Carnivorous plants arouse no less interest in him than shamanistic conjurations. His style is not nearly as vivid in his descriptions of native magical practices as in the pages on buckwheat and the pores of their leaves: "Cool dews and showers, by constricting their pores and thereby preventing a too free perspiration, may recover and again invigorate the languid nerves." His scientific approach and the minute, poetic exactitude of the language kept his reports on the Indians free of ideological distortion.

His son William, however, was a determined ideologist; in describing the Indians, he created a theatrical, maudlin Arcadia, an overembellished idyl. With considerable skill he tried to make the Indian nymphs appear as pure parts of the landscape, amid fields of strawberries, flights of turkeys, and fleeing herds of deer.

A vast expanse of green meadows and strawberry fields, a meandering river gliding through, saluting in its various turnings the swelling, green, turfy knolls embellished with parterres of flowers and fruitful strawberry beds, flockes of turkeys strolling about them, herds of deer prancing in the meads or bounding over the hills, companies of young, innocent Cherokee virgins . . . Some having already filled their baskets, lay reclined under the shade of floriferous and fragrant native bowers of magnolia, azalea, perfumed calycanthus, sweet yellow jessamine, and cerulean glycine, disclosing their beauties to the fluttering breeze and bathing their limbs in the cool, fleeting streams.

Alongside these sylvan delights, William Bartram described the horrors of drunkenness among the Seminoles, who for days on end drink, dance, and make love, and often in their intoxication mortally wound each other. Gradually, as they deplete their supply of liquor, a feeling of shame assails them. Only the chiefs and those who are in communication with the spirits resist the temptation of intoxication, but their prestige is not sufficient to restrain the community, which miserably succumbs. Except when under the influence of alcohol, the Indians behave with august calm; their small but reddened eyes are magnanimous; their conversation is circumspect, serious, but frank and joyous. They are both reserved and resolute.

In describing the events of the wars with the Spaniards and the English, Bartram quotes a passage of Indian oratory that explains the use of torture: it placates the manes of the war's victims (other travelers speak of the god of revenge). The communal system is suffused with a sense of openness and sincerity, does away with coercion and formality; it creates a society that fosters neither avarice nor ambition, where hospitality is generous and taken for granted. Bartram tells of having seen a young Indian, after witnessing certain white excesses, raise his arms to the sky and thank the Great Spirit for not having given the Indians the mentality of the whites, which degrades man's nature.

Natural rights, simplicity of nature: these locutions of Libertine ideology attributed to the native languages make one doubt the veracity of the entire narrative, which culminates in the exhortation to look among the aborigines for the civilized prudence and virtue known to us only by name. Divine wisdom dictates its oracles to them and they obey. The description of the highest levels of Indian society recalls Plutarch's *Life of Numa.* They have a king whose mysterious presence is likened to that of the beneficent sun; the king's dominion, imposed imperceptibly, comes from the Spirit, which they believe inspires all good counsel. Theirs is a democratic society according to the ideal of Jacobin simplicity, but also wise in the manner of Sarastro's rule in *The Magic Flute.* In fact, a seer presides over spiritual matters and also has a voice in military decisions, since the people are convinced that he communicates with powerful spirits, active in human affairs as well as in the play of the elements. Bartram reports certain stories of ecstasies and visions told by those who have risen from the dead, but adds, in a tone typical of the Enlightenment, reducing shamanism to a pedagogical expedient, that all these stories have a lesson for the reader and help to make him love virtue and favor the performance of civic duties. In the same way, the symbolism of tattoos, ornaments, and clothes is for Bartram reduced to a display of vanity, trimmings for an eighteenth-century pastoral ballet.

The only experience that Bartram cannot belittle is that of the candidates for priesthood, who carry a stuffed owl with eyes of glittering glass on top of their heads or in their hands, constantly murmur sacred songs, speak among themselves in an esoteric language, and are wrapped in white clothes. This lofty allegory does not seem to Bartram a mere "interesting" theatricality, but rather demands a respectful tone: "These bachelors are also distinguishable from the other people by their taciturnity, grave and solemn countenance, dignified step, and singing to themselves songs or hymns in a low, sweet voice as they stroll about the towns." But the feasts that mark the phases of the agrarian and zodiacal year are described by Bartram in such a way that they resemble the holidays of the Republican year imagined by the Jacobin Theophilanthropists, a society of French Deists.

Bartram was an associate of Benjamin Franklin's, with whom he founded the American Philosophical Society. His *Travels*, published in Philadelphia in 1791, was reprinted in England between 1792 and 1794, in Ireland and Germany in 1793, in Holland in 1797, and finally in France in 1799. It was read by the young English literary men and Jacobins, the followers of William Godwin, and from it they obtained pictures of primordial freedom that stuck in their imaginations.[20] In Wordsworth's poem "Ruth," we see the young Cherokee girls once again:

> Who quit their fold with dance and shout,
> Their pleasant Indian town,
> To gather strawberries all day long;
> Returning with a choral song
> When daylight is gone down.

And in *The Excursion* (book 3, 915) we see man immersed in virgin American nature:

> Pleased to perceive his own unshackled life,
> And his innate capacities of soul,
> There imaged.

Bartram's friend Franklin picked up some of his "practical teachings" from observation of the Indians. Resisting civilization, they seem to demonstrate that man tends by instinct to carefree idleness: "They visit us frequently, and see the advantages that Arts, Sciences and a compact society procure us, they are not deficient in natural understanding and yet they have never shown any Inclination to change their manner of life for ours, or to learn any of our Arts."[21] An Indian educated from childhood among whites gives up civilized customs soon after returning to his own people. But this is not a racial trait, since white prisoners adopted by the tribes, after living among them for some time, refuse to be freed and returned to civilization. This theme, so dangerous for the good progressive conscience, was taken up again by the idyllic Crèvecoeur in *Letters from an American Farmer*, in which he asks what there is in native customs that makes them so alluring. Perhaps they are marked by nature's very hand?[22]

Their secret, according to Franklin, lies in having few but natural wants, while in fact artificial wants force people to develop a technique of production. Franklin concludes that one must encourage industriousness, build factories for the poor to work in instead of leaving them to idleness. Why, then, his benevolent understanding of the Indians? The truth is that Franklin does not act or think without aiming at something useful. The Indian provides him with the occasion to invent a moral tale, but if Menenius Agrippa's tale illustrated the organic theory of the state, Franklin's confirms the relativism of the Enlightenment. Some American commissioners, he says, informed the native chiefs that a foundation was ready to subsidize the studies of their young men in a college. The Indians, knowing by experience that young men educated by the whites come back ill prepared to engage in hunting and war, rejected the offer, but in order to reciprocate they in turn offered to raise the sons of the English and make them into men. In *Remarks Concerning the Savages of North America* Franklin concludes with the famous declaration of his relativism: we call them savages because their customs diverge from ours, which we consider perfectly civilized, yet they are convinced of the same thing. On the other side of the Atlantic, the same banality was proffered by Joseph Addison in the *Spectator* of April 27, 1711.

But equality of rights did not prevent exploitation in reality. Franklin had his plan for utilizing the Indians, infiltrating them with emissaries: "They are People that think a great deal of their temporal, but little of their spiritual Interests and therefore, as he would be a most useful and necessary Man to them, a Smith is more likely to influence them than a Jesuit," so let us encourage "a Number of sober discreet Smiths to reside among the Indians."[23]

∴

Cadwallader Colden[24] admired the Iroquois, a masterful people whom he continually compares to the Greeks and Romans. Their two chiefs, one elected for his zeal as a warrior, the other for his mature wisdom, remain in their positions of leadership as long as their prestige lasts; their victory dances recall the victors of Marathon and Salamis; their custom of admitting the subjugated into their society recalls Roman policy. Colden sees in them proof of the lesson repeated by the moralists of the classic age: the principles of honor and love of country lift a people up, whereas the softness of luxury degrades it. We are offended by the practice of torture, but did not Achilles drag Hector around the walls of Troy? Did not the Phoenicians immolate their victims in flames? And did not the Spaniards burn heretics?

Even if Colden praises the equality that exists among the Iroquois, as Lahontan does, he views them nonetheless with the classically educated eye of a Girondist who cherishes the benefits of civilization, as a result of which the instinct of cruelty and revenge is overcome—"the curbing of these passions is the happy effect of being civilized."

∴

Hugh Henry Brackenridge, James Madison, and Philip Freneau, three famous patriotic leaders, were classmates at Princeton. For the first two, the Indian is a savage creature; for the third, he is a child enlightened by Nature. In the poem "The Rising Glory of America," written in 1771 by Freneau and Brackenridge, we find these verses:

> How much obscur'd is human nature here!
> Shut from the light of science and of truth
> They wander'd blindfold down the steep of time,
> Dim superstition with her ghastly train
> Of daemons, spectres and foreboding signs
> Still urging them to horrid rites and forms
> Of human sacrifice, to sooth the pow'rs
> Malignant, and the dark infernal King.

Roy H. Pearce has remarked that this proclamation of the Indian's bestial nature disappeared in the later edition of 1786.[25] In the interval Freneau had been converted to the cult of free instincts and the primitive life.

On the other hand, in 1782, Brackenridge wrote *Indian Atrocities,* a work concerned with the cruelty of the "animals, vulgarly called Indians," who have the form of men and perhaps are a human species, though certainly in their present state closer to devils, violate the laws of nature—as these are interpreted by Montesquieu—inflict torture, and so can be exterminated.

James Madison, the second of the Princeton classmates, was less violent but was also faithful to the idea of the Indian as a feral creature. Like other fathers of the Republic, he was a physiocrat and believed that "civilization" was bound up with agriculture. Generally, progressivism in America did not look to the future; the benefits of progress in the eighteenth-century agrarian republic were considered self-evident, and Jefferson, who advocated a periodic revision of the Constitution, was alone in this view. Progressive ideology was not animated by discontent and existed without millennarian dreams; progress was the present perpetuated.[26]

Madison tried to face up to the scandal of the young nation—the Indians who refused to be seduced by progress. Adams had ascribed this scandal to "bigotry" of a Platonic stamp. This bigotry is the cause of resistance or inertia that stands in the way of progress; the prosperity of the whites leaves the Indians indifferent, and not even sufferings and need can make them desire the benefits of civilization.[27] Whites brought up among the Indians rarely leave them, for the primitive, exciting hunting life is more attractive to them than the monotonous activity of civilized farming. Only an extraordinary intervention from outside, undertaken by reformers who would seem divine to the Indians, might reverse this natural tendency in favor of progress. The sudden change necessary to break the law of nature and bring about the inception of the life of the spirit, as Hegel would have put it, calls for the energy of capable, resolute men.

Freneau, the third of the Princeton classmates, wrote poetry of a smooth elegance somewhat in the manner of André Chénier. He described and held up for emulation the man inspired by science and equality, typified in the poem "On the Death of a Master Builder":

> By science enlightened, a friend to mankind,
> He came, for the purpose exactly designed;
> Like the Baptist of old, in the annals of fate,
> Precursor of all that is noble and great. . . .
> Designed as he was, to excel and transcend,
> Yet he courted the titles of brother and friend.[28]

Freneau believed that he applied these confused emotions also to the Indian. In the preface to *New Travels Through North America*, by Abbé Robin, which he translated in 1783, he protested, "It is mortifying enough, to see them constantly considered as mere beasts of burden."

He endeavored to identify with the Indian chief Tammany, and this is how he has him speak to the usurpers:

> But mark me, Christian, ere I go—
> Thou, too, shalt have thy share of woe, . . .
> A timid race will then succeed.

This prophecy would echo again in Melville's long poem, *Clarel*. Freneau's imagination delves even deeper into the Indian soul in "The Dying Indian: Tomo-Chequi."

> Relentless demons urge me to that shore
> On whose black forests all the dead are cast

exclaims the Indian who feels the call of death. What awaits him in the other world? A landscape of death to which Melville will go back again in *Clarel*, in order to describe the sandy wastes that border the Dead Sea:

> But all are empty unsubstantial shades,
> That ramble through those visionary glades;
> No spongy fruits from verdant trees depend,
>   But sickly orchards there
>   Do fruits as sickly bear,
> And apples a consumptive visage shew,
> And withered hangs the hurtle-berry blue.

Immortality can be understood only as the cosmic renewal of nature:

> Nature at last these ruins may repair,
> When fate's long dream is o'er. . . .

Still against a funereal background, Freneau writes "The Indian Burying Ground," depicting a neoclassical Indian hereafter:

> His imaged birds, and painted bowl,
>   And venison, for a journey dressed,
> Bespeak the nature of the soul,
>   Activity, that knows no rest. . . .

> And long shall timorous fancy see
>   The painted chief, and pointed spear,
> And Reason's self shall bow the knee
>   To shadows and delusions here.

Animal vitality is the unique essence of the world, Freneau repeats in "The Indian Student," in which an Indian student of theology rejects white civilization and its erudite abstractions:

> No mystic wonders fired his mind;
> He sought to gain no learned degree,
> But only sense enough to find
> The squirrel in the hollow tree.
> The shady bank, the purling stream,
> The woody wild his heart possessed. . . .

To please the imagination of the pre-Romantic Libertine, the noble savage must be a thoughtless child, a sylvan faun.

This apology for the Indian culminates in the famous verses of "The American Village":

> Nor think this mighty land of old contain'd
> The plund'ring wretch, or man of bloody mind:
> Renowned Sachems once their empires rais'd
> On wholesome laws; and sacrifices blaz'd.[29]

And yet the rather noble, emphatically neoclassical enthusiasm with which Freneau embraces the Indian is no less false than the embraces lavished by the French Assembly on representatives of the colored people: to deserve the benefits of fraternity, these people had to keep to the role that the Assembly assigned them. The Indian whom Freneau clasps to his bosom is a projection of his ideology—his reassuring and befeathered double. Freneau attributes to the Indian precisely his own Enlightenment idea of survival after death: Nature, which creates, destroys, and re-creates, is the sole truth, and men unite with it and become "children of nature" when they devote themselves fully to their work with fervid instinct and measured reason. Freneau sees vitality as an end in itself, and since illusions and hopes stimulate one to activity, he invokes them as excellent excitants. The wise man knows that the hopes for a hereafter are illusory, but the images of otherworldly hunts dear to the Indian are symbols of nature as incessant creation, destruction, and re-creation. Freneau's Indian must serve as another proof of Libertine ideology, and he is embraced so that he will be a witness in its favor. Fraternity has ideological interests at stake.

The one flash of truth about the Indians during the century spellbound by the Enlightenment appears in Alexander Henry's *Adventures*, which tells the story of his life as an adopted member of a Canadian tribe in the period that preceded the War of Independence and, above all, describes the enchanting friendship that tied him to the warrior Wawatam. During an ascetic retreat he had foreseen that predestined friendship in a vision. His experience of life among the Indians takes place in a completely visionary atmosphere, and Henry is unable to say why he ever left them. A bare sentence, a whisper, tears him away: "I was living among savages." And yet that sentence was strong enough to conceal for Henry the evidence of happiness; the curse of the epithet "savages" was more powerful than any enchantment exerted by real things.

Among the founders of the Republic, Thomas Jefferson, convinced that man was the mere product of circumstances, refused to condemn the Indian people, just as he refused to revere them. He rejected the legends of Buffon and De Pauw as contrary to experience. In his speech to the Congress in 1805 he identified a single front of the enemies of progress: the reactionaries Napoleon and Pitt in Europe, and those among the Indians who opposed the *reformation*—"They too have their anti-philosophers."

In a letter to John Adams of June 11, 1812, he recalls the chroniclers of Indian life: Joseph Lafitau (who likens the Indians to the nations of the ancient world) and James Adair (who calls attention to an order of Indian seers of the type of the Biblical scholars Gannes and Gambres and the gnostic Simon Magus). Without animosity for the race, he still is determined to destroy it (with compassion); he predicts that the Indians able to assimilate English economic and social techniques, such as the Cherokees, will have to be eliminated. *

John Adams replied[30] that the information on the Indians proved that they nurtured ideas similar to those of Philo of Alexandria: a striking intuition that could only come from the depths of admiration or contempt. As a true follower of the Enlightenment, Adams abhorred the Platonists as much as the Indians.

The opinions of the Indians and their usages . . . appear to me to resemble the platonizing Philo, or the philonizing Plato, more than the genuine system of Judaism.

The philosophy both of Philo and Plato is at least as absurd; it is indeed less intelligible. Plato borrowed his doctrines from oriental and Egyptian philosophers, for he had travelled both in India and Egypt. The oriental philosophy, imitated and adopted in part, if not the whole, by Plato and Philo, was 1. One God, the good. 2. The ideas, the thoughts, the reason, the intellect, the logos, the ratio of God. 3. Matter, the universe, the production of the logos, or contemplations of God. This matter was the source of evil.

Perhaps the three powers of Plato, Philo, the Egyptians and Indians, cannot be distinctly made from your account of the Indians; but

---

* *The Writings of Thomas Jefferson*, vol. IV, New York, 1898. The Irishman James Adair, in *The History of the American Indians* (1775), revived the theory of the descent of Indians from the Jews (as Boudinot did later on). He stated that they worshiped one God and that there was no sign of idolatry among them, their worship being, if at all, directed in their Sanhedrins to "cherubimical figures" and angels, among which they had knowledge of beneficent and malevolent hosts, especially the "concomitant holy angels" or guardians from whom they obtained premonitions and assistance. (Adair cites certain warriors he met, who received an angelic warning while resting in places supposed to be safe and then had immediately taken flight, escaping the enemy just in time.)

1. the Great Spirit, the good, who is worshipped by the kings, sachems, and all the great men in their solemn festivals, as the author, the parent of good.

2. The devil, or the source of evil; they are not metaphysicians enough as yet to suppose it, or at least to call it matter, like the wiseacres of antiquity and like Frederic the Great, who has written a very silly essay on the origin of evil, in which he ascribes it all to matter, as if this was an original discovery of his own . . . according to your account, the worship of the good spirit was performed by the kings, sachems, and warriors, as among the ancient Germans, whose highest rank of nobility were priests; the worship of the evil spirit by the conjurors, jongleurs, praestigiatores.

The persecutory violence of the Enlightenment zealot noted by Jonathan Edwards becomes evident in a grim letter written by Adams to William Tudor on September 23, 1818. The Indians are "bigots" (among the followers of the Enlightenment the term designated the object of their Inquisition) and for this reason do not want to submit. They are as bigoted as Mohammedans, Hindus, and Catholics, and have a mystical system of a Platonic-Philonian stamp: "It is a principle of religion, at bottom, which inspires the Indians with such an invincible aversion both to civilization and Christianity." In the eyes of an enlightened worshiper of progress and tolerance this was enough to consign them quietly to extinction.

∴

Another variety of Enlightenment thought, this time with a "Southern" stamp and combined with the romantic cult of the hero, inspired William Gilmore Simms's novel *The Yemassee.* The Yemassee Indians of South Carolina did not object to the proximity of the first English colonists, for they were protected by their defenselessness until 1715. In fact, the Yemassee had not been troubled by the worst of tyrannies, that is, the awareness of their inferiority in the face of a greater power, which somewhat later they would envy.

Sanutee, the Indian chief, was aware of the fate that hung over the two adjacent communities. He was one of those few who, fortunately for their compatriots, are found in all regions, as much in advance of history as aloof from the masses. Philosopher no less than patriot, as Simms describes him (and the very language he uses shows that the ideology of the Enlightenment was turning into the ideology of an oligarchy), he foresees for his people a destiny he deplores, knowing that the inferior race cannot help but succumb:

. . . in every case of a leading difference betwixt classes of men, either in colour or organization, such difference must only and necessarily eventuate in the formation of castes; and the ones conscious of any inferiority, whether of capacity or of attraction, so long as they remain in propinquity with the other, will tacitly become subjects if not bondmen.[31]

In the novel the same premonition comes to the young English aristocrat Gabriel Harrison, he, too, isolated among the English settlers— "thoughtless as ever, the great mass is always slow to note the premonitions and evidences of change which are at all times going on around them."[32] As a true, heroic patriot he runs the risk of paying with martyrdom for his prescience. The two heroes of the two races, in order to achieve their differing aims, must both play on the elementary emotions of the multitude.

When he finds himself deterred by his peers, Sanutee works the people up to a frenzy, evoking varying images and catchwords, to one man recalling past glories, threatening another with the vision of future calamities. Ultimately, he makes use of a witch doctor who, possessed by the god of evil and war, goes into convulsions.

The glare of torches around him showed the terrific distortion of every feature. His eyes were protruded, as if bursting from their sockets—his tongue hung from his widely distended jaws, covered with foam—while his hands and legs seemed doubled up like a knotted band of snakes, huddling in uncouth sports in midsummer.

This theatrically truculent tone appears to Simms the most appropriate to the subtle though Dionysian experience of the shaman, who infuses everyone with the sense of a divine presence. Standing erect, hands outstretched and eyes scintillating, he begins to sing:

> In my agony, he came,
> And he hurl'd me to the ground;
> Dragged me through the twisted bush,
> Put his hand upon my throat,
> Breathed his fire into my mouth—
> That Opitchi-Manneyto.[33]

By Opitchi-Manneyto's orders the chiefs opposed to the war are ignominiously degraded by having their tattoos skinned off. Sanutee, a consummate manipulator, knows how to combine fantasy with mass fury. On the English side, the young lord is also shrewdly maneuvering his people, those who "do not have any opinions of their own . . . or know the cause they contend for," as John Locke, who wrote Carolina's first constitution, said in his *Essay on Human Understanding*. Simms's white hero is a sagacious man not deceived by the monsters that trick the others, adept at divining the principles that rule men and their changing moods, "not at all troubled by the vague conjectures which a liberal courtesy would have agreed to call opinions." He seems to belong to the same breed as the "masterful figures" in Bulwer-Lytton's admirable *Zanoni* and Disraeli's novels. The magic he works is the aristocratic kind that uses ornate speeches embellished with quotations and gives a playful aura to the most tragic moment: a southern gentleman who puts the grim seriousness of the northerners to shame.

In the meantime, his Indian opposite number has aroused popular determination to go to war against the English, but he knows that he must intensify it, converting it into an insatiable passion. To this end it is necessary that "the principle of destruction" become dominant and that everyone in the tribe behave like dogs that have tasted blood and are trained to kill; they must be offered an Englishman who can be tortured. Sanutee will procure him. This begins the war, which after the initial Indian victories ends in the triumph of white Carolina.

The plot is often puerile and clumsy. Perhaps Simms's talents were more suited to the expository prose that examined the nature of the magical power which fascinates men and the interrelationships that are created when the mass of any people are manipulated by spellbinders. Is not the white man's imprecation akin to the Indian's ritual chant of death and challenge? And do not the Indians have a refined knowledge of the rhythms of both terror and blandishment?

The knowledge of the power of soothing, sweet sounds over the wandering mind, possessed, as the Hebrew strongly phrased it, of devils, was not confined to that people, nor to the melodious ministerings of their David. The Indian claims for it a still greater influence, when, with a single note, he bids the serpent uncoil from his purpose, and wind unharmingly away from the bosom of his victim.[34]

In his essays Simms shows that the need to justify the ferocious hunting down of the Indians suggested their denigration: "We must prove them unreasoning beings, to sustain our pretensions as humane ones—show them to have been irreclaimable, to maintain our own claims to the regards and respects of civilization."[35] Are not both the southern aristocrat and the Indian chief heroic figures destined to be swept away? The shared misfortune brings them together in Simms's heart and finally breaks the spell cast on him by Enlightenment ideas.

Simms's heroic but Enlightenment-influenced vision is revived in the frontier narrative of Alphonso Whetmore. Here are some of his views: "There is a small difference in the moral qualities that distinguish the white and red man." "Although the government of Indian tribes is generally of a democratic character, yet there are many instances where the popularity of a chief enables him to encroach on the freedom of his countrymen." "The ambitious red man, like a white prince, unites church and state in his strides to absolute power."[36]

Chapter V

——◆◆◆——

Enlightenment Zealots
and Romantics

The Indian world can be the Eden in which to stage Enlightenment fantasies about a place where the bonds of convention no longer constrict the free expression of the instincts (eventually ennobled, if one wishes, by gracious sentiments), but the Indian as he actually is does not matter. He merely serves to render credible the Utopia of absolute emotional and instinctual freedom.

How many elective affinities have been crushed by institutions, marriage, and the custom that prohibits multiple loves. Goethe speaks of this in his novel *Elective Affinities* and in *Stella.* But it is only in the gypsylike world of actors in which Wilhelm Meister lives—the European equivalent of a primitive tribe—that these erotic attractions can express themselves openly without catastrophe.

In 1790 the American Sarah Wentworth Morton, in her poem "Ouâbi, or the Virtues of Nature,"[1] imagined an Indian world that permits the happy solution of forbidden loves. A European exile, Celario, falls in love with the beautiful Indian girl Azâkia, who has saved him from death (the usual justification for novelistic love affairs and an episode dear to sentimental fantasizing, as in the case of the young David Copperfield). But Azâkia is the faithful wife of Ouâbi, the tribal chief, who, tied to Celario by a noble friendship, entrusts his wife to him when he has to go off to war. Now, how can the imagination be allowed to conclude its predictable journey?

Sarah Morton has Ouâbi taken prisoner, arranges for Celario to gather a band of warriors and free the friend who is just about to be sacrificed on a pyre and is already intoning his death chant:

> 'Midst the flames their fearless songs begin.
> Pain has no terrors to the truly brave.

Aware of his liberator's hidden passion, Ouâbi is grateful and gives him both his tribe and wife, as is permitted by Indian custom and the "virtues of nature." The "nobility" of the Indians was suggested to Sarah Morton by reading William Penn and perhaps the novel *L'Homme sauvage* by Louis Sébastien Mercier (1767), though she obtained her information about rituals and customs from the reports of General Lincoln.[2]

It was the Moravian John Heckewelder, however, who furnished the material for the greatest Enlightenment devotee of the noble savage, James Fenimore Cooper, in whose work the eighteenth-century ideological theme is colored by the new romantic tastes and enacted in a setting of somber tints and evanescent horizons.

Cooper's books give the impression of a fresh immediacy, while, in fact, they are of complex derivation. The philosophy of a vague deism and of tolerance is put into the mouths of innocent creatures of the woods, and the antimetaphysical *dullness* of the London cultural milieu satirized in Alexander Pope's *Dunciad* is attributed to the good common sense of woodsmen tempered by a hard and healthy life: in other words, a pious Enlightenment fraud. The noble savage is, of course, called upon to make a "supporting statement" in justification of this clever deception.

It is worthwhile following the journey from youth to death of the protagonist of a good many of Cooper's novels, Leatherstocking, who first appears in *The Pioneers* (1823), to be followed by *The Last of the Mohicans* (1826), *The Prairie* (1827), *The Pathfinder* (1840), and *The Deerslayer* (1841).

Leslie Fieldler has shown the Libertine and progressive philosopher in Cooper coexisting with the political conservative: Leatherstocking is a Faust impatient with all limits, and although he tries to define himself by denying Calvinist or Catholic theology, he nevertheless needs it to arouse the tensions on which he feeds, since he is blasphemous by nature. As such, he rejects original sin and, when he assumes the guise of the pioneer, this negation seems to him a virtue brought about by progress— "only a sign of 'progress.' "[3] Cooper manages to convince himself that he can reconcile admiration for the noble savage with belief in progress, denial of original sin, and his conservative political feelings. In America both conservatives and radicals believe in progress,[4] but in the sum of Cooperian contradictions the figures that must be added up are even more numerous than usual. Not by chance does he escape into fantasizing for long stretches of his novels.

It is in *The Redskins, or Indians and Injuns* that the Indian as a noble and natural figure takes on another dimension. No longer is he seen solely as representing the ideals of Libertinism—the propulsive force that will renew a faulty society. He also assumes certain qualities typical of conservatism, in order to put the antirent radicals to shame. The Indian's innate sense of justice is intolerable to these radicals because it disproves the omnipotence of the masses—"for nothing has more conduced to the abuses connected with antirentism than the widespread delusion that prevails in the land concerning the omnipotency of the masses."[5]

Leatherstocking (or Deerslayer or Natty Bumppo) is twenty-two years old when he first appears in *The Deerslayer*, which takes place between 1740 and 1745. The state of New York is still confined to its maritime counties; the virgin forest provides shelter "to the noiseless moccasin of the native warrior as he trod the secret and bloody warpath." Through these mazes stalks the young Deerslayer with a face expressing trust, seriousness, and open-hearted frankness, accompanied by the gigantic Hurry, discussing in a childish fashion the Delaware and Mohican tribes that have been defeated by the Mingos and are now intent on revenge. Deerslayer displays his knowledge of Indian life: the redskins honor those who are mad because the Evil Spirit prefers to inhabit the body of a shrewd man and God looks after the poor in spirit. He advises his companion not to give way to sudden, rash fits of anger. The Indians detest anyone who yields to sudden anger, and in fact he, who has lived among them, "did not resort to the artifice of louder tones, even by way of proving its owner's resolution." Thus Deerslayer instructs him in British superciliousness. His companion replies: "*You* may account yourself as a redskin's brother, but *I* hold 'em all to be animals, with nothing human about 'em but cunning."

Deerslayer has to meet his Delaware friend, the young chief Chingachgook, or Serpent, whose fiancée has been kidnaped by the Mingos; Hurry wants to see again the beautiful Judith, who lives on a large lake with her old father and a sister. The two men reach the solitary family just in time to fight the Mingos who have surrounded them, but the old man and Hurry are captured, and Deerslayer remains to defend the two young women on a scow in the middle of the lake. Here they are joined by Chingachgook, who announces that his fiancée is in the enemy's lakeside camp—all the threads of the story have been neatly tied together. Now the varied phases of fighting and negotiating between the opposing camps follow like a game of checkers; the various characters are shifted about in an hour from one side to the other with a dexterity that keeps the reader's apprehension at the highest pitch and has made Cooper so beloved from generation to generation. There are, together with all this, constant transitions from a realistic to a fantastic style of narration.

Deerslayer's character, superior even to that of his fellow Indians, holds the center of the stage. He is without baseness, the epitome of modesty, as stoic as a Marcus Aurelius of the forests, and he observes a chivalrous code of honor as faithfully as a monk observes the formalities established by his monastery's regulations. He is sustained by a pantheistic and tolerant deism. Thus the doctrines of John Toland and J. T. Desaguliers are translated into fiction; the discourses of London's proponents of the Enlightenment have been transformed into fantastic, sylvan, folklike fiction, taking on flesh amid the expanses of century-old American trees—the preferred site also of Chateaubriand's earlier and contrasting Catholic apologetic on the fate and fortunes of *Les Natchez*.

In *The Pathfinder* the young hero has evolved and now resembles Emerson's ideal man: "A fair example of what a just-minded and pure man might be, while untempted by unruly or ambitious desires and left to follow the bias of his feelings amid the solitary grandeur and ennobling influences of a sublime nature. . . ."

Chingachgook proves to be a pre-Christian Stoic and strikes a pose reminiscent of a neoclassical print when he bids farewell to his friend, who he fears is destined for certain death: "Drawing the light blanket he wore over his head, as a Roman would conceal his grief in his robes, he slowly withdrew into the dark, in order to indulge his sorrow and musings alone." Both men, the white and the redskin, re-create through their friendship the Rousseauian state of nature, where everything is open and authentic and nothing is subject to mediation. As Judith says when declaring her love to Deerslayer: "We are not here dwelling among the arts and deceptions of the settlements."

The Last of the Mohicans resumes the plot of *The Deerslayer* fifteen years later, at the moment of the Seven Years' War, and Uncas, the son of Chingachgook, joins the two heroes. The English army is encamped in the familiar forest:

At length the sun set in a flood of glory, behind the distant western hills, and as darkness drew its veil around the secluded spot the sounds of preparation diminished; the last light finally disappeared from the log cabin of some officer; the trees cast their deeper shadows over the mounds and the rippling stream, and a silence soon pervaded the camp, as deep as that which reigned in the vast forest by which it was environed.

Darkness . . . deeper shadows forms a succession of views alongside another parallel but waning one: *flood of glory . . . last light.* The two lines have superimposed on them a third, acoustical series: *sounds of preparation . . . rippling stream . . . silence . . . as deep as that* [other silence]. The second time the adjective *deep* appears in the sentence, it unifies by the echo of its first use the two parallel series, the visual and the acoustic.

Cooper knew how to paint, not only by laying color on top of color but also by giving breath to solid shapes, a vibration to shadows, by the use of deliberate, rhythmic, syntactical structures. For reasons of rhythm, the final relative clause replaces the more natural solution of a simple adjective, which might easily have been just as effective (try declaiming "the vast environing forest"); yet in that case the last phrase would not have been long enough to balance the bulk of the entire preceding sentence. Balzac urged writers to study the technique of the literary landscape in Cooper. But did he expend as much care in drawing his characters? And in probing the Indian spirit?

In *The Last of the Mohicans* two young girls travel through the forest escorted by an English army major and an Indian, Magua, who acts as their guide and will betray them. Their destination is a fort where the girls' father, an English colonel, awaits them. A preacher, David, joins the group, and soon after they meet Chingachgook and Hawkeye (the nickname now given to Natty Bumppo, the Deerslayer of fifteen years back), who are accompanied by Uncas.

The customary engrossing checker game with these characters and hidden enemies as pieces then begins, involving various shifts and counterattacks that verge on mere fantasizing; the outcome is that one of the Englishmen and young Uncas lose their lives. This narrative mechanism simply provides the background against which Cooper sets a Chingachgook endowed with inspired insights. This, for example, is how he explains the Indians' vulnerability to alcohol: their faith, nourished more by Dionysian excitement than Apollonian meditation, was easily seduced through a ruinous deception by what appeared to be a short cut to ecstasy. Chingachgook speaks of alcohol with horror: "Betraying his deep emotion only by permitting his voice to fall to those low, guttural tones, which render his language, as spoken at times, so very musical. . . ." When "musicality" is "guttural"—to recognize the possibility of such a connection is in itself a proof of real knowledge of the Indian world.

Here is the memorable passage: "The Dutch landed, and gave my people the firewater; they drank until the heavens and the earth seemed to meet, and they foolishly thought they had found the great Spirit. Then they parted with their land." Comprehension of the Indian permits him to grasp the true point of dissension between Indians and whites, a religious difference, which is manifested in the differing attitudes toward death in battle. The Indians push their fury all the way to paroxysm by praising and denigrating the enemy, stirring up the thirst for pain and revenge, and sometimes can even transmute that fury by torturing a courageous, impassive enemy. The Christians, however, prepare themselves for death in a spirit of humility and Apollonian forgiveness. The two kinds of religiosity are at loggerheads; while Chingachgook puts the enemy to the test, the Englishman tries to imbue his own spirit with serenity.

The affinities and differences between Puritans and Indians in *The Wept of Wish-ton-Wish* are demonstrated in the comparison between a family of colonists and an adolescent Indian who was captured while lying in ambush. The family has the austere ways that fit an insecure, probative condition in which the practice of self-mastery is the basis of virtue. The Indian surpasses them in self-mastery; yet his every act has the ease of childhood, whereas they have the artificial reserve that comes with age.

Cooper returns to the subject in Chapter XXV:

It would have been a curious study for one interested in the manners of the human species, to note the difference between the calm, physical and perfect self-possession of the wild tenants of the forest, and the ascetic, spiritually sustained, and yet meek submission to Providence, that was exhibited by most of the prisoners.

But in *The Deerslayer* Christian resignation is made more admirable than in its old-fashioned, Puritan form because of a touch of greater pride, which comes perhaps from Indian influence—the pioneers have adopted Indian ways. In *The Deerslayer* Hurry imitates the voices of nature in Indian fashion:

The quavering call of a loon arose from the opposite side of the lake, evidently at no great distance from its outlet. There was no mistaking the note of this bird, which is so familiar to all who know the sounds of the American lakes. Shrill, tremulous, loud, and sufficiently prolonged, it seems the very cry of warning. It is often raised, also, at night—an exception to the habits of most of the other feathered inmates of the wilderness, a circumstance which had induced Hurry to select it as his own signal.

The pioneers learn, too, as is explained in *The Pathfinder*, that the Indian is always grateful for his food, whether it be fat or lean, venison or bear meat, a turkey breast or a wild goose wing—"to the shame of us white men be it said that we look upon blessings without satisfaction and consider trifling evils matters of great account." And when in *The Pathfinder* Natty feels the pangs of love for Mabel, he says, as a true Indian would, that it is the devil or some Mingo witch doctor who has put into his mind the thought of the calamities that might befall her.

There are memorable examples in Cooper of speeches bedizened with metaphors that became the stock-in-trade of characters in the later popular Indian plays. Chingachgook says of his fiancée:

Among my people the rose dies on the stem where it is budded; the tears of the child fall on the graves of his parents; the corn grows where the seed has been planted.

The Delaware girls are not messengers, to be sent, like belts of wampum, from tribe to tribe. They are honeysuckles, that are sweetest in their own woods. . . . Set the pine in the bay and it will turn yellow; the willow will not flourish on the hill; the tamarack is healthiest in the swamp; the tribes of the coast love best to hear the winds that blow over the salt water.

So the sacred oratory, no longer Biblical but rather the deistic and Romantic oratory of "Indianized" whites, gives one a foretaste of certain passages in Melville:

When there's so many things about which it may be said we know nothing at all, why, there is little use and no reason in being difficult touching any one in particular. . . . Many's the hour I've passed, pleasant enough too, in what is term'd contemplation by my people. On such occasions the mind is active, though the body seems lazy and listless. An open spot on a mountainside where a wide look can be had at the heavens and the earth, is a most judicious place for a man to get a just idea of the power of the Manitou, and of his own littleness. At such times there isn't any great disposition to find fault with little difficulties in the way of comprehension, as there are so many big ones to hide them.

Cooper adheres strictly to the precepts of tolerance and the antitheological theology of deism, and his style, worthy of an English classicist, is the perfect dress for that ideology. Yet the closing paragraph of *The Deerslayer* would not be out of place in the mouth of a good Puritan:

We live in a world of transgressions and selfishness, and no pictures that represent us otherwise can be true, though happily for human nature, gleamings of that pure spirit in whose likeness man has been fashioned are to be seen, relieving its deformities and mitigating if not excusing its crimes.

This mixture of doctrines permits an equal love for purity in both the Indian and the white. Unfortunately, it also blocks Cooper's awareness of what John Adams with profound intuition called the Indian's mystical Neoplatonism—his most secret heart and most precious ark. Thus, in *The Last of the Mohicans,* shamanism is mocked with Enlightenment pettiness as a jumble of coarse rituals, the mask of ignorance and impotence, astutely tolerated by unbelieving, shrewd chiefs.

In *The Pathfinder* Chingachgook and Natty are again side by side during the phase of the war that is going in favor of the English, but in *The Pioneers* civilization has already won and has imposed its deformities upon nature. Old Natty must now defend himself against civilized regulations and endures the outrage of pillory and jail. His friend Chingachgook, converted by Moravian missionaries, "has acquired new needs"; alcohol degrades him, and a miserable death strikes him down.

Alone now, about eighty, reduced from hunter to trapper, Natty departs, in *The Prairie,* for the new, more remote frontier. The Pawnee is allotted the role of the good Indian, which in previous books had been filled by the Delaware. The opposite role of the bad Indian, in the past assigned to the Iroquois or the Mingo, is taken by the Sioux. The ever-repeated moral is the one that Thomas J. Farnham heard from a cultivated Indian whom he met in Arkansas:

As soon as you thrust the plowshare under the earth, it teems with worms and useless weeds. It increases population to an unnatural extent—creates the necessity of penal enactments—spreads over the human face a mask of deception and selfishness—and substitutes villainy, love of wealth and power, and the slaughter of millions for the gratification of some royal cutthroat, in place of the single-minded honesty, the hospitality, honour and the purity of the natural state.[6]

A reincarnation of Cooper.

∴

So much time had passed since the Puritan fury against King Philip, who had been cut to pieces in order to obtain horrible trophies, that the authors of the poem *Yamoyden, A Tale of the Wars of King Philip,*[7] the Episcopal minister James Wallis Eastburn and Robert Charles Sands, could finally resurrect him as a romantic, Schillerian warrior, a child of nature who could be usefully counterposed to repressive, debasing institutions, whether Calvinist or Catholic.

What destroyed the Indian race? Bigotry. The authors listened to the death cry of the defeated after having read in the Mathers the terrible story of the Indians wiped out, like the marks of their moccasins on the grass, by *soulless bigotry* "that tracked them to death, with mad, infuriate yell." They sing a funeral hymn to Philip, exemplar of a people's king who truly could wear the diadem of hereditary monarchs, those pawns of courtiers and priests intent on telling their beads—"Satiate dull sense, or count the frequent bead."

The Indian past is praised because it is irrevocable, a good pretext for a populist polemic. The image of King Philip is evoked to censure what seems to be the most opprobrious of acts—to "count the frequent bead"— and which in fact is the European religious custom closest to the Indian spirit.

The romantic vein is more pronounced in *Yamoyden* than in Cooper, who avoids witchlike shadows. In the poem's fourth Canto the authors actually try to reproduce by romantic rhythms the shudder that accompanies an evocation of spirits:

> Beyond the hills the spirit sleeps,
> His watch the Power of evil keeps;
> The spirit of fire has sought his bed,
> The Sun, the hateful sun, is dead.

And they gaze with fascinated smugness at the emblematic vultures:

> Moping and chattering round who fly
> Where the putrid members reeking lie,
> Piece-meal dropping, as they decay.

Cooper speaks again through the voice of George Catlin, the traveler and painter, who, in his long-winded, tedious letters, also shares his straining for an ornate style. Like Cooper, he criticizes the *horrible superstitions* (for example, the ritual tortures described in letter XXII), but he adds that long and cruel experiences prove the impossibility for "enlightened Governments or money-making individuals" to deal without injustice with such credulous and simple people.[8]

Cooper's romantic dreams are further perpetuated in William Cullen Bryant, the poet who rejected the tyranny of reason and taught reverence for more profound sources of inspiration: the conjunction of Jupiter and Venus is the sign and symbol of perfection in heaven as on earth.

"I would not always reason," begins "The Conjunction of Jupiter and

Venus," a melodious eulogy of the labyrinths of wild nature as counter-posed to the straight and narrow road of boring reason, ". . . for the spirit needs impulses from a deeper source than hers." This ideal conjunction of stars is close to being realized, Bryant believes, for it is promised by the chimera of progress. Every delight will be poured out as soon as the last, near promontory is negotiated. In promising this his verse becomes duly awkward:

> Ere long, the better Genius of our race,
> Having encompassed earth, and tamed its tribes,
> Shall sit him down beneath the farthest west,
> By the shore of that calm ocean, and look back
> On realms made happy.

But in "An Indian at the Burial-Place of His Fathers," which is enlivened by its lifelike mimesis of an imaginary Indian, the child of virgin nature, Bryant depicts, as Freneau does, the hero of a defeated race who prophesies the ruin of the victors, and gives free rein to his nostalgia for an untouched, ancient America. As the Indian contemplates his people's graveyard, a melodic consternation moves through the poem's stanzas. Bryant is letting the inspiration of the sign of Venus take over:

> A white man, gazing on the scene,
>   Would say a lovely spot was here,
> And praise the lawns, so fresh and green,
>   Between the hills so sheer.
> I like it not—I would the plain
> Lay in its tall old groves again.

Better the untouched virgin forests where one could see the deer go by and

> The forest hero, trained to wars,
> Quivered and plumed, and lithe and tall,
>   And seamed with glorious scars,
> Walks forth, amid his reign, to dare
> The wolf, and grapple with the bear.

The banks of the river were then sacred to the manes and

> Hither the silent Indian maid
>   Brought wreaths of beads and flowers,
> And the gray chief and gifted seer
> Worshipped the god of thunders here.

But now the wheat is green and high
On clods that hid the warrior's breast. . . .

In one of his late poems, "The Painted Cup," this same melody
becomes richer and is almost imbued with the Indian spirit evoked:

The fresh savannas of the Sangamon
Here rise in gentle swells, and the long grass
Is mixed with rustling hazels. Scarlet tufts
Are glowing in the green, like flakes of fire;
The wanderers of the prairie know them well,
And call that brilliant flower the Painted Cup.

. . . .

But leave these scarlet cups to spotted moths
Of June, and glistening flies, and humming-birds,
To drink from, when on all these boundless lawns
The morning sun looks hot. Or let the wind
O'erturn in sport their ruddy brims, and pour
A sudden shower upon the strawberry-plant,
To swell the reddening fruit that even now
Breathes a slight fragrance from the sunny slope.

But thou art of a gayer fancy. Well—
Let then the gentle Manitou of flowers,
Lingering amid the bloomy waste he loves,
Though all his swarthy worshippers are gone—
Slender and small, his rounded cheek all brown
And ruddy with the sunshine; let him come
On summer mornings, when the blossoms wake,
And part with little hands the spiky grass,
And touching, with his cherry lips, the edge
Of these bright beakers, drain the gathered dew.

In Gilbert Chinard's view, the Enlightenment idea of the noble savage
yields to Romantic dreams only for those incapable of recapturing freedom—ingenuous, gentle, noble, philosophical freedom.*

From now on, singularly ineffectual praise is lavished on the Indian.
During the nineteenth century, the primitive world will be destroyed
without the slightest wavering, but at the same time it will be depicted in
literature with the utmost tenderness of feeling. This is the hallmark of

* "Of all the travelers we have studied, there are only a few who, in the depths of
the forests, regretted their distant country and did not feel perfectly happy. . . . René
[Chateaubriand's hero], the first, will experience fully the impossibility of escaping
from himself and stripping away his ingrained characteristics." G. Chinard, *L'Amérique
et le Rêve Exotique*, Paris, 1913, p. 433.

the Romantic moment, embodied to perfection in Washington Irving. Here he praises the noble savage.

There is something in the character and habits of the North American savage taken in connection with the scenery over which he is accustomed to range, its vast lakes, boundless forest, majestic rivers, and trackless plains that is, to my mind, wonderfully striking and sublime

he declares in *The Sketch Book,* adding, however, that the Indian is not lovable and does not have in his heart the benign and fertile climate in which the most delicate and gentle virtues can flourish. Yet Irving was not deceived by his outward appearance of silent stoicism but actually discovered human sympathy and affection in the Indian.

The Indians had suffered two injustices: not only had they been dispossessed but their character had been described by "bigoted" or prejudiced persons. For the colonists they were beasts of the forest, for the writers an object of contempt. Public opinion was formed by the wretched hordes of degenerate and depraved men who infested the frontiers. All of Indian life rested on proud independence; when this collapsed, the Indians' morality went to pieces. What do we see today on the frontier, Irving asks, but the humiliated, offended, and deeply flawed remnants of a proud people, killed by an unnatural poverty, a lamentable and hopeless misery, "a canker of the mind unknown in savage life?" The first historians of Indian customs testify that in the Indian communities so perfect a charity existed that all preferred to starve rather than permit one of their neighbors to succumb to hunger.

In order to depict their dignified, imposing way of life one needs a true, pure "philosophy," says Irving, the believer in eighteenth-century common sense and humanity. But what is the Indian if not the product of his environment and social education? asks Irving, the disciple of the Scottish school of philosophy. Among the forces that molded the Indian temperament he includes superstition, without realizing that in doing so he reverts to the very slander he has just condemned. Of course, Irving is a humanitarian. He respects the cult of the dead, admires the tribes which, exiled for generations from their native soil and returning by chance to their old territory, are guided by miraculously preserved traditions; they head straight to a mound of earth, where they stand for hours in silence. "Sublime and holy feeling," he exclaims, and defends the Indians who revenged themselves on the Puritans for the violation of their burial grounds, the thefts of animal skins hung up in commemoration of the dead. Irving reports the speech of an Indian chief who exhorts his followers to revenge the outrage in a style that combines the cadences of a Protestant sermon and a speech to Congress, to which he adds certain rhythmical embellishments that are wholly his own. For example, he has the ghost of an outraged mother say: "See the breasts that gave thee suck, the hands that lapped thee warm, and fed thee oft."

The Indians were driven into their sudden wars by deep and generous impulses, even though they were guilty of ferocious acts and killed their prisoners. Irving invokes reasons of state: often it is enough to rid an enemy tribe of a few selected warriors to guarantee security for the future, though he attributes their ferocity in part to the superstitious belief that blood appeases the manes of the fallen. Yet those prisoners who escaped the massacre were adopted by their hospitable conquerors.

It is natural to the Indian to live in danger, which stimulates his faculties, gives vigor to his existence. Exposed to hunger, disease, the perils of the forest, he wraps himself in animal pelts and sleeps amid the roar of cataracts, thus becoming superior to the white man. He intones his death chant while the fire devours his tortured limbs, and yet the "bigoted" accounts of the first colonists saw in that lofty heroism only insensitivity and grim ferocity.

In his essay "Philip of Pokanoket," Irving further comments that in civilized life, where man's happiness and his very existence depend upon the opinion of his fellow men, he is compelled to strike a pose. He "is constantly acting a studied part," and bold, spontaneous personalities are smothered by having to practice petty deceptions, to affect generous sentiments for the purposes of popularity, so that one cannot distinguish his real from his artificial character. By contrast, the solitary Indian obeys his own impulses and judgments, which makes him both unusual and magnanimous. Such was King Philip, whose story Irving retells.

On his return to America after his long travels in Europe, Irving wanted to explore the world of the Indian, by now condemned to extinction, and he ventured as far west as Oklahoma. He described his journey in *A Tour on the Prairies,* published in 1835. Images of desolate plains crossed by herds of bison, of whitened skeletons on the edge of gorges, open the book: "Mouldering skulls and skeletons, bleaching in some dark raveen, or near the traces of a hunting camp, occasionally mark the scene of a foregone act of blood, and let the wanderer know the dangerous nature of the region he is traversing." Amid these symbols of terror the Indians, armed and wary, roamed about.

Watching one of the first Osage Indians he encounters, Irving amplifies earlier notations in *The Sketch Book* on the basis of direct observation:

the restriction of needs is the secret of freedom. Social life chains us to the superfluous, weakens the body, extinguishes the soul's impulses. "In society we are slaves less to others than to ourselves."

Irving discovers the Indians' sense of humor and their dryly satiric vein, their pleasure in improvising chanted descriptions of everyday events. Their gatherings are enlivened by criticism, irony, imitations, and gay mockery, especially of white men, but they become rigid as statues when observed by outsiders. The most ordinary events upset these hardy spirits. Almost any sign that appears "mystical and sinister" will make the warrior or hunter leave the trail, since the warnings of the prophet or "dreamer" take precedence over everything else. Here is an Indian seated before a fire on the plain, while his thoughts turn to his distant home; for two days now his left eye has quivered, and in his heart he decides that one of his family is dead or sick.

And yet Irving does not change the ideas expressed in *The Sketch Book*. As always, experience does not modify the ideal pattern prepared to accommodate it; form, whether it be good or bad, prevails over substance.

In *The Adventures of Captain Bonneville, U.S.A.,* the story of the famous pioneer, Irving to some extent rectifies and refines his portrait of the Indian. In the seventh chapter the expedition led by Captain Bonneville meets a band of exhausted Nez Percés—a miserable group that has only roots and the bark of trees to eat. Yet they refuse to join a hunt scheduled to leave on a religious feast day. They prepare to hunt a few days later, armed with only an old spear and their trust in God. Amazed, Captain Bonneville asks them how they can hope to kill game by such means; they smile to themselves and remain silent. Before leaving, they perform the hunting ritual and pray to the Great Spirit.

Accustomed as I had heretofore been, to find the wretched Indian reveling in blood, and stained by every vice which can degrade human nature, I could scarcely realize the scene I had witnessed. Wonder at such unaffected tenderness and piety, where it was least to have been sought, contended in all our bosoms with shame and confusion, at receiving such pure and wholesome instructions from creatures so far below us in all the arts and comforts of life. . . .

Here the language of the Puritans surfaces in the captain's mind.

A few days later the hunters return with large quantities of meat and share it charitably with the white men.

Simply to call these people religious [Bonneville says] would convey but a faint idea of the deep hue of piety and devotion which pervades their whole conduct. Their honesty is immaculate, and their purity of purpose, and their observance of the rites of their religion, are most uniform and remarkable. They are, certainly, more like a nation of saints than a horde of savages.

Other tribes of Nez Percé, the same ones that in *Astoria* Irving had declared, on the basis of other travelers' reports, to be sly and rapacious, remind Captain Bonneville of the golden age.

But though he repeats Bonneville's words of praise, Irving obviously has no wish to disconcert his reader. To him it is clear that this piety must have Christian origins. Did not the tribe adopt holidays and fasts, even certain rituals, from the Catholic calendar? "They have become blended," he says, "with their own wild rites, and present a strange medley, civilized and barbarous." The spell of the truth, so nearly established by the captain's story, has been broken.

The Indian adopted every rite and preachment from which he hoped to gain a spiritual advantage—a pragmatic conception of the religious life that was incomprehensible to the European. Thus the Sunday festival of the tribe that danced around a pole like "Shaker Quakers" seems to Irving "a wild fantastic ceremonial." And he remarks of another tribe that its members, like virtually all savages, believe in dreams, spells, amulets, or "medicine," as they call them. He reports that other tribes, too, in this way succeed in guaranteeing their safety, becoming invulnerable even to bullets.

The Blackfoot tribe, animated by a Dionysian and bellicose mystique, came into conflict with the Apollonian and pacific Nez Percé. Captain Bonneville tried in vain to excite these cultivators of serenity, who refused to seek revenge. A deserter, Kosato, the Blackfoot Coriolanus, also tried without success to rouse them with belligerent oratory interspersed with howls, dancing, and the beating of drums. Kosato later told his story to Captain Bonneville. Discovered to be the lover of the chief's wife, he had been degraded and deprived of his horse. From then on he thirsted for vengeance. Irving describes his anger in staccato prose punctuated by full stops and semicolons, like panting, laborious breathing, with swift transitions:

I sat brooding . . . until my heart swelled and grew sore, and my teeth were clinched. As I looked down upon the meadow I saw the chief walking among his horses. I fastened my eyes on him as a hawk's; my blood boiled. I drew my breath hard. He went among the willows. In an instant I was on my feet; my hand was on my knife. I flew rather than ran—before he was aware, I sprang upon him.

When the mild Nez Percé are compelled to fight, they prove to be as brave and capable in war as they had been meek and patient in peace. As for Kosato, he gives Irving the chance to coin a phrase worthy of Tacitus: "He fights more with fury than with valor." And yet such observations do not lead Irving to suspect that even in his material misery an Indian might hide invisible treasures. When he deals with the wretchedly poor Shoshone tribe, lovers of peace defended from attack by impregnable mountains, he feels only contempt:

Those forlorn beings, forming a mere link between human nature and the brute, having been looked down upon with pity and contempt by the creole trappers, who have given them the appellation of *les dignes de pitié* . . . They appear more worthy to be called the wild men of the mountains.

The Indian who behaves according to the logic of war will be branded a cruel monster, while the Indian who wants peace is equally scorned. The cowboy's procedure in rounding up the livestock, shutting them all indiscriminately in the same corral, is the equivalent of the progressivist method of argumentation.

Among Irving's hallmarks as an essayist one in particular has withstood the passage of time and the many changes in taste—the ability to pin down certain subtle, complex realities of political psychology, as in his description of the Regency, Louis XV and his circle of roués. Examining the Indian's life under the pressure exerted by the pioneers, he puts his finger on what is probably one of the most elusive reasons for decadence and disintegration: in a time of social upheaval religious impostors, inventors of ceremonies and doctrines are apt to prosper. They begin

by working on the women, the children, and the weak-minded. . . . The more knowing ones of the tribe look on and laugh, thinking it all too foolish to do harm; but they will soon find that women, children, and fools form a large majority in every community, and they will have eventually to follow the new light, or be considered among the profane.

Irving's orderly, disciplined political imagination permitted him to foresee the eventual adjustment of the balance of forces. Was it not possible, he asked himself, for a horde of nomadic, combative half-breeds and outlaws to form in the West and threaten the civilized settlements? The possibility was not remote. A central force that would organize society in the West was lacking, and so the government adopted the measure that Irving proposed: a network of military forts scattered throughout the territory.

The unifying principle of a newly formed horde or potential nation might well have been religious. It was on the verge of becoming a reality through the work of an eminently intelligent young Indian, William Blackbird, who had started negotiations in order to halt the advance of the whites in Michigan. About to be ordained a Catholic priest in Rome, from where he was to return to America to meet with the President, he was assassinated in 1832, in his room at the Pontifical College. The white press kept silent or pretended that his death was due to an accident, but the Indians of his tribe handed down the truth, which was later made public by his brother Andrew in his *History of the Ottawa and Chippewa Indians of Michigan.*

Another attempt to establish a native state was seriously considered by Sam Houston, the governor of Tennessee, who, after a scandal, had sought refuge among the Cherokees in 1830, though only in 1929 did this story give birth to a novel, James Marquis' *The Raven.* A similar attempt came close to realization in Texas; it is described in the appendix of the *Personal Narrative of James O. Pattie,* published in Cincinnati in 1833.

Later in the century the idea of the new, romantic nationality feared by Irving aroused the imagination of Charles W. Webber. In *The Gold Mines of the Gila* (1849) he described the vision of a beatific valley in the West, which progress had spared. Before that, in *Old Hicks, the Guide* (1848), he had created the most perfect villain that a democratic American could possibly imagine: a French aristocrat, accustomed to the courts of Europe, who with the help of savage bands organizes the society of which Irving had a premonition—the synthesis of decadence and primitivity. The novel, which to the reviewers of the time seemed better than *Omoo* and *Typee,* praised intuition and independence; the Indian shares these Emersonian virtues with geniuses. The greatest truths, which civilized man needed centuries to attain, became apparent to him in a flash: he bears the Gospel within himself, in his own free senses, and relies only on them. "The Indians," Webber writes, "equally scorn all shackles but those of the God-imposed senses, whether corporeal or spiritual, and, with like self-reliance, rule all precedents by the Gospel as revealed within themselves."

In the preface to his book, *Life Amongst the Modocs,* Joaquin Miller describes how, in 1855, he met the mysterious James Thompson, known as "The Prince," who wanted to establish a pure Indian republic around holy Mount Shasta, where the simplicity and integrity of their life could be preserved. Later on, Joseph De Bloney and the young Miller revived the plan. In *Life Amongst the Modocs* Miller narrates with much reticence the failed attempt to establish a sanctuary of the traditional life, a primitive, warlike state composed of savage Indians and Europeans. Miller was a favorite of the Pre-Raphaelites, and all of his work is an infelicitous, rhetorical, muddled attempt to glorify the vision of the Indian that Bonneville had had. His fiction begins with a hymn to Mount Shasta, solitary as God, white as the winter moon among the black forests—rising up almost in defiance of the Anglo-Saxon advancing across the bare, burning plains.

First of all, Miller promised to take up the defense of the Indians who lived at the foot of the mountain. He describes how he—"alone, a frail, sensitive, girl-looking boy"—while traveling to the gold fields of California, halted in ecstasy before the fatal mountain.

Wounded by the Indians, he was brought to their silent encampment, where he gradually recovered and stumbled on an incredible truth:

All the mind, or thought, or soul, or whatever it may be, which we scatter in so many directions, and on so many things, they centre on one or two. What if I told you that they talk more of the future and know more of the unknown than the Christian? That would shock you. Truth is a great galvanic battery. No wonder they die so bravely, and care so little for this life, when they are so certain of the next.

But the promise to reveal difficult and solemn truths is not kept.

The carefree life of the Indian seduced the young man. But his narcissism, reflected in an awkward, disjointed style, kept him from achieving any profound understanding of that life. In the same vein as Ik Marvel's best-seller, *Reveries of a Bachelor,* he chattered brashly about himself: "The world says you must not talk about yourself. The world is a tyrant." His love for the Indian is just as self-complacent as the love expressed by the eighteenth-century Libertines and Rousseauists, although it is influenced by attitudes typical of the decadent nineteenth century: ". . . whenever any man dared come out and talk freely, naturally and fully as he desired about himself, the wits nailed him to the wall with their shafts of irony, until the last man was driven from the green and leafy Eden of egotism. . . ."

One day, beside a stream teeming with salmon, Miller met a white man of proud and gentle bearing, who seemed like a prince in exile. Fascinated, Miller followed him, only to wind up in a pioneer town, where the alluring stranger vanished from sight. In complete bewilderment, he runs into a bearded, stocky Negro bedecked with gold ornaments and senses that he is being preyed on by a vampire, his sojourn among the Indians having made him sensitive to witchcraft:

I stood before him like a convict before his keeper. I felt that he was my master. . . . Understand that he had not said a word. I had not lifted my eyes. At last he hoisted his black fat hand to his black thick head and turned away. I walked with an effort out into the street. This man had taken my strength; he had absorbed me into his strong animal body.

The young man finally faints after days of vague fear spent roaming about the town, but fortunately he does so in the rediscovered "prince's" arms. The "prince" cares for him during his illness and then takes him to an isolated valley inhabited by a group of gold prospectors—very much like the new people whom Washington Irving dreaded.

An Indian girl, Paquita, and her small brother, the survivors of a tribe slaughtered by whites, live with the prince. But Paquita grows up, and the prince, feeling that he is in love with her, decides to leave. Once again, the protagonist is alone among the Indians, and from this experience comes the inspiration to write an ode to the "Arabic, Gypsy, Druidic" feeling that would lead everyone to wander through fragrant woods in a state of nature if the struggle for gold, the vicissitudes of commerce, and the rivalry of art did not predominate. In this puerile fantasy resounds the inveterate Enlightenment idea, expressing itself through languorous nineteenth-century effects. Miller's narcissism stood in the way of accurate observation, though he did discover a few scattered truths, explaining, for example, that the Indians refrained from climbing the holy slopes not out of fear of demons but in veneration of the Great Spirit.

Chapter VI

———◆●◆———

The Tradition of Benevolence
from the Seventeenth to
the Nineteenth Century

While the Libertines could achieve only a partial fellowship with the Indians, another European minority—the persecuted "enthusiasts," extremists of the Protestant Reformation—did, on the contrary, ally itself with them, with wholehearted rapture. Having solemnly burned the Bible, a Scottish shipowner, the Convulsionist Meikle John Gibb, was arrested. The Presbyterians vainly implored the Duke of York to hang him, and meanwhile those among them who were in the same cell with Gibb, having also been jailed for disobedience of the civil authorities, beat him. It was his custom to howl during his prayers, but the beatings kept him quiet. After being exiled to America, he became friendly with the Indians, won their deep admiration, and died there about 1720.[1] But that part of his life was not recorded in literary form, just as the whole encounter between Indians and Shakers was shrouded in almost complete silence.

Mother Ann Lee, founder of the Shaker society in America, was immediately recognized by Indians as the "good Mother"; it was an Indian who saw her head encircled by a halo of sanctity.[2] The Shakers received their supernatural songs from Indian spirits, and some Shakers were actually possessed by Indian ghosts. In the winter of 1842–43 a chance visitor to the Shaker village Niskayuna witnessed a religious dance during which two "sisters" began spinning around with their eyes closed inside a circle of motionless fellow worshipers and, behold! one sister announced that Mother Ann, the founder, was informing her of the arrival of an Indian tribe that wanted to be friendly. The following night the holy dance was resumed. Halfway through it the doors were flung open, and the Indians were invited to come in. The "sister" who had received the communication could see them, and the Shakers, possessed by their spirits, began to howl like shamans and, though usually chaste and austere, to perform a frenetic rite. They even wanted to be fed Indian food, which was prepared for them in the kitchen. Finally, the head of the community urged the Indian spirits to search for Shakers in the hereafter, and the living ceased to be possessed.

The communions that united Indians with Baptists and Quakers were less spirited. In 1636 the first Baptist settlement was established in Rhode Island by Roger Williams. A minister who had been a Puritan and had rebelled against the Massachusetts civil authorities' interference in the practice of religion, Williams was condemned by a court and, helped by Indian tribes, fled southward to Rhode Island. The chief reason for his flight was his belief in the separation of civil and ecclesiastical powers, which, he felt, should guarantee the purity of both without any need for "either explicit or implicit" agreements. In the new community he founded, Quakers and Jews, who were not allowed to settle in Puritan Massachusetts, were admitted.

Roger Williams, a friend of Milton's, believed in tolerance and rejected the notion of a special covenant between the community of Puritan saints and God, but, as Perry Miller observes, "As soon as the uniquely typical and visible state was translated into its antitype, which is the invisible church, all nations were left with no better guides than considerations of utility, prosperity, power or peace."[3] The authentic Puritans of Massachusetts felt betrayed by their English coreligionists, who in London gave a warm welcome to Williams, the liquidator of their intransigent theocracy.

In any event, the secularization of life, bereft of any notion of a covenant or election, broke down the barrier between colonists and natives. In 1643 the new coexistence gave birth to Williams's pamphlet *A Key into the Language of the Indians of America*,[4] a phrase book of the indigenous tongue, with a sort of list of opening sentences for missionary lectures. The prologue announces:

I present you with a key; I have not heard of the like, yet framed, since it pleased God to bring that mighty continent of America to light. Others of my countrymen have often and excellently and lately written of the country (and none that I know beyond the goodness and worth of it).

This key respects the native language of it, and happily may unlock some rarities concerning the natives themselves, not yet discovered. . . .

A little key may open a box, where lies a bunch of keys.

I know there is no small preparation in the hearts of multitudes of them. I know their many solemn confessions to myself, and one to another, of their lost wandering conditions.

But who are these natives whose language is about to be disclosed?

From Adam and Noah that they spring, it is granted on all hands.

But for their later descent, and whence they came into those parts, it seems as hard to find as to find the wellhead of some fresh stream which, running many miles out of the country to the salt ocean, hath met with many mixing streams by the way. They say themselves that they have sprung and grown up in that very place, like the very trees of the wilderness.

They say that their great God Cawtantowwit created those parts. . . . They have no clothes, books, nor letters, and conceive their fathers never had; and therefore they are easily persuaded that the God that made Englishmen is a greater God because He hath so richly endowed the English above themselves. But when they hear that about sixteen hundred years ago, England and the inhabitants thereof were like themselves, and since have received from God clothes, books, &c., they are greatly affected with a secret hope concerning themselves. . . .

They have many strange relations of one Wetucks, a man that wrought great miracles amongst them, and walking upon the waters, &c., with some kind of broken resemblance to the Son of God. . . .

Williams was evidently carried away by the allegorical style, a style later to be adopted by Edward Taylor and Jonathan Edwards. His symbolistic approach, which drew on a comparative philology of devotional English and Algonquin, produced a curious feeling of embarrassment among the Puritans, described by Perry Miller in a magisterial page.

To this mannerism Winthrop objected when he said that Williams' tract was full of figures and flourishes. It is actually an almost inescapable consequence of the typological method; he who once begins perceiving in the Old Testament not factual narratives but ingenious puzzles to be deciphered only in an imaginative realm outside history is bound also to find things or happenings around him lose their solidity and dissolve into inward communications. This emblemizing disposition is utterly different from the normal Puritan method of reading sermons in stones; theologians of the covenant studied events (exactly as did Winthrop and Bradford in their histories) in order to perceive the governing will of God at work. But they did not find in stone or beast an enigmatic symbol of a divine utterance, as they did not—as still today their successors do not—approve of the sort of people who do. Perhaps it explains the sneaking esteem for Williams which Cotton Mather could not keep out of his satire: at a time when Mather was seeking reinforcement for a piety which the covenant alone could no longer excite, when he was experimenting with novel ways of spiritualizing the commonplaces of existence, he let himself praise the *Key* because it "spiritualizes the curiosities."

But then Samuel Gorton, the Familist, turned up in Providence. Gorton had already been tried in Boston and banished in 1638, and later he was flogged in Rhode Island. Nathaniel Morton tells his story in *New England's Memorial* (1669). Gorton declared that Christ was a shadow, a similitude of what is experienced in every Christian, the image of God in whose likeness Adam was created, and that His suffering was the manifestation of His suffering in Adam. For Gorton the ministers of religion were necromancers; the eucharistic feast was a form of magic. To provide room for their revolution, more "advanced" than that of the Baptists, the Familists tried to establish relations with the Indians, as Williams had done. But they made the wrong move, forming an alliance with the chief of the Narragansett federation. Two members of the federation appealed to Boston, and the Familists' Indian adventure was cut short.

∴

The first two Quakers landed in Puritan territory in 1656. Their bodies were examined for demonic signs, and their books were burned by the public hangman. After a brief period of imprisonment they were put on a ship bound for England. During the succeeding years four Quakers were hanged for the crime of being Quakers. Some Quakers laid siege to converted Indians but without any effect, as Daniel Gookin relates; they taught them to have contempt for the ministers as priests of Baal and even for the Bible, which they felt was inferior to an inner light. George Fox visited the colonists, preaching also to the Indians from 1671 to 1672, and in 1678 a Quaker colony was founded in New Jersey. Finally, in 1681, William Penn attempted his "holy experiment." On October 10, just before taking possession of Pennsylvania, he wrote to his three commissioners: "Be tender of offending the Indians, and hearken, by honest spies, if you can hear that anybody inveigles the Indians not to sell, or to stand off and raise the value upon you. . . . Let them know that you are come to sit down lovingly among them."[5] God created the world, Penn stated. To Him all owe "their being and well-being"; to Him all must offer an accounting of their actions. This God has written in men's hearts His law, which teaches and commands us to love and to help. From this God also derives William Penn's authority, in whose heart He has placed a concern for this fragment of the world.

Penn concluded the famous treaty with the Delawares by declaring that he would not call them sons or brothers, for parents often chastise their sons, and brothers often quarrel. Nor would he compare the friendship that should join them to a chain, for rain can rust and trees fall and break chains. Instead, he considered them of the same flesh and blood as Christians, like two parts of one body. Penn's oratory strangely resembled that of the Indians, and it swayed them. In the same way, the silent language of trusting simplicity would persuade a band of marauding Indians not to break into the house of a Quaker who had left his door open at night. A long time afterward, one of the Indian warriors explained to this same man, so resolute about entrusting himself solely to Providence, that the band spared him precisely because it had interpreted his defenselessness as an act of faith in the Great Spirit. The unarmed Quakers never perished from the sword and were able to withstand the insults of those who, in the fury of war, goaded them on to defend themselves.

John Locke was the author of Carolina's laws, and William Penn framed the laws of Pennsylvania; both were liberals and tolerant, but they differed radically. Locke, as George Bancroft points out, looks for the truth through the testimony of the senses, while Penn finds it in God's direct revelations to the mind. Locke compares the soul to a sheet of paper on which sensations trace their signs; for Penn it is a musical instrument. Locke interprets conscience as the opinion one has of oneself, while Penn sees it as God's image and oracle. For Locke felicity is pleasure, and the greatest good is that which pleases. For Penn beatitude lies in the subjection of earthly instincts to the instincts of the divine; the greatest good is the supreme end, God in Himself and for Himself the object of love. The infinite is a negative notion for Locke, while for Penn it is an innate idea and of the same nature as truth, goodness, and God. Locke granted democracy only to large landowners, while Penn did not put any restrictions on the right to vote, since the light of God shone in everyone.[6] "Each man knows God," Penn said, "from an infallible demonstration in himself, and not on the slender grounds of men's lo here interpretations, or lo there"—man is an epitome of the cosmos, and by knowing Him one knows everything.

Pennsylvania's legislation was the faithful reflection of Penn's beliefs: everyone had equal rights, the law of entail was abolished, financial speculation restricted, and, as among the Puritans, cock and bull fights, the theater, carnivals, and profane amusements were forbidden. Penn admired the public life of the Delawares: "They speak little but fervently, and with elegance. I have never seen more natural sagacity, considering them without the help (I was going to say the spoil) of tradition."[7] The Quaker brimming with benevolence was as blind as the Puritan. As the Enlightenment zealot did, he projected on the Indian what he needed to see externalized in order to reassure himself about his own break with the past. In reality the Delawares were supported by a tradition and by a scripture quite similar to the Bible.

Francis Daniel Pastorius, the German Pietist, was active in the colony, and he pronounced Christian words that had never been heard from Puritan lips: the "so-called savages . . . live more contentedly and with less thought for the morrow than Christians." They do not know the tyranny of fashion, he said, are temperate, and apply the Senecan precept: "I desire ever more strongly what God wants as much as I."[8]

Quaker writings on the Indians are at times the very opposite of Puritan descriptions. In his *An Historical and Geographical Account of The Province and Country of Pensilvania in America* (London, 1698), Gabriel Thomas considers the Indians the remnants of the ten tribes of Israel because they look like the Jews, observe the new moons, offer the first fruits of their farming to a God—"to Maneto"—celebrate a feast of tabernacles, and rest their altars on twelve stones. As for their character, the Quaker avows that they are charitable among themselves, since they support the lame and the blind like all other members of the community and "are also kind and obliging to the Christians."[9]

John Heckewelder, a missionary for the Moravian Brethren who in many respects were close to the Quakers, reached America in 1754, lived with converted Indians in Ohio, and left a loving description of them.[10] He understood the supernatural roots of their communal generosity and their unusual hospitality: since the meat that was cooked had been taken from the forest, it was therefore common property before the hunter had appropriated it for himself. The grain or vegetables had been grown in everyone's soil, "yet not by the power of man, but by that of the Great Spirit."

Indian friendship, sensitive and steadfast, is praised at length by the honest missionary, who nevertheless does not succeed in penetrating the greatest truths of Indian life because he sees their customs as reflections of his own eighteenth-century concept of natural rights. He observes that in the Indian languages gender is not separated into male and female but rather into animate and inanimate, proof of their sense of a society that embraces men, beasts, and even plants: "from this they have not yet dared to separate themselves." In this spirit he observed their initiations, which seemed to him the excitation of deliriums that caused a lofty conception of self and courage for the most desperate exploits. Love and honesty, if divorced from intellectual understanding, avail as little as their opposites.

The Quakers' most characteristic literary genre was the diary, the Protestant substitute for confession. Their most famous diarist, John Woolman, was a preaching tailor who espoused the liberation of the slaves. His inner voice had also gently pushed him toward the Indians. He visited the Wyalusing settlement, where there was a tribe whose "prophet" had been converted by the Moravian Brethren and had then sent messages to the Quakers:

Having for many years felt love in my heart towards the natives of this land who dwell far back in the wilderness, whose ancestors were formerly the owners and possessors of the land where we dwell . . . and being at Philadelphia in the 8th month, 1761, on a visit to some Friends who had slaves, I fell in company with some of those natives who lived on the east branch of the river Susquehanna. . . . I believed some of them were measurably acquainted with that Divine power which subjects the rough and froward will of the creature. At times I felt inward drawings towards a visit to that place, which I mentioned to none except my dear wife until it came to some ripeness. In the winter 1762 I laid my prospects before my friends at our Monthly and Quarterly, and afterwards at our General Spring Meeting. . . .

So, having privately received the signs of destiny and then corroborated them by the community's consent, Woolman left his community, not only to spread evangelical teachings but also to learn, wanting to penetrate the life and spirit of the Indians in order to obtain instruction from them. This is the first occasion—and for a long time the only one—when this possibility is even entertained.

Thus inspired, Woolman, together with a companion, traveled to the Indians across the wild mountains, where God is manifest in all His solemnity, reaching the tribe just at the moment when war was about to overwhelm it.

A warrior raised a tomahawk to strike him, but he faced him with complete friendliness, and by speaking calmly made him put down his weapon. Yet, despite this propitious beginning, he wondered whether he should not return home, whether perchance his persistence in this undertaking originated in a vainglorious unwillingness to admit failure. Was he really propelled only by inspirations? Having examined this scruple for a whole night, he felt himself filled with a sense of peace and continued his journey. Finally, Woolman speaks lovingly to the "prophet's" sixty extremely gentle and taciturn followers, even though nobody understands him. The meeting could not be more Quakerish: all sit together in silence and each one makes a void within himself until a sudden impulse impels him to speak. "The silent meeting aimed not to cultivate even meditation but to subdue it. Not only the body but carnal mind was to be disciplined, suppressed, and got out of the way so that the light within might grow and dominate."[11] Silence can be broken only if the words pour out naturally, often accompanied by sobs and tears. Woolman discovered this spellbound silence and these sudden outbursts of the heart in the depths of the forest. Nothing else happened, but after all nothing else had to happen: the chain of Quaker love did not require external signs.

∴

However, no tender effusion is allowed in Jonathan Dickinson's "narrative of captivity," in which a group of shipwrecked survivors are attacked by ferocious warriors who are met with religious calm. Their assailants scornfully offer the naked Quakers pages torn from the Bible to cover themselves with, but they meet this affront with unperturbed composure. The prisoners are dragged from tribe to tribe and subjected to constant sufferings. The Indians seem to be nothing but brutes, their magical ceremonies repulsive:

Night came on; the moon being up, an Indian, who performeth their ceremonies, stood out, looking full at the moon making a hideous noise, and crying out, acting like a mad man for the space of half an hour; all the Indians being silent till he had done: after which they all made fearful noise some like the barking of a dog or wolf, and other strange sounds. After this, one gets a log and sets himself down, holding the stick or log upright on the ground, and several others getting about him, made a hideous noise, singing to our amazement; at length their women joined consort, making the noise more terrible.[12]

Another description is even more horrible: six warriors begin a dance around a pole stuck in the ground.

Whilst these six are thus employed, all the rest are staring and scratching, pointing upwards, and downwards on this and the other side every way; looking like men frighted, or more like Furies; thus behaving themselves until the six have done shaking their rattles. Then they all begin a dance, violently stamping on the ground for the space of an hour or more without ceasing. In which time they sweat in a most excessive manner, that by the time the dance is over, what by their sweat and the violent stamping of their feet, the ground is trodden into furrows; and by the morning, the place where they danced was covered with maggots.[13]

Regret that Quaker kindliness did not permeate relations between the two races is reiterated in the nineteenth century. In James Kirke Paulding's novel *Koningsmarke, The Long Finne* (1823), some Swedes of Delaware are captured and tortured in terrifying ways. The sadistic sequence is interrupted by the arrival of mild and generous Quakers, who placate the Indians' fury. However, admiration for William Penn in the nineteenth century is inspired by Enlightenment ideas and therefore is hardly religious. The Indian is depicted as a *philosophe* who criticizes the beliefs of the whites. The Quaker Helen Hunt Jackson, in her novel *Ramona*, published in the late nineteenth century, continues to echo the usual sentimental humanitarianism. But the Quaker tradition did not end with the loss of political power in Pennsylvania. Whittier's poetry and Bancroft's historical prose, and even some of Longfellow's mid-nineteenth-century poetry, may be considered of Quaker inspiration, not to mention the last Quaker pioneer, Thomas C. Battey. Woolman's spirit informs this nineteenth-century diary, *The Life and Adventures of a Quaker Among the Indians*, written by an elementary schoolteacher from the West and published in Boston in 1875. Actually, Battey was a fossil from the seventeenth century.

Prompted by a sudden Quaker inspiration, Battey felt called to live among the Kiowas:

Yielding to offer myself to go among the wild and roving Kiowas . . . I was favored to see that a whole surrender is required; that heretofore I had clung, with the arm of earthly love, to my precious wife and children, but that the time was near in which I must forsake all, make all that I hold dear upon earth as a "whole burnt offering," relinquish the thought of being joined by them in this land, and even of hearing from them with any degree of reliability. My very soul was solemnized within me, and I could but cry "Oh Most High and Holy One, whose right it is to rule and reign in the hearts of the children of men, enable me to say, in the depths of true and consecrated sincerity—Not my will, but thine, be done."[14]

Nothing could now turn him from his path, and despite horrifying stories about the tribes to which he felt attracted, he left and at last managed to pitch his tent in the Indian encampment. His newfound students come down with colds, and, as a consequence, he is suspected of the evil eye, but Chief Kicking Bird protects him. Not the slightest stirring of sympathy is kindled in Battey by tribal cultures; the dances seem to him diabolical and the religion superstitious. And yet some unspoken respect is reflected in his description of the holy ceremony for the elks in which the dancers worship holy objects:

They faced the medicine—shall I say idols? For it was conducted with all the solemnity of worship, jumping up and down in true time with the beating of the drums, with a bone whistle in their mouths, through which the breath escaped as they jumped about, and the singing of the women completed the music. The dancers continued to face the medicine, with arms stretched upwards and towards it—their eyes, as it were, riveted to it. They were apparently oblivious to all surroundings, except the music and what was before them.[15]

He admits: "I saw enough to cause my heart to swell with deep and conflicting emotions. . . ."[16]

∴

George Bancroft, born in 1800 in Worcester, Massachusetts, was the son of a Unitarian and Whig. He became a Transcendentalist and Democrat but recognized that the permanent values of truth, moral standards, and justice stand above all ideologies and creeds, and saw history as an organic process in which certain constant forms were active. By some weird alchemy of influences, his essential characteristics were somewhat akin to the spirit of William Penn.

In Bancroft's view the republican government owed its strength to the recognition of permanent transcendental values, and only by respecting them was a constant growth of freedom possible. When President Van Buren appointed him Collector of the Port of Boston, he gave positions on his staff to the utopian Orestes Brownson, who later converted to Catholicism, and the conservative Nathaniel Hawthorne.

His most important work, *A History of the United States,* started to appear in 1834. It was inspired by Quakerism, even though the ideology professed was Savigny's romantic, conservative, Germanic historicism.

Bancroft advocated compassion for the defeated race, but nevertheless he unintentionally denigrated it and gave a distorted picture of the native language, which

was held in bonds by external nature. Abounding in words to designate every object of experience, it had none to express a spiritual conception; materialism reigned in it . . . it had no name for continence or justice, for gratitude or holiness. . . . In another point of view, this materialism contributed greatly to the picturesque brilliancy of American discourse. Prosperity is as a bright sun or a cloudless sky; to establish peace is to plant a forest-tree, or to bury the tomahawk; to offer presents as a consolation to mourners, is to cover the grave of the departed; and if the Indian from the prairies would speak of griefs and hardships, it is the thorns of the prickly pear that penetrate his moccasins.[17]

The synthesizing quality of the native languages he saw as an apparent wealth that prevents abstraction, yet all languages, from these "savage and agglutinated" tongues to ours, share common traits. So, Bancroft concluded, linguistic structure is innate and comes from God: man can cultivate it, as he does the earth, but he cannot fashion it from nothing. Civilized—that is, cultivated—languages are ruled by analysis and brevity: "Men have admired the magnificence displayed in the mountains, the rivers, the prolific vegetation, of the New World. In the dialect of the wildest tribe, the wilderness can show a nobler work, of a Power higher than that of man."[18] Bancroft concludes emphatically and with a typical Emersonian staccato. In essence language contains every aspect of a people: the Indians' social life therefore is restricted to the life of the senses and is unaware of ascetic values. This reversal of the truth is perhaps due to certain eighteenth-century travelers whose reports Bancroft trusted. In fact, when he describes the Indians' war parties, he admits that they are preceded by rituals and fasts. This observation is based on Henry Rowe Schoolcraft's reports; when he writes of the warriors' continence, he follows James Adair's accounts.

What ancient legislator, Bancroft asks, could possibly have imagined that human society could subsist without laws or civil coercion, as it does among the Indians? Among them "the humiliating subordination of one will to another was everywhere unknown," and the chiefs often did not know how and when they had obtained their power. The Indian religion is simply animism and pantheism, Bancroft repeats, in agreement with Schoolcraft; only the missionaries conferred a certain refinement on this vague sense of the divine. But even from these false or vague notions Bancroft draws a kindly moral: it was not fear that gave birth, in Lucretian fashion, to their gods, but rather the faculty of awe in man and his need to communicate with nature. The search for the guardian spirit by means of terrible penances, which Bancroft notes on the basis of Schoolcraft's research, prompts other thoughts in keeping with the tradition of benevolence: "That man should take up the cross, that sin should be atoned for, are ideas that dwell in human nature; they were so diffused among the savages, that Le Clercq believed some of the apostles must have reached the American continent."[19]

Bancroft brings his treatise to a very ordinary conclusion: the Indian is savage and uncultivated yet still a man with many accompanying virtues.

They had the moral faculty which can recognize the distinction between right and wrong; nor did their judgments bend to their habits and passions more decidedly than those of the nations whose laws justified, whose statesmen applauded, whose sovereigns personally shared, the invasion of a continent to steal its sons. If they readily yielded to the impetuosity of selfishness, they never made their own personality the centre of the universe. They were faithless treaty-breakers; but, at least, they did not exalt falsehood into the dignity of a political science, or scoff at the supremacy of justice as the delusive hope of fools; and, if they made everything yield to self-preservation, they never avowed their interest to be the first law of international policy.[20]

The Indian did not give the coherence of a system to evil. He was not the Libertine who, on the Elizabethan stage, took the part once played by the devil in the medieval theater, and then later became the philosophizing "villain," the consistent follower of the Enlightenment.

Bancroft is inclined to celebrate the constant recurrence of permanent values in history, and the characteristics of a common humanity to be found in Indians and Europeans provide him with a very appealing illustration: "There is not among the aborigines a rule of language, a custom or an institution, which when considered in its principle, has not a counterpart among their conquerors."[21]

For Bancroft the hallmark of the highest civilization was a well-kempt courtesy, but European history was as far from that ideal as the history of the Indians: refined instruments of judicial torture were often used to punish crimes of opinion, and torture for religious reasons is a completely European feature. Yet despite the vehemence with which Bancroft denied Europe the right to set itself apart from aboriginal humanity, he nevertheless reproached the latter for lacking graceful dances or Raphaelesque decorations, which he considered the ideal purpose of all progress. When *Hiawatha* was published, Bancroft went so far as to write, condescendingly, saying that it depicted the infantile quality of Indian life, when the lower animals were the companions and equals of man and external nature was his friend. By now, benevolence had become Victorian.

∴

In John Greenleaf Whittier's poem "The Pennsylvania Pilgrim" Quaker benevolence again made its appearance in conjunction with the influence of German Pietists, Mennonites, and Rosicrucians. This serene region became the repository for occult knowledge; the herbarium of the

Reverend Pastorious was hermetic, and alchemy flourished in the depths
of the forest:

> About him, beaded with the falling dew,
> Rare plants of power and herbs of healing grew,
> Such as Van Helmont and Agrippa knew.

> For, by the love of Görlitz' gentle sage,
> With the mild mystics of his dreamy age
> He read the herbal signs of nature's page. . . .

> The pious Spener read his creed in flowers.

Johann Kelpius, the Transylvanian millennarian, arrived on the scene in
1694:

> Deep in the woods, where the small river slid
> Snake-like in shade, the Helmstadt Mystic hid,
> Weird as a wizard over arts forbid,

> Reading the books of Daniel and of John,
> And Behmen's Morning-Redness, through the Stone
> Of Wisdom, vouchsafed to his eyes alone.

Just as Stirke or Ireneo Filalete had done in New England, so Kelpius in
Pennsylvania actually produced the philosopher's stone, but legend has it
that he threw it in the river. The savants of Europe wrote to the gentle
Pastorius:

> Wise Spener questioned what his friend could trace
> Of Spiritual influx or of saving grace
> In the wild natures of the Indian race.

The Indian lived quietly, immersed in peaceful occupations:

> Giving to kindness what his native pride
> And lazy freedom to all else denied.

> And well the curious scholar loved the old
> Traditions that his swarthy neighbors told
> By wigwam-fires when nights were growing cold,

> Discerned the fact round which their fancy drew
> Its dreams, and held their childish faith more true
> To God and man than half the creeds he knew.

> The desert blossomed round him; wheat fields rolled
> Beneath the warm wind waves of green and gold. . . .

But that adjective "childish" is enough to taint everything poisonously. Must not a child be cajoled but at the same time tamed?

Indian virginal nature and fierceness are the two themes of Whittier's "The Bridal of Pennacook." Unmarred by the ideology of progress, the tone here achieves a melodic and chromatic perfection as in an archaic, untouched landscape where there is "no sound save the lapse of the waves on thy shores, / The plunging of otters, the light dip of oars." The consecutive rhymes link two exquisitely matched orders of sounds.

This landscape surrounds the enchanting life of the Indian village, over which the chief's magical powers threateningly hover:

> In their sheltered repose looking out from the wood
> The bark-builded wigwams of Pennacook stood,
> There glided the corn-dance, the council fire shone,
> And against the red war-post the hatchet was thrown.
>
> There the old smoked in silence their pipes, and the young
> To the pike and the white perch their baited lines flung;
> There the boy shaped his arrows, and there the shy maid
> Wove her many-hued baskets and bright wampum braid.

But the idyl cloaks the fierceness of the domineering chief, Bashaba:

> Nightly down the river going
> Swifter was the hunter's rowing,
> When he saw that lodge-fire glowing
>   O'er the waters still and red;
> And the squaw's dark eye burned brighter,
> And she drew her blanket tighter,
> As, with quicker step and lighter,
>   From that door she fled.
> For that chief had magic skill,
> And a Panisee's dark will,
> Over powers of good and ill,
>   Powers which bless and powers which ban . . .
>
> All the subtle spirits hiding
> Under earth or wave, abiding
> In the caverned rock, or riding
>   Misty clouds or morning breeze;
> Every dark intelligence,
> Secret soul, and influence
> Of all things which outward sense
>   Feels, or hears, or sees,—

These the wizard's skill confessed
At his bidding banned or blessed,
Stormful woke or lulled to rest
　　Wind and cloud, and fire and flood;
Burned for him the drifted snow,
Bade through ice fresh lilies blow,
And the leaves of summer grow
　　Over winter's wood!

The Indian's heart is hard and cold,
It closes darkly o'er its care,
And formed in Nature's sternest mould,
　　Is slow to feel, and strong to bear.

In a number of poems Whittier shows himself an alert Quaker friend of the Indians, and yet his poem "On the Big Horn," addressed to the surviving conquerors of General Custer, offers only assimilation and white education as their lodestar and does so with stolid, slovenly, humanitarian fervor:

The Ute and the wandering Crow
Shall know as the white men know,
　　And fare as the white men fare,
The pale and the red shall be brothers,
One's rights shall be as another's,
　　Home, School and House of Prayer![22]

The dreadful repressive urge animating these horrid verses was much more lethal and efficacious than the counterenchantment that Whittier had imagined in his novella *The Pow-waw*, where the Indians' exorcisms are broken by a New York priest using a polyglot Bible. Custer's old vanquisher, Sitting Bull, countered Whittier's exhortation with a final, patient, desperate act of passive resistance, which he paid for with his life.

∴

Longfellow, having read Heckewelder as a young man, was steeped in the climate formed by the Moravian, Quaker tradition. In a letter to his mother dated November 9, 1823, he noted that the Indians "are a race possessing magnanimity, generosity, benevolence, and pure religion without hypocrisy." In 1850 he invited an Ojibwa chief to tea. In 1854, after having read Schoolcraft, his experiences and observations began to find expression in the octosyllabic verses of *The Song of Hiawatha,* which he completed the following year.

The monotonous rocking-horse beat of his verse, modeled after the Finnish epic *Kalevala* (Holmes justified this meter on the grounds that verse measured to fit the breath is appropriate to oral literature), may have dissuaded many from meditating upon its subject matter. Another obstacle is the lack of ethnological precision. Yet a poem is not a report; it must simply give form to a myth, and a mythical structure is not altered by the addition or subtraction of this or that element.[23] The myth of the god Hiawatha had been described by Schoolcraft, yet Daniel Brinton denied its credibility, since in the Onondaga dialect the god Atorarho was alternately called Tahiwagi-Hiawatha and Tahionwatha.* The poem's images are, however, woven together with a grace and coherence that called forth a number of versions: Freiligrath's German, Bunin's Russian, and Newman's Latin (the *Carmen Hiawathae* of 1862).

Carl Gustav Jung was later to see a process of individuation in the unfolding of the scenes and therefore a method of psychic therapy by means of symbols, although Longfellow, as Stith Thomson was to prove, had fallen into the trap of his prejudices, abolishing those parts of Indian tradition in which Hiawatha appears as both civilizer and clown.† This

---

* "The confusion," he says, "seems to have begun more than a century ago; for Pyrlaeus, the Moravian missionary, heard among the Iroquois (according to Hecke-welder) that the person who first proposed the league was an ancient Mohawk, named Thannawege. Mr. J. V. H. Clarke, in his interesting *History of Onondaga,* makes the name to have been originally Ta-oun-ya-wat-ha, and describes the bearer as the Deity that presides over fisheries and hunting-grounds. He came down from heaven on a white canoe, and after sundry adventures, which remind one of the labors of Hercules, assumed the name of Hiawatha (signifying, we are told, 'a very wise man'), and dwelt for a time as an ordinary mortal among men, occupied in works of benevolence. Finally after founding the confederacy and bestowing many prudent counsels upon the people, he returned to the skies by the same conveyance in which he had descended. His legend, or rather, congeries of intermingled legends, was communicated by Clarke to Schoolcraft, when the latter was compiling his *Notes on the Iroquois.* Schoolcraft, pleased with the poetical cast of the story, and the euphony of the name, made confusion worse by transferring the hero to a distant region and identifying him with Manabozho, a fantastic deity of the Ojibwas.

". . . And thus, by an extraordinary fortune, a grave Iroquois lawgiver of the fifteenth century has become, in modern literature, an Ojibwa demigod, son of the West Wind, and companion of the tricksey Paupukkeewis, the boastful Jagoo, and the strong Kwasind." *The Iroquois Book of Rites,* Library of American Aboriginal Literature, vol. II, ed. Daniel G. Brinton (Philadelphia, 1883), pp. 35–36.

† "The double character of leader of the people and foolish dupe does not appear to strike the Indian as incongruous, but Longfellow would undoubtedly have spoiled his poem for white readers had he included the trickster incidents." Stith Thomson, "The Indian Legend of Hiawatha," *Publications of the Modern Language Association,* 1922, p. 137.

double aspect of its hero was too profound for what Daudet called the stupid nineteenth century.

Where are the legends of the poem found?

> In bird's-nests of the forest,
> In the lodges of the beaver,
> In the hoof-prints of the bison,
> In the eyrie of the eagle!

And what is their significance?

> Every human heart is human,
> . . . in even savage bosoms
> There are longings, yearnings, strivings
> For the good they comprehend not,
> That the feeble hands and helpless,
> Groping blindly in the darkness,
> Touch God's right hand in that darkness
> And are lifted up and strengthened. . . .

The first canto puts into verse the depiction by the painter George Catlin of the Red Pipe-stone Quarry. The Great God or Manito sends a message of peace to the fiercely warring tribes, while posed like a model for a conventional allegorical painting. The second canto (which versifies Heckewelder's account of a bear hunt) tells how Mudjekeewis killed the great bear of the mountains, the terror of the nations, receiving the four winds as his reward. He keeps the west wind for himself and gives the other winds to his children. The east wind goes to Wabun:

> Though the birds sang gayly to him,
> Though the wild-flowers of the meadow
> Filled the air with odors for him,
> Though the forests and the rivers
> Sang and shouted at his coming.
> Still his heart was sad within him,
> For he was alone in heaven.

His solitude is alleviated when he beholds a maiden; he clasps her to his heart, changing her into the morning star.

The north wind falls to the fierce Kabibonokka. Rushing from his freezing caves toward the south, he encounters Shingebis, the fisherman, whose indifference annoys him:

> And though Shingebis, the diver,
> Felt his presence by the coldness,

> Felt his icy breath upon him,
> Still he did not cease his singing,
> Still he did not leave his laughing. . . .

Then the fierce north wind challenges him to combat. They fight on the snow, and the courageous, gay Shingebis wins.

Fat, lazy Shawondasee lives in the south, where the smoke from his pipe infuses the land with gentleness:

> From his pipe the smoke ascending
> Filled the sky with haze and vapor,
> Filled the air with dreamy softness,
> Gave a twinkle to the water,
> Touched the rugged hills with smoothness . . .

Mudjekeewis, keeping the west wind for himself, wanders through the meadows and impregnates the maiden Wenonah, the daughter of Nokomis, a virgin mother descended from the full moon.

Wenonah gives birth to Hiawatha and then dies, desolate because of Mudjekeewis' abandonment. Longfellow's romantic *cantabile* makes of this nymph impregnated by natural forces something that simultaneously suggests an evanescent figure from a ballad and Faust's Gretchen.

Nokomis raises the child Hiawatha, teaching him to read the heavens:

> Showed the Death-Dance of the spirits,
> Warriors with their plumes and war-clubs,
> Flaring far away to Northward
> In the frosty nights of Winter;
> Showed the broad, white road in heaven,
> Pathway of the ghosts, the shadows.

Hiawatha grows up and becomes a hunter, transfixing his first deer with an arrow:

> And a deer came down the pathway,
> Flecked with leafy light and shadow.
> And his heart within him fluttered,
> Trembled like the leaves above him,
> Like the birch-leaf palpitated.

Now the young hero learns about his father's betrayal of his mother, and his heart burns in his breast like a red-hot coal. He ventures into the realm of the west wind and meets his father, awesome in aspect, like a comet:

> On the air about him wildly
> Tossed and streamed his cloudy tresses,
> Gleamed like drifting snow his tresses.

The two talk and for a time Hiawatha dissimulates, but at the mention of his mother he begins the battle. Mudjekeewis retreats to the edge of the West:

> To the earth's remotest border,
> Where into the empty spaces
> Sinks the sun, as a flamingo
> Drops into her nest at nightfall,
> In the melancholy marshes.

After three days of struggle Mudjekeewis announces to his son that the trial he has had to inflict on him has lasted long enough. Now he must go back home and defeat monsters and magicians, reclaim the land's uncultivated wastes, and return on the day of his death to rule over the northwest wind.

> Homeward now went Hiawatha;
> Pleasant was the landscape round him,
> Pleasant was the air above him,
> For the bitterness of anger
> Had departed wholly from him,
> From his brain the thought of vengeance,
> From his heart the burning fever.

The fifth canto tells of Hiawatha's seven-day fast, which is undertaken not for his benefit but for the good of the people; Longfellow's myopic Victorian vision cannot see beyond the two terms of the self and the nation. On the first day Hiawatha contemplates the wild game and asks God if life must depend on these things. The second day he contemplates the fruits of the earth and asks the same question. The third day he devotes to the fish. On the fourth he lies there exhausted, dreaming with his eyes half closed. A young man appears before him:

> Dressed in garments green and yellow
> Coming through the purple twilight.

He announces that his prayer has been granted and that he should rise and fight. Hiawatha, though almost fainting, obeys:

> From the twilight of his wigwam
> Forth into the flush of sunset
> Came, and wrestled with Mondamin. . . .

The struggle is renewed for three twilights. Mondamin announces that on the seventh day of his fast Hiawatha will conquer, kill, and bury him. Hiawatha will then return to the grave of the man he killed (as the protagonist does in Hawthorne's *Septimius Felton*) and remain there until green sprouts shoot up from it and finally corn has been formed (on the grave in Hawthorne's story a kind of bitter grass sprang up). And so the canto concludes on a note of tenuous poetic felicity:

> And still later, when the Autumn
> Changed the long, green leaves to yellow,
> And the soft and juicy kernels
> Grew like wampum hard and yellow,
> Then the ripened ears he gathered,
> Stripped the withered husks from off them,
> As he once had stripped the wrestler. . . .

To what extent Longfellow reworked his sources can be easily measured by comparison with Schoolcraft's text in *The Myth of Hiawatha*. There the hero is presented, in the manner of a Victorian fable, as a measly little man:

Although poor, he was a man of a kind and contented disposition. He was always thankful to the Great Spirit for everything he received. The same disposition was inherited by his eldest son, who had now arrived at the proper age to undertake the ceremony of the Ke-ig-uish-im-o-win, or fast, to see what kind of a spirit would be his guide and guardian through life.

He starts the fast and during the first days meditates on the trees in the woods:

On the third day he became weak and faint, and kept his bed. He fancied, while thus lying, that he saw a handsome young man coming down from the sky and advancing towards him. He was richly and gaily dressed, having on a great many garments of green and yellow colors, but differing in their deeper or lighter shades. He had a plume of waving feathers on his head, and all his motions were graceful. He then told the young man to arise, and prepare to wrestle with him, as it was only by this means that he could hope to succeed in his wishes.

They fight for three days.

On the third day he again appeared at the same time and renewed the struggle. The poor youth was very faint in body, but grew stronger in mind at every contest, and was determined to prevail or perish in the attempt. He exerted his utmost powers, and after the contest had been continued the usual time, the stranger ceased his efforts and declared himself conquered. For the first time he entered the lodge, and sitting down beside the youth, he began to deliver his instructions to him, telling him in what manner he should proceed to take advantage of his victory.

They will fight for one last time, the god tells him, and as soon as the young man has defeated him he is to take off the god's clothes, throw him onto the ground, clear it of all roots or weeds, and bury him there. In this way, he will achieve the goal of helping his neighbor. A tall, graceful plant with colored, silky tassels will then spring up. From this modest version, so homely in its essential spirit, Longfellow's decorous art takes its most moving effects.

Hiawatha's most notable exploit is his expedition against Pearl-Feather, who lives in the region of the sunsets:

> "Yonder dwells the great Pearl-Feather
> Megissogwon, the Magician,
> Manito of Wealth and Wampum,
> Guarded by his fiery serpents,
> Guarded by the black pitch-water. . . .
> He, the mightiest of Magicians,
> Sends the fever from the marshes,
> Sends the pestilential vapours,
> Sends the poisonous exhalations,
> Sends the white fog from the fenlands."

Nokomis exhorts Hiawatha to avenge his grandfather, who descended from the moon and was killed by Megissogwon, the spirit of wealth. Hiawatha, after smearing his canoe with oil, goes into the swamp. He kills the fiery serpents that try to stop him:

> Weltering in the bloody water,
> Dead lay all the fiery serpents. . . .

So he passes into the night:

> Sailed upon that sluggish water,
> Covered with its mould of ages,
> Black with rotting water-rushes,
> Rank with flags and leaves of lilies,
> Stagnant, lifeless, dreary, dismal,
> Lighted by the shimmering moonlight,
> And by the will-o'-the-wisps illumined,
> Fires by ghosts of dead men kindled,
> In their weary night-encampments.

The new struggle with the master of wealth and pestilence who is encased in a suit of wampum at first goes against Hiawatha until the woodpecker gives him the idea of wounding the giant on the crown of his head.

Hiawatha's next adventure is an amorous one. He woos Minnehaha, Arrow-maker's beautiful daughter, from the hostile Dakota tribe. The handsome Pau-Puk-Keewis dances at their wedding, and the description of his sacred dance is one of Longfellow's bravura pieces:

> Rose the handsome Pau-Puk-Keewis,
> And began his mystic dances.
>   First he danced a solemn measure,
> Very slow in step and gesture,
> In and out among the pine-trees,
> Through the shadows and the sunshine,
> Treading softly like a panther,
> Then more swiftly and still swifter,
> Whirling, spinning round in circles,
> Leaping o'er the guests assembled,
> Eddying round and round the wigwam,
> Till the leaves went whirling with him,
> Till the dust and wind together
> Swept in eddies round about him.

The storyteller regales the guests with the story of Osseo, son of the evening star (one of the legends taken from Schoolcraft). Though he is old, broken, and continually coughing, the lovely Oweenee marries him because he vibrates with the spirit of Venus, the evening star. One day he sees a dead, moldering tree. He cries out in anguish, leaps into the tree's hollow, and comes out with his youth restored; but Oweenee immediately shrivels and turns into a little old woman. Osseo hears the voice of the evening star, which summons him on high, and then finds himself in heaven, where Venus restores youth to his bride and explains to him:

> In the little star that twinkles
> Through the vapors, on the left hand,
> Lives the envious Evil Spirit,
> The Wabeno, the magician,
> Who transformed you to an old man.
> Take heed lest his beams fall on you,
> For the rays he darts around him
> Are the power of his enchantment.

But when one of the couple's small sons shoots a bird with an arrow, the spell is broken: they come back to earth and henceforth make up the "Little People."

During the long peace of his reign, Hiawatha teaches his people the art of writing and ceremonies to protect the planted fields:

> Gitche Manito the Mighty,
> He, the Master of Life, was painted
> As an egg, with points projecting
> To the four winds of the heavens. . . .
>   Mitche Manito the Mighty,
> He the dreadful Spirit of Evil,
> As a serpent was depicted . . .
>   Life and Death he drew as circle,
> Life was white, but Death was darkness. . . .
>   For the earth he drew a straight line,
> For the sky a bow above it;
> White the space between for daytime. . . .
> On the left a point for sunrise,
> On the right a point for sunset,
> On the top a point for noontide,
> And for the rain and cloudy weather
> Waving lines descending from it,
>   Footprints pointing toward a wigwam
> Were a sign of invitation. . . .
> Bloody hands with palms uplifted
> Were a symbol of destruction. . . .

Then Hiawatha assigns a totem to every family; the prophets, the magicians, and the medicine men paint figures representing their songs:

> Figures strange and brightly coloured;
> And each figure had its meaning,
> Each some magic song suggested.

To take revenge for the benefits lavished on the people by Hiawatha, the spirits of evil kill Chibiabos the singer, and only songs and magical potions will restore reason to the afflicted demigod. Pau-Puk-Keewis, the clown, then tests Hiawatha, forcing him to hunt him and transforming himself into a series of animals in order to outwit him. Other gloomier adventures herald the approach of Hiawatha's death, which takes place with the arrival of black-robed missionaries. Hiawatha has carried out his mission and disappears, going off to the happy hunting grounds. This last part is completely Longfellow's invention.

Almost without a break in continuity the diluted romanticism pervading *Hiawatha* also colors Edna Dean Proctor's floriated, *fin-de-siècle* verses, which explain

> Why the Rainbow, A-mi-to-lau-ne
> From the Medicine lilies drew
> Orange and rose and violet
> Before the fall of the dew,
> The dews that guard the Cornmaids,
> And the field kemp fair to view;
> But the Rainbow is false and cruel,
> For it ends the gentle showers,
> And the opening leaves and the tender buds
> Like the ruthless worm devours,
> And still its stolen tints are won
> From the blanching, withering flowers.

∴

Henry David Thoreau, who seemed destined to unveil the mystery of Indian life rather than halt in the limbo of benevolence, died just when he had begun to write his major work on the Indians, after having accumulated eleven notebooks densely filled with preliminary notes.[24]

There remain, however, some anthology pieces in *A Week on the Concord and Merrimack Rivers,* of which it is hard to say whether they should be considered noble oratory or truly poetic. Thoreau describes the whites' slow and lethal advance:

The white man comes, pale as the dawn, with a load of thought, with a slumbering intelligence as a fire raked up, knowing well what he knows, not guessing but calculating; strong in community, yielding obedience to authority; of experienced race; of wonderful, wonderful common sense; dull but capable, slow but persevering, severe but just, of little humor but genuine; a laboring man, despising game and sport; building a house that endures, a framed house.

By contrast, the Indian is shown to have a stellar nature:

We talk of civilizing the Indian, but that is not the name for his improvement. By the wary independence and aloofness of his dim forest life he preserves his intercourse with his native gods, and is admitted from time to time to a rare and peculiar society with nature. He has glances of starry recognition to which our saloons are strangers. The steady illumination of his genius, dim only because distant, is like the faint but satisfying light of the stars compared with the dazzling but ineffectual and short-lived blaze of candles.

In *The Maine Woods* Thoreau had noted how that absorbed, haughty, and distant disposition is reflected in laconic ways: "Indians like to get along with the least possible communication and ado. He was really paying us a great compliment all the while thinking that we preferred a hint to a kick."

At Concord in 1860 Alcott, Thoreau, and Emerson had discussed the fate of the Indian. The Orphic but Hegelian Alcott, who denied the spirituality of nature, did not hesitate to condemn him: "I say that he goes along with the woods and the beasts, who retreat before and are superseded by man, and the planting of orchards and gardens. . . . Man's victory over nature and himself is to overcome the brute beast in him." Thoreau rebelled against this brutal struggle of man with nature, which is the Hegelian formula of progress: "We would not always be soothing and taming nature, breaking the horse and the ox, but sometimes ride the horse wild and chase the buffalo. The Indian's intercourse with nature is at least such as admits of the greatest independence of each."[25] These thoughts are similar to some in Carlyle:

How little I know of the *arbor-vitae* when I have learned only what science can tell me! It is but a word. It is not a *tree of life*. But there are twenty words for the tree and its different parts which the Indian gave, which are not in our botanies, which imply a more practical and vital science. . . . The Indian stood nearer to wild nature than we. The wildest and noblest quadrupeds, even the largest fresh-water fishes, some of the wildest and noblest birds and the fairest flowers have actually receded as *we* advanced, and we have but the most distant knowledge of them.[26]

Herman Melville also seemed capable of deciphering the mysteries of Indian life, but all that remains is his anonymous review of Parkman's *The California and Oregon Trail*, published in *The Literary World* of March 31, 1849. His devout, kindly feelings condemn Parkman's expressed contempt for the Indian, but they do so without passion or conceptual rigor: "Why, among the very Thugs of India, or the bloody Dyaks of Borneo, exists the germ of all that is intellectually elevated and grand. We are all of us—Anglo-Saxons, Dyaks, and Indians—sprung from one head, and made in one image."

Melville's perfect savage—the harpooner Queequeg in *Moby Dick*—is a Polynesian, but the model that suggested this extraordinary character was Paul Cuffe, a man of mixed Indian and Negro blood and the harpooner who wrote *Narrative of the Life and Adventures of Paul Cuffe,* published in Vernon, New York, in 1839. Like the Indians of America, Melville's Queequeg has a supernatural guardian (Yojo), who takes the substantial form of an idol. Queequeg pays homage to Yojo in his "evening prayers" with a fire of wood shavings, and once a year, he communicates with his guardian by maintaining a protracted, absorbed immobility during a sleepless fast. In Indian fashion, Queequeg smokes a ritual pipe, symbol of peace. (In Chapter XXX the satanic white man, Captain Ahab, throws his own pipe into the sea because he no longer enjoys it: he smokes by taking "nervous whiffs" . . . "like the dying whale".) Queequeg is tattooed, so that touching his belly or thigh is like touching the sun: he bears the zodiac incised on his skin (Chapter XCIX).

On board the *Pequod* there is also an Indian from Gay Head, the harpooner Tashtego. He has an "Antarctic" eye, tawny, lithe, snaky limbs, so that looking at him, Melville says, "you would almost have credited the superstitions of some of the earlier Puritans and half believed this wild Indian to be a son of the Prince of the Powers of the Air." (This vision of the man-serpent will be obsessively perpetuated in the American imagination, even in the figure of Elsie Venner in Oliver Wendell Holmes's novel of that name.)

Tashtego goes down with the *Pequod,* clinging to the top of the mainmast, though in his final death agony he nails the wings of a "sky-hawk" to the mainmast, and so the "bird of heaven" with "archangelic shrieks" is caught and, wrapped in the ship's flag, sinks into the sea. Like Lucifer, the *Pequod* (modern civilization, the titanic child of the Enlightenment) descends into its inferno dragging "a living part of heaven along with her." And the diabolical figure is an American Indian. The American imagination demands that the cosmic man Queequeg must come from Polynesia, while the emblem of satanism must be taken from a tribe on the North American continent.

The "Indian hater" and exterminator of Indians in Melville's *The Confidence Man* also mentions the subject of Indian diabolism. In Chapters XXVI and XXVII of this sublime treatise on the metaphysical conception of fraud written in the form of a novel, the Indian is the symbol of evil, his exterminator the personification of the ascetic exaltation that lives by perpetual watchfulness and struggle. But the exterminator, too, is the symbol of evil, of destruction as an end in itself (as Djuna Barnes has said, "There's nothing like destruction for an aim"). He represents a satanic exaltation that detaches one from the world, from all human warmth, and is pursued with the same intransigence as that with which the saint strains toward the angelic and divine. Melville creates symbols that can be interpreted in several ways, and the Indian, like Moby Dick, is at the same time the evil as well as the innocence of Nature. As all perverse men do, the satanic protagonist of *The Confidence Man*, "the cosmopolitan," talks unceasingly of brotherhood, charity, and faith. Above all, he tries to discredit the idea that men might do evil for its own sake, without ulterior motives. He declares his disbelief in the hater of Indians; such a man can only be a misanthrope who most likely conceals a kind heart. A perfect scoundrel, he insists that one must have faith in man.

From the Indian traditions that go back to the time when the continent was an earthly paradise, Melville, in *Moby Dick*, evokes only the blazing white steed of the prairies. Imperial and angelic, it led large migrant herds of wild horses, an object of sacred veneration and ineffable terror for the Indians. Melville's imagination cannot take in anything else, as if, quite against his own wish, the barrier erected by his ancestors prevented him from understanding the Queequegs of his own continent.

∴

Melville kept the tradition of benevolence free from the contamination of Enlightenment or Rousseauian humanitarianism. The odious Enlightenment assumptions were also screened out by John Adams's great-nephew, Henry Adams. Together with Hawthorne and Melville, he was one of the few nineteenth-century rebels against the idea of progress. After three generations, the Enlightenment conception was prodigiously hated and rejected in the very family that had so authoritatively championed it. To Henry Adams the fathers of the country appear in the full nakedness of their rapacious nature. The most seductively charming and neoclassically impeccable of them, Thomas Jefferson, is diligently stripped of all prestige in the pages of the *History of the United States During the Administrations of Jefferson and Madison*. His hypocrisy is demonstrated when he likens the "bigotry" of such European conservatives as Pitt and Napoleon to the policies of the Indian chiefs and uses "the mask of Indian philanthropy to disguise an attack upon conservatism."[27] Jefferson exhorts the Indians to apply themselves to the cultivation of the soil: this in fact was "progress" for the founding fathers. But since progress must harmoniously join with feelings of humanity and brotherhood, the good President wanted the transition to be smooth and gradual: the Indians must be protected from contact with whites, from alcohol, swindles, and the purchase of their territories. Certainly there were many problems:

Even the reform would be difficult, for Indian warriors thought death less irksome than daily labor; and men who do not fear death were not easily driven to toil.

There President Jefferson's philanthropy stopped. His greed for land equalled that of any settler on the border, and his humanity to the Indian suffered the suspicion of having among its motives the purpose of gaining lands for the whites. Jefferson's policy in practice offered a reward for Indian extinction.

No one would have felt more astonishment than Jefferson had some friend told him that this policy, which he believed to be virtuous, was a conspiracy to induce trustees to betray their trusts.[28]

The quiet sarcasm of this passage is expressed by the short, abrupt paragraphs; rarely has humanitarian hypocrisy been confuted with more vehement pauses. In his *Historical Essays* of 1891 Adams outlines a history of the family, which is a synthesis of his cyclical, Vico-like vision of history. From free primitive communism one passes to the rigor of the religiously established family, and any excess in one direction leads to an automatic reaction that propels in equal measure in the opposite direction. The Indian world has affinities with the Germanic and democratic. The future can only reconfirm its celebrated prototypes: Luther and Cromwell were conservatives because from the height of Catholic civilization they swerved sharply back to its opposite, the primitive Germanic past.

∴

The illusory nature of the concept of a dialectical unfolding of history, a constant advance, is demonstrated by the indifference with which, even after Adams's unrefuted, anti-Enlightenment lesson, writers go right on grinding out the old stereotypes. Humanitarian benevolence will have a pitiable though undaunted prolongation in literary Naturalism. Indeed, Hamlin Garland's primary objective was the defense of the Indian. Unfortunately, this well-meant intention was that of a man who could write unblushingly: "Rise, o young man and woman of America! Stand erect! Face the future with a song on your lips and the light of a broader day in your eyes."[29]

At one time, hypnotized by the Hopi snake dance,[30] he had fallen into near ecstasy, and the Indian theme then appeared to him more powerfully attractive than the quest for naturalistic documentation. Later on, he visited the Sioux and Cheyenne tribes, acquiring a feeling of benevolence toward them and evoking the joy of their past life:

The Indian was alternately continent and lax. When work was done, he was careful to take care of himself—the hunt took up all his time—taxed his energies to the utmost—but when the hunt was over and his lodge was filled with food—he relaxed and enjoyed himself. This twofold life made him spartan and dissolute—active and indolent—persistent and irresolute. These were his habits of mind—and they handicapped him when he came to take the white man's road.[31]

His Indian stories, replete with accusations against the government, were published in 1923 in *The Book of the American Indian*, in which the place of honor is given to "The Silent Eaters," the name given to the followers of Sitting Bull who remained loyal to him to the end.

Just as Helen Hunt Jackson had written *A Century of Dishonor* and her lachrymose pro-Indian novel, *Ramona*, so Garland, in 1902, drew up a project for the improvement of Indian conditions, suggesting that missions be discouraged and the old handicrafts revived.

However, in line with the government's vicious program, the Indian was called upon to abandon his forest home, take off all his ornaments, and stop singing and dancing. It was as though the conqueror had said: "Every form and symbol of the past is vile—put them away. . . . Smoking is expensive and leads to dreaming—stop it. To do beadwork or basketwork is heathen; your wife must abandon that." In exchange, he was offered sermons and hard labor.

In "The Red Man as Material,"[32] Garland denounced the scholarly missionaries and the entire policy of the Anglo-Saxons in terms reminiscent of Benjamin Franklin's Enlightenment emphasis: they want to suppress all customs different from their own. But, in fact, Garland's progressivist benevolence is often as offensive and vulgar as the iniquity he denounces. He describes an encounter between a rough pioneer and some Indians in these revolting words: "It was in absolute truth the meeting of the modern vidette of civilization with the rear-guard of retreating barbarism. . . . From the barbaric point of view, the Indian is as true and noble as the white man."[33]

Chapter VII

❧

The Tradition of
Progressivist Hatred in
the Nineteenth Century

Side by side with the tradition of benevolence there exists a tradition of
hatred or contempt, and its ancestry is Puritan only in the case of Emerson's scornful coldness (or Hawthorne's suspicion of diabolism). The
tradition is not a matter of racism, since this is found only in Schoolcraft
and his collaborators. Indeed, even this horrifying attitude is simply the
emotional sedimentation of progressivist ideology, which by the nineteenth century is regarded as an accepted fact, a datum instead of a
result. Progressivism forms the very climate of the nineteenth century.

In the tradition of benevolence, Melville had confronted the unpleasant
reality of a steadfast, often obstinately silent hatred for the Indian, the
frontier's great passion, which James Hall codified in his writings on
Colonel Moredock.[1] This enmity is often expressed as a violent protest
against the success of Cooper's books, to which are counterposed those of
Charles Brockden Brown. "We believe that Indian life and character have
never been more finely presented than by Brown," a critic wrote in
refutation of the Cooperian notion of the noble savage.[2] However, in his
novel *Edgar Huntly*, Brown gave only scant attention to the Indians. In
this work the Delaware Old Deb, or Queen Mab, makes her appearance;
she has refused to leave her ancestral land and lives in a hut with three
mongrel dogs, precursor of the lonely dog lover in Melville's story "The
Encantadas."

Old Deb considers herself the ruler of the territory, and it is even
rumored that she has murdered a colonist; she incites her tribe to take
revenge on the white usurpers, and her savage appearance is in itself
subversive. The novel's Indian warriors are implacable, fear-inspiring,

bloodthirsty. "Endowed with strenuous and lofty minds," they exude pure energy, bloodcurdling yet admirable. Leslie Fiedler has observed that as they drift before Edgar's somnambulistic sight, they seem akin to ghosts. The Indians have become as unreal as the leading figures of the feudal, ecclesiastical world in Enlightenment Europe. Indeed, Brown declares in his preface that there is an equivalence between, on the one hand, "puerile superstition, and exploded manners; Gothic castles and chimeras" and, on the other, "the incidents of Indian hostility, and the perils of the western wilderness." And, actually, the Indians in *Edgar Huntly* are as imaginary as Lewis's Spanish monks or Walpole's lords of Otranto. In 1837 Robert Bird criticized Cooper by mimicking him in his novel *Nick of the Woods.* Yet in his novel, as in Brown's, the gallant Indian is absent; to support his thesis he features a Quaker disdainful of all struggle, who in the end is transformed into an exterminator—"the man of amity and good will [turned] into a slayer of Indians, double-dyed in gore."

Proof of the natives' inferiority is demonstrated, according to Bird, by the swift changes in their moods. He does not see that this might be a quality painstakingly striven for, a childlike trait that Indian upbringing tried to preserve. He speaks of an Indian who, standing before a grave, begins his lamentations, "addressed to the insensible mountain or perhaps equally insensible corpse in it." Then the Indian displays the contents of his medicine bag, his fetishes—bits of bone, wood, and feathers—and praises the dead man in a lugubrious voice, shedding tears that presumably are produced by genuine sorrow. But, once his lamentation has ended, he immediately turns to a white prisoner, threatens him furiously, then quickly quiets down at the sight of whisky and begins to laugh uproariously.

These vacillating moods, which the narratives of captivity keep stressing with horror, come from an impatience with all superfluous delay and at the same time from a pliant surrender to impulses that spring from the heart. The Indian's time is completely vital, instantaneous. Between one moment and the next, each lived at the peak of intensity as though it were the goal and end of an entire life, there is not that link typical of "clock time" (Melville's "horologicals"). Life "instant by instant" is pure time, time unrelated to space, that is, not seen as a continuous succession from "point to point." The Indian rejects the solidified, organizable, exploitable coherence of time; on the contrary, he wants to keep it discontinuous so that it can remain at the highest pitch of intensity. Sorrow is followed point-blank by ferocity and joy because he shrinks from contiguous, blended emotions, from bitter-sweet melancholy, from things that are loved and hated, from systematic repression, all of which give the illusion of a rational (or at least associative) progression from one mood to the next. It is not surprising that Edgar Allan Poe's Dupin is a thrilling hero to the modern mind and that his character becomes the point of departure for a whole new literary genre, the detective story, for he observes the transitions from one emotion to another as a mathematician observes the successive numbers of a series. He is the man for whom clock time has suppressed the vital impulse.

The Journal of Julius Rodman, Being an Account of the First Passage Across the Rocky Mountains of North America Ever Achieved by Civilized Man,[3] was written by Edgar Allan Poe in a petty spirit. He took as his model Washington Irving's *Astoria,* telling the story of an exploratory mission into unknown regions "infested with Indian tribes . . . whom we had every reason to believe ferocious and treacherous." As could be expected, the Sioux are an "ugly, ill-made race . . . their eyes protruding and dull": the doctrines of De Pauw are partially revived. Their bodies are smeared with grease and charcoal; they wear shirts of animal skins and are wrapped in buffalo mantles adorned with rattling porcupine quills and military emblems, while tufts of human hair hang from the seams of their antelope-skin leggings. They attack the expedition's boat but do it so ineptly that the explorers escape, leaving the Indians "in the most ludicrous amazement." The negotiations that follow the failed attack show them to be even more savage and grotesque: they ask whether the small cannon aboard is a giant grasshopper. A shot from this cannon scatters them, and the explorers explain to a wounded prisoner that the cannon was indignant at hearing itself called a "large green grasshopper." Later on, part of the expedition is captured but manages to escape after the stampede of a panic-stricken herd of antelopes that bursts into the Indian camp. As the journey proceeds, other tribes appear. The Assiniboins attack in order to see the Negro servant Toby at closer range, and when they do they admire him so much that "he might then have made his fortune by ascending the throne of the Assiniboins." The Indian is used by Poe to excite in his public the most dreadfully vulgar hilarity, and, indeed, one cannot find in his entire work the slightest sign of any other intention.

∴

One could perhaps believe that the extermination of Indians carried out on the "frontier" was the work of men without ideology or culture, a pure fact of nature, as the historian Turner liked to assert. In this "theory of the frontier" there crops up again the fallacious belief that man is exempt from history, crude and practical, skillful at seizing and manipulating material goods, inventive, spontaneous and intolerant of the burdens of civilized life.[4] If this man exterminated the Indians, enlightened, progressive culture was somewhat less responsible. The horrible deed was the work of an independent, unleashed force, the disreputable rabble that, as the Quaker in Robert Bird's novel *Nick of the Woods* explains, "can think it legitimate, as many believe, to shoot at a wandering Indian as at a furtive bear."[5]

But what human force is entirely untouched by ideas and, in the final analysis, independent of language and tradition? It should be enough to recall the names of the pioneers' towns, their architecture, which was still neoclassical at the time of the Civil War, the number of colleges scattered along the frontier. Even their vaunted Jacksonian anti-intellectualism (interpreted as a kind of reflex) is more a product of empiricist culture than primordial crudity. It is true that in 1858 a Wisconsin legislative committee declared: "It is not by pouring [*sic*] over the dreaming and mystical pages of classic lore that the student is to develop the energy of character and strength of purpose to enter manfully into the great battle of life."[6] But this anticultural ideology is the culmination of progressivist ideology, not an instinctive precultural outburst.

One of the nineteenth-century explorers, Henry Marie Brackenridge, published in 1814 his *Views of Louisiana,* which contained extracts from the journal of an expedition undertaken in 1811 into the territory of the Arikara tribe. The stench of the villages is noxious, the Indian religion unintelligible, based on certain "tricks" regarded as supernatural by the rabble, and the tortures that the Indians inflict are barbarous. Yet Brackenridge admires the display of shields, quivers, red cloths, and cloaks of buffalo skins covered with designs. He wittily notes the cunning of a chief who loves a horse and, not wanting to make a gift of it yet unable to refuse to do so—an act that would be proof of scant magnanimity unworthy of a great man—announces that he has consecrated the horse to his own supernatural guardian—"to his magic."[7] Nor does the Jesuit priest Pierre-Jean de Smet[8] see anything in the Indians but a source of laughter and pity. Is not the loving protection they accord the beavers, their relatives, an absurd belief? Is it not repulsive to sacrifice to the gods the things they hold most dear, even their very limbs? "To this dark picture," he says, "we can add a passionate love of gambling, an innate inclination to deception, gluttony, and to anything that could flatter sensuality."

Father de Smet was later to serve an intermediary between government authorities and the Sioux led by Sitting Bull. He succeeded in winning over the Sioux, so he tells us, by appearing among them with a flag of peace bearing the image of the Virgin Mary, similar to their Virgin of the Buffaloes. But since his winning good humor concealed such deep-rooted contempt, one can readily believe what the old Sioux used to repeat even a short while ago: "The Black Robes were Sitting Bull's best friends while he was on the prairie, but when he came to the agency, they were the first to turn against him."[9]

From 1840 to 1843 Audubon, the great and sensitive naturalist, followed the itinerary of the painter Catlin and kept a journal in which he upbraided his predecessor for his Cooperian benevolence toward the Indians. Everything about them appears to him either contemptible or ridiculous. This, for instance, is his description of a medicine man's tent:

We had entered this curiosity shop by pushing aside a wet elk skin stretched on four sticks.

Looking around I saw a number of calabashes, eight or ten otter skulls, two very large buffalo skulls with horns on, evidently of great age, and some sticks and other magical implements with which none but a "Great Medicine Man" is acquainted. During my survey there sat, crouched down on his haunches, an Indian wrapped in a dirty blanket with only his filthy head peeping out.[10]

The starving, filthy Indians eat putrefied animals, and Audubon exclaims: "Ah! Mr. Catlin, I am now sorry to see and to read your accounts of the Indians you saw. We saw here no 'carpeted prairies,' no 'velvety distant landscape.'" Every contact with the Indians is repulsive. They approach some famous warriors: "Their very touch is disgusting—it will indeed be a deliverance to get rid of all this 'Indian poetry.'"[11]

∴

At a century's remove from the last missionary exploits, Ralph Waldo Emerson, that true epigone of the Puritan spirit, in his essay on Concord[12] recalls that the patent of Massachusetts stipulated the Indian be converted, but depicts him as he still appeared to the Puritans—a remote mystery, part of inconvertible nature.

The man of the wood might well draw on himself the compassion of the planters. His erect and perfect form, though disclosing some irregular virtues, was found joined to a dwindled soul. Master of all sorts of woodcraft, he seemed a part of the forest and the lake, and the secret of his amazing skill seemed to be that he partook of the nature and fierce instincts of the beasts he slew. Those who dwelled by ponds and rivers had some tincture of civility but the hunters of the tribe were found intractable at catechism. Thomas Hooker anticipated the opinion of Humboldt and called them the "ruins of mankind."

Emerson notes the first questions of the catechumen: "In 1644 Squaw Sachem made a formal submission to know God aright"; and finally Eliot's great mission: "There under the rubbish and ruins of barbarous life, the human heart heard the voice of love, and awoke as from a sleep." He also lists the neophyte's memorable questions; but "I confess what chiefly interests me . . . is the grandeur of spirit exhibited by a few of the Indian chiefs under torture." The story of the converted Indians ends miserably. "The Indian seemed to inspire such a feeling as the wild beast inspires in the people near his den. It is the misfortune of Concord to have permitted a disgraceful outrage on the friendly Indians." But this reproach to the past is a mere act of courtesy; in fact, he continues to be cold to the Indians. William Green, a mystical follower of Böhme and Madame Guyon, whom he met in New York (and whom he mentions in a letter dated March, 1842), tried to convince him that in the West there were Indians who "had known the Spirit."

∴

Indeed, the persistence of Puritanism in Emerson—with, however, an antinomian shading—is so great that he reacted with all the force of his atavistic prejudices to the appearance of *Hiawatha* and felt impelled to write to Longfellow:

I find this Indian poem very wholesome; sweet and wholesome as maize, very proper and pertinent for us to read, and showing a kind of manly sense of duty in the poet to write. The dangers of the Indians are, that they are really savage, have poor, small, sterile heads, no thoughts; and you must deal very roundly with them, and find them wanting in brains. And I blamed your tenderness now and then, as I read, in accepting a legend or a song, when they had so little to give. I should hold you to your creative function on such occasions.[13]

∴

Francis Parkman, born in Boston in 1823 and educated at Harvard, first traveled in Europe and then, around 1846, in the wild regions of the

American West. The adjectives that occurred to him upon meeting the Indians expressed his horror and contempt, though gradually, living among them, his Gothic vision became less murky, and he managed to draw some reasonably accurate profiles of them. Among the portraits in *The Oregon Trail* is one of a young hunter who, as proof of his attainment of manhood, has just killed a deer and, despite his excitement, is able to maintain a semblance of indifference. Parkman realized that this feat derived from a strength that checks expression but does not mar the fullness of feeling, quite different from English "self-control," which inhibits the expression of all emotion.

Parkman's objectivity is due above all to his prose style, at its best, for instance, in this description of a tribe crossing a mountain ridge on which a forest fire is blazing:

We were on the eastern descent of the mountain, and soon came to a rough and difficult defile, leading down a very steep declivity. The whole swarm poured down together, filling the rocky passageway like some turbulent mountain-stream. The mountains before us were on fire, and had been so for weeks. The view in front was obscured by a vast dim sea of smoke and vapor while on either hand the tall cliffs, bearing aloft their crest of pines, thrust their heads boldly through it, and the sharp pinnacles and broken ridges of the mountains beyond them were faintly traceable as through a veil.[14]

One must read Parkman's page with some attention to discern its texture; the use of metaphor is subtle. He presents himself as a man offering a flat report, yet stamped like a watermark on the page a framework of three superimposed planes is discernable: the Indians, the sea of smoke, the shapes of the mountains in a jagged line, seen as if through a veil. The description continues, settling finally on the central animated scene after a sweep of the horizon in accordance with the rules of the most complex perspective: "The scene in itself was most grand and imposing, but with the savage multitude, the armed warriors, the naked children, the gaily apparelled girls, pouring impetuously down the heights, it would have formed a noble subject for a painter. . . ."

When the book appeared in 1849, this whole picturesque world was about to collapse, and in 1872 Parkman looked back at a completely irretrievable past:

We knew that there was more or less gold in the seams of those untrodden mountains; but we did not foresee that it would build cities in the waste and plant hotels and gambling-houses among the haunts of the grizzly bear. We knew that a few fanatical outcasts were groping their way across the plains to seek an asylum from Gentile persecution; but we did not imagine that the polygamous hordes of Mormon would rear a swarming Jerusalem in the bosom of solitude itself.[15]

In 1892, after another twenty years, Parkman contemplated the utter ruins:

For Indian teepees, with their trophies of bow, lance, shield, and dangling scalp-locks, we have towns and cities, resorts of health and pleasure seekers, with an agreeable society, Paris fashions, the magazines, the latest poem, and the last new novel. The sons of civilization, drawn by the fascinations of a fresher and bolder life, thronged to the western wilds in multitudes which blighted the charm that had lured them. . . . The wild Indian is turned into an ugly caricature of his conquerer, and that which made him romantic, terrible, and hateful, is in large measure scourged out of him.[16]

Parkman himself feels the hatred—the hatred for an enemy—yet, enunciating what he has seen in his classical, Latin-nurtured prose, he achieves a redeeming precision, with the result that he is not an "Indian hater" of the sort he himself described in *The Conspiracy of Pontiac*. And when he defines, in a manner worthy of Sallust, the characteristics of these detested men, revulsion disappears and the purest attention dominates his prose. Thus he coins this epigram: "The Indians, who, though often rapacious, are utterly devoid of avarice." And this is how he sets forth the religious beliefs of the Indian, who worships

an all-wise, all-powerful Spirit, the supreme Ruler of the universe, yet his mind will not always ascend into communion with a being that seems to him so vast, remote and incomprehensible; and when danger threatens, when his hopes are broken, when the black wing of sorrow overshadows him, he is prone to turn for relief to some inferior agency, less removed from the ordinary scope of his faculties. He has a guardian spirit, on whom he relies for succor and guidance. . . . Among those mountains not a wild beast was prowling, a bird singing, or a leaf fluttering that might not tend to direct his destiny or give warning of what was in store for him; and he watches the world of nature around him as the astrologer watches the stars.[17]

In *The Jesuits in North America* Parkman accused various authors of having attributed their own ideas to the Indians, who were accustomed to assenting automatically and scornfully to any question that concerned their spiritual life. Loskiel and Heckewelder distorted according to their missionary intentions; Adair in order to bolster his thesis of the descent of the Indians from the lost tribes of Israel; Jarvis with the aim of demonstrating that every religion deforms the original Revelation.[18] Finally,

Schoolcraft lacked philological accuracy and style; even his collection of legends in *Algic Researches* was not faithful to the letter. But Parkman himself judged the devout fervor of Marie de l'Incarnation in *The Jesuits in North America* in terms of all the preconceptions of the "philosophy of common sense." Her mystical exclamations, such as *"Allant à l'oraison, je tressaillois en moi-même, et disais: Allons dans la solitude, mon cher amour. . . ,"* seem to Parkman erotic extravagances. In his opinion, meditation opens up a dreamland. It is "contemplative fancy," an abnormal tension of the faculties, he says, oblivious to the collective testimony of the mystics which had unanimously defined their experience as the very opposite of fantasizing, nervous tension, and eroticism. As for the "dark night" of the mystic, to the presumptuous Parkman, it is an "exhaustion that produced common sense." He is amazed that a woman whose habitual state was "mystical abstraction" could be endowed with extraordinary practical abilities, as though all mystics, from Mohammed to St. Theresa of Ávila, had not been eminently practical. In a note clearly added to the text after having acquired further, though still very meager, information on the subject,* he admits that the combination of practical talents and religious enthusiasm is in fact far from rare, as is shown by the founders of the various orders. And how could Parkman have understood the shamans of America if he could not even distinguish their visionary experiences, their explorations of the *mundus imaginalis,* from ordinary dreams?

His epitaph on the death of the indigenous civilization is frigid:

> The Indians melted away, not because civilization destroyed them, but because their own ferocity and intractable indolence made it impossible that they should exist in its presence. Either the plastic energies of a higher race or the servile pliancy of a lower one would, each in its way, have preserved them: as it was, their extinction was a foregone conclusion.[19]

A century later something of the Roman quality of Parkman's style echoes at times in the prose of his disciple Bernard De Voto, particularly in certain pages of *The Course of Empire*. It can be seen when he delineates the "magical" reasons for the superiority of a French pioneer like Duluth, in whom the Indians "are to see the disregard of death and the will to use force without stint regardless of the consequences which the civilized mind could focus instantly but to which the primitive mind

---

* Parkman's blindness to spiritual values was acquired, for as a young man he had praised the effect on one's mind of the Benedictine rites observed in Catania, adding that anyone who denied this must be "stupid or insensitive" by nature or through prejudice.

could be worked up only by a long series of religious exercises." Parkman's influence can also be detected in De Voto's description of the antithetical behavior of A. J. La Barre: "La Barre treated them with a mixture of threat, bluff, and anxiety which they understood at once. With stately insolence, they ridiculed him and defied him." But stylistic incisiveness is not enough to overcome the obstacles that the Enlightenment put in Parkman's path (as later in De Voto's, who actually accused his master insufficient progressivism).

∴

A third great figure of the American Renaissance neither wanted nor knew how to approach that almost domestic enigma. In his review of Parkman's *The Jesuits in America* in *The Nation* of June 6, 1867,[20] Henry James cast only a cursory glance at the Indians. His affection goes to the Jesuits, and so, by contrast, the Indians seem "obstinate, intractable, and utterly averse to the reception of light. . . . Their piety was more discouraging than their obduracy." Unlike Melville, James supports Parkman:

. . . the old-fashioned portrait of the magnanimous and rhetorical red man is a piece of very false coloring. Mr. Parkman knows his subject, and he mentions no single trait of intelligence, of fancy, or of character by which the Indian should have a hold on our respect or his fate a claim to our regret. The cruelty of the Canadian tribes is beyond description. They had no imagination in their religion; they confined what little they possessed to the science of torture.

Even their mythology is unacceptable; James attacks "the utterly graceless and sterile character of their legends and traditions." The Jesuits, by contrast, came near to overcoming the laws of nature and certainly those of their own temperaments. In his mature phase, James rose above certain skepticisms of his youth, but he never looked more discerningly at this reality condemned with such hasty disdain.

∴

Mark Twain's aversion, however, was and remained uncontrollable. His contempt for the Indians often knows no bounds, despite rhetorical, intimidating, or foolish statements like the following:

I have no race prejudice, and I think I have no color prejudice, nor caste prejudice, nor creed prejudice. Indeed, I know it. I can stand any society. All that I care to know is that a man is a human being—that is enough to me; he can't be any worse. I have no special regard for Satan but I at least claim that I have no prejudice against him. It may even be that I lean a little his way, on account of his not having a fair show.[21]

In "The Noble Red Man" Mark Twain attacks the image of the good savage and the sentimentality of those who deprecate the white advance, digging up again the old theme of Indian atrocities, although William Ellery Channing had pointed out that "the Indian . . . when he tortures his captives, thinks of making an offering, of making compensation to his own tortured friends." Channing had also asked: "What, indeed, is this free spirit of which we so much boast? Is it not much more a jealousy of our own rights than a reverence for the rights of all? Does it not consist with the inflictions of gross wrongs? Does it not spoil the Indians?"[22]

Twain mistakenly thought that he could despise humanitarian sentimentality, as though despite his sarcastic or facetious manner, he were not a product of precisely the same ideology.

Twain wrote a critical satire on Cooper, in which he violently denounced his lamentable tendency to fantasize. "A work of art? It has no invention; it has no order, system, sequence or result; it has no life-likeness . . . its characters are confusedly drawn . . . its humor is pathetic; its pathos funny. . . ." Nothing of this celebrator of the Indians must be left standing. Twain cannot bear the thought that even a shred of Cooper's Edenic dream should survive. He objects to Cooper's intuitions. "To these reverberations," it has been said, "Mark Twain is deaf. Nor is he aware of the ritual initiation through which Natty passes."[23] How, then, could he admit the existence of much profounder rituals, which are integrally woven into Indian life?

The tradition of contempt is not necessarily bound up with a fierce or skeptical nature. Elizabeth Madox Roberts was a delicate, melodious stylist. In her novel *The Great Meadow*, which deals with the pioneers' conquest of Kentucky in 1770, the female protagonist, presented in a light recalling an Impressionist scene, sets her spinning wheel in a humming motion that evokes, prayerlike, Berkeley's pages:

They, these things, or any small part of the whole mighty frame of the world, are withouten any kind of port or shape until somebody's mind is there to know. Consequently, all the ways you wouldn't know, all you forgot or never yet remembered, mought have a place to be in Mind, in some Mind far off, and he calls this Eternal Spirit.

These lines might have been suggested by a passage in Berkeley's treatise *Concerning the Principles of Human Knowledge:*

. . . that all the choir of heaven and furniture of the earth, in a word all those bodies which compose the mighty frame of the world have not any subsistence without a mind, that their *being* (*esse*) is to be perceived or known . . . they must either have no existence at all, *or else subsist in the mind of some eternal spirit.* . . .

This is the motif articulated by the softly flowing narrative in *The Great Meadow*. But when the Indians come on the scene, all warmth vanishes and the absorbed, meditative tone is replaced by the surliest frigidity.

There are people who dare remember the Indian's right to the land, but they are immediately silenced (actually, more in the accents of the nineteenth than of the eighteenth century):

If the Indian is not man enough to hold it let him give it over then. . . . It's a land that calls for brave men, a brave race. It's only a strong race that can hold a good country. Let the brave have and hold there.

Yes, sir, yes. . . . If he can't hold, if he's afeared and frighted to stay there, let him cry for't. If he sees ghosts there and hears noises and is frighted by the Alleghewi . . . Stronger men are bound to go in there, more enduren men.[24]

Having become a prisoner of the Ojibwas, the heroine's husband is spared because of the courage with which he undergoes torture. He then stays with his savior, Dahsing, who lives by heeding his visions, renouncing all his belongings because of his belief in a promise received in a vision. But during a terrible winter, when the tribe's good fortune seems almost at an end, some of the Indians propose to break the spell by sacrificing the white man and eating him. He saves himself by saying that not his strength but his weakness infuses the limbs they intend to eat and by announcing the end of the freezing cold. So, as the result of a facile deception at the expense of this inferior race, he can leave and go home. "They're a poor sort, under all their paint and war-noises. If you guard yourself against surprise he has got a mighty little advantage."

∴

Up to the first years of the twentieth century (when Pound was writing *Patria mia*) poetry was a marketable commodity, and so commercial poetry with an Indian background began to be written.* It consisted

---

* Its origins can be traced to Eastburn and Sands's *Yamoyden* (1820), together with a great deal of octosyllabic verse studded with cumbersome repetitions, such as *Frontenac, or the Atotarho of the Iroquois* by Alfred B. Street, *Songs of the Sierras* by Joaquin Miller, *The Songs of the Ancient People* by Edna Proctor, and the poems about Sitting Bull by John G. Neihardt.

chiefly of narrative verse based on pathetic tales in which the Indians are molded to fit sentimental languors utterly alien to them[25] and included a series of plays about Indians that exploited the figures of Pocahontas, King Philip, Pontiac, Tecumseh[26] and featured *cabalettas,* which were a mixture of Ossian and indigenous oratory.

An evaluation and review of this enormous bulk of material was undertaken by Albert Keiser in *The Indian in American Literature* (1933) and again in R. H. Pearce's *The Savages of America* (1953), and it is unlikely that anything of worth remains to be unearthed in this heterogeneous mass.

The first phase of this commercial literature ends with the Civil War (in Europe the watershed is established with the advent of heavy industry). What follows is in a different style; to the exploitation of sentimentality other manipulations of the consumer's psychic mechanism are added, in particular, the stimulation of violence. Gradually there evolves the most successful plot formula of commercial literature since the detective story was invented by Poe—the Western. Both originated in America, two formulas for a literature that is repetitive, just as music that is repetitive—obligatory syncopation—would come into being there.

For more than a century the culture industry has exploited these unvarying recipes for story construction: the world dominated by the ideology of novelty is surpassingly static. The puritan narrative of captivity was the progenitor of the Western, which first took shape in 1836, with James Strange French's *Elkswatana, or The Prophet of the West.* In it are two romantic adventurers—the Virginian Rolfe (whose name, perhaps not by chance, is the same as that of the protagonist in Melville's *Clarel*) who wanders through the forests to forget an unhappy love affair, and Barth, a rough Western type. They go out in search of a girl stolen by the Indians, who later proves to be the Virginian's beloved.

Charles W. Webber's *Old Hicks, the Guide* is also close to the Western, though the genre really came into being when the publishing apparatus for the dime novel was set up in New York. Provided that the narrative machinery is assembled in a stereotyped fashion—with a villain to be beaten, a pure man to beat him, and a chase—the Indian may figure either as the Cooperian good savage or as the detestable beast of the narrative of captivity. Violence is the essential element. In Owen Wister's *The Virginian,* published in 1902, the formula is still intact. But along with the Western that hinges on the healthy, chaste, and strong hero, the publishing industry began selling a parallel story in which the fermentation of sin is added to give birth to all values.

Around 1880, with Philip S. Warne's *A Hard Crowd*, the parallel Western began also to be tinged with eroticism. Besides the familiar swooning, virginal heroines there appear such erotic amazons as Calamity Jane—the good heroine who must be pure "in heart," yet still may behave as brutally as the villain.

Insofar as it is a vehicle devised for mass fantasizing, the Western does not have many variations. The hero in this literature must fulfill the same function as the commonplace in society, that is, play a role onto which neurotic images, identifications, and pathetic desires can be projected. He is no longer devout, as in the pious centuries; he has only the most tangible good qualities. He is a loner and a sterling example of "self-reliance." He abounds in good sense but at the same time is impetuous, metes out justice on his own, and scorns the urban agglomerates and people who work in offices. After 1920 he becomes more uncertain, trapped by advancing civilization, and nothing is left for him but to remain faithful to the gallant gestures demanded by his role, but with despair in his heart.

When, in this context, the Indians are the faithful companions of Cooper's tradition, they appear inexpressive, static, with an automatic, doglike loyalty and devotion. But even when they are granted a certain nobility, as in Zane Grey's novels, their exterminators are not criticized.[27] More often Indians are seen as the *Topeka Weekly Leader* described them in 1867: "a set of miserable, dirty, lousy, blanketed, thieving, faithless, gut-eating skunks as the Lord ever permitted to infect the earth and whose immediate and final extermination all men, save Indian agents and traders, should pray for." In April, 1877, Leander P. Richardson in *Scribner's Monthly Magazine* imparted the following wisdom: "The coyote is the only animal that is meaner than the Indian, and the two have many traits of character in common."[28]

Chapter VIII

———◆◆◆———

Listeners to the Indian
in the Nineteenth Century

Although the Quaker tradition tried to approach the Indian with loving-kindness and the Libertine dealt with him in a spirit of equality, nobody had as yet broken through the barrier that separated whites from Indians, a barrier formed not so much by feelings and manners as by diametrically opposed orientations of the spirit. For a true comprehension of the Indian much more was necessary than benevolence and sentimental fraternity, namely, an intelligence informed by love, *amor intellectualis*. Spurred by ardent hatred, which is also a force, John Adams, as his letter to Jefferson shows, had glimpsed the hidden essence of the Indian spirit, yet during the nineteenth and twentieth centuries only a slow, gradual approach would finally lead to acceptance of the Indian heritage.

At the beginning of this long process—and actually running counter to it—stands the *oeuvre* of Henry Rowe Schoolcraft, one of the major bodies of work to spring from racist ideology grafted onto progressivism. Yet in this work were hidden the seeds of a radically different fruit—that of loving and intelligent comprehension. And from Schoolcraft's quarto volumes, which condemned a defeated race with scientific arguments, came the mediocre but memorable poem of benevolence *Hiawatha,* as well as a great deal of objectively observant research into the Indian by a pleiad of ethnographically interested writers, each working on his own. But the talented essayist Charles Godfrey Leland was the true pioneer of the new epoch. From the ever-growing interest in Indian esotericism would arise a new American literature, still imperfectly known, whose beginnings were noted by Franz Boas in an essay in 1902:[1]

The symbolic significance of complex rites [Boas says] and the philosophic view of nature which they reveal, have come to us as a surprise, suggesting a higher development of Indian culture than is ordinarily assumed. The study of these doctrines conveys the impression that the reasoning of the Indian is profound, his emotions deep, his ethical ideals of a high quality.[2]

This was the culmination of a whole new direction in thought begun in 1839, when Schoolcraft had first written about the Indians: "Hitherto our information has related rather to their external customs and manners, their physical traits and historical peculiarities, than to what may be termed the philosophy of the Indian mind."[3]

∴

Henry Rowe Schoolcraft, born in 1793 in Albany County, New York, studied chemistry and mineralogy and spent his youth working at first in his father's glass factory and then traveling for a geological society. Gradually, almost involuntarily, he passed from the study of the rocks of Lake Superior to the study of the natives, and in 1823 he became the government agent for Indian affairs. His marked mimetic talent and intense empathy led him to a familiarity with the Indian dialects and local myths and also into marriage with an Indian chief's granddaughter. After a few travel books, there appeared in 1839 *Algic Researches*, which was followed by *Notes on the Iroquois* (1847), *Scenes and Adventures in Semi-Alpine Regions of the Ozark Mountains* (1853), and, finally, *Historical and Statistical Information Respecting the History, Conditions and Prospects of the Indian Tribes of the United States* (1851–57).

Ironically, it was this white man assimilated by the Indians who contributed to the disastrous expansion of federal territory; his negotiations on behalf of the Federal Government further restricted the area on which the indigenous population could live. And when in 1853 this pedantically meticulous, if not always accurate, ethnologist allowed himself to be carried away by his fanciful imagination and wrote *Alhalla, or The Lord of Talladega. A Tale of the Creek War* in trochaic tetrameters, he catered to popular taste by including some edifying recognition scenes. A traveler, a missionary, and a trader meet Alhalla, the surviving chief of a tribe exterminated by the perfidious white man. The chief is accompanied by a daughter in mourning for the death of her betrothed. But did they not see an Indian wandering about nearby? They find him: it is in fact the fiancé. The two young people embrace, happily reunited.

Schoolcraft also attempted the imitation of Indian poetry, though actually he was copying the mincing, affected grace of Romantic verse. Little of the delicate Ojibwa magic can be guessed at from what remains in this simplistic, jog-trot, juvenile verse (reminiscent of "Twinkle, Twinkle, Little Star").

FIRE-FLY SONG

Flitting white-fire insects!
Wandering small-fire beasts!
Wave little stars above my bed!
Wave little stars into my sleep!
Come, little dancing white-fire bug,
Come, little flitting white-fire beast!
Light me with your white-flame magic,
Your little star-torch.

Precisely because of his strong mimetic talent, Schoolcraft could not escape the attraction that fashionable poetic forms exerted on him; he transposed the Indian legends into suave, smooth prose that recalls the language in which Lamb rewrote Shakespeare's tragedies. Whatever purely oral and roughly sketched elements the originals may have had, he was sure to polish. Occasionally, however, the outcome is delightful, and the neat, genteel lines preserve the profound allusions of the original. In retelling, for instance, the story of "The Magic Circle in the Prairie,"[4] Schoolcraft becomes an American Perrault. The measured, classic French prose of the seventeenth century similarly preserved certain horrifying tales of initiation rites that were still being handed down in the countryside.

In Schoolcraft's tale, the hunter Algon notices a circle of footprints in the middle of the prairie, but there is no sign of steps leading to it. As he stares at the inexplicable circle, music is heard from on high, a vague gleam appears, and Algon finally sees a basket descending from the sky containing twelve sisters, who step out of it and dance in a circle. He lunges and tries to capture the youngest sister, but she escapes and the entire group leaps back into the basket, which rises into the sky. The next day it all happens again, the descent, the dance, his attempt to capture the girl, but this time as the basket rises into the sky one of the older sisters, alluding to the creature they have met, wonders aloud: "Perhaps it is come to show us how the game is played by mortals."

The scene is repeated, and this time Algon, with a trick, succeeds in capturing the youngest girl. She is the daughter of a star, and they live a joyful life together. A little boy is born to the two lovers. One day she becomes nostalgic for her celestial home and, getting into the basket with her little son after having sung the right song, finds herself back among her own people. When she returns to her despairing terrestrial spouse, she brings him a message from the boy's grandfather in heaven: he too should come up, bringing with him the required gifts, one of each animal species.

After a long hunt, Algon collects the great wedding gift and makes his appearance in heaven. A grand celebration takes place among the sky dwellers, and those who choose tails or paws from the gifts are changed into earth-bound animals, while those who choose other parts are turned into birds. Algon and his family choose a white hawk's feather, and that becomes their totem: they spread out their wings and return to earth.

This is an example of a legend gracefully and faithfully retold. But many tales in these collections were outrageously distorted by Schoolcraft, for instance, "Leelinau or The Lost Daughter" (in the second volume of *Algic Researches*), the rather widespread story of a girl who prefers a spiritual presence to an earthly spouse. Schoolcraft distorted it to the point of changing an initiatory search into a romantic reverie, the sacred fear of the protagonist's parents into emotions that Monsieur Homais might have felt toward a daughter tempted to become a nun:

The effect of these visits was to render the daughter dissatisfied with the realities of life, and to disqualify her for an active and useful participation in its duties. . . . She had permitted her mind to dwell so much on imaginary scenes, that she at last mistook them for realities, and sighed for an existence inconsistent with the accidents of mortality. The consequence was, a disrelish for all the ordinary sources of amusement and employment, which engaged her equals in years.[5]

It seems an unreal caricature of a sententious, self-satisfied philistine conceit.

.·.

In his preface to the legend of Hiawatha, Schoolcraft demonstrated how the ideas of Carlyle and Emerson about the Anglo-Saxon's racial mission could be supported by the material on the Indian religion he had collected. The comparison between ancient Germans and American aborigines had often been made, so much so that Samuel Borchart and other philologists imagined that the two peoples were of the same race. Schoolcraft, however, denied the existence of any such bond. Scandinavian mythology, he stated, is incomparable:

That mythology is of so marked and peculiar a character, that it has not been distinctly traced out of the great circle of tribes of the Indo-Germanic family.

Odin, and his terrific pantheon of war-gods and social deities, could only exist in the dreary latitudes of storms and fire, which produce a Hecla and a Maelstrom. These latitudes have invariably produced nations, whose influence has been felt in an elevating power over the world; and whose tracks have everywhere been marked by the highest evidences of inductive intellect, centralizing energy, and practical wisdom and forecast. From such a source the Indian could have derived none of his vague symbolisms and mental idionsycracies, which have left him, as he is found to-day, without a government and without a God.[6]

This racist denigration was contested by Daniel G. Brinton in the preface to his book, *The Iroquois Book of Rites:*

Instead of a race of rude and ferocious warriors [he states], we find in this book a kindly and affectionate people, full of sympathy for their friends in distress, considerate to their women, tender to their children, anxious for peace, and imbued with a profound reverence for the constitution and their authors. We have become conscious of the fact that the aspect in which these Indians have presented themselves to the outside world has been in a large measure deceptive and factitious. The ferocity, craft and cruelty, which have been deemed their leading traits, have been merely the natural accompaniment of wars of self-preservation. . . . The sentiment of universal brotherhood which directed their polity has never been so fully developed in any branch of the Aryan race, unless it may be found incorporated in the religious quietism of Buddha and his followers.[7]

Brinton asserted that the impetus toward freedom came to the Germano-Celts from the people they had supplanted in Europe, the Iberians (from whom the Basques are descended), whose stock is the same as that of the American Indian. And so he put the blame for an insensitivity to political rights on the Aryans: "To humble themselves before some superior power—deity, king, or brahmin—seems to them a natural and overpowering inclination."[8] Thus one should admire not the intellectual and servile Aryans but rather the proud Basques and the American Indians, to whom goes the credit for free institutions which guarantee, so Brinton believes, genuine civilization and genuine progress.[9]

But it was Aryan racism that inspired the Indian Commission placed under Schoolcraft's guidance by Congress. According to Schoolcraft, after his marriage into the tribe, the Indians entrusted him with all their secrets: the fears and hopes that led them to celebrate their seemingly shocking rites. Fear and hope were interpreted by Schoolcraft as the prime reasons for all religions; hampered by this prejudice, he never was able to get to the heart of these rituals. As a result, the questions he framed for the commission were captious (much more powerful than the person queried is the man who formulates the questions): "Do certain adepts really think they are inspired by devils?" "What positive proofs exist for these hallucinations?" Thus supernatural reality would be a perversion of sensibility, interesting to the degree that it has sociological repercussions. In fact, one of the questions concerned the effects of mysticism on the Indians' character, behavior, and destiny: "And their sacred hieroglyphics, what advantage do they offer the people?"

In July, 1850, most of the documents gathered by the commission were handed over to the War Department. In 1851 three quarto volumes were issued in Philadelphia: *Information Concerning the History of the Indian Tribes Published by Authority of Congress.* The editor of the volumes expressed the official ideology—the middle path between the various theses on the Indian—in fact, the most hypocritical of all, that is, the Indians are brothers, made in the image and likeness of the common Creator, but deflected, by an act of fate, from the path of progress we are following. Not by chance does the particle dividing the sentence introduce an adversative clause; the second assertion annuls the first or, to use the language of legal sophistry, it leaves its validity intact but removes its efficacy. It bestows on the Indian all the rights of fraternity but forbids him to exercise them. This outrage was implicit in the commission's preliminary questionnaire, in which the Indian's metaphysical certainties and intellectual intuitions were brushed aside as hallucinations. This was truly a strange dialogue, with one of the interlocutors pre-empting the privilege of decreeing the borderline between hallucination and truth. All these reports added up to an apology for American methods; the government appears motivated by impeccable ideals, and the enforced migration is presented as an act of generosity on its part. Comparison with European colonies should render these positive American qualities all the more evident. In fact, has not everything possible been done to arouse the Indians from their lethargy? Have not the missionaries tried to rid them of their superstitions? And, finally, are not the Indians afflicted by a disposition hostile to "progress?" They constitute "a nonprogressive mental type"; hence they are mere objects.

In *Algic Researches* Schoolcraft had already accused the Indian of this Unforgivable Sin:

He does not seem to open his eyes on the prospect of civilization and mental exaltation held up before him, as one to whom the scene is new or attractive. These scenes have been pictured before him by teachers and philanthropists for more than two centuries; but there has been nothing in them to arouse and inspire him to press onward in the career of prospective civilization and refinement. He has rather turned away with the air of one to whom all things "new" were "old," and chosen emphatically to re-embrace his woods, his wigwams, and his canoe.[10]

As for the origin and nature of Indian civilization, Schoolcraft and his committee strove to demonstrate that they are wholly identical with those of Hindu and in general Oriental civilization; migrations across the Bering Strait would explain the kinship. Because of its simplicity, this theory of a Pan-Oriental American religion, argued by means of a series of analogies drawn between Hinduism, Zoroastrianism, and America's indigenous cults, was to become widely accepted. In his "Traditions of the Natchez," T. B. Thorpe, taking the doctrine for granted, later remarked: "As fire-worshippers, the Natchez displayed their Oriental origin, and they were more sincere in this most poetic of all idolatries than the Magi of the East."[11] In Melville's *Clarel* the idea of a Magi tradition, kept alive among the contemporary Parsi Indians and reaching Europe by way of the Gnostics, forms one of the poem's connecting threads.[12]

∴

Schoolcraft's report is a comprehensive and violent racist text, which defines the somatic and spiritual traits of the race and finds it guilty of an unforgivable discrepancy between lively individual intelligence and an incapacity for collective "progress." The members of such races have a refined sensibility and impeccable reasoning powers, yet the society to which they belong remains "static" and "infantile," and not even contact with civilized peoples has awakened it to the satisfactions of perpetual development. Is not India itself arrested, static? And what is responsible for this? Is it not perhaps the race's essential nature, which stifles emulation, the impulse to invention, novelty, education? It is race that is the cause of resignation and prevents the striving for constant improvement.

Moreover, that the factor of race is detrimental to progress is demonstrated by science, indeed by the Academy of Natural Sciences in Philadelphia, which offers decisive proof of this theory. The microscopic examination of the cross-section of a body hair reveals that it is round in Europeans, ellipsoidal in Negroes, and always oval in the Indians of Asia and America. Those creatures whose hair section is oval are characterized by a "static" social spirit "and are alien to progress." Nonetheless, they do possess a few estimable traits and are not wholly destitute of virtue. Indeed, their family feelings seem perhaps too ardent, as is shown by the

Hindu widow who immolates herself on her husband's funeral pyre, and by the rigorous mourning customs among American Indians. As for their valor, that is an outstanding quality among them.

The religions of both the Hindus and American Indians share the same defect: they fail to promise rewards or punishments after death. This deprives man of a sound moral incentive and denies God or the Great Spirit the attribute of justice. Further, the Parsis worship by offering hymns and the flames of pyres on the mountaintops to the Great Spirit, rejecting any image or likeness of Him as unworthy. The American Indians worship His power in the sun, waterfalls, and mountains, and as an offering burn their sacred, sweet-smelling leaf in the holy pipe. But below the Great Spirit stand Ormuzd and Ahriman, the good and evil deities, who contend for the world in a perpetual unstable equilibrium figuratively represented to the multitude: Evil as a serpent coiled around an egg, which is the symbol of Good. Is not this Parsi image also found at the headwaters of the Ohio River, on a pyramidal hill, whose stone sides bear the carving of a snake opening its jaws to swallow an ovoidal stone? Thus the Magi, the Brahmins, the Chaldeans, and the American Indians are all linked together by a shared cosmic dualism.

The Celto-Germans, by contrast, did not regard the god of darkness as one of the dynamic principles of the universe, of disintegration and unmitigated evil. Instead, he became Rhadamanthus, the punisher of evil men and the welcomer of good men in the Elysian fields.

Metempsychosis is another dogma that originated on the banks of the Ganges and is alien to the Celto-German races; only the Pythagoreans professed a belief in it. Yet, among the Indians, the belief that the soul migrates from body to body, from human to animal, and vice versa, is widespread. However, they often believe that the shades of the dead torment the living and that food must be offered to them. According to this conception, two substances exist in men, both distinct from the body—one migrating from body to body and the other hovering around his mortal remains. The worship of innumerable gods and natural powers —the sources of fear and awe—is common to both Orientals and American Indians. Do not the Indians try to obtain the protection of a tutelary divinity, of a Manitou who would defend them from the evil Manitou? And do they not also submit to superstitious torments to beseech its help?

Besides discussing profane pictography, the editors of these large Indian Commission tomes speak of the secret esoteric language and its hieroglyphics used by the initiates, the medicine men. These men are armed with "medicine bundles," that is, bags of cloths, feathers, stones, and metals. The bundles serve to concretize and symbolize the magical power of the chants with which they heal the sick who have been treated ineffectually with secular remedies. The construction of the lodges in which they perform their cures is minutely regulated, since each detail is symbolic and magical. Thus, for example, the top must be open (in *Clarel*, Melville emphasizes this aspect of the Roman Pantheon and stresses its religious significance). After the ritual circumambulation and the consecration of the lodge, the medicine man begins his musical, rhythmic struggle with the morbid, demonic disharmony. The prophets, distinct in their function from the medicine men and shamans, also have recourse not only to the chants but to the rhythmic beat of the ritual drums and the sound of bells or rattles.

Schoolcraft boasted of having succeeded, in 1820, in being initiated by two adepts in the mysteries of a shamanistic fraternity. In explaining the esoteric mysteries, the adepts made use of a table of twenty-two fundamental figures (similar to Germanic runes, and endowed at once with mnemonic and magical functions). Each figure had its corresponding song, which explained it and translated it into a specific rhythm.

The first figure depicts an eagle with wings outstretched beneath a semicircle; this represents the Great Spirit, which stretches across the heavenly vault and is full of grace. The second figure represents the catechumen with eagle feathers on his head, his right arm raised to the celestial vault that curves before him, his left arm adorned by a maniple, or an open bag, signifying that his hunger for esoteric knowledge is much greater than his desire for money. The third is a series of capsules within capsules and signifies an interval in the initiation ceremony during which a meal is prepared and the singing stops. Other emblems follow, which one must meditate upon during the subsequent phases of the initiation. The fourth is an outstretched arm that holds a dish in its hand. As it is being contemplated, the chief, whose wrists are adorned with feathers, sings an invitation to the meal, which must be consumed with the gods. The fifth emblem is the steam bath and marks the point at which the candidate must purify himself by sweating. The sixth shows a hand with its fingers extended: the moment when the candidate is welcomed by the initiated. The seventh is a parcel, symbol of the gifts that the catechumen now gives to the initiator, who has become his father. The eighth is the tree of life, from which spurts a therapeutic jet; ideally, it is around this tree that the round dance is performed. The ninth is a stuffed stork, from which many smaller birds are brought forth: the image of fecundity. The tenth is a circle pierced by an arrow to signify that the medicine man traverses the entire cosmos with the speed of an arrow. The eleventh is a small bird, the spirit carried by the wind to the borders of the world. The twelfth is the outlines of a mountain over which hovers a bird, the celestial vault on which the Great Spirit is enthroned; below it a medicine man's arm strains to reach it. The thirteenth is a sign of pause. The fourteenth is a blossoming tree of life, to which praises are sung. The sixteenth is a quarter of a circle, the course of the sun from dawn to midday, and a medicine man is touching it. The seventeenth is a beplumed circle, the Great Spirit that speaks to men in thunder by clapping his hands. Hieroglyphs of sacred drums are the eighteenth and nineteenth signs, while the twentieth and twenty-first are two ravens, the birds that communicate (as in the mysteries of Mithra) the decrees of destiny. The last figure is an ecstatic medicine man, levitated above the earth and touching the sky with his fingers. This corresponds to the phase in which a supplication to be lifted to the heights is sung.

In one of the preliminary questions concerning Indian symbolism in this vast inquiry, Schoolcraft had already mentioned ancient mnemonics. It is a mysterious subject, as the second chapter of the eleventh book of Quintilian's *De institutione oratoria* reveals. How did American-Indian pictography relate to the fetishism of the East, to Egyptian hieroglyphics, and, finally, to the rhetorical mnemonics of classical antiquity. Schoolcraft cleverly connected the table of shamanistic symbols with the ancient techniques of the rhetoricians, and, had he not been hampered by his common-sense prejudices, he might have gone even further in the discovery of mnemonic devices, a field opened up so productively in our century.

∴

Schoolcraft labored under the illusion that he had disclosed the secrets of the esoteric fraternity. After having obtained other, greater revelations, W. J. Hoffman, in *The Mide Wiwin or 'Grand Medicine Society' of the Ojibwa* (published in the seventh Annual Report of the Bureau of American Ethnology), denounced the superficiality of Schoolcraft's information in his presentation of the ritual texts. Although he tried hard to conceal his merely curious attitude, it must have discouraged Schoolcraft's initiators into the mysteries. Later he wrote about the sorcerers with a skeptical undertone, noting that they were regarded as men of great sanctity, wisdom, and self-denial. They affected to live poorly, he said, were above selfish motives, and communicated with the spirits of the elemental world. At all times they were under an influence that would have been "the extreme of human folly to resist."

Besides extracting some (modest) initiatory secrets from the medicine men, Schoolcraft was also able to obtain an autobiography from an Algonquin seer, Catherine Wabose (Hare), the first of a series of those astonishing hybrids produced by the spirit of the Indian who confides and the style of the amanuensis (primly Victorian in Schoolcraft's case).[13]

Early in life, when she was twelve years old, Catherine's mother warns her that she must remain alert to receive a supernatural visit. Her trepidation is so great that during the day she becomes dizzy, while at night she feels she is being visited by ghosts, precursors of the great ecstasy. Suddenly one night she is lifted up by a spirit of the air and carried into the heart of the forest. Here, she is joined by her mother, who sets to work and builds her a small lodge. When it is completed, she tells the girl to enter it, ordering her to remain shut up in it in silence, without tasting anything, not even snow. After two days she returns but does not bring food of any kind, and when the girl complains of her hunger and even more of her thirst, her mother reminds her of her family's poverty and the children still not old enough to work. She urges her to bear her suffering and to observe a strict fast so that the Master of Life might have pity on all of them. Then the mother leaves, promising to return within two days, during which her daughter should watch to see what the Great Spirit might send, accepting the good visions and rejecting the bad ones. All alone, Catherine starts to cut firewood with a little hatchet and twist the cords for mats, and while her pangs of hunger decrease, her thirst continues unabated. She resists the impulse to suck snow; she knows that supernatural presences are watching her.

On the fourth day her mother appears punctually, bringing a tin dish on which she melts some snow that she gives to her daughter to drink. Before leaving again, she tells the girl that the vision will benefit not only their family but also mankind.

Finally, on the sixth day of her trial, a voice from on high calls to her, expressing pity and urging her to follow it. She obeys, and there appears before her a thin, silvery path leading upward. After she walks a short distance, the new moon, with a flame rising from its top, appears on her right hand, and on her left the setting sun. On the right the Everlasting Woman appears before her and reveals her name to her, allowing her to give it to another. Then she bestows on her everlasting life. Finally Catherine is told: "Go, you are called on high."

She sees before her a man standing with rays like horns rising from his head and a large circular body. He is the Little Man-spirit, the friend of man. He commands her to give his name to her first son and urges her to continue the ascent. She follows the path, which leads her to an opening in the sky. There she hears a voice and near the path sees a man whose head is surrounded by a brilliant halo and whose breast is covered with squares. He tells her that he is called Bright Blue Sky, exhorts her to listen and not to be afraid, and announces that he wants to endow her with the gift of life. Immediately she sees herself encircled with bright points descending like needles, which fall at her feet. This is repeated several times. Bright Blue Sky exhorts her to bear it without fear. Now there are showers of nails and darts, but they too give no pain and drop at her feet. This is repeated several times. Bright Blue Sky tells her that her trial has ended, predicts a long life for her, and urges her to advance a little farther.

Now she finds herself at the threshold of the opening in the sky. Bright Blue Sky tells her that this is the limit beyond which she cannot pass; he also tells her that a mount will carry her back to the lodge and that she will then be able to care for her physical needs. The conveyance is a kind of fish swimming in the air; getting upon it, she is carried back with such velocity that her hair streams behind her. The next day, the sixth of her fast, her mother returns with some dried trout. Catherine's sense of hearing and smell have become so acute that she is aware of her mother's coming from a long way off. Indeed, the smell of the fish nauseates her, and she refuses to touch it. Her mother encourages her to persevere and leaves. Catherine again starts to cut firewood but falls down in a faint. When she regains her senses, she drags herself into the lodge and once again has the same vision, meets the same persons, hears the same promises and songs. On the seventh day of her fast a third vision is granted her: a round object descends from the sky, and when it is near her she sees small hands and feet protruding from it. The globe announces to her the gift of prophecy for herself, her family, and her tribe, and then it departs on wings, similar now to a woodpecker. In the evening her mother returns with a wooden bowl of corn boiled in melted snow, since it is forbidden to use water from the stream. Catherine eats and tells her mother what she has seen, and her mother instructs her to continue her fast for three more days, and then takes her home. Many guests welcome her with a celebration, but she barely eats, since her senses are still so acute that all animal food sickens her.

After a certain time Catherine is initiated, and when the rigors of the winter became harsher and the tribe, tormented by starvation, is about to succumb, the chief urges her to try her skill to relieve them. A prophet's lodge is built according to her directions, with a prescribed number of posts made from certain kinds of wood and with a roof of deer skin. The population of the encampment encircles the lodge. She enters it, carrying a small drum. She kneels and bows her head to the ground, beating the drum and singing her incantations. Soon the lodge begins to shake and the air to whistle around it. Then she stops playing and silently presses her ear against the ground. To the question of where game can be found, the response given by the globelike spirit is that they must go toward the west. The next day, obeying the instruction, the hunters obtain provisions for the tribe.

After a few years Catherine, now the tribe's prophetess, marries a great hunter, Strong Sky, and has two children with him. They live peacefully until in 1822 they happen on a French settlement, where her husband goes into the tent of a certain Gaultier. She tries in vain to stop him, knowing that he has drunk liquor and sensing imminent misfortune. A niece of Gaultier's rouses her in the middle of the night, and she runs to the stranger's tent; it is empty. Outside she sees a faint gleam in the darkness—her husband's earrings. Believing that in his drunken state he has probably fallen asleep, she goes to him in the dark, but slips and falls on something wet: blood on the grass. Her husband is lying dead, killed in a brawl.

Later she remarries and has two children, but her second husband also dies. One of her children falls ill, and during his death agony he sees the Christian God handing him white garments. Another of the children also dies. Soon after, John Sunday, a missionary, arrives, and his preaching of the Gospel converts her; she takes the name of Catherine. The serenity with which she endures the death of her children is exemplary.

Her third husband, an Ojibwa and a Christian like her, was called Wabose (Hare). Schoolcraft became the helpful friend of the family and adopted one of the daughters. He managed to persuade the prophetess to intone the magical hymns revealed to her by the celestial beings. Upon hearing those sounds, now drawn out, now hurried, alternately whistling and guttural, Schoolcraft concluded that they seemed calculated to excite terror in the spirit and proved that she was in a state of obsession and delirium. This is how he replied to the question he had asked himself about native mysticism: its adepts think that they are visited by spirits and suffer the deliriums in good faith.

The wonders of Catherine's story are innumerable. Her mother's figure looms large precisely because it is immersed in shadow, while Catherine's conversion is a mystery precisely because it is free from any shadows. The sole manifest sign of her new inner life is a negative one: the absence of all human weakness at the death of her children. The transition from Dionysian mysticism to the Apollonian calm for which this female Indian Prospero sacrifices her powers has been perfect. Not since the medieval *Book of Marjorie Kempe* has there been a text in which the supernatural is so densely and closed intertwined with everyday life. Alongside the shadows furrowed by a silvery line in the mystical ascent stands the darkness of the place of the crime, where the earring faintly gleams, both realities fused in a single exalted surrender.

∴

Catherine's chant made Schoolcraft experience a moment of consternation which he was unable to explore, hampered as he was by Enlightenment prejudices, just as he saw the exultancy of Indian warfare but was unable to grasp its sacred meaning. When the warriors go off to war, the chief intones his fearsome chant:

The songs are brief, wild repetitions of sentiments of heroic deeds, or incitements to patriotic or military ardor. They are accompanied by one or more choristers, by the drum and rattle, and by the voice of one or more listeners. They are repeated slowly, sententiously, and with a measured cadence, to which the most exact time is kept. The warrior stamps on the ground as if he would shake the universe. His language is often highly figurative and he deals with the machinery of the clouds, the flight of carnivorous birds, and the influence of spiritual agencies, as if the region of space were at his command. He imagines his voice to be heard in the clouds; and while he stamps the ground with well-feigned fury, he fancies himself to take hold of the "circle of the sky" with his hands. Every few moments he stops abruptly in his circular path, and utters the piercing war-cry.

He must be a cold listener who can sit unmoved by these appeals. The ideas thrown out succeed each other with the impetuosity of a torrent. They are suggestive of heroic will, of high courage, and a burning sentiment.[14]

Schoolcraft cannot imagine that beyond these martial sentiments there might exist an interpretation of the war's events as symbols of inner conquest.

His racism was not overtly bloodthirsty, but it put blinders on his intelligence. In his judgment of *Hiawatha* he wrote that the Indian "is a warrior in war, a savage in revenge, a stoic in endurance, a wolverine in suppleness and cunning. But he is also a father at the head of his lodge, a patriot in the love of his country, a devotee to noble sports in his adherence to the chase, a humanitarian in his kindness and an object of noble grief at the grave of his friends and kindred."

The Indians' essential quality, though so clear to Captain Bonneville, is not mentioned.

∴

In 1842 the American Ethnological Society was founded and in 1846 the Smithsonian Institution, and so it seemed that a radical renewal, an intellectual rigor heretofore unknown, would reform Indian studies. It is inevitable that every twenty years the illusion spreads among ethnologists that unprecedented developments are about to take place. Just as Jefferson dreamed of revising the Constitution every sixteen years, so methodological opinion regularly surrenders to these cycles. But the basis of Indian studies remained unchanged, no matter how much the method seemed to alter. Pearce has perfectly summed up the illusions that marked the transition from the period of Schoolcraft's researches to the new ethnology:

Yet even while scientists moved towards the modern study of the Indian as a normally complex and difficult human who possessed a tolerably respectable civilization of his own, they continued to think of him literally as a primitive, as one whose way of life was somehow earlier than their own. They continued to try to comprehend that way of life historically, in its relation to the long evolution of man toward high civilization.[15]

∴

Lewis Henry Morgan was the most famous among the innovators, and from his school also came a novelist *artifex superadditus ethnologo*, Adolf F. Bandelier. Morgan's work, inspired and in part directed by the Iroquois Ely S. Parker, an engineer and army general, also supplied all the categories of judgment to Friedrich Engels, then engaged in creating the ethnology and critical exegesis of the Marxist religion. If the idea of the American Constitution is partly indebted to the Iroquois, their role in the creation of Marxism is far from insignificant.

Marxist doctrine, which was to replace the vaguely Utopian American doctrines, was the almost inevitable development of typically American theoretical premises, which originated in the need to redefine attitudes toward the Indian that had already crystallized among followers of the

Scotch school of Robertson and Scott. Morgan formulated his history of progress chiefly by making use of Iroquois material. Man could be traced back, so the new paleontological sciences seemed to demonstrate, to a more remote epoch than had once been thought. From this he drew the conclusion that for all peoples three successive phases must be posited: savagery, barbarism, and civilization. Between the first two, society everywhere had been organized in clans, phratries, and tribes, and this was the embryo from which, by an ineluctable law, civil society must finally develop. It was precisely in America that one had the privilege of ascertaining this truth in the quick of life, since the aborigines were at the point in history corresponding to that of our barbarian ancestors. That humanity's inception was savage Morgan proved on the basis of the progressive increase in the production of goods and the ever more complex political and linguistic organization. The language of primeval men, so Morgan thought, must be the same as that imagined by Lucretius in *De Rerum Natura* (V, 1020), whom he quotes:

> And urged for children and the womankind
> Mercy, of fathers, whilst with cries and gestures
> They stammered hints how meet it was that all
> Should have compassion on the weak.

Architecture developed from the crude hut in successively more elaborate forms, and, slowly, over the course of millennia, property took shape. There remained religion, whose evolutionary course Morgan found difficult to measure against any known parameters, since it is tied to imagination and emotion. However, he felt certain that the deeper we look into the past, the more grotesque and unintelligible religion becomes.

Morgan chose fishing and the use of fire as signs of the first steps beyond the savage state; before this, fruit and nuts were the sole food, and language was not yet articulated. However, he had to admit that no people had ever been observed in this phase, which thus remained hypothetical, no more scientific today than when it was formulated by Lucretius:

> As yet they knew not to enkindle the fire
> Against the cold, nor hairy pelts to use
> And clothe their bodies with the spoils of beasts;
> But huddled in groves, and mountain-caves, and woods,
> And 'mongst the thickets hid their squalid backs,
> When driven to flee the lashing of the winds
> And the big rains.

In the next phase there were the Romans, divided among clans, curias, and tribes, and the Iroquois. The Iroquois gentes or clans had to unite in phratries to perform certain common tasks, and so phratries of the same dialect came together in tribes. The confederation of the Iroquois was evidence of the moment of transition from the tribe to the state. Such was the model Morgan applied to the entire history of humanity, with an extension not so much analogical as imaginative. This operation was performed in *Letter On the Iroquois, by Skenandoah,* published in the *American Review* in 1847.

The Iroquois noble chiefs, rather advanced in the production of goods, had communistic productive relations; hence the common lodges that gathered together as many as twenty families. These formed the primitive, "infantile" model of the Marxist "reign of liberty," which was to be the beacon of evolved, conscious, and mature humanity. So, to Iroquois society fell the privilege of lighting the way to the future at the very moment of its own destruction. Progressivist theories have their particular ways of formulating a theory of sacrifice.

Democracy was born with the clan, where the post of chief or sachem was elective and revocable and was conferred in a ceremony that centered on either bestowing or removing animal horns from the chief's head. The ownership of goods, the duty to avenge members killed by enemies, the burying ground, and worship were all held in common. Certain activities were the responsibility of the collectivity of related clans or phratries; others were the responsibility of the collectivity of unrelated phratries or tribes; and finally others, the most important, fell to the confederation of all the tribes. Morgan studied the balance of forces in this political system that had at one point made the Iroquois arbiters of the wars between France and England. He was not interested in the Indian but rather in the functioning of their social structure. It is this aspect that, in Morgan's opinion, determines all of existence. In *A View of the Progress of Society in Europe,* William Prescott also refused to recognize any other cause—efficient or final, material or formal—for Indian spiritual reality but that of "society."

These are concepts that by and large are still taken for granted today, even to the point of ignoring the fact that at the very most they might have been acceptable merely as hypotheses in their own time, when Friedrich Engels appropriated them. Engels welcomed the conjecture of progressive phases but emphasized that all progress was at the same time a regress, since the aggrandized political and economic organization diminished freedom and the institution of property degraded the use and enjoyment of goods. Progress was a good thing because it released man from the subjugation of nature and from fantasies about the supernatural by means of which primitive man had tried to console himself or compensate for his vulnerability and the stalemate in which nature kept culture. But the splitting up of work into specialized tasks and the division into classes consecrated by the right of property at the same time brought about a regression from primitive communism; Engels is one of the most sentimental celebrators of the noble savage. Only by carrying the progress-regress dialectic to the extreme of its ultimate reversal could man hope to combine the advantages of a superabundance of all goods and of free primitive existence.

These key Marxist tenets, which are based on a fusion of the two myths of a primordial golden age and the bestial origin of man, counterposed to each other since the Renaissance (although both stimulated ideological, and therefore social, unrest), were given their main theoretical expression in Morgan's *League of the Ho-Dé-no-sau-nee, or Iroquois* (Rochester, 1851). Morgan shared with Engels an admiration for the fine human qualities of the primitives (though he seems ignorant of the work of Pernety, the eighteenth-century abbé and alchemist, who, in a polemic with De Pauw, praised the aboriginal arts). Morgan stressed that it would be pointless to look in rude epochs for high intellectual qualities, the fruit of civilized refinement, but that it would be equally irrational to believe that the Indian lacked man's noble traits.

In his late work on aboriginal architecture, Morgan's praise of primitive communism alternately recalls William Morris or Marxism at its purest. His fervent acclaim of Indian houses, for instance, vibrates with the tension inherent in the juxtaposition of the use value of wealth and the exchange value of commodities, and establishes the mode of connecting aesthetic judgments with the analysis of economic relations. Here were buildings not put up by forced labor; their elegant and alluring spaciousness proclaims that the Indian constructed them for his own use and occupied them under a regime of complete equality.

Liberty, equality, and fraternity are emphatically the first great principles of the *gens* and this architecture responds to these sentiments. . . . As a key to the interpretation of this architecture, two principles, the practice of hospitality and the practice of communism in living, have been employed.[16]

But his preliminary assertions concerning "primitive man's" lack of intellectual qualities were almost all gratuitous. In man's megalithic and neolithic beginnings, the cyclopean structures and other monuments reveal an advanced knowledge of engineering and astronomy, and even their huts were rich in complex symbolic meaning. This was to be proved by the work of Joseph Norman Lockyer.[17]

Primordial religion seems grotesque only to those who refuse to interpret the data. It is probable that the primitives were often indifferent to economic development, which is entirely compatible with the greatest spiritual culture, poverty being an ideal in religious societies. As for the progressive development of language, and thus of thought, structural ethnology has relegated this notion among the many fragile legends on which progressivist ideology was nourished.

These small truths need to be kept in mind in order to achieve the necessary detachment in considering Morgan's hypotheses. Recent ethnology has refuted them, but they remain rooted in seemingly ineradicable ways in the common mind, mostly in the form of subliminal prejudices, as unavowed as they are effective.

∴

Adolf F. Bandelier, Morgan's colleague, embarked on a reform of narrative fiction that was intended to parallel the ethnographic one.

We have, Mr. Morgan, and I under his directions, unsettled the Romantic School in Science; now the same thing must be done in literature on the American aborigine. Prescott's Aztec is a myth, it remains to show that Fenimore Cooper's Indian is a fraud. Understand me: I have nothing personal in view. Cooper has no more sincere admirer than I am, but the cigar-store man and the statuesque Pocahontas of the "vuelta abajo" trade as they are paraded in literature and thus pervert the public conceptions about the Indians—these I want to destroy first if possible.[18]

The Delight Makers[19] presents an account of life in a village, or pueblo, locked in a deep gorge. The obsession with black magic is predominant. Cooper's romantic naïveté is definitely a thing of the past; in fact, it will survive now only in the commercial Western. Obsolete also is the cavalier imprecision exemplified in George W. Kendall, who described the same places and people in *Narrative of an Expedition across the Great South West Prairies* (published in London in 1845), with its fanciful tales about promiscuous ritual orgies in the caves of New Mexico.

Bandelier's narrative is woven in accordance with the same ideological pattern as Morgan's work. There is a network of correspondences and antagonisms among the people of the tribes and the underlying framework of the secret societies. This closely knit fabric, which provides the dynamic equilibrium of the community as revealed by Morgan, in Bandelier becomes the very air his characters breathe. Even the Latin quotations to which Morgan is addicted appear in Bandelier's narrative context (the Indians' funeral lamentations remind him of Tacitus' sentence about the Germans: "It is right for women to mourn and for men to remember"). Morgan's prejudices hold undisputed sway in Bandelier's mind. The Indians are infantile; they belong to a historical phase that represents mankind's childhood. Their religion must either be regarded as a product of the social structure or reduced to hallucination. Thus:

> In most cases of importance the shaman is honest. He really believes that what he says is the echo from a higher world. This firm belief is the fruit of training; and the voices he hears, the sights he sees when alone with Those Above are the products of honest hallucination. His training and the long and painful discipline he undergoes in rising from degree of knowledge to degree of knowledge, the constant privations and bodily and mental tortures, prepare him for a dreamy state in which he becomes thoroughly convinced that he really is a medium.

If one wished to theorize in a less evasive manner about these positivistic (and Enlightenment-influenced) commonplaces and attempted to define the concept of hallucination, so indiscriminately extended to every perception of the supernatural, it would become quite clear how frivolous and merely reassuring it is to believe that substantially diverse events can all be lumped together simply by giving them the same label. (What characteristic distinguishes perception from collective hallucination? Constancy? And what is more constant than a traditional order of visions?) All the literature on the subject has always and everywhere emphasized the distinction between a prophetic or gnostic-ecstatic vision and a "dreaming state," which is its opposite and must be destroyed (the aim of self-torturing ascetic practices), so that the former can come into being.

Bandelier's thought, like Morgan's, is based on the German philosophy of the historic and historicist development of the human spirit. Thus he fell into the trap of mistaking the solid substance in Indian metaphor for a deficiency in the power of abstraction (as if everything could not be defined as the lack of its opposite, as if the capacity for abstraction were not completely distinct and separate from a paucity of metaphors, as if, finally, by virtue of the laws of analogy, metaphors and similes could not be the vehicles of pure ideas). "The Indian speaks like a child, using figures of speech, not in order to embellish, but because he lacks abstract terms and is compelled to borrow equivalents from comparisons with surrounding nature." Oddly enough, Bandelier did not realize (but neither did Hegel, whom he most likely echoed) that when he said "abstract," he was using a metaphor. In describing a mental operation he used a word for a physical operation—that of drawing one thing from another by muscular effort. The word "compelled" suggests the action of physical force, and expresses analogically a mental obligation. He produced metaphors without knowing it, just as Monsieur Jourdain produced prose without knowing it, and the only difference between him and the Indian "infant" was that he repressed the awareness of using metaphors.

What was the origin of this "subconscious ingenuity" in Bandelier (or in Morgan, or in their masters in classic German philosophy)? What was the origin of their unconscious desire to blind themselves and repress reason, to give resolving, pacifying, magical values to such words as "hallucination" and "infancy"? If one looks closely, Bandelier was led to these mystifications and deformations in order to defend his anti-Christian theology, which was identical with that of German idealism. For Hegel the Serpent in Genesis was the "positive" character and its exhortation to the progenitors of humanity the inception of the Spirit. He exalted the desecration of and the revolt against nature and above all cultivated the hatred of piety, of surrender to the divine will and to providence. This was the origin of those pages in Bandelier where he enlisted the help of one of the Fathers of that "church of the Serpent," that is, classic German philosophy, to bolster his judgment of an Indian summer solstice dance. This ritual dance

gives public expression, under very strange forms, to the idea that has found its most perfect utterance in the German philosopher's [Schleiermacher] definition of "abject reliance upon God"; whereas in its lowest form it is still "a vague and awful feeling about unity in the powers of nature, an unconscious acknowledgment of the mysterious link connecting the material world with a realm beyond it."

Hegel's invective against the religious alienation of the Spirit and the man who conforms to celestial rhythms and those of vegetable growth form the persistent undercurrent of Bandelier's objections concerning the Indians. He could have brought the same charges against the pious Aeneas and the saints of the West, with their sense of destiny guided by divine providence: the very opposite of the unrest prized by the followers of the Serpent.

This implicit, slavish obedience to signs and tokens of a natural order to which a supernatural origin is assigned, is the Indian's religion. The life of the Indian is therefore merely a succession of religious acts called forth by utterances of what he supposes to be higher powers surrounding him. . . . The Indian is a child whose life is ruled by a feeling of complete dependence, by a desire to accommodate every action to the wills and decrees of countless supernatural beings.

The metaphor of the Indian as a small child is comforting for the person who with brute force has acquired the right of guardianship over him. The convenience of the colonialist is wedded to the inverted religion of German philosophy.

A long analysis of Bandelier's ideology may be justified also by the light it throws on the salutary limitations of every ideology, which never fully absorbs the man who adopts it. Though completely convinced and dominated by his system, Bandelier had an extraordinary mimetic imagination. He learned the indigenous languages and dialects with great facility, assimilated the emotions of others,[20] and with something like clairvoyance heeded the ascendancy, the magnetic power of men's gaze. His imagination followed its own laws, grasping instantly the shape of things before the mechanical application of ideology had time to stamp them with its crushing imprint, lacerating the delicate, iridescent tissues, their very life. Thus the frigid, violent, arrogant, and blind pedant was altogether transformed when he began to breathe narrative life into the forms that his imagination drew from his memory, becoming compassionate, responsive, farsighted. And *The Delight Makers* is a truly alive novel filled with real people, trees, and rocks and not, save for brief, irritating moments, the cartoons of ideological propaganda.

The life of the Quere village rising on a canyon wall in New Mexico is, as we said, an interwoven fabric of various forces. Its individual gentes or clans are divided, but their members join in marriage and in religious fraternities; thus each person is involved in a communal bond of hereditary and acquired forces, of distinct loyalties and obediences that define it. The noble chiefs form the council, the civil and military authority, and are assisted and guided by the corps of shamans, while the worship of the gods of peace and harmony is entrusted to priests. They are not even permitted to hear of quarrels or misfortunes and live in a constant state of propitiatory asceticism. In this context various fraternities operate. The most mysterious is that of the *Koshare,* the delight makers or clowns, who are hated, feared, and revered. From the first conversation the weight of their presence is felt throughout the whole novel. They perform crude pranks at certain festivities and everyone laughs, but the laughter is mixed with an undercurrent of terror; they seem to know everything about everyone, and no one can be sure that he may not, owing to some hidden sin, become the object of their mockery. A patriarch warns: "When I was young and a boy like your son . . . I cared little about the Koshare. Now I have learned more," and he tells the legend of the fraternity's origin. It appears that when the people were drawn from below the ground and directed to their present land, the gods also made sure that they would not become weary on the exhausting journey by summoning the Protoclown from the nether regions to entertain them. His "body was painted white and black, and [he] carried on his head dried corn leaves instead of feathers." He was the first of the Koshare. Besides playing pranks, the Koshare also fast and pray to make the crops grow.

The Koshare are by definition ambiguous, deadly and clownish, religious and blasphemous, quite different from the shamans, who are divided into various fraternities: the Shyayak, shamans of the hunt, who know the spell by which one attracts game; the Uakani, who perform magic in wartime; the Chayani, doctors and magical healers; and finally the Yaya, both prophets and priests, who know the essence of all these forms. By contrast, the Koshare, during their summer and autumn exhibitions, attain moments of satanism: "The pranks of these fellows are simply silly and ugly; the folly borders on imbecility and the ugliness is disgusting, and yet nobody is shocked; everybody endures it and laughs."* What is the relation of these obscene trivialities to the task of stimulating fruitfulness? The Cuirana, members of the society charged with assisting the sprouting of the seed, indulge in no such pranks.

The villain of the novel, Tyope, is for good reason a Koshare, and while there are also benign Koshare in the novel, their connection with the fraternity and its secrets always assumes a sinister aspect. Tyope covets the command of the tribe, and the only way to obtain it is to slaughter his competitors. He comes to an agreement with a Navajo warrior, but the conspiracy is too complicated to succeed. He also wants the disgrace of his repudiated wife, Shotaye, a sensual, crafty woman, devoted to black magic. Bandelier cannot help seeing Shotaye with a gleam of sympathy, much as that other Hegelian, Michelet, described European witches in

* D. H. Lawrence sensed the sinister essence expressed in the very costumes of the Koshare—"like blackened shocks of a dead corn-knole, tufted at the top."

his lyrical essay *La Sorcière*. The result is a complicated, almost appealing character who rushes to the side of a frail young bride consumed by fever and seemingly about to die. Shotaye overpowers her, instills her with strength, and by questioning a corncob adorned with an owl's feathers, fascinates her with dark rites, and cures her. The price paid for these rites is a drought and the failure of the Koshare dances. Tyope suspects the healed woman and plots to obtain proof of the use of witchcraft. The counterposed machinations of Tyope and Shotaye bring on catastrophe. The Queres separate because of dissensions between a rich and an impoverished clan that Tyope has fostered. As a result, they fall into the trap set by the Navajos and attack a village of their own tribe, where Shotaye, who has found refuge there from her impending trial for witchcraft, gives the alarm. The Quere warriors are exterminated. In the meantime, the Navajos have destroyed the undefended Quere village. The sad epilogue in which the survivors try to salvage a few remnants of the past has overtones of an almost Manzonian sense of providence.

Bandelier's art excels in the confrontations, the dialogue of looks and threats, the battle between strong wills. We see it in the sudden collapse of Tyope's violent, cold energy, similar to that of the dying Don Rodrigo in Manzoni's *The Betrothed*: "Everything manly and strong had left his heart; nothing of it remained but a faintly putrid core, whose former fermentation had produced the effervescence that took the shape of energy, shrewdness, and daring." And again in the story of the spell cast on a young man by a female Koshare who wants him as a husband for her daughter. She shows him the pots her daughter has painted:

"Lightning," said she, indicating with her finger a sinuous black line that issued from one side of the arches resting on a heavy, black dash.

"Cloud," he added, referring to the arches.

"Rain," concluded the maiden, pointing at several black streaks which descended from the figure of the clouds. Both broke out in a hearty laugh.

The young man asks what the pots are for, and the woman tells him that they are for the Koshare and leads him to believe that they can make it rain. She also assures him that their dances, fasts, and prayers can make the crops grow: "In these words she artfully shrouded the true objects of the Koshare. It enhanced their importance in the eyes of the uninitiated listener by making him believe that the making of rain was also an attribute of theirs." The seductiveness of the Koshare mystery, similar to that of the society of the Tower in Goethe's *Wilhelm Meister*, the appealing beauty of those symbolic vessels and their decipherment are all interlaced with the lovely young woman's amorous charm (and is not Goethe's Wilhelm trapped in similar convergences?). Then the mother continues: "On this bowl you see painted everything that produces rain. . . . Here you see the tadpole, here the frog, here the dragon-fly and the fish; they, as they stand here, pray for rain. . . ." To this skill Bandelier adds the minor one of skillful narration of ambushes and thrilling pursuits, learned from Cooper.

So a ruinous ideology has vainly offered its crippling services to a supple and subtle imagination: *The Delight Makers* is a gracious introduction to the Indian life of New Mexico, the inspiration of a large school in the twentieth century, and even if the story were not so artfully devised to keep the reader's interest, the book would still stand on its own merits, as in this scene of a meal:

> To enjoy this meal both lads squatted, but Shyuote, still half asleep, lost his balance and tumbled over. Angry at the merriment which this created, the boy hastily grabbed the food, but his mother interfered.
>
> "Don't be so greedy, uak,—'urchin.' Remember Those Above," she said; and Shyuote, imitating the example of Okoya, crossly muttered a prayer, and scattered crumbs before him. Then only, both fell to eating.

Or this scene of a pursuit:

> He dipped some water from the brook and moistened his parched lips, taking care not to touch his face or body with the liquid. Tyope was tired and worn out, but at the same time angry; and when the Indian suffers or when he is angry he neither washes nor bathes. . . . Physical or mental pain, disappointment, and wrath, are with him compatible only with lack of cleanliness. . . .

Chapter IX

———— •◦• ————

The Literature of Reverence

The first man to approach the Indians with true reverence was an Episcopal minister, Samuel Farmar Jarvis, on the occasion of an address given at the New York Historical Society on December 20, 1819. Jarvis was open to such feelings since his tenets were entirely divorced from progressivism. He believed that God had bestowed on early man a revelation that subsequent history had adulterated but which had been elucidated, developed, and brought to its consummation in the doctrine of the Incarnation. In the beginning was the Church of the Fathers, from which man had fallen away by creating confusion in both ideas and rituals, except for periodic descents of the divine into the human. Hence the fundamental resemblance of all religions (and in fact a century later the same certainty informed the ethnographic school headed by the Austrian ethnographer Wilhelm Schmidt and the work of the magazine *Anthropos*).

However, in the New York of 1820, where Jarvis's address was published, it did not have the power to dissipate the fury of prejudices, even though it was shrewdly and sarcastically presented as a call to Enlightenment duty: ". . . the religion of the Indian tribes of North America, had not been viewed with that largeness of observation, which is the characteristic of enlightened philosophy."[1] The Indian, he continued, is vanishing, so the fear that inhibited knowledge of him should also come to an end. But when fear ceases, contempt takes its place. To complicate matters further, the Indians are secretive, especially when it comes to their religion.

They were undoubtedly blessed by the Revelation or Tradition common to all men, which was subsequently corrupted by the human tendency to "contract everything within the compass of our understanding, and to subject it, if possible, to the scrutiny of our senses. A Being purely spiritual, omniscient, and omnipotent is above our comprehension, and we seek, by the multiplication of subordinate deities, to account for the operations of his power."[2] But the idea of Tradition persists, as is proven by the King of Gerar near whom Abraham lived, the Pharaoh with whom Joseph discussed dreams, Balaam, and Job's Arabian homeland. More abundant evidence of this is encountered among the Indians described by Charlevoix, Loskiel, and Heckewelder than among all the nations of antiquity, and the degree of their idolatry is probably not much greater than that found among the ancient Jews. The immortality of the soul was also part of Tradition; the purity with which this revealed truth was felt by the Indians is especially evident in the reports of Mackenzie's travels. Rituals, or visual transmissions, are an excellent method of preserving Tradition, more reliable than oral transmission, for visual transmission endures even when the dogmatic expression is not grasped or is distorted. Rituals center around oblations, which still exist among all Indians. Mackenzie reported certain lavish sacrifices or *potlatch* among the northern tribes, and few peoples are so generous in frequent tributes on every sort of occasion. It is a fact that sacrifice is by definition an act that reason cannot conceive without the help of Tradition; providentially, it prepares the mind for an understanding of the sacrifice of God to God—the cross. Moreover, except for the Aztecs, aboriginal sacrifices were extremely mild, in accordance with unadulterated Tradition. The Indians also maintained a priesthood, though often combining it with the civil authority, just as King Anius in Vergil was "both king of men and priest of Apollo." This leaves the problem of the medicine men, whom Charlevoix called satanic and Heckewelder considered impostors, but who simply fulfill a prophetic office like Elijah, Balaam among the Gentiles, and also Job, who can pray and so save Eliphaz. The gift of prophecy is granted to the degree that one is close to Tradition, and only when the Tradition goes into decline does it become confused with superstitious practices. If the Indians are idolaters, Jarvis concludes, they are less so than any other people and more than any other faithful to the Tradition. In America, Jarvis's ideas are in accordance with European proponents of the Tradition, which was defended in France by De Bonald, Bautain, and Bonnetty, and in Italy by Gian Francesco Finetti, the author of *Difesa dell'autorità della sacra Scrittura contro G. B. Vico* ("Defense of the Authority of Sacred Scripture Against G. B. Vico, 1768"; reissued by Benedetto Croce in 1936). Using the same arguments as Jarvis would, Finetti illuminates the concept of sacrifice:

Having with his positing of a savage state prevented the flow of perennial tradition, Vico, together with the wisest authors, was unable to derive the origin of sacrifice from the doctrine handed down by the first fathers to their descendants. . . . Moreover, it seems clear that, instead of being caused by stupid superstition and monstrous cruelty, the use of human victims was the result of a false refinement of reason, owing to which man believed that sacrifices were all the more welcome to God when the victims were more precious. . . .

∴

Charles Godfrey Leland, the major essayist in the generation after Emerson, was the first to uncover the secret nucleus of Indian life. Born in Philadelphia in 1824, he was graduated from Princeton and continued his studies at Heidelberg and Munich. As a boy, he searched in the woods for the arrowheads dear to Thoreau and for stones of unusual shapes, similar to the voodoo cult stones of which his family's Negro servants had told him. Emerson notes that Thoreau seemed to attract Indian relics; in much the same way, Leland attracted esoteric experiences. During his youth, which mirrored prophetically his future passions, he visited Peale's Museum, in Philadelphia, where a collection of oddities as well as portraits was housed. He became friendly with Algonquin farmhands during his vacations and, having learned from Carlyle's *Sartor Resartus* to strip away the "outer garments" in order to understand the true character of men, he refused to be distracted by the Indian's (and later, the gypsy's) wretched appearance. Before him, in the same spirit, the soldier, philosopher, and student of alchemy Ethan Allen Hitchcock had observed Indian religiosity in its essential purity, remarking that Carlyle himself would have enjoyed separating heart and essence from clothes.[3]

Leland was initiated into the Kaw tribe of Kansas aborigines. He played a part in the Paris revolution of 1848. When he returned to the United States, he worked as a journalist and wrote humorous verse, which was collected in *The Breitmann Ballads* (1871). President of the Gypsy Lore Society, he was to be the first to divulge the esoteric language, Skelta, used by the coppersmith gypsies. He spent his last years in Florence transcribing the revelations of a sorceress named Maddalena in his book *Etruscan Magic and Occult Remedies*, which was followed by *Legends of Florence* and *Arcadia or the Gospel of the Witches*. He died in Florence in 1903.

"A gypsy camp near Budapest, or ravelling the hem of tidy Philadelphia; an Indian reservation in Passamaquoddy, a decaying Florentine palace—the whole bucolic repository of sub-culture . . . here our pioneer researcher panned his gold."[4] About 1882 Leland began to gather the legends of the Indians of New Brunswick, making use of manuscripts in Anglo-Algonquin, often of an esoteric nature. He sensed around them the atmosphere of the Nordic saga and counterposed the noble, Nordic Algonquins to other Indians, just as Cooper had contrasted the Mohicans (Algonquins) with the Iroquois.

Unlike Hiawatha, Glooskap, the Algonquin god, is a Thor or Wotan— "congenial to a reader of Shakespeare and Rabelais"—and all around him moves a world of giants who resemble the Nordic Jötuns. The ideas of Carlyle and Emerson on Germanic myths are the lens through which Leland observes the world of Algonquin mythology. All that does not fit into this picture of dreadful Nordic divinities, this flock of minor natural forces, seems to him "strangely like that of the Rosicrucians."[5] First came the god of good, Glooskap, and then came the evil god, the androgynous Wolf, both in Algonquin mythology and in the *Edda*. And just as for the ancient Germans, so for the Algonquins was the first man held captive in the ash, the Tree of Life, before God breathed life into him.

Leland composed a memorable Emersonian-style speech in defense of the savage:

Living as he does in the woods, becoming familiar with animals, and learning how much more intelligent and allied to man they are than civilized man supposes, be believes they have souls, and were perhaps originally human. Balaam's ass spoke once for every Christian; every animal spoke once for the Indian. If a child can be put to sleep by singing to it, why cannot insensibility to pain or a cure be caused by the same process? He is told that the wafer becomes the body of Christ; this may confirm his belief that the Indian god Manobozho turned bits of his own flesh or his wife's into raccoons, for food. . . . But the greatest cause of all for a faith in magic is one which the white man talks about without feeling, and which the Indian feels without talking about it. I mean the poetry of nature, with all its quaint and beautiful superstitions.[6]

The second part of his speech has inflections reminiscent of Hawthorne, while preserving the Emersonian staccato in the brief, incidental phrases:

To every Algonquin a rotten log by the road, covered with moss, suggests the wild legend of the log demon: the Indian corn and sweet flag in the swamp are the descendants of beautiful spirits who still live in them. . . . And how much of this feeling of the real poetry of nature does the white man or woman possess, who pities the poor ignorant Indian? A few second-hand scraps of Byron and Tupper, Tennyson and Longfellow . . . Joe, or Noel, or Sabattis may seem to the American Philistine to be a ragged, miserable, ignorant Indian; but to the *scholar* he is by far the Philistine's superior in that which life is *best* worth living for.[7]

Power, which is synonymous with the Algonquin word for magic, manifests itself in capricious, eccentric, malicious children. In a grown man it can terrify by his overwrought voice and face; his voice can be softened into a soothing chant or explode in a frightening howl, and as the Algonquin medicine man emits these sounds he seems to sink into the ground like the Nordic wizard in the saga of Thorstein (Leland suggests that there might be a particular way of moving that gives this impression). The Algonquins know ways very different from the usual ones of obtaining magical power, for instance by sleeping chastely for seven nights beside a pretty, desirable virgin. Other Indians dive into the water and stay under it for a long time; yet others meet an aggressive ghost and struggle with it until dawn. Dead to its promises and pleas for peace, they struggle until the ghost enters into them together with all of its power. "When the true magician 'gets mad,' and continues to get madder till the end, he is invincible. Allied to this is perseverance."[8] Finally there is the supreme method: penitence. As among the Hindus, it can give one strength for both good and evil; the most usual practice was a seven-day retreat fasting, without sleep and in continuous prayer. "The highest ambition of an Indian was to become a *Megumoowessoo,* a mystical being, which is explained differently as fairy, faun, sylvan deity, but which means one who enjoys all the highest privileges of humanity allied to the supernatural."[9]

Before Leland, only some pages of Minnie Myrtle's *The Iroquois, or The Bright Side of Indian Character* (New York, 1855) had grasped these truths and confuted the widespread lies. For example, why not intervene between nations that were exterminating each other anyway? In that case, what about the Christian nations that were continually at war with each other? And in response to the statement that the Indians "inflicted tortures upon the enemy taken in battle," Minnie Myrtle cited the tortures inflicted because of differences of opinion in which European history abounds.

She also explained the particular difficulties in translating the Indian language. As a metaphorical language, it is filled with allusions, each important event having been handed down by naming a person after it or by giving its name to a mountain, lake, or river. Thus the clumsy attempts to translate Indian speech in the modes of Ossian rhetoric were brought to an end. Every language reflects the essence of a way of life, and in the case of the Indian language it is a spiritual life in which praise of the divine is more important than entreaty and in which attentive openness to religious experience is all-pervasive.

The author of "principalities and powers" could not more thoroughly believe in guardian angels, and "princes of the powers of the air," than these simple people, who never heard of Revelation; and whose Theology, though systematic and well-defined, never causes them any wars of words, or of more "carnal weapons."[10]

This experimental, detached, and thus never persecutory character of Indian devoutness is evident in Stanley Vestal's description of Sitting Bull's last years.

. . . when the agent tried to dragoon him into the Church and the system there, he found the old man "incorrigible." As to putting away one of his wives, he said, "I like both; I do not wish to treat them differently." When the ban on medicine men was discussed, he answered, "The main thing is to cure the patient; any method that works is a good one." When the missionaries urged him into the fold, he smiled tolerantly: "What does it matter how I pray so long as my prayers are answered?"[11]

Sitting Bull urged the Indians to take from the whites all the good they had to offer, and to do it with tolerance; but the tolerance proclaimed by the whites, their protestations of fraternal feeling, were flawed. This was evident when the authorities, using deceit and violence, suppressed the new Indian ghost-dance religion (very different from the one cultivated in the bare chapel Whittier had dreamed of, which was actually imposed on the Indians in the name of tolerance). Sitting Bull inspired the ghost dancers with the power to see their dead by moving an eagle's feather over their faces.[12] Later on came the peyote cult, which was also opposed. Of course, just before this, traditional tribal priests opposed to the peyote cult had been persecuted in the name of progress and tolerance (the benefits from both being deferred till the day the Indian became completely civilized).

∴

Stimulated by the Iroquois Ely S. Parker, who had been Lewis H. Morgan's inspirer, the poet Harriet Maxwell Converse followed in Leland's footsteps. Her dedication led to her initiation into an esoteric fraternity, or Medicine Society, and later into the Seneca tribe. She died in 1903, honored by the funeral lamentations of the Iroquois, and leaving behind her notebooks, which Arthur Caswell Parker edited and published.[13]

She defended the Iroquois against the old accusation of devil worship, testifying that the fraternities gave not the slightest sign of evil influences: "Their chants are entirely free from human passions or grossness of superstitions. In fact, if a member evidences a spirit of evil, he is excluded from the meetings, until he is purified." The Iroquois do not know profanity or obscenity and, in contrast to the whites, "do not understand the efficacy of prayer with a view to material things." Harriet Converse described her own initiation into the fraternity, which transmitted from generation to generation a medicine composed of parts of animals and plants in powder form.

She also wrote down a series of legends and stories, among them the legend of Hiawatha, the opponent of Ot-to-tar-ho, a mild young man who one day while out hunting kills a bird of sumptuous plumage, which, however, is poisonous to the touch. The poison transforms Ot-to-tar-ho, who becomes an enraged murderer with convulsed features, his head covered with snakes instead of hair.

The people fast and perform incantatory dances, but all in vain; the mind of the possessed man becomes so powerful that he can kill at a distance, read thoughts, dominate assemblies. Finally, he establishes his rule over the people, shattering their hearts. Only Hiawatha is able to dispel slowly the tyrannical enchantment by creating the league of the Iroquois. Harriet Converse also understood the astronomical essence of the myths, just as Haile later was to discover the spiritual astronomy of the Navajos.[14]

One myth described the Pleiades. After teaching the secrets of the forest to his eleven sons, a hunter lies down with them to sleep. Harriet Converse tells the story:

As they slept, soft singing voices floated through the still trees, nearer and nearer approaching till they awakened Hai-no-nis, the eldest of the eleven brothers. Charmed by the weird chanting, he aroused his brothers to listen to the sorcerous song, and they followed as it led through bewildering paths to a large tree where under its branches a great circle widened its moon shadows. For a time the voices ceased, but as the brothers waited, the song was resumed in a quicker strain that turned them to swift dancing till in the frenzy of its measure, they could not cease. They implored the Night Wind to guide them back to their father, but it passed heedlessly by, and the voices led the brothers still further as, delirious with motion, they danced onward and upward till they left the earth far beneath in their skyward flight.[15]

The moon later fixed them in the firmament as the Pleiades, which are celebrated at the feast of the New Year. The hunter Go-do-waas threw his magical belt into the sky and formed the Milky Way, to which he now leads souls; each star of the constellation guides a soul. Tireless hunters who, unaware of being caught in a net, continue to pursue a bear, form the Great Bear (or Big Dipper). Parker notes that both in America and in Europe the Great Bear designates this constellation. The same mental process leads to certain conclusions: the group of four stars suggests a track, the boreal crown a cave, and what animal turns on its back (in autumn and winter the constellation turns upside down) and then rises again? When it turns, the leaves grow red and yellow: a sign of the blood and fat that drain away; the stars that pursue it have killed it. It will be resurrected in the spring.

.·.

The speculative interest in Indian religious secrets was not always friendly. In *The Medicine Man of the Apache* John G. Bourke observed that the white race has been slow to learn and the redskin has not been adroit in his reticence. Fortified by his readings of Dupuis and Higgins, Bourke pointed out parallels between Indian religious customs and ancient classic mystery cults, criticizing the mistakes of Adair and Custin. His outrageous conclusion is that one must extirpate the priesthood that guards these mysteries.[16]

What will be needed to attain the truth is not merely intellectual curiosity but emotional empathy, a quality that is found in G. B. Grinnell, the first to describe in detail the method by which the Cheyenne obtain their visions. This was done by means of painfully torturing needles stuck in their skin while their eyes stared at the sun.[17] Dreaming the old dream of a dawnlike, absolute naturalness, Grinnell went into ecstasies over a Pawnee Hunt:

Here were eight hundred warriors, stark naked, and mounted on naked animals. . . . For the moment they had put aside whatever they had learned of civilization. Their bows and arrows they held in their hands. Armed with these ancestral weapons, they had become once more the simple children of the plains, about to slay the wild cattle that Ti-rá-wa had given them for food. Here was barbarism pure and simple. Here was nature. . . .

Each naked Indian seemed a part of his steed, and rose and fell with it in the rhythmic swing of its stride. The plain was peopled with Centaurs. Out over each horse's croup floated the long black hair of his rider, spread out on the wings of the breeze. Gradually the slow gallop became a fast one. The flanks of the horses showed here and there patches of wet, which glistened in the slanting rays of the westering sun.[18]

What a difference in tone between this thirst for sensual barbarism and Victorian times, when William G. Simms, writing about the close-fitting garments introduced by the whites, remarked that the Indian ". . . until this improvement . . . had been compelled, in battle or the chase, to throw aside the cumbrous covering which neutralized his swiftness and to exhibit himself in that state of perfect nudity, which was scarcely less offensive to the Indian than to more civilized communities."[19]

Grinnell persuaded these mythical and at the same time very real beings to tell him their stories. Though he did not succeed in penetrating their mystical life, he nevertheless understood the "perfect ignorance" that afflicted the public. And since he noted down the Pawnee tales with great exactness, he preserved precious vestiges of their mystical world. Thus the story of "The Boy Who Was Sacrificed" reads like an introduction to the mysterious origin of sacred immolations.

There was a time, far back, when some people thought that it was good to sacrifice to Ti-rá-wa whatever they had that was most precious to them. The sacrifice of the animal, the burnt offering has always been made by all the Pawnees. . . . The Skidi have always performed the sacrifice of the captive. Each one of these is sacred and solemn, but it is not like giving up something that belongs to you, and that you love. . . . Many years ago . . . there lived a man, who believed that if he sacrificed his son to Ti-rá-wa, it would be a blessing to him. He thought that if he did this thing, perhaps Ti-rá-wa would speak to him face to face . . . and that in this way he would learn many things that other people did not understand.[20]

The man performs the frightful deed and returns to the village, not saying a word about it to anyone. The dead boy is resurrected by the *Nahu'rac*, birds (angels, Grinnell explains) who reveal their mysteries to him through dances and endow him with healing powers. He returns to the village and from it brings back some meat for the *Nahu'rac*, who dance and confer additional powers and knowledge on him. The young medicine man never reveals what had happened: ". . . the boy never told anyone. He knew that he could never have learned all these wonderful things unless his father had sacrificed him."

This brief story encompasses a multitude of possible meanings. Everything may be seen from the viewpoint either of the father, the son, or Ti-rá-wa, who actually arranged it all; one can meditate on the relationship of prayer, sacrifice, and destiny almost endlessly. One can even read into it (more simply) an edifying discourse on the essence of pedagogy and the heterogenesis of goals.

Another story, "The Ghost Bride," tells of a man who meets his dead bride again and wants to take her back to the village, but she tells him: "You must go first to the village, and prepare a place for me. Where I sleep, let it be behind a curtain. For four days and four nights I must remain behind this curtain. Do not speak of me. Do not mention my name to any one."[21]*

The man follows these instructions. After four days the woman comes out from behind the curtain. "His relative asked him: Who is the woman? And to avoid speaking her name, he told who were her father and mother." This breach of her instructions is enough: the girl disappears; she will not live again. That same night the young man dies in his sleep. And this is the enigmatic conclusion: "Then the people were convinced that there must be a life after this one."

What inspires the certainty of a hereafter? An absence? A death that occurs as if through a summons from the world of the dead? The possibility of resurrection if man can only avoid error and sin? Or, as a structural equation of the story would explain, the equivalence between the improbability of an impeccable innocence and the improbability of a resurrection of the dead? If so, then one can *stand for* the other, transforming the earthly desire for perpetual life and resurrection into a spiritual search for eternal life. Only by admitting the continued existence of the dead can one explain the fact that a young man vainly sends someone to look for a ghost and dies the same night. Moreover, one learns that secrecy is the sole guarantee for the fruition of spiritual experience.

Among the many stories gathered by Grinnell among the Blackfeet, "Scarface,"[22] has the same qualities. In it a young girl refuses all the most prestigious suitors and confesses to her exasperated parents: "Father! Mother! . . . Pity me. I have no secret lover, but now hear the truth. That Above Person, the Sun, told me, 'Do not marry any of those men, for you are mine. . . .'"

One day a miserable young man with a scar on his cheek is being mocked by the girl's suitors; they dare him to go and propose marriage to the haughty girl. He does so, and she consents, but first he must obtain

---

* Among the Blackfeet and the Cheyenne, Grinnell informs us, the search for the guardian angel entailed a fast of four days, which few could bear. Among the Sioux everything was divided by four: infancy, youth, maturity, old age; a bull sitting, leaping, with cow, and alone. "To die" and "to come" can merge in meaning.

the Sun's permission. As a sign that he has done so, the suitor's scar has to vanish.

The betrothed man sets out on his journey to the Sun. An old woman presents him with provisions. First, he meets the wolf, who sends him to the bear, who sends him to the badger, who sends him to the wolverine. By now the pilgrim is exhausted, but the wolverine comes to his aid and shows him, beyond a great expanse of water, the trail that leads to the Sun. On the bank he collapses in despair, but two swans offer to ferry him across. On the other side he sees weapons, a bow and a quiver, but he does not touch them, and behold, there appears before him a young man of great beauty, who praises him for not touching them and, revealing himself to be Lucifer, the son of the Sun, takes him into his father's house. There he is welcomed by Lucifer's mother, the Moon, and the Sun, having returned after sunset, entrusts Lucifer to him. He must not let Lucifer approach the great water, where other sons of his have already been devoured by ferocious birds. In exchange, the Sun consents to his marriage to the girl and adds: "I am the only chief. Everything is mine. I made the earth, the mountains, prairies, rivers, and forests. I made the people and all the animals. . . . I can never die. True, the winter makes me old and weak, but every summer I grow young again." He also shows him how he should have his wife build him a cosmic lodge, with a steam bath that represents the sky, painted half red to symbolize the sun, half black to symbolize the night. And he adds that between heart and brain, the latter, which never lies, is the better. The young man returns to earth by the trail of the wolf (the Milky Way), and the married couple lives happily ever after.

A wealth of cosmological and spiritual meanings is contained in this hermetic little fable. The several stages of meditation are marked by the encounters with the various helpful animals. Lucifer, for instance, represents the occasion for dangerous risk, and the Sun, as in every tradition, is the symbol of intellectual knowledge.

In *The Iroquois* (1855), Minnie Myrtle had noted: "It is very difficult for a stranger to rightly understand the morale of their stories, though it is said by those who know them best, that to them the story was always an illustration of some important event or principle." Grinnell responded emotionally to this illustrative background, though he never understood it.

From the same sympathy and the same limitations came the strength and fragility of the accounts, similar to Grinnell's, furnished by Walter McClintock, who was adopted by the Blackfeet and wrote about them in *Old Indian Trails* (1910) and other books. The narrative pace of certain descriptions of winter vigils brought to life by storytellers is also similar to Grinnell's, and the solemnity of his adoption into the tribe manages to come through despite his diligently Victorian, descriptively slovenly style. This, for example, in his book *The Old North Trail* (1968), is a moment of the ritual whose solemnity can be guessed at rather than re-experienced through subtle, rhythmic affinities (the effect of the relative clauses is actually downbeat).

> Taking a sacred stick decorated with red paint, representing a cane, Mad Wolf placed it upon his right and left shoulders in turn, and prayed for long life. Blessed Weasel did likewise, handing the cane to me. I laid it upon both of my shoulders while they prayed that I might live to be old. . . . Mad Wolf brought forth a small buckskin bag from which he took some red clay, the sacred paint which the Blackfeet believe has power to ward off sickness and to bring long life. . . . There was an impressive silence as he motioned to me and said: "Here comes my white son." While kneeling before him, he painted my face on the forehead, chin and both cheeks, representing the Sun's daily course through the heavens. The forehead represented the rising, and the left cheek the setting Sun. Then taking the beaver skin, he passed it down both sides of my head, shoulders and arms to the hands, ending with an upward movement by which he imparted his blessing and prayed. . . .[23]

Work closely akin to Grinnell's was done in the Southwest by Charles F. Lummis, a Yankee, who, during his long trek from Ohio to California in 1884, visited San Ildefonso, where he was deeply moved and impressed by the grace and hospitality of the Indians. He returned in 1888, living among the Tewas of Isleta, and was the first white man to descend into a kiva, the underground ceremonial chamber. In a sketch he described his awed reverence before the nine chiefs, who displayed qualities of beauty, grace, rationality, and authority. The magazine *Out West,* which Lummis edited in California, defended the Hopi Indians in accents that recall those of Captain Bonneville:

> These people are far more law-abiding, and far more religious, than any American community whatever . . . and not only their dances, but the planting of their fields and the harvest, the building of their houses, the lighting of their fires, even their smoking, are sacraments.[24]

But in a sketch on the Navajo medicine men included in *Mesa, Cañon and Pueblo* (New York–London, 1925), he related their exploits in a tone of banal superiority. He observed that they must perform before people whose eyes are "incomparably less easy to fool than ours," but who have a much narrower "intellectual horizon." And with an amazement reminiscent of Schoolcraft's he added that even they are convinced that they are aided by supernatural forces. Finally, he listed the things that he had seen and that could not be explained: they make lightning flash and thunder roll in a room; they go on a hunt for wandering evil spirits and come back bearing certain small beings similar to fetuses, tiny witches killed by arrows that have pierced them through and through. "Of course they are manikins of some sort; but the deception is sickeningly perfect." They fling themselves into the fire and swallow swords; they dance, and a feather stuck in a basket follows each of their movements; by observing certain leaves in the spring, they can foretell the harvest; they give their blessing with a corncob from which pours an endless cascade of grains. Lummis did not see the famous transformations into animals or the spectacles of Navajo magic: the creation of a sun that rises and circles the lodge, the planting of a seed in the earth that is made to grow during one revolution of the sun so that at midnight it appears as a full-grown plant.

∴

Mabel Dodge Luhan, a writer hampered by narcissism, and married to a Taos Indian, succeeded by her insistence in bringing D. H. Lawrence to Taos. Convinced that she was a sorceress and that she had captured Lawrence by a spell, she also intended to give herself to him, but Frieda, his wife, frustrated this wish. The whole story has been told in Mabel Dodge Luhan's book *Lorenzo in Taos*.

D. H. Lawrence, having thus been drawn to the high plateau, in "The Hopi Snake Dance," one of the sketches in *Mornings in Mexico*, penetrates to the core of Indian life. He sees it centered on the sun, the great living source of life, from which emerge "the great potencies . . . Dragons, Rain, Wind, Thunder, Shine Light." From these potencies, "emerge the seeds of life itself, corn, and creatures like snakes." The richest creature of all is man, "the highest thing created, smelted between the furnace of the Life-Sun, and beaten on the anvil of the rain, with hammers of thunder and bellows of rushing wind."

Lawrence perceived the presence of the wronged and afflicted Indian in the spirit of the American earth, in the strange brutality that emerges from it; similar perceptions are found in Hart Crane, who in his poem *The Bridge*[25] presents allegorical visions similar to those of Blake (or

Shelley). He sees the American earth in an emblematic Pocahontas, akin to the Hertha of German mythology:

> Papooses crying on the wind's long mane
> Screamed redskin dynasties that fled the brain,
> —Dead echoes! But I knew her body there,
> Time like a serpent down her shoulder, dark,
> And space, an eaglet's wing, laid on her hair.

And in order to enter into that earth spirit, to let himself be pervaded by Pocahontas, Crane must first identify himself with the Indian chief Maquokeeta, who possessed her, creating a dance of springtime that has the same frenetic pitch as Stravinsky's *Sacre du Printemps*. Just as Stravinsky did, Crane aimed at Dionysian frenzy, but a persistent skepticism vitiated this effect the more he turned to it as a stimulant for the desired ecstasy:

> Dance, Maquokeeta! snake that lives before,
> That casts his pelt, and lives beyond! Sprout, horn!
> Spark, tooth! Medicine-man, relent, restore
> Lie to us—dance us back the tribal morn!

"Lie to us" has the same quality of affectation that led Oscar Wilde to wear a green gardenia in his buttonhole, and could easily be a line from *Salomé*. The dry, stripped context should not deceive us.

Crane participates voluptuously in the torture of the Indian chief, the Dionysian immolation that opens up the road to Pocahontas and fertility—to the rhythmic uprush of life.

Indeed, never before has the setting of aboriginal America been so completely imagined, or seen by the white man's eye with such "Indian" attentiveness. Though Crane could not help being a child of his time, he came close to capturing the aboriginal truth:

> Over how many bluffs, tarns, streams I sped!
> —And knew myself within some boding shade:
> Grey tepees tufting the blue knolls ahead,
> Smoke swirling through the yellow chestnut glade. . . .
>
> A distant cloud, a thunder-bud—it grew,
> That blanket of the skies: the padded foot
> Within,—I hear it; 'til its rhythm drew,
> —Siphoned the black pool from the heart's hot root!

The resemblance of Lawrence and Crane in this quest for ecstatic rhythms is obvious. Yet both men are much more the disciples of

Nietzsche, who counterposed the spirit of the earth to that of the heavens, than of the Indians they admired.

∴

There is a neglected corpus of work from the first part of the twentieth century that has a power equal to any of these famous revelations: the fiction and essays of Mary Austin.

D. H. Lawrence, who met her in Taos in 1923, mocked her in an unfinished play, *Altitude*,[26] and showed her intoning *Om* like a Hindu holy man as she faces the sun and then commenting with unrestrained pedantry on all the smallest incidents of the day. Is the fire being lit? It is a homage to the god of fire, the task of the woman in the house, of the man in the fields. Is there anyone who is unaware of these truths? If so, he has need of a Feminine Mediator or Redeemer. Is food being cooked? No, this is worship at an altar. And when an Indian comes in, she immediately points out that he is a burning coal, while the Anglos are burned-out ashes. He feels the rhythm of the earth. All this is intolerable, but no more so than D. H. Lawrence at his most vulgar.

Mary Austin, who was born in Illinois in 1868 and died in 1934, lived for a long time in the California desert near the Shoshones and Paiutes before settling in Santa Fe. In 1903 she published *The Land of Little Rain*, depicting the arid soil and its plants "turning their foliage edgewise toward the sun, growing silky hairs, exuding viscid gum. The wind, which has a long sweep, harries and helps them . . ."; its quadrupeds and insects, ". . . strange, furry, tricksy things dart across the open places, or sit motionless in the conning towers of the creosote"; its sultriness, ". . . the air breathes like cotton wool. Through it all the buzzards sit on the fences and low hummocks, with wings spread fanwise for air. . . . Their heads droop, and all their communication is a rare, horrid croak."[27]

The Shoshones live in a volcanic landscape that resembles the mouth of Avernus: ". . . old red cones of craters, wasteful beds of mineral earths, hot, acrid springs, and steam jets issuing from a leprous soil. After the hills the black rock, after the craters the spewed lava, ash-strewn, of incredible thickness, and full of sharp, winding rifts," encircled by blue-gray bluffs, "blue because thickly wooded with *ceanothus* and *manzanita*." These are rare, singing words that would have delighted the English brought up on Pater, just as they were enchanted by the landscape of accursed Syrtis. Yet how many writers would have been capable

of combining this sumptuous material with a taste for the starkest incisiveness, describing the *manzanita* as "thorny, stocky, close-grown and
iron-rooted"? Mary Austin is rich and precious, but never self-indulgent
or languid, never enamored of rarity as an end in itself. The same stylistic
privilege can be seen in T. E. Lawrence.

The Shoshones (so scorned by Irving) resemble the flora of their
region: "The solitariness of the life breeds in the man, as in the plants, a
certain well-roundedness and sufficiency to its own ends." Above all, they
enjoy prodigious springtimes: "the beginning of spring . . . is a misti-
ness as of incense smoke, a veil of greenness over the whitish stubby
shrubs, a web of color on the silver sanded soil," when their arrows strike
the quail beside the springs. They revere the sorcerer, but he knows that,
if three of his patients die, his life must be sacrificed. Every ailment that
is not a wound or a dislocation is caused by a spell that he must know
how to break.

Near them live the Paiutes, who "have the art of reducing life to its
lowest ebb and yet saving it alive on grasshoppers, lizards, and strange
herbs." She describes them in "The Basket Maker," a story that presents a
portrait of Seyavi, an artist who weaves baskets. Each moment in her
work is ritualistic, beginning with the cutting of the willows: "Twice a
year, in the time of white butterflies and again when young quail ran
neck and neck in the chapparal, Seyavi cut willows for basketry by the
creek where it wound toward the river against the sun and sucking
winds." She does not weave the baskets for money but out of dedication,
often burning them in honor of the dead. Now she is blind and is going to
die and enjoys wrapping herself up in her shroud:

> So in her blanket Seyavi, sometime basket maker, sits by the unlit hearths of
> her tribe and digests her life, nourishing her spirit against the time of the
> spirit's need, for she knows in fact quite as much of these matters as you who
> have a larger hope, though she has none but the certainty that having borne
> herself courageously to this end she will not be reborn a coyote.[28]

Among the stories about mountain flora, where the luxuriant, chaste
style creates a feeling of sober inebriation, one story, "Other Water
Borders," contains a passage that shows how much Mary Austin had
learned from the Indians:

> The Indian never concerns himself, as the botanist and the poet, with the
> plant's appearances and relations, but with what it can do for him. It can do
> much, but how do you suppose he finds it out; what instincts or accidents

guide him? How does a cat know when to eat catnip? Why do western bred cattle avoid loco weed, and strangers eat it and go mad? One might suppose that in a time of famine the Paiutes digged wild parsnip in meadow corners and died from eating it, and so learned to produce death swiftly and at will. But how did they learn, repenting in the last agony, that animal fat is the best antidote for its virulence; and who taught them that the essence of joint pine (*Ephedra nevadensis*), which looks to have no juice in it of any sort, is efficacious in stomachic disorders. But they so understand and so use. One believes it to be a sort of instinct atrophied by disuse in a complexer civilization. I remember very well when I came first upon a wet meadow of *yerba mansa*, not knowing its name or use. It *looked* potent; the cool, shiny leaves, the succulent, pink stems and fruity bloom. A little touch, a hint, a word, and I should have known what use to put them to.

Quite understandably, someone who knew her wrote:

Mary Austin was not only gifted with a degree of ESP, but she practiced some kinds of homely "magic" she had doubtless learned from her Indian friends. Again and again she recurs to her intimacy with the Paiutes. From them, she tells us, she learned how to write.[29]

Mary Austin wrote the history of aboriginal American literature for the *Cambridge History of American Literature*. In the final chapter of this history she describes not only the transcription of indigenous material in works like Frank Hamilton Cushing's *Zuñi Folk Tales* but also Indian influences that, unknown to some authors, permeate certain of their works. They can be seen in some of Mark Twain's prose burlesques or in the epitaphs of Edgar Lee Masters' *Spoon River*, which have a pithy gravity and a preference for the succinct phrase.

The Uncle Remus fables must also be included in this literature infused with an aboriginal spirit:

Joel Chandler Harris did not himself know, when he wrote them, that his Br'er Rabbit and Br'er Fox were original Cherokee inventions. In the reports of the Bureau of Ethnology, where you will find their Amerind forebears, the tales have a grim quality, a *Spoon River* quality, which to our understanding misses the humouresque which they had to the Indian.[30]

Here are spanned the two extremes of the gamut over which Mary Austin's work ranged effectively. For though she was an exquisite writer of prose in *The Land of Little Rain* and a rigorous essayist, her novels and her play *The Arrow Maker* were woefully inept. When she was involved in novelistic or theatrical creation, her obsession as a protesting feminist—not merely sentimental but often petulant—had a distorting effect. In *Outland* narcissistic exaltation and fantasizing smother the storytelling intention. *The Arrow Maker* (1911) is the appropriate descendant of the clumsy series of Indian dramas originating in 1766. A priestess does not want to remain chaste. She falls in love with a warrior and helps him to become chief of the tribe. When she repents and asks the gods for the return of her magical powers, the beloved man, who benefited from her help and yet betrayed her, fears the consequences and kills her. The preface that Mary Austin wrote for this abominable play, however, is an extraordinary refutation of those distorted vitalistic and decadent notions which look for the violence of "primitive" passions in the Indian, just as Stendhal looked for a similar violence in the Italian woman.

We are always hearing from the people farthest removed from it, of "great primitive passions," when in fact what distinguishes the passions of the tribesmen from our own, is their greater liability to the pacific influence of Nature and their greater freedom from the stimulus of the imagination. . . . The two greatest themes of modern drama, love and ambition, are modified, the one by the more or less communal nature of tribal labour, the other by the plain fact that in the simple, open-air life of the Indian the physical stress of sex is actually much less than in conditions called civilized.[31]

After this plain and peremptory refutation, what remains of the imaginary Indian on whom the morbid, Alexandrian excitations of the devotees of "primitive passion" are foisted?

But why should the author of a minor masterpiece like *The Land of Little Rain* be unable to meet the test of the play and novel? Her humanitarian, "ameliorative" viewpoint had not been wholly burned away by the air of the California desert, and when she returned to a polluted atmosphere, these banal ideologies weighed her down. The sorceress in *The Arrow Maker* speaks as if she had absorbed the slogans of the feminist press and the tense, breathless ideology of the "common man." An old Indian woman is made the mouthpiece for modernist complaints against sacerdotal virginity ("Why should she not have a husband and children as other women? How can she go before the gods for us until she knows what we are thinking in our hearts?"), and the heroine is given to exclamations straight out of the mass-circulation ladies' magazines: "Oh, I am weary of the friendship of the gods! If I have walked in the midnight and heard what the great ones have said, is that any reason I should not know what a man says to a maid in the dusk? . . . " The alternation of registers of so different a quality is disconcerting, all the more so since in the years following she was to write her most subtle book-length essay, *The American Rhythm*.[32]

Rhythm is the innermost vital reality, shaping the form of every substance that stamps an imprint, "leaves a track, a mold, by which our every mode of expression is shaped." Man is a web of pulsations or physiological and psychic rhythms—"an orchestration of rhythms which, subjectively coordinated, produce the condition known as well-being."

The rhythms of the human organism "are given by the blood and the breath. What is the familiar iambus but the *lub*-dub, *lub*-dub of the heart, what . . . the trochee but the inhibition of the blood by the smaller vessels?" All organs have their specific rhythm, and rhythm is a factor in thought formation, particularly in the poetic quest: "The poet falling into it [a rhythm] will find the whole sum of sensory material enriched by association."

These rhythmic forms, invisible substance of the visible, are for the Indian the most vivid, palpable reality. He perceives binary rhythm (systole and diastole, rising and subsiding) as the essence of the universe, the law of symmetry and of opposites.

And are not Taker and Holder the protagonists of the first drama, even as the Amerind conceived them, Ahayuta, Matsalema, the eternal Twin Brethren, right and left hands of the Sun Power? One of them pulls the life-force up through the dust to corn, and the other pulls the corn back to dust.

This is the source of all art:

If we go back in the history of the dance we find the pattern by which men and women, friends and foes, welded themselves into societies and became reconciled to the Allness. Here we find economy of stress giving rise to preferred accents, and social ritual establishing the tradition of sequence.

Man probably first danced out of a deep sense of well-being:

Thus he discovered that, by the making of rhythmic movements and noises, power comes. The senses are keyed up. That mysterious awareness of his prey, the instant intake and response to the environment, which is traceable to no discoverable sense, but is of the utmost importance to the hunting kind, appreciates. . . . Man learned to resort to the dance when he felt helpless or fragmentary. . . . As he learned to know such states of psychic completion for states of power, he danced for the sake of the meal or the mate. Who can doubt that the Allness is moved by our singing, since it immediately begins to throb in us as the dance progresses? Will not the corn fill out in the ear even as the soul fills?

Thus magical practice is born as the art of producing appropriate rhythms. For the Indian,

streams of impressions of perennial freshness flow across the threshold of sense, distinct, unconfused, delicately registering, *unselected*. . . . It is this impersonal extension of the faculty of awareness which has brought the Indian the reputation of superior sense perception, which is not borne out by scientific tests of sense reaction. The Indian sees no better than the white man, but he sees more, registers through every sense, some of which have atrophied in us. . . . It is upon this enlarged reservoir of sensory impressions that he draws in his poetic dance dramas, every one of which comprises an orchestration of subjectively coordinated rhythms which the white man cannot always perceive and not easily resolve into mathematical indices.

Mary Austin introduces us, by means of brief scenes, into that polyrhythmic world. One winter at the Tesuque pueblo, while watching the Eagle dancers, she saw how they, feeling the wind through the tips of their wingstretched plumes, wove that rhythm into the pattern of their ancient dance, "to the great appreciation of the native audience."

The Indian responds to his own inner life and expresses it in rhythms that then combine with the rhythms of the environment. He feels that "the fringes of his consciousness are lapped by ripples of energy that proceed from the life process going on within himself." These pulsations, the reverberating motions of the universe, are influenced by rhythms corresponding to the reality one intends to evoke. This art of suggestion is known to Indian medicine men much more fully than to our psychologists, even though they may be unable to formulate its principles in Western terms.

The secret of their power is simply the inflexible, concentrated will:

In the making of magic spells . . . it is important to exclude everything but the goal of intimate desire. Even as the mother keeps out of her lullaby all color of anxiety or impatience, so the magic maker allows no doubtful or contradictory concept to intrude in the composition of the spell.

Mary Austin described several magical ceremonies, among them a Paiute ceremony in which, after a purely instrumental prelude, the voice of the narrator rose, hovering like a bird in flight above the melody: "Over it, the narrative rode like a bird on running water, now carried by it, now putting its wings down for a firm forward stroke. . . ."

∴

Frances Densmore had been collecting Indian songs since 1910, record-
ing them among the Chippewas.* One of them was the chant of the Mĭdé
(Grand Medicine) society:[33]

>In form like a bird
>It appears.
>
>The ground trembles
>As I am about to enter.
>My heart fails me
>As I am about to enter
>The spirit lodge.
>
>The sound of flowing waters
>Comes toward my home.
>
>Now and then there will arise
>Out of the waters
>My Mĭdé brethren
>The Otters.
>
>Beautiful as a star,
>Hanging in the sky,
>Is our Mĭdé lodge.

In 1915 she had recorded chants of the last of the Teton Sioux. The
following chant was intoned while painting one's body for battle:[34]

>At the center of the earth
>I stand
>Behold me
>At the wind center (where the winds blow toward me from every side)
>I stand
>Behold me
>A root of herb (medicine)
>Therefore
>I stand
>At the wind center
>I stand.

* Frances Densmore's work fills twelve volumes of the collection of the Smithsonian
Institution's Bureau of American Ethnology. Yvor Winters and Kenneth Rexroth have
praised this extraordinary work, which encompasses the music and songs of nearly all
the tribes.

Indian songs are not true songs but rather the potentiality of song. Mary Austin quotes Frances Densmore, who says that Indian song is "not a song but the stuff from which songs are made."

This is a Paiute "Song in Time of Depression":

> Now all my singing Dreams are gone
> But none knows where they are fled
> Nor by what trails they have left me.
>
> Return, O dreams of my heart
> And sing in the summer twilight
>
> . . . .
>
> By the creek and the almond thicket
> And the field that is bordered with lupins!
>
> Now is my refuge to seek
> In the hollow of friendly shoulders,
> Since the singing is stopped in my pulse
> And the earth and sky refuse me;
> Now must I hold by the eyes of a friend
> When the high white stars are unfriendly.
>
> Over sweet is the refuge for trusting;
> Return and sing, O my Dreams,
> In the dewy and palpitant pastures,
> Till the love of living awakes
> And the strength of the hills to uphold me.

This is an admirable Shoshone song, also in Mary Austin's version:

> Come not near my songs,
> You who are not my lover,
> Lest from out that ambush
> Leaps my heart upon you!
>
> When my songs are glowing
> As an almond thicket
> With the bloom upon it,
> Lies my heart in ambush
> All amid my singing. . . .[35]

Mary Austin pointed to some parallels in Western literature. Did not Dickens give voice to a similar free, rhythmic song when deeply perturbed by the death of Little Nell? Did not John Livingston Lowes find traces of such lyrical outbursts in Hardy and Meredith? And have not

many representatives of the new poetry returned to the Indian conception of poetry? "Is it," she asks, "the 'polyphonic prose' which Miss Lowell
found lurking in a dim, ancestral corner of her mind, and brought
forward as a new discovery?"

Mary Austin was the only one to comprehend the living theory of
Indian rhythm, where others described only its outward appearance.
Dorothy Brett, for instance, in her book on D. H. Lawrence, regards the
cult of rhythm at Taos as mere local color:

> No sound, not a twig moves, the Indians are sitting in a row on a log, facing
> the setting sun. One of them rises and throws a great log on the fire, the flames
> leap high. The Indians are softly beating a small hand-drum, like a tambourine,
> and singing in their strange, haunting voices to the setting sun. As the light
> fades, we all slip into shadow. The firelight catches your red beard and white
> face, bringing it suddenly out of the darkness. You are brooding, withdrawn,
> remote. Remote as the group of dark Indians are remote in their ecstasy of
> singing, the firelight playing on their vivid blankets, the whites of their eyes. I
> am caught and held by your brooding face. All of us are caught and held by
> the rhythm, the Indian rhythm, as if the very earth itself were singing.[36]

Neither does Margot Astrov, editor of *The Winged Serpent,* an anthol-
ogy, go beyond a vitalistic, Lawrencian interpretation of Indian songs.
But the first comments in her introductory essay continue the discourse of
The American Rhythm:

> When Old Torlino, a Navajo priest of *hozónihatál,* was about to relate the
> story of creation to Washington Matthews, he made the following pronounce-
> ment, addressing as it were his own conscience, solemnly affirming that he was
> going to tell the truth as he understood it. And he said:
>
>> I am ashamed before the earth;
>> I am ashamed before the heavens;
>> I am ashamed before the dawn;
>> I am ashamed before the evening twilight;
>> I am ashamed before the blue sky;
>> I am ashamed before the sun.
>> *I am ashamed before that standing within me which speaks with me.*
>> Some of these things are always looking at me.
>> I am never out of sight.
>> Therefore I must tell the truth.
>> *I hold my word tight to my breast.*

This declaration is nothing but a succinct statement of the Indian's relation
to the "word" as the directing agency that stands powerfully behind every

"doing," as the reality above all tangible reality. It is the thought and the word that stand face to face with the conscience of the native, not the deed.[37]

An educator and poet, Eda Lou Walton, collected and transposed Navajo and Blackfoot prosody in *Dawn Boy* (New York, 1926) without, however, achieving more striking results than the other translators, as may be seen in the "Prayer for Harvest":

> I enter into the House of the Red Rock
> Made holy by visiting gods,
> And into the House of Blue Water
> I am come.
> Enter me, Spirit of my forgotten Grandmother,
> That curtains of rain may hang
> All dark before me,
> That tall corn may shake itself
> Above my head.[38]

Because of his study of Celtic magic (and his association with the mystical society, the Golden Dawn), W. B. Yeats was the one poet to unfold and develop that mystery. "The purpose of rhythm," he says in *Ideas of Good and Evil,*

it has always seemed to me, is to prolong the moment of contemplation, the moment when we are both asleep and awake, which is the one moment of creation, by hushing us with an alluring monotony, while it holds us waking by variety, to keep us in that state of perhaps real trance, in which the mind liberated from the pressure of the will is unfolded in symbols. If certain sensitive persons listen persistently to the ticking of a watch, or gaze persistently on the monotonous flashing of a light, they fall into the hypnotic trance; and rhythm is but the ticking of a watch made softer, that one must needs listen, and various, that one may not be swept beyond memory or grow weary of listening; while the patterns of the artist are but the monotonous flash woven to take the eyes in a subtler enchantment.[39]

Mary Austin strove to graft Imagism onto the trunk of magical Indian chants,* and one issue of the magazine *Poetry* was devoted to the mirage of an indigenous revival in the heart of white American culture, taking its inspiration from D. H. Lawrence. There is permanent value in her intuition of the mystical character of every Indian song, the contemporary of every archaic age in which art still lived in the womb of the "Great Mystery" and had a practical, psychic purpose, establishing contact with

---

* In her preface to *The Path on the Rainbow* Mary Austin declared that the Imagist revolution resumed poetic discourse at the point where the last witch doctor had interrupted it.

the rhythm of those things that occasion song. This rhythm carries us into the impersonal world of which the comment of John E. Brown speaks and which Mary Austin quotes so appropriately:

It is this inherent power of poetry to raise the psychic plane above the accidents of being, which gives meaning to the custom of the Death Song. As he sees his moment approaching, the Indian throws himself, by some profound instinct of self-preservation, into the highest frame of mind attainable.[40]

Hence the Indian's indifference to the effect that a composition has on others, and, above all, the stenographic character of indigenous poetry, which is "a phrase out of the heart of the situation." The singer weeps by singing, though not for what he enunciates but rather for what the words bring to mind. Mary Austin compares it to the "death song" on the cross, the quotation from the Psalm: "Why hast thou forsaken me?" No other writer, during the first part of this century has given so much thought to the essence of rhythm.

∴

In 1927 Willa Cather was staying with Mary Austin as a guest in her house at Santa Fe. She was working on a novel about New Mexico and was to succeed precisely where her friend Mary Austin, the victim of ideology, had failed so miserably.

Though inferior to her friend as an essayist, Willa Cather had greater formal vitality. In *Death Comes for the Archbishop* she encompassed in her view the Indians of New Mexico, but the core of the book is devoted to the life of a French cleric. She assimilates the luminous desert country in pages indicative of long elaboration and subsequent polishing, and defines with equal diligence the relation between the Indians and that earth:

It was as if the great country were asleep, and they wished to carry on their lives without awakening it; or as if the spirits of earth and air and water were things not to antagonize and arouse. When they hunted, it was with the same discretion; an Indian hunt was never a slaughter. They ravaged neither the rivers nor the forest, and if they irrigated, they took as little water as would serve their needs.[41]

But a screen prevents her from entering intimately into the lives of these discreet presences; only once does one hear their inner secret reverberate. The bishop takes shelter with his Indian servant Jacinto in a cave filled with a fetid, nauseating smell. Jacinto stops up a fissure in the rock wall with mud and then burns some aromatic branches. The stench is gone. He then leads the bishop to the end of a tunnel, opens up another crack, and makes him listen to the roar of a river running deep below.

The bishop would like to explore the first fissure while Jacinto sleeps, but as he is getting up he sees that the Indian has forestalled him; he is pressing his ear to the opening, his entire body flattened against the rock wall. A pit for sacrifices? The abode of a holy snake? The quavering echo of these unanswered questions is all that Cather tells us of the indigenous world. She has transformed some of Lummis's remarks on the mysteries of New Mexico into an adventurous episode.

It is not surprising that she halts at the threshold. Despite her extraordinary sensitivity, she dare not delve beyond a certain point into the mystical spirit of her characters. She does not lack love or subtlety; yet she did not want, dare, or know how to make the leap beyond the emotional life of the modern world. At the novel's apex the bishop begins to live in a time no longer circumscribed, which resembles that of certain hagiographic paintings where all the events of a life are contiguous. "He sat in the middle of his own consciousness; none of his former states of mind were lost or outgrown. They were all within reach of his hand, and all comprehensible."

This experience is presented as a human, not a religious, illumination. At the beginning of the book, half asleep, hearing the silvery peal of a bell, he sees himself in an Oriental setting. When he wakes up he remembers that the bell was brought from the East and that the *Angelus* was most likely a Templar devotion, taken over from the Moslems. Such thoughts seem to his coadjutor to lessen piety, whereas for him they increase it. They are the author's hints at something beyond the pure religious life, a kind of human knowledge of events not contained in everyday experience. This presumption of superiority is perhaps the obstacle that prevents her from accomplishing that qualitative leap not only into the Indian world, whose fearfulness and delicacy is nevertheless suggested, but into the mystical world of her protagonist.

Of course she knows a great deal about devout life and reports it with great charm. The bishop, in his early years, suffered from thirst while crossing a desert in Texas. "Empowered by long training, the young priest blotted himself out of his own consciousness and meditated upon the anguish of his Lord. The Passion of Jesus became for him the only reality; the need of his own body was but a part of that conception." Farther on he visits the Acoma pueblo on top of a cliff, an impregnable refuge. "The rock, when one came to think of it, was the utmost expression of human need; even mere feeling yearned for it; it was the highest comparison of loyalty in love and friendship." And so, thanks to contemplation of that Indian village, there is revealed the metaphor of the church as a rock, which was to nourish the poetry of T. S. Eliot.

Chapter X

———◦•◦———

The Last Decades and
Poetic Ethnography

In the period immediately after the First World War the conviction, pervasive not only in Faulkner and Hemingway but also in a long succession of commercial writers, was that the Indian possessed a secret, not indeed of a metaphysic but of a more intense reality, in which it would be exciting to be shipwrecked. However, the tradition of intellectual communion and of listening to the Indian was to be carried on by the many ethnographers turned storyteller (or storytellers nourished by ethnographic research) and by the followers of the Southwest school. Later, Edmund Wilson was to attempt to assimilate this particular approach into the categories of brilliant journalism, while John Barth and other writers adapted it to a genre of ironic Libertinism.

∴

Faulkner rejected progressivist illusions associated for him with the northern invaders and exploiters; but neither did he cling nostalgically to sentiments of gallantry peculiar to his South, traceable to the light-hearted partisans of the Stuarts. An urge for knowledge drew him to the exploration of the subtle, more mysterious and savage reality that reveals itself in moments of mortal danger, be it in hunting, war, or daring exploits, a reality at once exhilarating, saddening, and proud, creating a link between generations and by its nature assuming dashing, chivalrous forms, yet going deeper than its external trappings. Faulkner dedicated to the Indians a cycle of stories with a unitary plot; the cycle can best be viewed as an organic whole by ignoring, as was done with Cooper's Leatherstocking tales, the sequence in which the stories were written or published.

Despite the rapture and *élan* with which he tells the story, as though, like the bard of some oral epic, he were carried along by a rhythmic, tonal wave, Faulkner's taste inclines to the Baroque. The Indian world that captures his imagination is a hybrid merging with a decaying, criminal Europe. His eighteenth-century Choctaws have been corrupted by the habit of keeping Negro slaves and fall under the sway of Ikkemotubbe, later named Doom, one of their own people who has successfully steered his way through the gambling dens of New Orleans. When he becomes chief, Doom is joined by a West Indian Negro woman he seduced in New Orleans, and together with her reigns in the wreck of a gilt-corniced steamboat that he has had transported overland all the way to the center of their realm by the tribe's black slaves.

This clearing in the virgin forest, with the huge pens of the Negro slaves adorned with fetishes, the cabins of the lazy, ferocious Indians, and, at its center, the crumbling, rococo steamboat bedecked with Louis Quatorze furnishings and strewn with garbage, is a masterpiece of decadent scene setting. Here, Doom's dynasty controls the fate of the tribe; Doom is succeeded by his son Issetibbeha, and he in turn by Mokketubbe, a Mongoloid suffering from dropsy.

Fascinating people as much by his bravery as by his fierceness, Ikkemotubbe, the "founder," rides about bareback on a horse, his torso smeared with bear's grease, and vies with a white man for a girl's favors. While the tribe looks on admiringly, the two men have their bodies oiled with bear's grease mixed with mint and then go to a cave to fight their duel. It is a hole in a distant hill, from whose vicinity the spoor of wild animals turns away; even dogs refuse to enter the cave. Adolescent boys go there to test their courage beneath the cave's vaults, of which, it is said, just a whisper would be enough to bring parts of the roof down. In fact, part of the cave's roof falls on the dueling men, who help each other to get out alive; from that moment on they no longer give a thought to the girl for whom they have risked their lives.*

Doom has brought back from New Orleans some puppies and a small box of poison. He terrorizes people by killing a puppy instantly with a poisoned pellet. He then poisons the rightful chief (the Man), and the chief's son; his succession is assured. His ferocity and commanding presence are unconquerable.†

Ikkemotubbe's son goes to Paris and after his return begins decorating the barbaric seat of the small kingdom. At his death, according to the

---

* "A Courtship."   † "A Justice."

custom, his son and heir, the Mongoloid degenerate, has to sacrifice the dead man's favorite servant, a Negro who flees into the forest.* Two squat Indians enter the slave quarters, talking nostalgically about the past. "In the old days there were no quarters, no Negroes. A man's time was his own then. He had time. Now he must spend most of it finding work for them who prefer sweating to do." Astonished, they stare at the dark cabins in which the white eyeballs of the Negro slaves gleam, "wild, subdued" slaves who "would even rather work in the sun than to enter the earth with a chief." Carried on a litter, the Mongoloid monster guides the chase, which is conducted with decadent lethargy. The agile victim is finally overtaken. He asks for and is given water, and the Indians watch "his throat working and the bright water cascading . . . down his chin and breast." They wait, "patient, grave, decorous, implacable."

A century later, all that remains of the tribe is an old man, Sam Fathers, the son of a Negro slave and a Chickasaw chief, who preserves the cult of the Chickasaw past.†

Sam Fathers transmits his ineffable heritage to a white boy, consecrating him to the ferocity of the hunt, after teaching him how to kill his first deer. The boy cuts the animal's throat, and Sam

stooped and dipped his hands in the hot smoking blood and wiped them back and forth across the boy's face. Then Sam's horn rang in the wet gray woods and again and again; there was a boiling wave of dogs about them. . . . They were the white boy, marked forever, and the old dark man sired on both sides by savage kings, who had marked him. . . .

Thus the childless old man, "whose bloody hands had merely formally consecrated him," will be perpetuated in the boy's life. Since the death of Jobaker, a full-blood Chickasaw and a hermit no one but Sam dared approach, he is the last man who still feels himself to be something of an Indian.

Sam also wants to die a hermit. Faulkner's fleeting allusions capture succinctly and truthfully the vestiges of Indian life lingering on after the race's extinction in Mississippi. In the same period Hemingway, in his short story "Fathers and Sons," can do no better than describe an Indian girl with cold and sentimental lubricity; later he parodied this vein in *The Torrents of Spring*. Even William Carlos Williams, despite his good will, was handicapped by his humanitarian sentimentality and unable to penetrate the Indian world. Brief sketches of Indian women in his poetry, quotations from old chronicles in his long poem *Paterson* or his cultural essay *In the American Grain* are the traces of his application. Only the

* "Red Leaves."   † "The Old People" and "The Bear" in *Go Down, Moses*.

Aztec and Nahuatl worlds come to life under his scrutiny, and in fact he imitated the patterns of Nahuatl poetry gathered by Daniel G. Brinton.

∴

With the publication in 1929 of a masterpiece of American kitsch, Edna Ferber's *Cimarron*, commercial literature, until then the custodian of a certain wholesomeness, displays a thoroughly "decadent" tendency. The hero, Yancey, a pioneer in the Oklahoma of 1889, himself "savage and overcivilized," rather than use the savages' wretched shapes for target practice, dares to love them. His wife, however, like everyone else, has learned to keep them at a distance. ". . . Sabra had picked up odds and ends of information about these silent, slothful, yet sinister figures. She had been surprised—even incredulous—at her husband's partisanship of the redskins. It was one of his absurdities. He seemed actually to consider them as human beings." He dares even to weep over the end of the peaceful, home-loving Cherokees, who were driven from Georgia, dares even to investigate unpunished crimes in their wretched, violence-ridden Oklahoma settlement.

Yancey is a fighter for justice, the knight-errant of a nonideological democracy, beleaguered but inevitably triumphant. What's more, he has something of the Indian in his nature, and thus a touch of magic, which occasionally makes the reader's flesh creep (upbraiding a cowardly character, he summons up the unearthly cry of the aborigine—"a sound between the gobble of an angry turkey cock and the howl of a coyote").

His wife, true heroine of a decadent Western, is erotically curious about the Indians, and Yancey explains to her that they are a cold, almost passionless race. "They work themselves up, you know, at those dances. Insidious music, mutilations, hysteria—all kinds of orgies to get themselves up to pitch." Although Ferber probably does not realize it, she is evoking the horror of the witches' sabbath with its gelid, frenetic couplings; the truncated phrases and such clumsy interjections as "you know" only help to make it more sinister. And did they not use a diabolical substance at those gatherings, "the little round peyote disk or mescal button" swallowed at a ceremony that ended with the singing of an eerie song? But Yancey says that the whites have deprived the Indians of their gods, reduced the Sun to a "dying planet" and "the Stars [to] lumps of hot metal." "Man cannot live by bread alone."

His wife then stares at him questioningly, and Yancey nods his "magnificent head slowly, sadly." Besides stringing together the most pedestrian quotations, the hero of the new Western also admits to taking drugs. His love for the Indians is a facet of his Luciferian desire to accept the dark side of life, a desire that gradually, in the logical development of this literary genre, will become a blissful disintegration. In this process the Indian will assume the role of go-between, the same role that the Berber will play in Paul Bowles's *A Sheltering Sky,* or indeed any other primitive, right down to those natives of various breeds who help William Burroughs act out his tedious daydreams.

The counterhero of the novel of disintegration (and often it is a counterheroine like the protagonist in D. H. Lawrence's *The Plumed Serpent* who, in a state of utter intoxication, sinks into a fetid world of blood, death, and sensuality) defends the Indian or some other outcast with the clichés of Enlightenment humanitarianism. But actually he is defending himself while using the Indian as a screen. Thomas Morton's Libertine thought, like the water gushing from the spring of Arethusa, surfaces again in the decadent Western. The Indian is used by the "disintegrated" hero, just as he had been used by that figure's ancestors or Libertine forerunners. But this counterhero is quite remote from the Indian spirit. In *Cimarron* he interprets it as an escape into an exalted dream, as a cheap opportunity for fantasy and visceral pleasure, a mistake that will also be made by Antonin Artaud, the most mythologized of the counterheroes of programmatic disintegration, even though he understood the "philosophical" nature of Indian life.

In *Cimarron* one witnesses the collapse of the great big Western hero, whose slitlike eyes subjugated opponents and whose thoughts were few, violent, and pure. White Protestant America has begun to feel the first tremors announcing its end: "The great shoulders sagged. The splendid head lolled on his breast." Yancey's son, in love with an Indian girl, also participates in the peyote ritual. It is as though the Indians had succeeded in dragging the victors into their own death agony:

Their lips were gently smiling. Sometimes they swayed a little. The sacred fire leaped orange and scarlet and gold. Old Stump Horn wielded his eagle feather fan, back and forth, back and forth. The quavering cadences of the Mescal song rose and fell to the accompaniment of the gourd rattle and the unceasing drum.

∴

The gap between literature and ethnography, already bridged by Bandelier, was spanned again by almost all the major ethnographers.

They had been solicited by Elsie C. Parsons, who asked each of them for a story to include in her book *American Indian Life* (published in 1922), after she herself had written the biography of a typical Zuñi girl.[1] Robert H. Lowie wrote the life of the Crow Indian Takes-the-Pipe, an impeccable grab-bag of characteristic traits. Clark Wissler, using a similar method, depicts the life of the Blackfoot medicine men, Smoking-Star. He explains the overwhelming effect on the Indian caused by the effort to obtain, through the imbalance produced by intoxication, a break with the usual bonds and an experience of the transcendent. Some of them had visions during intoxication and became medicine men. Wissler comes close to understanding the trap into which the Indian fell, attracted as he was by hopes of a Dionysian liberation, for whose accomplishment, however, he had no traditional spiritual rules.

In his relating of the initiation of a Menominee into the esoteric procedure imposed by the Grand Medicine Society, Alanson Skinner brings to mind certain sections of *Hiawatha*. The master welcomes the neophyte by saying: "These songs may appear to partake of the ways of children—yet they are powerful. I understand you well; you desire to imitate the ways of our ancient Grand Master, Mä'näus, who was slain and brought to life that we might gain life unending!" Though the actual form of the ritual is diligently reproduced, Skinner's account conveys to some degree the sense of a sociable yet ritualistic white fraternity. By contrast, Paul Radin shows himself to have been moved and influenced well beyond the mere precision of material facts. In his brief profile, "Thunder-Cloud, A Winnebago Shaman Relates and Prays," the tone is struck by the awesome opening chord: "I came from above and I am holy. This is my second life on earth."

Thunder-Cloud fell in battle during his previous life, returned home, but realized that nobody noticed his presence and so he knew that he was dead. He tries in vain to return to his original, heavenly home and so passes through several animal existences as a fish, a bird, and a buffalo. Only after this long probation can he return to his "spirit-home," but a second birth as a man tempts him. He subjects himself to a long fast in order to obtain the consent or mandate of the superior powers, even those as high as the fourth heaven. They put him to the test in the center of the earth, and he succeeds in magically killing an almost invulnerable bear. (It is with delight that one meets here the theme of alchemical regeneration in the bowels of the earth that lies at the core of Tasso's *Jerusalem Delivered,* placed again at the core of an adventure reminiscent of the Greek Orphic and Pythagorean practices as we know them from Plato's

Phaedo and the Empedoclean prescriptions.) Thunder-Cloud is shown capable of resuscitating the bear, or piercing a stone with his breath. These feats are proof that he knows how to cure with his breath and heal with his saliva (as he was taught by an eel living at the bottom of the ocean). Thus he proceeds to his reincarnation: "I thought that I had entered a lodge, but it was really my mother's womb I had entered."

After a clumsy, fanciful opening, M. R. Harrington sketches the usual yet vivid story of a quest for vision in "The Thunder-power of Rumbling-wings" (in Elsie C. Parsons's *American Indian Life*). The boy in the story is harshly treated by his parents, who wish to force him to become an exile, an outcast on whom the spiritual powers will look with pity. He departs for his tormenting retreat. On his return his father explains to him in detail all of his dream's symbolic meanings, and the revelation burst upon him with the impact of an exciting dénouement.

Among the various ethnographers of Arizona and New Mexico only Alfred Louis Kroeber achieved the level of literature in the savage, grim biography of *Earth-Tongue, a Mohave*. For good reason the Mohaves' conception of the witch doctor's nature is distinctly gloomy and fearful; although Kroeber does not seem to be consciously aware of this, he transmits it to us quite unmistakably.

In addition to her ethnographic works Alice Marriott wrote a series of sketches, *Greener Fields* (1953), in the gently humorous style favored by *The New Yorker* magazine. Still, a veneration for the Indian world predominates, and the difficulty of ever penetrating its religious secrets is made obvious. Elizabeth, a completely indifferent and assimilated Kiowa, is suddenly shown accepting the world of invisible presences, exemplified in the "ten grandmother gods" (they "work rather like vacuum cleaners. They suck up all the evil that might come to the tribe. . . ."). In another of Alice Marriott's books, *Ten Grandmothers*,[2] memorable stories about the Kiowa are gathered, in which ethnological fidelity is united with an unalloyed aesthetic strength unhampered by a preoccupation with entertainment. These are succinct, spare sketches recalling Hemingway's short stories. This, for example, is the beginning of a war party: Sitting Bear, the chief, makes a speech before the young men leave and sings the song of the Crazy Dog, since they all ought to fight as bravely as Crazy Dogs:

> I live, but I will not live forever,
> Mysterious moon, you only remain,
> Powerful sun, you alone remain,
> Wonderful earth, you remain forever.

Then the women make their throaty war whoop that "fairly lifted the young men into their saddles."

After days of prayer, weeping, and fasting a young man achieves his vision:

Sometimes tears were running down his face when he was praying; sometimes his eyes were dry and burning, and there seemed nothing left in the world but him and the heat of the sun that was sucking him dry.

It was just at daybreak that he heard the voice—daybreak that was coming very slowly, not shoving the night aside like the earlier dawns he remembered at this place, but trying to slip past the darkness and get into the world without being noticed.

The voice was like the light. It slipped into his mind from somewhere, and it seemed all around him yet nowhere. . . . He had to work hard, trying to make his mind make words of the tiny sounds. At last they came.

"Look down," the voice was saying. "Look in the grass at your feet. That's where a man must look for power. He has to make himself humble before it will come to him."

It seemed hard work to pull his eyes down from the edge of the world and the seeping light to the ground directly in front of him, but he did it.

There then appears before him a little lizard who tells him by sign language to imitate it, becoming as if invisible by dint of being unnoticeable, indistinguishable—like anything else that grows. Other powers will then come to him to teach him and confer their power on him.

∴

In *An Anthropologist at Work,* Ruth Benedict's book edited by Margaret Mead (1959), several essays of high literary value stand out among the ethnographic dryness. The Indians lament the ravaging of their homeland; the white man stripped the earth bare and polluted the rivers that were the spirits' abodes. White men purchased land for prestige. Indians purchased songs for that purpose, songs attained perhaps through fasting and self-torture. Men have come unscathed from arrows through the help of a song; poor boys have become chiefs. They are worth horses, beaded robes, and blankets. A Blackfoot would buy visions.

The Indian would buy magical songs to sing at gatherings of his peers; the white man yearned for a different kind of prestige, equally intangible if one examines it closely, but based on "progress" and the "glories of civilization."

Ruth Benedict defends the cannibal by contrasting the bleak ferocity of the whites to the devoutness with which the Indian devoured the hearts of heroes who, confronted by instruments of torture, were capable of laughing and of singing the death song through the most terrible torments. On Vancouver Island, the cannibalistic ritual was a way to break the ecstasy.

.·.

In her book *Ishi in Two Worlds* (1961) Theodora Kroeber, wife of Alfred Louis Kroeber, somewhat awkwardly tells the story of the last solitary Indian of an exterminated tribe, the Yana. He had been living warily in the woods, untouched by contacts with the whites, when in August, 1911, worn out by hunger, he was captured by chance near a slaughterhouse in California. Terrified, but with a firm countenance, he was finally entrusted to Kroeber, with whom, after being calmed and reassured, he lived at the Institute of Anthropology.

Theodora Kroeber documents the revolting massacre perpetrated by the pioneers in California, describes the bureaucratic difficulties caused by Ishi's appearance and his slow adaptation to his new life. The best part of her book, however, is the last section, in which she outlines Ishi's calm and independent character and sets forth his judgments on the life of the whites. Like every Indian, he is his own physician, but knows only one operation, the scarification of the hunter's arms and legs to infuse him with strength. He also perforates the nasal septum in order to insert a decorative bone or a twig of laurel or juniper as protection against colds. When bitten by a rattlesnake, he ties a toad or frog on the injured flesh. He avoids sleeping naked under the moon.

The white man's diseases, Ishi believed, come from living in cramped places—automobiles, offices, even houses.

The white man seemed to him to have become excessively a victim to the ever present evil spirit, the Coyote doctor. . . . This could be due, in Ishi's opinion, to the white man's carelessness in failing to protect himself from the unwilled malignity and danger of the *sake mahale,* the woman whose moon period is upon her.[3]

Menstrual blood and corpses are the two corrupting forces against which the white man does not guard himself. Moreover, surgery seemed to Ishi a shameless presumption and anesthesia an outrage, an estrangement of the soul ("to induce sleep is to cause the soul to leave the body. . . ."). The removal of tonsils seemed to him one of the most stupid of operations, since it would be enough to smear the inside of the throat with honey and to blow ashes over the larynx.

An even more striking encounter is that of Carlos Castaneda, at the time a graduate student in anthropology at the University of California, Los Angeles. While classifying the hallucinogenic plants used by the Indians in the Southwest, he encountered a Yaqui medicine man, Don Juan, who took him under his tutelage in order to transform him, if possible, into a "man of knowledge." Out of this came *The Teachings of Don Juan, A Yaqui Way of Knowledge.* The reader immediately comes to share the opinion of Leo W. Simmons, who reviewed the work for the New York *Times,* that the narrative effects are so skillful that had it been published as a novel it would certainly have achieved fame. One could easily produce for it a fine genealogical tree, with Gérard de Nerval's *Aurélie* at its root and among its ascendant branches the Artaud of the Mexican writings and the Yeats of the prose tales.

But it is not a novel. In fact, it is accompanied by an outline of structural analysis—just enough to put the herd of lowly academics on the alert. Yet Don Juan is an excellent character (he can even be compared to Poe's Inspector Dupin and Yeats's Robartes, for, like them, he understands acutely the workings of the human mind). He leads Castaneda by the hand up the paths of Yaqui knowledge, also making use of ingestions, fumigations, and lotions made from dangerous herbs. Whoever wants to understand something about shamanistic life will find this a text of prime importance and will encounter in Don Juan an incomparable teacher. With him Castaneda travels the paths of the peyote, pipe, and lizards, experiencing visions that shake him so violently that they finally uproot him from the world he knows. At the end, Castaneda, overwhelmed by terror, ceases his investigations, but he departs with a fine hoard of discoveries.

Among other matters, Don Juan taught him that in the sphere into which he has led him what one learns depends on why one wants to learn it. In a certain sense, his entire role as a teacher is a reiteration of the maxim *respice finem:* "You must define your purpose clearly." He is not satisfied with vague words and demands a very clear goal and yearnings that are meticulously detailed. To clarify these things in one's mind one must use words, but one must also know that these words are only metaphors. It should be remembered that a proposition is true or false depending on whether the inner goal with which it must tally is true or false. To inculcate this in his pupil, Don Juan uses the methods of the Zen masters. He begins by enjoining him to "find his spot." And the pupil

must grotesquely search for it—his unmistakable spot. He will learn that
to sit on one's spot creates superior strength and happiness (something
like this is found in the medieval English mystic, Richard Rolle). Don
Juan advises him to lead "a truthful, deliberately lived life free of fear or
ambition," and imparts so vehement a faith that it transforms the mere
recital of myths into the risk of death. He also teaches him a kind of
alchemy based on simples.

But his description of the enemies that one encounters on the "path" is
certain to become classic. First of all, there is fear; everyone experiences
it (but it is better to experience it than not to have any "knowledge" of
it). He who succumbs to it will become a conceited bully or a frightened
man. But he who overcomes it will become lucid with a clarity of mind
that erases fear (without knowing it, Don Juan is quoting a Greek ecclesiastical historian, Evagrius) and gives man a knowledge of his desires.
But clarity is the second enemy; it blinds him, "forces the man never to
doubt himself." The man defeated in this way becomes a buoyant warrior, or a clown; he no longer desires to develop further. The man,
however, who regards true clarity as a mere instrument can control it.
Then he attains true power. But this, too, can change into an enemy, and
he who gives into power can be turned into a cruel, capricious man. The
man who learns that "power is only a burden upon his fate," that in
reality "power is never his," can defeat it. Here, finally, man has reached
his goal; but it is precisely here that the last enemy waits, the desire for
rest, old age. Once that is overcome, the world of knowledge opens up.

∴

Yet one must not hope for beneficial results from this diffusion of new
ethnological information on the Indian's spiritual life. The ominous
animosity first expressed in Mather's *Magnalia Christi Americana* perpetuated itself in different guises but unchangeable substance through the
eighteenth-century Enlightenment (which at the end of the nineteenth
century still shaped the minds of the Indian commissioners, who saw
their task as assisting "in the great work of redeeming these benighted
children of nature from the darkness of their superstition and ignorance . . .") and the "Caucasian" racism of the nineteenth century. In
the twentieth century this feeling becomes a sociologism which, though it
recognizes the structure of Indian civilization, sometimes in a subtle
fashion, aims at deforming it all the more effectively. Typical of this
attitude is a book of some literary value: *The Hopi Way* by Laura

Thompson and Alice Joseph. In his preface to it John Collier observes: "Does one seek to influence an individual or a group? Let him discover what is central to the being of that individual or group. . . . Remember that deep and central preoccupations, devotions and views of life can be helped to apply themselves to new practical ends." The entire series of Indian monographs published by the United States Indian Service in collaboration with the Committee on Human Development of the University of Chicago was compiled with the aim of identifying the keystone of the various Indian social edifices (Hopi, Navajo, Sioux, and Papago) in order to direct them at will.

No longer is there an attempt to denigrate Indian spiritual reality. John Collier, former Commissioner of Indian Affairs, gives full recognition to its marvels, its particular vivid and eternal time in contrast to our fragmentary and contingent time. It is absurd, he says, for anyone to imagine that he can reduce the sacred dramas of the Pueblos to nothing more than an operation to make the corn grow or to bring a sense of security to the afraid and insecure. One might as well say that all man's spiritual summits can be reduced to this banality and so admit the bankruptcy of one's capacity for perception.

In the foreword to Thompson and Joseph's monograph on the Hopis, Collier wrote:

> The nature world of the Hopi is one of the most perilous and severe of all nature worlds. The Hopi have met this changeless fact by building this difficult nature-world into the center of their psychic and social life. With the Elizabethan they could say: "Deep in that lion-haunted inland lies / A mystic city, goal of high emprise. . . ."
> The Hopi have achieved peace, and not through policing but through the disciplines and the affirmations planted within each of their several souls. . . . And the Hopi pay for their peace, severe payments.
> The Hopi, without using a single one of the forms of democracy which distinguish (and limit) the European tradition, live in democracy. . . . Though individual shortcoming may wreck the society and even the universe (so the Hopi believe) yet the individual's conduct and his thought, his emotion and his choices, are finally left to himself.[4]

Thompson and Joseph were able to capture "Hopi life": the rules of conduct that prescribe acts and thoughts for each person in every circumstance. The ceremonies that give a rhythm to Hopi life call for *na'wakna*, a "good heart," that is, the absence of anger, fear, sadness, or preoccupation; in the Hopi language *na'wakna* also means "to will" and "to pray."

Diametrically opposed to the "good heart" is the "two-heart" or witchcraft, which comes from close association with black ants, coyotes, owls, crows, dogs, cats, and bull snakes. Powers of every kind, including evil powers, are bestowed by the grandmother-spider who is poised at the center of the cosmic web. The year is a dense network of festivals that reweave the cosmos.

For the Indian, reality must be translated into rhythms. If Mary Austin was the first to understand this musicality, it was also recognized by Oliver La Farge, an Easterner who went to Santa Fe; an ethnologist and novelist, he was the author of *Laughing Boy.*[5] Music pervades the Navajo protagonist's life, and "song followed song." The state of mind that opera induces in a white audience is here an everyday matter. And, besides, this prayer is pure musicality or, according to the Navajo expression that recurs in the novel, *hozoji nashad,* "traveling in beauty." Goethe had grasped this very state, so rare in Western literature, noting how "inwardly it often seems to me that a secret genius whispers something rhythmical, so that while roaming about I move to a rhythm and at the same time seem to catch faint sounds accompanying some song which somehow appeals to me" (*Wilhelm Meister,* III, I).

La Farge's tale is dominated by the figure of a young Navajo girl determined to turn her back on her degrading "assimilated" past; she tenaciously ensnares a jeweler among her people, Laughing Boy, and becomes his wife. Meanwhile, she continues to exploit a white lover. After the first "singing" happiness, a feeling of malaise seizes Laughing Boy. What has he done? How has he strayed from the "trail of beauty?" He subjects himself to steam baths, fasts and sings, but all in vain; he senses impending disaster. Now the story becomes purely and vulgarly functional. He shoots an arrow into his wife's lover, whom he has caught on the threshold of his house, then wounds her, too, but not so severely that she cannot give him a full report on her past life and obtain his forgiveness. However, a former suitor of his wife's solves their quandary by killing her with a rifle shot.

In a stiffly contrived novel, *Enemy Gods,* La Farge narrates somewhat haphazardly the story of a young Indian, a Navajo, unrooted from his tribe to become a "civilized man." He feels his rootlessness above all when he hears his native music:

Song rose in a shining spiral, out of his mouth he created, participated in creating a substance in which the thread of his own voice ran gleaming. It was a state of being, union, submission, mastery, and outlet into which one entered, floating upwards, the drum in him and he enfolding the drum, solitary and entirely one with the others.

After having followed the path of the whites, the protagonist returns to his ancestral customs, learns the true ceremonies, and in this atmosphere even his loves are clothed in hidden meanings: "The paint on the girl disturbed him no longer, it had ceased to disguise her face and served only to set her apart. Dawn Girl, Pollen Girl, perhaps. Over her face they had drawn morning light, evening light, and soft darkness. Her hair hung down like the rain, with the eagle plumes beside it."

∴

The same translucent, aromatically scented region, rich in tradition, which had inspired Bandelier, D. H. Lawrence, Willa Cather, and Mary Austin, provides the setting for *The Man Who Killed the Deer* (1942), a novel by Frank Waters, who is both a novelist and ethnographer. Martiniano, the Indian protagonist, has been designated since childhood to go to the white man's degrading public school. Uprooted in this way from the life of Taos, he has not received initiation in the kiva, the underground ceremonial chamber in the heart of Taos. Born a rebel, he feels impervious to the fascination of that numinous spot. The opening of the novel quietly communicates the aura of absorbed, dense life in a Taos house, the ample rhythm: "The last piñon knot crumpled in the small conical fireplace. Its coals blazed redly alive, then slowly clouded over with a gray film like the eyes of a dead hawk. The white-washed adobe walls began to lose their pinkish pallor and dim outlines." A few pages later the metaphor of the eyes of the hawk returns, like a secret cadence: "Something was wrong. It tainted the air. Yet no man, shrouded in his impenetrability, betrayed himself by anxious questions. . . . Children ducked into the willows bordering the stream like baby chickens at sight of a hawk." The hawk is the symbol of the restlessness that ruffles the surface of the pueblo with its sacred planimetric layout: "The two opposite halves of the pueblo appeared like the fragments of a great headless drum, like the walls of an ancient kiva unearthed after a thousand years . . . as something living with a slow serpent-pulse. . . ." The uprooted Martiniano has killed a deer out of season and defied the forest ranger. This is but one link in a long chain of misdeeds, a sign of his disturbed state. He too will fall into the clutches of a missionary of the peyote cult that the old guardians of tradition had suppressed through public beatings. His destiny has a totem: the deer, a presence that returns again and again in his life. In some strange way it is as though from that presence Martiniano would learn how to free himself from peyote.

One of the old men says:

How is it we can forsake the four-fold world of which we are a part? From the fire element of the first world we hold the heat of animal beings. That of air gave us the breath of life. That of water produced our life-stream, our blood. And from that of the earth we derived the solid substance of our physical forms. From each of these worlds we have had our successive emergences. We are all that we have been. So we ask: what kind of religion is it which would refute that which we are; that falsely subjugates the body, inflames the mind with dreams and leads away the spirit.[6]

At the beginning of the nineteenth century the Winnebago chiefs had already taught that peyote, an infernal demon, sweeps away the ancient barriers within which the spirit is given the space to grow. The Taos road is quite different, the road to order and informed joy, and it is traveled in the dances that re-evoke Genesis, such as the dances of the Koshares:

Their loose flexible arms with gentle motion drew up the deep power from the blackness of the earth with which they were painted, drew up the hidden juices into the roots, drew up the corn shoots. Then at a change of rhythm, their heads raised. They drew down the rain like threads, drew down from the sky its star-power and moon-glow, its pink-tipped arrows of fire, its waters.[7]

The traditional religion gradually possesses Martiniano, moderates, muffles, and eventually puts an end to the turbulence of his spirit, and his return to tradition goes hand in hand with his ever more intelligent reading of the signs of his destiny. Was not his totem, the deer, incarnated in his wife? Was she not a doe in human guise and therefore of the same animal substance as that which gives its names to the Pleiades, whose hoofs form the ceremonial rattles and who "complemented at once the eagle above and the snake below; gave rise to Deer Clan and Antelope Priests, and lent the mystery of their wildness, swiftness and gentleness to all men?" And so, Martiniano, without an initiation, attains the wisdom that is imparted in the kiva: "It was like a great coiled serpent sleeping within him. Like the legendary earth-serpent of his people, heavy with wisdom and power, that someday would awake, uncoil and strike from the torn and tortured flesh the rending, screaming eagles of desire."[8]

In *The Return of the Vanishing American*, Leslie Fiedler accuses Waters of making concessions to Hollywood taste, and in fact he extracts from the novel a few sorry, stereotyped statements on the evolution or ineluctable history that will eventually destroy not only the surviving Indian civilization but also white materialism.[9] An equally vulgar aspect of the book is the sensuality—reminiscent of D. H. Lawrence—in which Martiniano's conversion is steeped. And yet the novel's extraordinary success (as well as the esteem in which it is held by the people of Taos) is fully deserved. Time and again, knowledge and charity interweave in its fabric, and Waters' pages show an early glint of the lavishly ornate style later to become the hallmark of Lawrence Durrell's Alexandria Quartet. The ability to explain the Indians' speculative principles simply is demonstrated in Waters' modest ethnological work, *Masked Gods: Navaho and Pueblo Ceremonialism.* Two sentences of his, which sum up Navajo unity of being, viewed as a system of correspondences, are eminently worth remembering: "This belief leads to associations of the most unexpected things. For example, lightning, snakes, arrows, winds, clouds, cacti, jewels, and locusts are associated in function."[10]

Later, Waters settled for some time in the small Hopi reservation in Arizona and there gathered the invaluable material that went into the making of his masterpiece, *The Book of the Hopi* (1963), in which Hopi cosmogony is revealed, their ceremonies are explained, and their esoteric conception of the centers of energy in the human body is unveiled. We owe to Waters the knowledge of a Hopi physiology of the invisible body quite similar to that of Hindu and Buddhist Tantrism.

The Indian world of New Mexico reappears in the work of William Eastlake, in whom Faulkner's image of the Indian is reflected. As Delbert E. Wylder has observed,

Eastlake's Indians are closer to Faulkner's Ikkemotubbe, Herman Basket and Crawford. . . . Eastlake has taken the Indian's distrust of change and his harmonious relationship to nature, to construct Indian characters that reflect the most ridiculous aspects of the twentieth century Anglo's frantic need for material progress with its resulting destruction of the Anglo's own psychological balance.[11]

In the scenes of *Portrait of an Artist with Twenty-Six Horses,* he succeeds in re-creating indigenous magic by showing us the Indian's singular faith in destiny, a natural faith which is the tacit premise of all the visions of succoring spirits that sustain Indian life. From this interest derive the scenes of shamanistic prophecy in his novel *Go in Beauty,* where a few memorable lines satirize the white woman who sees Picasso in Indian sand painting and instead of opening herself to the Indian's self-reliant metaphysics, indulges in psychoanalytic ponderings. "When she saw one of the Indians' sand paintings she did not think of The People, she thought of Picasso . . . and when one of the Navaho People talked to her she did not listen to what he said but wondered what went on in his subconscious."[12]

∴

Just as Waters in the Southwest used the materials offered by the prairies, so Mari Sandoz planned a series of narrative documentaries or historical novels—whatever one wishes to call them—on the Indian resistance from the arrival of the iron plow and gunpowder down to the final submission. *The Buffalo Hunters, Cheyenne Autumn, Old Jules,* and *Crazy Horse,* among other titles, compose the grand succession of books.

The fabric is dense, and the events are almost all taken from actual accounts of the survivors or culled from obscure diaries and archives. This close-packed sequence of events has the fascination of a chronicle almost palpably, implacably propelled forward by the sheer force of time. In fact, time in its inexorability is the most imposing protagonist. The major characters who emerge from the jumble of events are almost figures of pure, ineluctable time; like the cycle of seasons, they have become strong and indifferent yet nourishers of their people. Among them Crazy Horse, one of the victorious Oglala chiefs at the battle of Little Big Horn, has a certain Roman soberness—an Alberto of Giussano, the twelfth-century knight, transported to the prairies beyond the Missouri River. We follow his childhood, adolescence, and maturity step by step, all the way to his murder at the hands of the whites after the tribe has been subjugated—the same fate as that suffered by Sitting Bull. Like Black Elk, Crazy Horse lives his vision, and time and again, as his destiny gradually unfolds, it makes him foresee the situations he encounters. In the uniform and dense texture of the plot supernatural events are given no more prominence than any other; this is true even for the description of the shooting ceremony. Here, the medicine men prove themselves invulnerable to lead bullets and by ritualistic means extend their charisma to a war party. The warriors were instructed to advance against the enemy slowly, singing and holding up their palms to stop the bullets. But the enemy did not shoot; instead, a cavalry charge swept down on the Indians with drawn swords, scattering them in all directions. Even sacred moments, such as the ceremonials of the holy clowns, the *heyokas,* the thunder dreamers, stand out no more than other events in the saga.

They had let the things that protected them go too long and this spring, when the antelope were dropping their young, one of them was killed by lightning and several horses were struck. So they made the old, old ceremonials before the people, doing everything backwards and mixed up, as they must—wearing their clothes wrong side out or turned around, all singing together instead of one at a time, shivering in the heat of the sun, crawling through mudholes instead of jumping them, pointing their arrows at themselves and falling like dead when they missed, taking meat from the boiling kettles with their hands.

All these things brought much laughing to the people, made them feel new and strong, and yet among the leaders there was a splitting as when a great cloud is suddenly hit by many winds.[13]

Or: ". . . in the hostile country the time was a good one, with the cherry bushes bending black for the *wasna*, the young buffalo plentiful, and the *heyoka* making the people laugh and grow strong with the power of the thunders in the sky."[14]

By an adroit use of metaphor Mari Sandoz succeeds in evoking the atmosphere of the various places in her extremely sober chronicle: "So the wild young warriors went away like dogs caught at the meat racks."

"So the fall moved slowly by, plump and fat as a prairie dog."

"At one of the many little fresh-water lakes of the sandhill country the trails came together once more like the wing-tip feathers of an eagle."

"When another moon stood in the evening west, thin as a drawn bow . . ."

.·.

Among recent inspirations born of the encounter with the Indians one of the most felicitous is apparent in Jaime de Angulo's collection, *Indian Tales* (New York, 1953). These are re-creations and fusions of Indian legends, evolved in much the same way as *Hiawatha* in the last century. *Indian Tales* was praised by Ezra Pound, William Carlos Williams, and Marianne Moore. Born in Spain, De Angulo went to Maryland and then lived for forty years with the Indians of California, describing them in ethnographic reports[15] and translating their myths. His literary portrait of his favorite tribe appeared in the *Hudson Review* in the autumn of 1950 and was well received because of its deliberate crudity, in tune with the realistic narrative of the Hemingway period. Indeed, this somewhat brash, folklike style can be most subtly effective when one has to present things and events involving the esoteric faculties, which are bound to encounter deep resistance in the modern reader.

Blind Hall called his medicine "my poison." The Indian word is *damaagome*. Some Indians translate it in English as "medicine," or "power," sometimes "dog" (in the sense of pet dog, or trained dog). . . . Blind Hall was groaning and bellyaching about the pain in his ribs. We were sitting in the sun. "Give me a cigarette, white man. Mebbe I die. I dunno. The autocar he knock my shadow out of me . . . tonight I doctor myself, I ask my poisons. . . . I got several poisons. . . . I got Raven, he live on top mountain Wadaqtsuudzi, he know everything, watch everything. . . . I got Bullsnake, he pretty good too. . . . I got Louse, Crablouse, live with people, much friends, he tell me lots things. . . . I got Jim Lizard, he sit on rock all day, he pretty clever but not serious, he dam liar. . . .

The session in which, after the choral liturgical chants, Blind Hall evokes these presences, speaks with them, feels their replies form inside him and immediately repeats them aloud, is one of the best stories of this kind that have been told since the seventeenth century.

De Angulo's imaginative tales reweave the cycle of the coyote, the ambivalent Mercury of Indian faith, in a rhythm learned from the narrators of the period between the two World Wars, and as so often happens when a story draws on mythological archetypes—*Robinson Crusoe* and *Gulliver's Travels* are cases in point—the book was soon absorbed into children's literature.

.·.

For the first time since *The Delight Makers* a white man immersed himself in a shaman's life. I refer to the novel by N. C. McDonald, *Witch Doctor*, retitled *Shaman* in its second printing. It was also the first time that Tlingit life had been depicted. With the means of narrative rhetoric the author penetrates deeply into the minds of the people of the northern Pacific coast, whose arts, with their impressive symmetries and stylizations, whose astonishingly complex religious customs, similar to those of the Egyptians, verge on the terrifying.* And it was, finally, the first time that the comic vein was blended with a story of witchcraft and war without marring its frightful, arcane quality. True enough, some passages are too burlesque and cinematic, and at times the transposition of archaic

---

* The next year *Indian Primitive*, by Ralph W. Andrews (New York, 1960), was published: a series of sketches describing the tribes that live on the northern Pacific coast. The first report on the Northwest had been given by Alexander Ross in *Adventures of the First Settlers on the Oregon or Columbia River*, published in London in 1849. This book describes an unusual shamanistic session in which the healer presses with all his might against the pit of the sick man's stomach, then begins to pray, stamping his feet on the ground; his assistants, who have supplied the accompaniment to his song beat the drum only now and then, "by way of an omen." Having thus expelled the demon, the medicine man sucks the diseased part and miraculously draws the sick blood through the pores.

conversations into the tempo and style of a contemporary American squabble is too much of a corruption of the original, but these are flaws that McDonald's art induces us to let pass.

The protagonist, Kwak, is the shaman of the Tlingit. He is about to be killed; he has been unable to stave off the famine. Almost resigned to dying, he tries vainly to communicate with the divine powers and, exhausted, dozes off.

A change awakened him. There was a great quietness about, and as he raised his head to listen a crow called and was answered. Looking up through the hollow snag he saw centered in the opening a large yellow star. A great sigh went out of him. His prayers had been answered. He knew exactly where he stood in time.[16]

He feels revived. We participate in his sustained tremulous attentiveness, straining to catch clues, appeals, correspondences, and we admire his determined cunning in manipulating man, equal to the strength with which he is able to dominate himself. McDonald is familiar with the use of tricks to reinforce prestige: the witch doctor's worldly glory does not impair the reality of his ecstatic concentration, his "body of glory" in the strictly mystical sense. On the contrary, the first exalts and magnifies the second. It is McDonald's great merit that this profound intuition is seriously understood and represented. To this he adds, to complete the tour de force, the ability to show how much of the absurd and funny can be mingled in a shaman's sublime, intense life. Subsequently, Kwak senses the approach of schools of fish, orders the tribe to start fishing, overcomes the famine, and so saves his life.

The community is thrown into an uproar by a young girl of exquisite aristocratic bearing, a fugitive from a northern tribe. Kidnaped and put aboard an American ship, she escaped from it after many vicissitudes. She refuses to accept a servile role, although she does not possess the ritualistic qualities of noble breeding and is neither marked nor tattooed. The shaman is irritated by her deceit, though from the top of his tower he has seen a ship similar to the one the young girl has described. He begins to plot the capture of the ship and plans to sacrifice her as a propitiatory act for the success of the exploit. He walks toward a large canoe under construction on which he has decided to sail: "He walked on, not hurrying. One who is guided by supernaturals does not rush about."

A quarrel erupts when the slaves are ordered to seize the girl, and the shaman is astonished by the boldness of her reaction:

Kwak was staggered, though not by her threat. A small demon of fear was fluttering its black wings in his bowels. It had flown in when he realized suddenly that this girl was protected. . . . Was he going against his vision? Forgetting his high office and allowing himself not only to act and talk like a head chief but to think like one? . . . A chant rose in his throat and burst from his lips: "O Mother of Chiefs, O Mother of Chiefs, O Mother of Chiefs—lift me up high, lift me up high, lift me up high."

The girl's body seemed to wilt, the fierceness going out of her. She lowered the axe and laid it gently aside. Her expression softened to a look of deep study. . . . Then her face shone with the light of memory, and she spoke correctly a phrase belonging to the secret rite of the Cannibal Society in appropriate response to his own. Kwak, stunned with surprise, was slow with the answer, but gave it and then added, "May the Great Mother Bear bless and protect you, Princess, until you are returned to your aunts and uncles. We will feast and dance the great steering paddle into your hands and give thanks that the wrong-idea-demons have been vanquished."[17]

So the canoe leaves with Kwak and the young girl to fight the American ship and the first rifles the Tlingit have ever faced. The girl soon recognizes the ship and the captain who kidnaped her. Kwak sees the change:

When he glanced back over the heads of the crowd to see how the girl would answer he saw with surprise that the demons of hate had taken charge of her—or perhaps the spirit of one of her slain relatives—probably a younger brother. Very unusual. A mistake on the part of some supernatural overseer, decided the shaman. A female has not the strength of mind to control a warrior's spirit. Too bad this one couldn't have taken hold of one of the untried young fellows. It was too much for the girl. She had the savage, hating look of a grounded hawk, downed by an arrow through his wing, that knows he is about to be finished off.[18]

He and the princess agree to go aboard the ship. The captain is burning with desire for her and wants to keep her and her companion. Kwak scorns him; no Indian would demean himself by showing his desire for a woman. The man must be insane, but the insane are in touch with the spirits and so must be treated with respect; even the shaman must at times go mad in order to establish certain contacts.

Lifted onto the main deck, the shaman and the girl succeed in stabbing the captain. His boatswain a Congolese slave, already the princess's friend, takes command of the crew, and the three of them steer the ship so that it is stranded on a beach. The crew, which tries to revolt against the new rulers, is exterminated by the Tlingit warriors. The entire episode is handled with the technique of a Cooper who has learned from his critic Mark Twain. It is, at bottom, only an entertainment, a piece of childishness or an Elizabethan interlude of clowning, which runs parallel to the very subtle description of the shamanistic spirit confounded by overwhelming, radically new events.

Kwak is forced to act as a leader and, thinking of his spiritual vocation, murmurs to himself: "I don't know whether half of me has split off and become district chief, or if the spirit of my late cousin crowds in every now and then to take charge." He fears, with a shiver, that the ghosts of the stabbed white men may be suggesting some of these new impulses to him. "It couldn't have happened if he'd kept his mind on his medicine instead of letting it be filled with battle and slaughter. *They* had taken advantage of his lack of vigilance."

At the end of the adventure Kwak realizes how dangerous is the new wealth of the ship's cargo with which he has endowed his people and decides to renounce it, sacrificing the ship itself. He does not have the boldness of great leaders who throw caution to the winds and stand up naked, reborn, trusting totally in supernatural beings.

He announces the sacrifice at the height of the feast of gifts (potlatch), while the ship is in fact casting off: the Congolese and the princess have ordered the slaves to sail to some other shore.

∴

In 1959 Milton Lott, a writer of Westerns, based a novel on the story of Wovoka, the founder of the ghost-dance religion, which enabled its followers to enter the realm of the dead and speak with them. It was a last gust of prophecy, bloodily suppressed by the troops in 1890. Sitting Bull was one of its martyrs.

A conversation between the government agent and a few of the native soldiers employed by the whites preserves something of the spiritual reality that was annihilated:

The agent looked up, startled. "What do you mean, sacred? They're only men—like you or me."

"No. They have done what you and I cannot do: they have caused many to die in the dance and have brought them back after they have seen and talked with their relatives in the world of spirit. We have seen them do these things and are afraid to interfere. . . . Some of the dancers, young people, have seen men who died long ago. . . . There is mystery here and power."[19]

The small Sioux encampment that Lott describes will be destroyed by the soldiers; the ensuing massacre is narrated with craftsmanlike skill. But the slow progress of the story toward this depth of iniquity is told in a style that does not fulfill the author's intentions of spare incisiveness. The characters are merely sketched: the neurotic, intolerant Protestant minister, his wife, who, in contrast to him, respects the natives and inevitably, dangerously, is attracted to the young scholar who loves and studies their civilization and sympathizes with the new religion.

Yet the novel has its shrewd moments. Lott made good use of the treatises of Ruth Benedict and Clark Wissler and the books of John G. Neihardt. The state of mind of the minister intent on praying for the dead Indian child is a paradigm of the instinctive horror felt for the Indian world:

Before he began praying he was afraid he might faint. The slanting, conical walls without windows oppressed him; the smells of incense, leather, smoke— all the trappings of savagery—and above all, the disquieting presence of death seemed to constrict his breathing, to weigh on his heart and lungs.

But as he prayed, his strength renewed. A sense of power lifted him up, sustained him.[20]

Here we see the Puritan sensibility re-created.

∴

Full of good will after a careful study of the Indian verities, Hal Borland wrote *When the Legends Die*[21] somewhat in the style of La Farge, with his combination of realism and a mimesis of native poetic inwardness. A Ute worker kills a confidence man, runs away, and hides in the forest, where he is joined by his wife and small son. Here they return to the archaic, happy life.

One morning they saw that Pagosa Peak to the east was white with snow. He said: "Soon the leaves will fall. I am going to make a place where we will be warm this winter." He went over to the south side of the mountain and came back and said: "We are going to go to that place." . . . She said: "I do not want a house. I want a lodge that is round like the day and the sun and the path of the stars. I want a lodge that is like the good things that have no end." . . . Then she chanted the old song of the lodge, which is round like the day, and the year, and the seasons.[22]

A joy that bursts forth in the ancient songs, ready from time immemorial to lift up and ennoble every emotion, now suffuses each reverent act of hunting, building, and gleaning. Misfortune inevitably strikes the paradise. The two parents die; the orphaned child manages to procure food in the company of a small bear and birds who join him out of instinctive, totemic affinity. Once again paradise is lost. He goes into the city to barter some wicker baskets and falls into the hands of white barbarians; he is thrown into a school where the stench and vulgarity torture him even more than the beatings. He must chase away his brother the bear and, after a useless flight, also gives up all thought of resistance. He survives the trial, becomes a cowboy, and is hired by a gambler who bets on rodeos; his ability to speak silently to the horses makes him a champion. Cold, harsh, inaccessible, he thinks that he is now far from his origins, yet one day he is attracted by a secret force into the old forest, imagining that he wants to kill a bear whose tracks he has seen. But for him the bear is like the deer for the man of Taos in Waters' novel: the personification of the return to paradise. His finger cannot pull the trigger; he spares the bear and returns to live in the hermitage of childhood—a victorious Ishi. The identical theme of an Indian's return to forest life is also at the center of Peter Matthiessen's novel *At Play in the Fields of the Lord.*

Lumpish and lumbering because of its insistently facetious tone, *Piegan,* by Richard Lancaster, is the diary of a long interview with the chief of the Montana Blackfeet. This was the tribe that Grinnell had tricked by a great display of affection and which later was decimated by hunger and a fourth of its members destroyed by alcohol. The best pages are those in which the horror drowns out the mechanical laughter.

The Chief once asked me to explain to him why the White Man had been so anxious to trap all the Underwater Persons (all the beavers). I told him it had been because the White Man was crazy and thought that everybody should wear a hat of beaver fur. . . . What really motivated the extinction of the buffalo was the development in 1871 of a new tanning process. . . . I have never had the courage to tell the Chief that his people and his culture were sacrificed so that some stinking machine (the older Blackfoots still refer to the automobile as a "skunk wagon") could keep on turning out beer bottles, silk umbrellas or patent leather shoes.[23]

Beavers were indeed sacred to the Blackfeet, for they were the chieftains of the "underwater beings" to whom the Indians gave presents each time they had to cross a body of water and who appeared in their visions as blond, blue-eyed creatures. Lancaster gives some accounts of ceremonies but omits more useful information, protesting indignantly against those who claim to be able to define the ineffable.

∴

The number of books encompassing both literature and ethnology, and free from any progressivist arrogance toward the Indian, has grown enormously; the survey given here is necessarily limited. However, the new spirit that pervades these books continues to be opposed by the rooted force of progressivist persuasion, the tradition of benevolence, or obsolete Libertinism.

To counter the vogue of the negative heroes of *Cimarron,* Conrad Richter has recourse to a compromise and a somewhat bizarre theory: each cell group in an organism tends to establish a harmony that permits the greatest vibratory power and arouses its neighbors, thus forcing them to search in some way for more potent harmonies. One is reminded of P. D. Ouspensky (who fascinated a number of English writers around 1930), especially when Richter tells us that mystics are the greatest manipulators of energy. In his novel *The Mountain on the Desert* a hermit explains that the basic primal motive is hunger for energy, that activity releases energy and not vice versa; crying, kicking, laughing, acting, and praying all seem to be forms of vibratory activity. For Richter, the Indian is above all a teacher of energy. *The Light in the Forest* is dedicated primarily to the Indian. In it young Butler, kidnaped in the second half of the eighteenth century by a tribe of Delawares, to his great sorrow is returned to his parents. Every symbol of the oppressive civilization revolts him: "You might as well ask a deer to dress itself in the hide of its enemy, the wolf."

Richter wants to maintain the two warring conceptions in equilibrium so that at the end Butler will also condemn the Indian's savage, cruel nature as intolerable. Indeed, the native's admirable, intense energy is destined to give way before the more discordant energy of European civilization, which, however, is a premise for the evolution of other, new forms. In spite of everything the ideology of progress somehow wins out.

∴

Edmund Wilson, a skillful blender of literary criticism and political doctrine, always up-to-date, never audacious, an impeccable journalist, was suddenly attracted by the remnants of the bastardized, weary Indian world. He confronted it in a modernized spirit of Enlightenment benevolence.

He discovered that the Constitution of the United States was influenced by the unwritten constitution of the Iroquois Confederation, that Benjamin Franklin had been inspired by it to unify the American colonies. He got to know some Iroquois, learned that a nationalistic movement existed, and noted, at its roots, a religious revival.

Gan-yo-die-yo (Handsome Lake), the eighteenth-century reformer, after a life of dissipation, had a series of visions and restored the native morality destroyed by the use of alcohol, imparting the teachings of a new faith. Between 1860 and 1865 the text of the revelation, until then passed on only orally, was written down in Seneca language, then translated into English and published by the Seneca Arthur C. Parker in 1913. In *Apologies to the Iroquois* (1960), Wilson records the major sections of this Scripture (known as the Good Message), and also the tribes' recent political struggles against the inexorable harassments of the authorities.

One of the Indians he presents is Philip Cook, an ironworker, accustomed to keeping his balance on vertiginously high narrow steel beams, giving, by his very appearance, the impression of being assimilated to the materials with which he works, a calm, disciplined man. A Catholic, he had no tribal feelings until he became involved in politics. In 1948 he espoused the cause of Indian nationalism and, delving deeper into the history of his people, discovered the story of white treachery and iniquity. As a result, he left the Catholic Church, rejected Protestantism, and became an adherent of the religion founded by Gan-yo-die-yo; his ancestors, he found, were not polytheists, as he had been taught by the priests. They had worshiped the sun, moon, and other natural forces only as deputies of the Creator. But Cook had a vocation as a restless reformer, and so the guardians of the cult expelled him. He ended up a Mormon.

Mad Bear, a Tuscarora and another Indian nationalist, is portrayed with the technique of the polished *New Yorker* profile. Enlisting in the navy at sixteen, he fought at Okinawa and later in Korea. Because he lived on a reservation, he was denied a veteran's loan under the G.I. Bill of Rights. He told Wilson of an ancient prophecy concerning a great white serpent who would become so powerful that he would choke the Indian people and then become enormous. A red serpent would then appear to oppose the white one, while a black serpent would defeat them both, after which a great light would shine forth. Mad Bear interprets this vision as the announcement of a struggle between America and

Soviet Russia; the black serpent stands for the African peoples, and the light for the final appearance of a Savior.

William N. Fenton, the anthropologist and Iroquois scholar, helped Wilson gain entry into the religious world of the Senecas faithful to the teachings of Gan-yo-die-yo, taking him along so that he could witness a "Dark Dance." This is an oratorio, a song cycle sung in the dark, born from the vision of a boy hunter who lived among the "Little People," the pygmies who preside over the flowering of the plants. The boy later returned to his village only to discover, like Rip Van Winkle, that he had been gone not for just a few days but for decades.

The "Dark Dance" calls the Little People back among men. Wilson says that in witnessing the ceremony he experienced a sense of excitement, even fear; the music opens out to something larger than those who released it, as though it were independent of the performers. And Indian people normally involved in active, everyday life, "gay and easy," become silent and thoughtful when the subject is introduced.

In his description of this and other rituals Wilson, bolstered by the confused notion of man's merging with nature, is unable to go beyond psychological notations. Moreover, he seems unaware of most of the literature on the subject: his knowing, informed air, his touches of "live" experience, disguise the limitations of his reportage, which amounts to no more than a skillfully put together sketch. He scrupulously adheres to the standards set by that sector of the culture industry that fabricates "brilliant reportage."

Wilson takes for granted the accepted Enlightenment axiom that there is nothing in Indian culture that cannot be fathomed with the help of modern categories (psychoanalysis or such facile formulas as the primitives' fusion with nature). The objective quality of spiritual experience is not even entertained as a hypothesis. One makes a show of impartiality, provided that the Indians keep their resistance within the framework established by political groups (possibly masked as apolitical).

The sketches scattered throughout the book (profiles of persons, telling details, such as the Indians who are watching television in the room next to the hall where the sacred dances are being performed), are supposed to persuade the reader that "he has seen all that there is to see." At the same time, he is not even given a bibliography. But he will nurse the illusion that he has actually touched the essence, will repeat it all as if he himself had experienced it, for the level-headed tone of the reporter "with his tongue in his cheek" has persuaded him that he is fully up to date.

At any rate, this is also obvious in other writings by Wilson; for instance, he analyzes Symbolism with only a minimal understanding of Villiers de L'Isle-Adam's *Axel.*

∴

Wilson's amiable deference to the Indians is wholly absent in the Libertine novelists of recent years. In *The Sot-Weed Factor* John Barth sees the Indian as a savage of staggering lubricity, but he is not held up to derision, since the white man himself is civilized only on the surface. In a feeble parody of eighteenth-century style Barth rewrites the ancient story of Pocahontas, decked out in all the obscenity that is considered obligatory among naïve, sex-obsessed adolescents.

Still in the role of an importunate prostitute is the archetypal Pocahontas who, in Leslie Fiedler's opinion, appears in a series of fictional works—Fiedler's own story "The First Spade in the West," *The Ballad of Dingus Magee* by Davie Markson, *Sometimes a Great Notion* by Ken Kesey, and *Midnight Cowboy* by James Leo Herlihy. These daydreams sparked by images of eroticism and degradation find a concrete release in the figure of the Indian woman and are simply a new form of the old insult to the savage (even though these new writers no longer counterbalance the savage Indian with an example of white decency—be it even hypocritical.)

Fiedler thinks that the latest comer in this series, Leonard Cohen, who in his novel *Beautiful Losers* gives free rein to fantasies of rape committed on the memory of the saintly Catholic Mohawk Katari Tekakwitha—the Canadian counterpart of St. Rosa of Lima—succeeds in transforming a dead tradition into a living myth. The intent here is to transform an edifying memory alien to the author into material for imaginary erotic exploits, hoping to shock and also to infuse some vitality into his work with this display of sacrilegious fantasies.

Indeed, one of the most frequent weapons with which the modern spirit defends itself against the fascination of ancient and august spiritual reality is that of folk derision, a formula invented in America by Mark Twain.

The re-emergence of Indian spirituality in recent years was subjected to precisely this kind of attack in Thomas Berger's picaresque novel *Little Big Man,*[24] amply nourished with the latest ethnographic information. The picaro-protagonist lives alternately as a white man and as a Cheyenne at the time of the last Sioux resistance. This, for example, is a scene in which the Indian soothsayer become familiar by the spread of ethnological studies is made ridiculous by a speciously candid tone:

. . . while riding along he muttered prayers and incantations to bring us bad medicine, but so ran his luck that he never saw any of the animal brothers that assisted his magic—such as Rattlesnake or Prairie Dog—but rather only Jackrabbit, who had a grudge against him of long standing because he once had kept a prairie fire off his camp by exhorting it to burn the hares' homes instead. . . . Ever since that incident the rabbits all knew him, and when encountering him alone would stand up on them enormous hind legs and say "We think bad thoughts for you."[25]

Apart from the tone, Indian wisdom is well formulated: "You should never feel sorry about beating anybody, unless having conquered his body you want his spirit as well," or of an Indian orator: "The . . . remark was developed deep in the chest, but came out high and quavering after having fought a passage through his tightened throat . . . it could get the wind up in you once you caught the style." But Berger's sensibility is incapable of grasping the essence of invisible Indian life. His tone of quiet, implied mockery is relinquished only once, when the protagonist, following Cheyenne custom, has spent the night making love to all of his sisters-in-law. At dawn his wife returns with their newborn infant, and he—at peace, absorbed, and content ("I had medicine then") sees the rising sun in the sky as a favorable portent. To have imagined this scene arouses a great, sorrowful, celebratory urge in Berger (not by chance highly praised by Henry Miller). Once again the Indian has served to corroborate the dreams of European Libertinism.

In his novel *The Track of the Cat* Walter Van Tilburg Clark has his hero, an Indian hunter, accompanied by a mysterious totemic animal with Melvillian overtones—the magical mirror in which each hunter can read his real nature. In the story "Anonymous" which forms part of the volume *The Watchful Gods*,[26] Clark mocks an enthusiast of the "bone-deep realities" of Indian life, drawing the portrait of a vacuous, affected young Navajo whom everyone obeys because of some inexplicable feeling of subjugation. Is this a symbol of the new feeling of subjugation among whites when confronted by those who were persecuted in the past? The lunatic asylum in Ken Kesey's *One Flew Over the Cuckoo's Nest,* where an Indian and a white man join to fight against being lobotomized, was already emblematic.

Chapter XI

─●◦●─

Indian Literature

In a speech quoted by Cotton Mather in his biography of John Eliot (included in *Magnalia Christi Americana*), Richard Mather reports the sermon of the Indian Nishohon, written in a perfect "plain style" worthy of the Puritan masters:

. . . what sacrifices shall we offer? My answer is, we must offer such as Abraham offered. And what sacrifice was that? We are told in *Genesis* XXXII: 12, "Now I know that thou fearest me, seeing thou hast not withheld thy son, thy only son from me." It seems he had but one dearly beloved son, and he offered that son to God; and so God said: "I know thou fearest me!" Behold, a sacrifice in deed and truth, such as we must offer. Only, God requires us not to sacrifice our *sons*, but our *sins*, our dearest *sins*. God calls us this day, to part with all our sins, though never so beloved; and we must not withhold any of them from Him. . . . Let us part with such sins as we *love best*, and it will be a good sacrifice!

This is the sole example in English of an indigenous Puritan literature from the seventeenth century.

In 1665 Caleb Chaesahteaumuk was graduated from Harvard, delivering a Latin oration that is preserved in the archives of the Royal Society. And in 1675 the Indian Eleazar, who studied at Harvard, wrote a Greek poem, which has been lost.

However, the Indian biography, a minor, devotional genre, was cultivated by the Puritans, and through it filtered a little of the spirit of the Indians themselves. *A Summary Account of the Life and Death of Joseph Quasson, Indian,* by Samuel Moody, published in Boston in 1726, tells the story of a drunkard sentenced for murder, to whom God grants the time to repent. *Indian Converts,* by Experience Mayhew, published in London the following year, contains a series of edifying accounts of providential interventions in the lives of converted Indians. Born into a family of missionaries in 1673, Experience was preacher to the converted

229

Indians of Martha's Vineyard. He gathered all the anecdotes handed down in his family and told the story of Hiacoomes, one of the first Indians to convert despite the opposition of both his temporal leaders and his spiritual authorities. A dreadful psychic epidemic seemed to condemn such disturbances of religious peace, yet Hiacoomes persisted in the new faith.

There was this Year 1643 a very strange Disease among the *Indians*, they ran up and down as if delirious, till they could run no longer; they would make their Faces as black as a Coal, and snatch up any Weapon, as tho they would do Mischief with it, and speak great swelling Words, but yet they did no Harm. . . . Now this, and all other Calamities which the *Indians* were under, they generally then attributed to the Departure of some of them from their own heathenish Ways and Customs.

Hiacoomes redoubled the fervor of his preaching and, "remembering Jehovah," stood up to the tribe's wise men.

In the life of Miohgsoo a hint of the very voice of the converted Indian comes through. He narrates with mystical Indian enthusiasm:

. . . true Believers did live above the World, and did keep worldly things always under their Feet; . . . when they were either increased or diminished, it was neither the Cause of their Joy nor of their Sorrow; neither did they stoop so low as to regard them, but stood upright, with their Hearts heavenward.

Thus, thanks to the works of the Holy Spirit, they feared the Father and revered the Son.

The same mystically Indian and stringently Puritan tone can be fitfully heard in the life of Noquittompany, who, though guilty of human wickedness, nevertheless had an edifying death: "He with great chearfulness entertained that King of Terrors. . . . He professed his Hopes in the Mercy of God." A group of boy saints also died in this way, among them Jedidah Hannit, who predicted calamitous times for his people.

One of the religious women, Abigail Kosoehtaut, so Mayhew recounts, was sleeping one day next to a sick sister when she heard a voice in the air repeating: *"There is Favour now extended in* Canaan," and, as she was rejoicing, grateful for those heavenly voices, she felt herself wake up,

but she could not find that any Person called her. However, she then went to her Sister, and said, *Now, Sister, you are going into everlasting Happiness;* to which, her Sister being now speechless, could make no Answer, save that by a Sign she consented to what was said to her, and with a smiling Countenance lifted up her Eyes and Hands towards Heaven; after which she said no more, but the next Morning dy'd.

A crucial page in this first book of Indian biographies gives the reason for the collapse of native civilization upon the arrival of the white men: the loss of the traditional repository of religious wisdom handed down from generation to generation by the holy men. In fact, Mayhew relates an Indian chief's—Tawanquatuck's—story:

A long time ago the *Indians* had wise Men among them, that did in a grave manner teach the People Knowledge; but they, *said he,* are dead, and their Wisdom is buried with them; and now Men live a giddy Life in Ignorance till they are white-headed.

One could also compile a special literature that recorded the oratory of the Indian chiefs during negotiations with the Dutch and English, who were obliged to conform to the Indians' ritual if they wanted to reach any agreements with them.[1] Cadwallader Colden praised the Attic urbanity of these speeches.

Following the orators, the "Praying Indians," and the authors of Puritan sermons (a *Sermon* was published in Boston in 1773 by Samson Occom), some Indians in the nineteenth century, such as David Cusick, wrote the histories of their tribes.[2]

William Apes, a direct descendant of King Philip, was born in 1798 and became a Methodist preacher in 1829. In the same year he wrote his autobiography, *A Son of the Forest,* and in 1836 delivered a peroration in Boston against the Puritans who had despised his ancestors because of their kindness and resignation. Just as they were about to perish of starvation in 1623, the Puritan colonists pretended they were friends of the natives, but they did so with perfidious, insidious intention. The list of Puritan iniquities reverberates throughout his painful, outspoken harangue: men tricked into lining up in front of a cannon and then fired on, other men degraded by alcohol. King Philip was the avenger of innumerable outrages, a great leader on a par with George Washington. The rightly famed Indian eloquence divested itself of its epic, metaphor-laden style and adopted the simple appeal to the heart so characteristic of English oratory, together with its particular humanitarian insistence on the atrocities of the accused. Only one argument remained to the people who listened in Boston's Odeon; after the speech Apes disappeared, and his body was never recovered.

An autobiography of Chief Black Hawk (1767–1838) was published in 1833: *The Life of Ma-ka-tai-me-she-kia-kiak, or Black Hawk* (reissued in

Urbana, Illinois, 1964). It is studded with accounts of war parties and revolves around the futile resistance to the advancing Americans. The style, though modern and succinct, is Biblical in its cadences, the prose, dense, compact, and solemn. The opening paragraph immediately establishes the lofty, laconic tone:

My great grandfather Na-nà-ma-kee, or Thunder (according to the tradition given me by my father, Py-e-sa) was born in the vicinity of Montreal, where the Great Spirit first placed the Sac nation, and inspired him with a belief that, at the end of four years, he should see a *white man,* who would be to him a father. Consequently he blackened his face and ate but once a day (just as the sun was going down), for three years, and continued dreaming throughout all this time whenever he slept—when the Great Spirit again appeared to him, and told him that at the end of one year more, he should meet his father.

So the arrival of the first French galleon was religiously awaited. After the French it was the turn of the English, with whom the tribe had only brief contacts, being forced by the threat of many enemies to retreat to the south, toward Louisiana.

His father having died, Black Hawk in his turn became an eminent warrior. The Americans then arrived and the first clash occurred. An irremediable lack of communication ruined their relations, and Black Hawk exclaims that it was impossible to make oneself understood by them, "as it appears that their feelings are acted upon by certain rules laid down by their *preachers!*—whilst ours are governed by the monitor within us." Among the many war adventures (the Sauk or Sac tribe was an ally of the English) there was one directed by a mysterious monitor —an inner voice that in a vision advised Black Hawk to find a hollow tree, watch a snake issue from it, and follow its track in order to surprise the disarmed enemy leaders. He did so and came upon two American officers, but the opportunity went up in smoke because of the excessive caution of the ambushers.

Another section that stands out from the account of clashes and ambushes is the description of a fertile island, the tribe's vegetable garden and orchard watched over by a good spirit and desecrated by the building of an American fort—a graceful metaphor for the common reader. But Black Hawk is clearly aware of what would remain vague or merely verbal to a white man, and so he informs him that the good spirit

lived in a cave in the rock immediately under the place where the fort now stands, and has often been seen by our people. He was white, with large wings like a *swan's,* but ten times larger. We were particular not to make much noise in that part of the island which we inhabited, for fear of disturbing him. But the noise of the fort has since driven him away and no doubt a *bad spirit* has taken his place.

Black Hawk furnished what is perhaps the first precise description of the Algonquin religion in his account of the Sauk ceremonies at the ripening of the wheat. At this time all the people pay each other visits.

Some lodge in the village makes a feast daily, to the Great Spirit. I cannot explain this so that the white people would comprehend me, as we have no regular standard among us. Every one makes this feast as he thinks best, to please the Great Spirit, who has care of all beings created. Others believe in two Spirits: one good and one bad, and make feasts for the Bad Spirit, *to keep him quiet!* If they can make peace with him the Bad Spirit will not hurt them! . . .

Black Hawk has a lesson to teach: each man must find his own path.

∴

Black Hawk's Biblical qualities were not borrowed, which was proved during those very years by the discovery of the tribal chronicle of the Delawares, the Walam Olum. Its hieroglyphics lend themselves to a depth of interpretation rivaling that of the Hebrew characters in the cabalistic exegesis of the Old Testament; the text has a metaphysical profundity equal to any other sacred scripture. In 1820, Constantine S. Rafinesque, professor of botany in Kentucky, received the manuscripts in Delaware ideograms from a certain Dr. Ward; in 1822 he obtained from another source the songs that accompanied the text. After having learned the native language, he translated the entire work into English in 1833. In 1836, after his death, his version appeared in his work *The American Nations.*

Other versions, the work of Ephraim George Squier, appeared in 1848, and then again in 1885 under the editorship of Daniel G. Brinton, who also furnished proofs of its authenticity. The first reproductiom of the hieroglyphics themselves was issued by the Indiana Historical Society in 1954,[3] so that we finally possess the text of the Delaware Bible. It begins with a Genesis somewhat more Gnostic-Dualistic in character than the Hebrew one and continues with the history of the Delaware people up until their settlement in their homeland.

The beauty of the hieroglyphic syntheses unites in a perfect whole with the power of the text.

The initial verses and symbols describe the origin of the cosmos:

1. "There at the edge of all the water where the land ends." The symbol is composed of two parallel semicircles, which represent the arch of the heavens, and two horizontal lines, representing the earth that borders the sea:

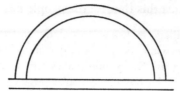

2. ". . . the fog over the earth was plentiful and this was where the Great Spirit stayed." The symbol is:

A head spiked with rays is the Great Spirit, the parallelogram with diagonal lines is the earth with its four corners, the semicircle is the water.

3. "It began to be invisible everywhere, even at the place where the Great Spirit stayed."

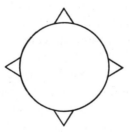

The circle is holiness, while the four cardinal points indicate the four quarters of the earth.

4. "He created much land here as well as on the other side of the water." A parallelogram with diagonal lines represents the four corners of the earth. Rolling land is denoted by the segments of circles at the top of the glyph in the lower quadrant.

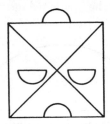

5. "He created the Sun and the stars of night."

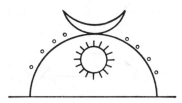

The symbol includes sun, moon, stars, and the arch of the heavens.

6. ". . . all these he created so that they might move." The sun, moon, the arch of the earth, and the land. The curve of the stars perhaps indicates motion. There are most likely twelve points above the arch.

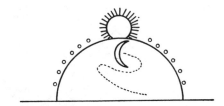

7. "Accompanying good deeds the wind blew, the sky cleared, and water rippled in many places."

The circle is a head, the lateral lines are two arms and signify "clear" in the language of gestures. The lines in the semicircle are the sign of the wind.

8. "It looked bright, for he made islands, and having done so, he remained."

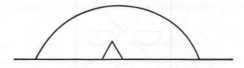

The open-ended double horizontal lines indicate the sea. The small triangle stands for an island, and the curve is the celestial arch.

9. "Then again, the one who is the Great Spirit, a Manito, created Manitos."

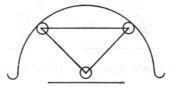

The curlicues at the extremities of the celestial arch indicate spiritual power; the circles are the Manito or spirits.

10. "And persons who die, and souls for all of them."

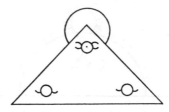

The winged circles represent souls; the dotted circle in the upper point of the triangle is divine. The triangle indicates invisibility, while the circle at the top is the sun.

11. "Thereafter he was a Manito to young men, full grown men, and their grandfathers."

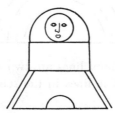

The circle that surrounds the first ancestor signifies his spirituality.

14. "But another powerful Manito created powerful men and those water monsters."

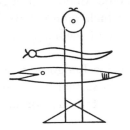

The point in the circle signifies divinity, the long body, power, the two small curved lines on the head, evil. Two sinister evil beings and the two intersecting lines signify contest.

15. "He created the flies and he created the mosquitoes."

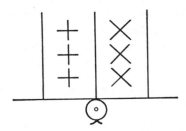

The crosses are flies, the X's mosquitoes. The emblem of the evil spirit is seen below the ground line, the position conveying the idea of absence or death.

After a happy period, the serpent, having been entrusted with the task by the Evil One, gives rise to evil, which is represented by red marks, the color that prisoners to be sacrificed are painted, and then the story of the Lênapés and their migrations begins, just as after Genesis the history of Israel commences. The Walam Olum and the Delaware religion seem to have influenced Joseph Smith and the Mormon religion.[4]

∴

In 1847 *The Life, History, and Travels of Kah-Ge-Ga-Gah-Bowh* (George Copway) was published in Philadelphia and Albany. Its meek tone, ashamed of its pagan past, still belongs to Puritan times; yet

Copway* denies that the ancestral religion worshiped the devil. On the contrary, as the Walam Olum makes clear, for the Lênapés it recognized a power at the origin of evil, to which offerings of dogs, whisky, and tobacco were made.

He also mentioned the Grand Medicine Lodge, in "some way similar to the Masonic institution,"† which grouped its followers in four distinct grades, teaching them the use of medicinal fetishes and a morality quite similar to Christian precepts.

The precepts of the Medicine Lodge were aimed at inculcating charitable impulses in the followers so that "the spirit that sees you will bless you," and also urged them not to harbor animosity and thus become victims of its reflection.

Gradually one begins to suspect that Copway protests he is a humble, converted, and assimilated Indian in order to be able to smuggle into the threatening world of the whites a notion terribly inimical to them, namely, the purity of the natives' life and their knowledge of truths usually considered the province of the conquerors. If one accepts this hypothesis, his book, though quite chaotic on the surface, becomes coherent, carefully elaborated to demonstrate without ever openly saying so, the superiority of the natives. Are they not unfamiliar with cursing, so common among the whites? And is not the vision that Copway confides he has had after fasting and praying a lofty one?

I saw, in my dream, a person coming from the east; he approached, walking on the air: he looked down upon me, and said, "Is this where you are?" I said

---

* Born in 1818, Copway, an exceptionally robust athlete and warrior, converted to Methodism in 1830 and studied at Ebenezer Academy in Illinois. He was a friend of Longfellow and Parkman. He died in 1863. Besides his autobiography, he wrote *The Ojibway Conquest* (1850), *Organization of a New Indian Territory East of the Missouri River* (1850), *Running Sketches of Men and Places in England, France, Germany, Belgium, and Scotland* (1851), and *Traditional History and Characteristic Sketches of the Ojibway Nation* (1851).

† This theme of Indian Masonry is undoubtedly motivated by a desire to play up to the white Masons. It was touched on by Robert C. Wright in *Indian Masonry* (Ann Arbor, Michigan, 1907), in which he denies that an Indian Masonry in the strict sense can exist. Chief Joseph Brant was an Indian Mason, but *The Masonic Review* (Cincinnati, 1863, vol. XXVIII) in its obituary of him remarks that Brant was a member of an English lodge, not an American one. The author says that he had examined the archives of the lodge to which Brant's patron, Sir William, belonged: "It does not appear from the records of this lodge that Brant or any of the Indians were made Masons in it, nor have we met with any written evidence to show that at this early period the American lodges made Masons of any of their Indian neighbors. These wild noble men of the forest had themselves their own mystic organizations, some of whose features and ceremonies were so akin to the Royal Art, that they have been denominated Indian Masonry." Brant worked fruitlessly for his race: "There was an handwriting on the wall, which even if he could decipher, he could not obliterate, and the red men have fallen like the leaves of their native forest."

"Yes." "Do you see this pine?" "Yes, I see it." "It is a great and high tree." I observed that the tree was lofty, reaching towards the heavens. Its branches extended over land and water, and its roots were very deep. "Look on it while I sing, yes, gaze upon the tree"; he sang, pointing to the tree; it commenced waving its top; the earth about its roots was heaved up, and the waters roared and tossed from one side of their beds to the other. As soon as he stopped singing, and let fall his hands, everything became perfectly still and quiet. "Now," said he, "sing the words which I have sung." I commenced as follows:

It is I who travel in the winds,
It is I who whisper in the breeze,
I shake the trees,
I shake the earth,
I trouble the waters on every land!

While singing, I heard the winds whistle, saw the tree waving its top, the earth heaving, heard the waters roaring, because they were all troubled and agitated. Then said he, "I am from the rising sun. I will come and see you again. You will not see me often." Thus spoke the spirit, and then turned away towards the road from which he had come. I told my father of my dream, and after hearing all, he said, "My son, *the god of the winds* is kind to you; the aged tree, I hope, may indicate long life; the wind may indicate that you will travel much; the water which you saw, and the winds, will carry your canoe safely through the waves."

I relied much on my dream, for then I knew no better. But however little reliance can be placed in dreams, yet may not the Great Spirit take this method, sometimes, to bring about a good result?

The question was intended to stick in the memory, whereas the cautious protests that precede it would be forgotten. And certainly the interpretation given by his father is completely esoteric.

In fact, two pages later, in the next chapter, Copway calls to mind what ethnologists have rarely understood: "The *traditions* handed down from father to son, were held very sacred; one half of these are not known by the white people, however far their researches may have extended. There is an unwillingness, on the part of the Indians, to communicate many of their traditions."

Copway's acceptance of Christianity was also mediated by a vision: at a Methodist sermon he fell unaccountably ill, the weight of sin oppressed him, and he felt like a wounded bird flapping its wings to reach safety:

Presently and suddenly, I saw in my mind something approaching; it was like a small but brilliant torch; it appeared to pass through the leaves of the trees. My poor body became so enfeebled that I fell; my heart trembled. The small brilliant light came near to me, and fell upon my head, and then ran all over and through me, just as if water had been copiously poured upon me. I knew not how long I had lain after my fall; but when I recovered, my head was in a puddle of water, in a small ditch. I arose; but O! how happy I was! I felt as light as a feather. I clapped my hands and exclaimed in English: "Glory to Jesus."

There is no hiatus between his own inherited religious experience and the Christian one, but Copway was careful not to say that. His pathetic book was an appeal to tolerate a Christian Indian state, in line with the principles and language of humanitarianism; therefore he is careful never to disconcert the average, arrogant reader. Copway's itinerary is paralleled in Schoolcraft's biography of the lofty mystic Catherine Wabose.

Modern Indian literature in the English language begins with Simon Pokagon's *O Gi Maw Kwe Mit I Gwa Ki—Queen of the Woods* (Hartford, Michigan, 1890). This novel, which candidly borrows its bizarre themes from the first phase of Romanticism, stirred the modest talent of Luella D. Smith to the short and, alas, unheeded poem "The Cry of Cain," in which the victorious race admits its guilt in the cruel treatment of the Indian Abel. To begin with, Chief Pogakon regrets that he cannot delve more deeply into the Algonquin heritage to tell his story. Then he begins to remember the life in the woods spent in the company of his mother during his holidays from the white school. There are pleasing episodes throughout the bucolic idyl. Having killed a deer, he returns to his retreat, hears his mother singing in the distance, halts in ecstasy, and is visited by a vision: "Jesus standing with one hand on the sinner's head and the other resting on the throne of the Great Spirit, saying, 'Come to me.'" Familiar with visions, he doubts his own eyes when he sees a girl on the other bank who imitates the song of the birds.

Sometimes in her songs, in fancy I could hear and see close by, in bush or brake, the bobolink tuning his voice to cheer his nesting mate. At other times I would look up almost convinced that I could see him dancing in the air, on wing, rising and falling with time and tune, then at the close alighting on the bush from whence he rose. . . . At times a snow-white deer about the maiden played in circles like the lamb.

He reaches the virgin on the other bank and discovers that their destinies are already intertwined, for their mothers have been brought up together.

He goes back to school, but love torments him; he feels like a panther caught in a trap. Then he becomes engaged and obtains his beloved's secret, who confides:

"You ask for the sacred secret of my heart which never yet has been told . . . while watching in a hazel bush one bright morning in spring, a robin came, and lighted just above me, pouring forth its joyful song of praise, so close that I could plainly see every motion of his bill and swelling throat. Unconsciously I too began to sing its warbling song."

Their marriage, however, will be ruined, their only son becoming a drunkard and dying prematurely.

The Apache Geronimo, who had been captured after he had led a spectacular campaign against the whites, toward the end of his life dictated his autobiography,[5] in self-defense and in condemnation of the American army.

But it is the autobiography of the assimilated Christian and physician Ohiyesa, or Charles Alexander Eastman, a strong yet serene Sioux, that sounds the saddest note of indignation. Ohiyesa was born in 1859 in a Minnesota tribe that was slaughtered a few years later. He was among the few fugitives who reached Canada, where he studied in the white schools and finally earned a degree in medicine. Returning to the United States in 1880, he took the name of Charles A. Eastman. Later on, he began to write his autobiography in a clean, primping, Victorian style. *Indian Boyhood* was published in Boston in 1902.

All customs were described as of divine origin, and all of life conformed to that origin; a pregnant woman concentrated on exalted images and scenes and took only what was considered noble food as nourishment.

The child was taught the art of solitude and that extraordinary attentiveness that whites took to be instinctive. Ohiyesa's uncle posed difficult problems to him to get him used to meditation. How, for example, does one see whether a lake is full of fish? The boy learned the significance of the wavy lines on sandy bottoms. He was taught to observe the behavior of animals from a hiding place, to imitate the wolf who, before taking flight, transfixes his enemy with a penetrating look, or the bear, who pretends obliviousness before he pounces.

This familiarity with animals furnished Eastman with the material for another book, *Red Hunters and the Animal People,* tales that easily stand comparison with Kipling's much more famous animal stories. The barrier of language separating men from beasts dissolves in this Indian reflection:

"Do we not talk with our eyes, lips, fingers? Love is made and murder done by the wink of an eye or by the single motion of the hand."

Ohiyesa's uncle made him take long runs and exhausting marches, startled him from sleep with a war cry, challenged him to protracted fasts. From these strenuous trials the young man was to go on to the wretched American school. But his fidelity to the loftier, austere life of his youth never faltered.

In his various books Eastman makes it clear that the Indian's religion remains incomprehensible to a man of another race, mainly because the Indian, as long as he believes, does not speak of it, and once he has ceased to believe discusses it mockingly and disparagingly. Even if he is induced to speak of it, the white man's racial and religious prejudices act as a kind of screen. And, finally, all the studies were made in a period of transition, when Indian beliefs and philosophy were disintegrating.[6]

Unfortunately, Eastman himself is imbued with Enlightenment deism, a Freneau in Indian guise. Still, he succeeds in correcting certain confused ideas about visionary experience, the heart of Indian life.

That solitary communion with the Unseen which was the highest expression of our religious life is partly described in the word *hambaday*, literally "mysterious feeling," which has been variously translated "fasting" and "dreaming." It may better be interpreted as "consciousness of the divine." . . . In this holy trance or ecstasy the Indian mystic found his highest happiness and the motive power of his existence.

Since this is the supreme value, the Indian scorns wealth, worldly zeal, and large agglomerations of men.

Not less dreaded [Eastman says] than the pestilence following upon crowded and unsanitary dwellings was the loss of spiritual power inseparable from too close contacts with one's fellow-men. All who have lived much out of doors know that there is a magnetic and nervous force that accumulates in solitude and that is quickly dissipated by life in a crowd.

The spirit "concerned only with the essence of things" was cultivated by means of prayer and fasting, and kept distinct from the "physical mind," which casts spells and enchantments. The sun, the earth, and other visible things were symbols and revered as such. For the Indian the sun was a sign of Goodness, as the cross is for the Christian. The souls of animals, guided by their divinely bestowed instincts, were therefore the object of veneration, and their bodies, sacrificed to provide food and life to men, were accepted with humility, and gifts and prayers were offered to their souls.

Responding to the ambiguity of the missionaries, Eastman rivals Melville in incisiveness: "I believe that Christianity and modern civilization are opposed and irreconcilable, and that the spirit of Christianity and of our ancient religion is essentially the same."

Indian education was simple: young children were inculcated with the trinity of silence, love, and reverence, and generosity, enthusiasm, ardor, and chastity were instilled in adolescent boys. In educating her children, the Indian mother not only followed the precepts of her people but also learned from the birds, ants, spiders, beavers, and moles.

Old age was considered the happiest stage in life, the time to enjoy a new, gentle freedom. Yet, in his own home, even the fiercest warrior behaved with almost feminine delicacy, speaking gently and softly. The supreme obligation was prayer from the moment the day began.

During the hunt every impressive scene brings the Indian to a halt and induces him to prayer.* The killing of the game is a new cause for prayer: the hunter stands before the killed animal, lifting his pipe to signify that he has honorably liberated the spirit of the brother whose body he has been forced to appropriate out of harsh necessity.

The trauma of commerce and European proselytism shook native institutions, and so a good part of the rites later studied by whites were corrupt mixtures—even music suffered from hybridization. The trauma whipped up a wave of cruelty; the sun dance—which had originally been a glorification of God, who in response to a vow saved a man already destined to die—became a display of tortures in the nature of a bullfight or a boxing match. Instead of a rite of expiation and thanksgiving, it became the setting for a supplication to win victory in war or to succeed in stealing horses from an enemy.

From the "Shawnee Prophet" Tenskwatawa (late eighteenth century) to the Paiute Indian Wovoka, who founded the "Ghost Dance" (c. 1889), hybrid cults were created, based on the authority of the Gospels, while the Algonquin "Medicine Lodge," created to resist the missionaries, "in some respects not unlike the free Masons, being a union or affiliation of lodges, each with its distinctive songs and medicines," secretly taught the virtues of herbs and elicited the psychic energies of its members with ceremonies and collective prayers, usually of white origin.

---

* The hunter must be completely alert, responding to and diligently observing everything on his trail as well as disposing himself, so Eastman teaches, to prayer. If he kept his mind fixed exclusively on the prey he would fail in his purpose, his subliminary sensibility becoming disturbed and in turn alarming that of the animals (according to Paul Coze in *L'Oiseau-Tonnerre,* Paris-Geneva, 1938).

The impostures produced by decadence have obscured manifestations of real prophetic power, but in the old days "a Sioux prophet predicted the coming of the white man fully fifty years before the event, and even described accurately his garments and weapons. Before the steamboat was invented another prophet of our race described the 'fire boat' that would swim upon their mighty river. . . ." And were not the details of a war party against the Ojibwa foreseen by a prophet? A prophet among the Dakotas who died at the age of a hundred predicted every move of their enemies. Eastman relates that his grandmother could sense with precision the presence of buried bones and could tell, by a special sensation in her breast, what was happening to children who were far away.

Many Indians believed in metempsychosis, and some declared that they could remember their former lives. Others conversed with a twin soul that was never seen and had been born in another tribe or another race. Thus a Dakota prophet foresees that his band would encounter a band of hostile Sioux led by his spiritual twin, who had the same totem as he himself. Instead of fighting, the two bands sue for a truce and

Lo, the stranger prophet advanced to meet them, and the people were greatly struck with the resemblance between the two men, who met and embraced one another with unusual fervor. . . . The prophet asked his twin brother to sing one of his sacred songs, and behold! it was the very song that he himself was wont to sing.

∴

Edward Goodbird dictated the story of his life to Gilbert L. Wilson in 1913—*Goodbird the Indian* (New York, 1914). He was a Hidatsa who had lived in the days when the tribe was still free and proudly scorned the Sioux, who subsisted on hunting and lived in tepees. The naïve, heavy-footed style tried to depict the subtle processes of shamanistic revelation, when by dint of sufferings a man's spirit appeared before him in the shape of a beast. After returning home and regaining his strength, the man would capture a beast like that which had appeared in his vision, and keep its skin or some other part, addressing his prayers to it, nourishing it at times on food, at other times on the smoke of burning cedar branches. The awkward, often skeptical tone suddenly vanishes when the narrator becomes immersed in the amazing episode of the man who for reasons of propitiatory penitence drags four heavy buffalo skulls behind him, clambering up steep places. The man laments and begs the gods for a vision; he starts to ford a river, where he soon finds the water up to his throat and has to start swimming. And behold, he suddenly feels light and hears a bellow behind him; the buffalo skulls have turned into living beasts that now keep him afloat.

∴

A Croatan, Chief Buffalo Child Long Lance, who became a captain in the Canadian army during the First World War and was afterward named the chief of a tribe of Blackfeet, described traditional tribal life in his book *Long Lance* (1928), beginning his account with the education of the young men who grew to enjoy ice-cold baths and flagellations during the long winter, thus learning to be thankful for the coming of the warm season and its attendant labors. They carefully learned their language with its eight declensions and nine conjugations, whose perfect use was a condition for every public speech (the man who had not mastered it had no right to be heard, since he would corrupt people by his mistakes). Long Lance also related how the priest of the tribe picked his successor in the boy who had charisma, an understanding of character, and could get himself out of scrapes. The priest took him with him to live in solitary places for six months, teaching him utter indifference for his body. Then there were the journeys through the "seven tents of medicine," seven courses of a year each, the last course being devoted to the ability to kill by sheer will power.

Long Lance also describes the ceremonies that put the priests in communication with spirits. First, they have themselves swathed like newborn infants, and then, constricted and impeded in this way, they leap between sharpened stakes. Terrible voices are then heard and, flung by an invisible hand, the priests find themself in some high and dangerous place.

The high point of the book is a description (at second hand it is said) of the awesome Sun Dance: the preparations, with the warriors charging at a gallop, shooting among the gathered people who raise a clamor with rattles and bells, and the priestess, who has fasted for five days, having the participants kneel before her and painting their faces black. The priest then attaches the nest of an eagle (the "thunderbird") to the top of a pole, which is raised up with the priest clinging to it. When he returns to the ground, he makes incisions in the breasts of the participants, inserts skewers of wood to which thongs of rawhide are attached, which are then tied to the pole. The men are suspended from the pole and dance around it until they free themselves from their bonds by atrociously lacerating the muscles of their breasts.

Even at second hand Long Lance's account gives an impression of truthfulness that one looks for in vain in an authentic, firsthand autobiography that was published the same year—*My People the Sioux* (Boston, 1928)—in which an Indian demeans himself in order to see himself as a white man might. It is the autobiography of Luther Standing Bear, chief of the Oglala Sioux—a book without a touch of supernatural life.

He describes his childhood amazement at the whites, their waste of precious meat, their filth—people who live "in dugouts, just like wild bears, but without the long snout"—but he has had no supernatural experiences and so is easily assimilated and amalgamated into the white world. He conceived of his life as a "success story," in which various banal experiences as a student, a collaborator of Buffalo Bill's, and a movie actor all find their place. Indian nationalism of a European stamp is the shabby tribute he pays to his origins.

True enthusiasm has a comeback in the biography dictated by the eighty-year-old Crow, Plenty-Coups, to Frank Linderman: *American: The Life Story of a Great Indian, Plenty-Coups, Chief of the Crows* (1930), in which the asceticism of the warrior and supernatural visions again assume their original, rightful place. Plenty-Coups vindicates the reality of shamanistic powers; nobody now knows what the medicine men knew before the coming of the whites, when they obtained such miraculous cures. Plenty-Coups tells the story of a warrior shot through the heart by a bullet, on whom a medicine man performed an exorcism by imprinting him with a new rhythm (by means of leaps, songs, waving a buffalo's tail in front of him, puffing, and spitting on his wound after chewing certain secret flowers). He finally healed him by the sheer force of his gaze. Plenty-Coups himself had to work for a long time before he could acquire this power.

His grandfather started him on his path as a boy when he suddenly ordered him to strip. When he saw him naked, he told him to capture a butterfly that was flying nearby.

Panting, but concealing my shortness of breath as best I could, I offered it to Grand Father, who whispered, as though he told me a secret: "Rub its wings over your heart, my son, and ask the butterflies to lend you their grace and swiftness." . . . We were eager to learn from both the men and the beasts who excelled in anything, and so never got through learning. . . . Whenever a boy's father caught a beaver, the boy got the tail and brought it to us. We would take turns slapping our joints and muscles with the flat beaver's tail until they burned under our blows. "Teach us your power in the water, O Beaver!" we said, making our skins smart with the tail.[7]

His grandfather gives him a bear's raw heart to eat so that he will re-member the alert awareness of the bear, quick to fight even when just aroused from sleep.

Plenty-Coups fasts for long periods and sweats on the mountain peaks, but all in vain—no message comes to him. During one of his vigils in the mountains (it was the custom for a herald to ride on horseback through the encampment, exhorting the young men to seek power on the nearby peaks), he finally received the longed-for vision. After four days of fasting, he had amputated a finger, and at the call of the blood four eagles came and alighted near him. But they do not tell him anything.

However, in the sleep that overtakes him in his exhaustion, the vision reveals itself: a presence directs him to a bison seated in the plain, and he reaches it (some time later he will find a bison's skull at that point on the plain). He then burrows underground in a tunnel where he brushes past hundreds of bison in the darkness; then he re-emerges on a plain crowded with these beasts, which suddenly vanish. The countryside is covered with cows and cultivated fields. He sees himself as a very old man, on a farm.

So he prophesies the disappearance of the bison and the coming of the whites. His tribe, the Crows, will follow his advice and ally themselves with the whites against the Sioux and the other unsubmissive tribes. But the long alliance did not bind them together: ancient customs were wise. The rule that forbade marrying a man who had not distinguished himself in battle guaranteed healthy children, and in fact in the old days one never saw deformed Indians. The whites used their religion and their laws when it suited them; they had no faith, and yet they fooled only themselves. The Indian knows how to live with the concentrated steadi-ness of a star: everything changes, but Indians act as though they were the seven stars (the Big Dipper) in the sky that live forever.

The shamanistic powers have been lost; miraculous cures are mere memories.

Our Wise Ones learned much from the animals and birds who heal themselves from wounds. But our faith in them perished after the white man came, and now, too late, we know that with all his wonderful powers, the white man is not wise. He is smart, but not wise, and fools only himself.

Around 1930 a pleiad of Indian biographers studded the literary sky, and this vogue for publication brought its own debasement, as in the case of James Paytiamo's *Flaming Arrow's People,* which makes one think of a children's book of the Art Nouveau period. It recounts the usual events in the life of the young Acoma Indians: the preparations for the dance of the spirit fetishes (katchina), then the dances themselves, fights, and races—"their bodies covered with clay containing powdered bird feathers make them imagine they are on wings." Equally Art Nouveau and childish is *I Am a Pueblo Indian Girl*, by E-Yeh-Shuré (Blue Corn), which deserves to be mentioned only because of its closing poem:

BEAUTY

Beauty is seen
In the sunlight,
The trees, the birds,
Corn growing and people working
Or dancing for their harvest.

Beauty is heard
In the night,
Wind sighing, rain falling,
Or a singer chanting
Anything in earnest.

Beauty is in yourself.
Good deeds, happy thoughts
That repeat themselves
- In your dreams,
In your work,
And even in your rest.

In 1931 the autobiography of the Cheyenne Wooden Leg was published.[8] It was compiled by a physician, Thomas B. Marquis, who had spent a long time interviewing the survivors of the battle of Little Big Horn in 1876, when General Custer's troops had, as if by magic, been thrown into confusion. Unlike the other autobiographies, it is a series of lively sketches, either humorous or adventurous. Its definition of religious fasts and their purpose has an admirable simplicity: the aim is to subdue the passions of the flesh and to further the individual's spirituality. Abstinence of the body and concentration of the mind on elevated thoughts cleanse body and soul and promote or assure their health. "Then the individual mind gets closer toward conformity with the mind of the Great Medicine above us."

The description of the four days of fasting in the darkness of a ritual lodge has a limpid, rhythmic quality: "Fitful slumbers, prayers, smoking, efforts at meditation, these alternated in my quiet activities. I was hungry and thirsty, especially thirsty. My body was hot. My heart was heavy. My

ears constantly were listening, listening to every faint whisper of Nature."
Then comes the immersion of the young boy, covered with red paint,
with a black sun on his chest and a black moon on his scapula, after the
trial and ritual steam bath presided over by the priest:

He released from the stones the vitality put into them by the burning wood
that had got it from the sun, the material representative of the Great Medicine.
The stones hissed their protests as the water compelled them to release into the
air their spiritual curative forces. Our bodies were enveloped by the steam
wherein floated the vital energy. The vivifying and purifying influence soaked
into our skins. Bad spirits were driven out of us and drowned in the water that
dripped from us.

The chapter titled "Worshiping the Great Medicine" is one of the most
splendid in Indian literature, constructed musically, mounting in a cre-
scendo from one ascetic trial to another—the protagonist's and those of
famous medicine men—until it reaches a climax in the image of the
warrior in his war paint advancing toward the enemy, guided by memories of his supernatural exploits, telling himself over and over that he is
protected by the Highest Power.

The battle of Little Big Horn, in which the pitiably armed Sioux and
Cheyenne warriors routed General Custer's hand-picked troops, gave
Wooden Leg the opportunity to describe one of the most exciting battle
scenes in all literature. The whites killed each other, shooting like
madmen. The prayers of the Indian holy men had robbed them of their
wits, although, Wooden Leg adds, joking grimly at white incredulity, he
now prefers to think that they were drunk on their whisky.

In Chief Luther Standing Bear's *Land of the Spotted Eagle* (1933), the
carefree happiness of Lakota life is also reflected in the ease and simplicity of the style. Diseases were generally unknown.

Now and then a man or woman would become afflicted with a crooked mouth
or one that dropped at the corner. The explanation for this condition was that
the person so troubled had at some time spoken unkindly or maliciously of
another who had passed on to the land of the ghosts. The spirit of the injured
one returning in the state of resentment would come close to the offending one
and startle him with a quick whistle.

The main occupation was study, not the bookish kind of the whites but
the reading of the actions, gestures, and intonations of men and beasts,
together with the deciphering of each object, whose existence—even if
only a stone—might prove either baneful or propitious.

Only to the white man was nature a "wilderness" and only to him was the land "infested" with "wild" animals and "savage" people. To us it was tame. Earth was bountiful and we were surrounded with the blessings of the Great Mystery. Not until the hairy man from the East came and with brutal frenzy heaped injustices upon us and the families we loved was it "wild" for us. When the very animals of the forest began fleeing from his approach, then it was that for us the Wild West began.

Constantly living in the fresh air, the Lakotas (like the English before the reign of Edward VI, as Polydore Vergil, the sixteenth-century historian, asserts) knew neither colds nor influenza. For these tempered men everything was fraught with meaning: each spring led them to meditate on the force that moved water and induced them to pray while quenching their thirst at it. The sight of an animal would invest them with its qualities; the sight of a rock gave them its strength.

The Stone Dreamer sang a song about the night sun, or moon, and also one about the day sun, which was taught him by stones. The stones were possessed of extraordinary knowledge, for they were on the earth, in the earth, and in the sky visiting the sun and moon, so they taught [a] song to the dreamer, that he might derive power from these heavenly bodies.

A life wholly suspended above material events, in colloquy with one's own daimon, is told in *Two Paiute Autobiographies* transcribed by Julian H. Steward,[9] in which the very diction reverberates with elation:

I became so sick that I gave myself up for dead. My soul admitted that I would have to die.

I died and my soul started southward, toward tüpüsi witü. While I was traveling, I looked down and my soul saw a stick in the ground not quite as tall as a man. . . . I turned to the stick and said, "This is the soul stick." I seized the stick and looked back toward my mountain, which was my power. I knew then that I would be all right and live forever, for whenever a soul going south sees the soul stick, it knows it will come back. . . . Whenever I dream, especially when it is a bad dream which means trouble, I talk to something in the darkness. I talk to my power. That is why I have lived so long. . . . Even when I have sex dreams, I talk to the night, because if I should not pay attention to them, they would continue and lead to fits. . . .

But if the greatest merit of these autobiographies is their archaic, remote quality, their succinctness, then *The Autobiography of a Papago Woman*,[10] dictated by the ninety-four-year-old Chona to Ruth Underhill, certainly excels in these respects. Chona, a chief's daughter, apprehended the essential things as if she had dreamed them; her father whispered them in her ear as she slept. She learned to leap out of bed at the first white streaks on the horizon—the hairs of the Creator.

The tribe's life is described with force and succinctness: the Papago religious libations so similar to those of Germanic warriors ("Making themselves beautifully drunk, for that is how our words have it. People must all make themselves drunk like plants in the rain and they must sing for happiness"), the wars and the magical preparations for them, when they sing:

> Oh bitter wind, keep blowing
> That therewith my enemy
> Staggering forward
> Shall fall.

And then the priest who had had a vision of an owl and conjured the dead in the shape of owls, who would inform him of the enemy's movements. The battles with the Apaches were often brought to a halt, for the dead are dangerous:

They stopped fighting right away because an enemy's death lets power loose. You must take care of yourself until you have tamed that power or it will kill you. . . . You would be like a sick man. You would fall. So they painted their faces black to show what had happened. . . . They stood away from the others, and other men who had killed came to join them.

An old warrior set those who had killed for the first time on the right path, directing them to the necessary vision. It was good to have the slain enemy's scalp, which attracts rain from the top of a pole, but woe to anyone who tore it down: he could no longer dance until he was painfully purified.

Chona's brother often fainted: he was learning, the priest said, that he was singled out. Her father killed three Apaches, and so he kept in his house three dummies that resembled them, which he fed. But the dead were not placated; on the contrary, they caused sickness among his relatives. Her father taught Chona that the holidays were established by the Creator at the beginning of time, and he also revealed to her how creation took place, but he did so only in the depth of winter when the snakes were asleep. When the summer came, her father sang at night: "I saw the tassels waving in the wind / And I whistled softly for joy."

The older women taught the truth of thoughts to the young girls: "If we thought too much about any boy before we were married, that boy would seem to come and make love to us. But it would not be he, it would only be a snake."

Chona married a priest who received his powers from a coyote. He resisted the white scourge, whisky, which crushed the Papago's spiritual strength, so different from the fermented juice of the cactus, which was drunk ritually once a year during the great rains.

Chona was forced to separate from her first husband and married again. In her old age she too acquired powers and succeeded in healing children.

.˙.

In comparison, *Son of Old Man Hat,* the life of a Navajo transcribed by Walter Dyk, is far inferior in quality. Almost entirely bereft of spiritual inspiration, it is at the same time virtually erotomanic, a rare thing in Indian literature. The praises lavished on it in Edward Sapir's preface appear offensive to us, mainly because of the presence of purer books. But he defines very well the aura that generally surrounds Indian literature: "What this singularly untroubled narrative does for us is to destroy all the turbulent dichotomies of self and not-self. It is as far removed as possible from the romantic spirit, the self-exploitive phase which is the sign manual of contemporary American feelings."[11]

The discovery of the Indian's wholly mystical world was made possible in the sphere of ethnography as soon as it had freed itself from preconceived, sociologically oriented notions of the origin of religious and ritual life. Sometimes the discovery was implicit in some of the splendid recordings of rituals made by Alice C. Fletcher's collaborators in the Bureau of American Ethnology. Among them is the faithful transcription of a ritual that equals aesthetically Carl Sandburg's versions published in the issue of *Poetry* devoted to indigenous poetry.[12] "The Hako: A Pawnee Ceremony" is a revelation bearing comparison to the works dictated in *Black Elk Speaks.* It was given to Alice Fletcher by a Pawnee priest, Tahirussawichi, who speaks in a tone of distress resembling that of the final farewell of the Sioux initiate, Black Elk:

I have done what has never been done before. I have given you all the songs of this ceremony and explained them to you. I never thought that I, of all my people, should be the one to give this ancient ceremony to be preserved, and I wonder over it as I sit here. . . .

I think over my long life. . . . I did not fall but I passed on, wounded sometimes but not to death, until I am here today doing this thing, singing these sacred songs and telling you of those ancient rites of my people. It must be that I have been preserved for this purpose, otherwise I should be lying back there among the dead.

The reading of this ritual, if it explains to the scholar rites and mythologies from every part of the world, also lifts the ingenuous reader to the same level of intensity and grace as a tragedy by Aeschylus.

∴

Francis La Flesche was the most noted among Indian ethnologists. Mary Austin tells how she had barely finished speaking at a conference when La Flesche took the floor and said that finally what he had always known and always puzzled about had been rendered "intellectually clear to him." "Not only did he agree," Mary Austin says in *The American Rhythm*, "with my rendering of the Indian rhythm, but he adduced an interesting instance of the recitation of tribal lays, which, in eleven divisions, were given in recitative simultaneously, and yet produced an harmonious effect. I doubt if any such rhythmic orchestration of spoken verse is possible among moderns, even in duet, to say nothing of eleven voices."[13]

The Indian whom Mary Austin helped to attain discursive consciousness of the polyrhythmic essence of art and ritual, the very core of the inner life of his people, who "need to dance as we need to laugh to save ourselves," delved further and more deeply into Osage rituals. He translated the initiatory chants in which the person goes through stages, identifying with bears and other animals and, finally, with the pipe. "Of the Peace Pipe I have made my body: when the Initiate make of it their bodies, by making it their life symbol they shall live without anger or violence. . . ."

La Flesche understood exactly the separation of material power from spiritual authority in the warrior's mystique: the spiritual leader left for battle, not to guide the struggle but rather, like Moses, to mediate by means of the pipe between the combatants and the divinity.

∴

The genre of the Indian autobiography is closely intertwined with ethnological research, especially in the work of Paul Radin, whose inventiveness as an ethnologist-poet we have already seen in Parsons' anthology. His ethnology was, above all, intent on revealing the order of space in which the Indian moved: a web of relations among the different clans that formed a complex structure, studied by ethnographers from Morgan to Lévi-Strauss. Radin was able to grasp this structure of Indian life by describing the form of the Winnebago village.[14] Two buildings stand out prominently: on the left the house of the chief, the member of the clan called Thunderbird, the creature that causes thunder by shaking its wings and shooting flashes from its eyes.

The inhabitants on this side of the road could not intermarry. The chief never left for war, and his authority found expression in the increase of general prosperity, in composing conflicts, and encouraging hospitality, moderation, and silence. In the summer he celebrated a feast day and sounded the call of a female bird that has fed all her little chicks. If necessary, he had to risk his life to bring peace and charity among contenders. Once order was restored and he was found lying dead, his hand still holding the sacred pipe, symbol of reconciliation, he would be recognized by all as a true chief.

In the other large building to the right of the axial street, running east and west, lived the chief of the Bear clan, whose members were also forbidden to intermarry. To him fell the tasks of war, and just as the other chief held a pipe in his fingers, so he held a rod or scepter with which he beat the recalcitrant. Helped by his Bears and by the closely related Wolf clan, he warded off visible and invisible enemies.

The chief of the Vulture clan lived not far from the chief of the Bears and watched over weapons, emblems, and prisoners of war.

Still on the left side were gathered the clans of the Pigeon and Eagle who, together with the Thunderbird, formed the Sky or Upper People. On the right side, or Earth, lived the clans of the Wolf, the Elk, the Water Spirit, and the Moose; these were the reserve police, the messengers, the chief's coadjutors, and the makers of fire. Scattered around them were the clans of the Deer, the Snake, and the Fish.

In the temple, divided into twelve sectors, all members participated in the worship of the many forms the spirits can take and which can be revealed to those who are able to entreat them by a protracted fast.

Radin penetrated into the inwardness that projected its sense of order on this enclosure of space. He secured an authoritative statement which is a classic among all those that have been preserved: the memorable autobiography of the Winnebago Crashing Thunder.[15] It begins with his devotional exercises as a child:

During childhood my father told me to fast and I obeyed him. Throughout the winter, every morning, I would get up very early, crush charcoal, and then blacken my face with it. As soon as the sun rose would I go outside and there gazing steadily at the sun make my prayer to the spirits, crying.

Thus I acted up to the time I have memory of things.

From then on, Radin explains, Crashing Thunder remembers; what he does not remember, the Winnebago relegates to nonexistent things.

But the boy's religious life is impeded by his conceit and his lack of honesty; he lies, pretending that the spirits have visited him. Soon his other weakness, an erotic obsession, begins to manifest itself (his parents have fruitlessly warned him that "only those boys who had no connection with woman would be blessed by the spirits"). At night he roams about the camp, hoping to sneak into a lodge and sleep with a young girl; he does not succeed; all he gets are some smiles, yet he brags about his conquests to his companions.

He strives in vain for mystical experiences, saying that even though he had tried to render himself pitiable in the sight of the spirits, his thoughts were centered upon women.

He even undergoes an initiation, without having any faith in what is being taught him. He has a number of temporary marriages, and together with his wives begins to drink a lot. With the strength he gains from intoxication he pretends that he has been blessed by a meeting with a bear, that he is filled with the fury of this simulated "guardian," and even succeeds in deceiving everyone.

He signs up with a rodeo, passing himself off as a cowboy, but at one of the stops he gets into a brawl and is badly beaten up. By now his life is filled with violence and disorder; he continually changes wives, and one day he decides with a friend to kill a man so that he might feel he is a warrior.

The frightful expedition takes place. His friend murders a sheep herder. Crashing Thunder is in a state of delirium tremens when he is arrested and put on trial.

After being acquitted, he becomes interested in the new peyote cult, to which the traditional Winnebagos are opposed. An attraction he tries vainly to resist leads him to a gathering, where he takes the drug, and "after a while I looked at the peyote, and there I saw an eagle standing with outspread wings. It was as beautiful a sight as could well be observed."

The eagle then dissolves and in its place he sees a lion, which is replaced by a soldier, and finally by a flag, a great waving of flags. For the first time, moved by the beauty of these visions, he prays to God. No sooner has he prayed than he begins to understand new things, shares in the silent thoughts of all those seated around him, and thinks: "I shall only regard Earthmaker as holy."

From then on he wants to devote himself completely to religion, but his incessant sexual imaginings stand in his way. He hopes by marrying again to be freed of them to devote himself wholeheartedly to the ceremonies. In a new vision he sees himself tied up; he understands that his erotic thoughts are the ropes that bind him. In another vision he sees the end of the world: the good are separated from the evil and he, not yet purified, is among the latter.

His life now changes; he finds a wife who says to him with delicacy and archaic simplicity: "I wanted a man who ate peyote and who paid attention to the ceremony." He sees his entire past as false and evil; with his new wife he will live devoutly happy.

∴

In 1945 Nancy O. Lurie began to transcribe the confidences of Crashing Thunder's sister, Mountain Wolf Woman. The simple, chaste life of an Indian girl indifferent to what remains of the ancient religion passes quietly until her marriage and her first pregnancy, but one day she and her husband attend a peyote ceremony and suddenly—hearing "solar thunder"—the sphere of the supernatural is opened up to her.

I was sitting with bowed head. We were all sitting with bowed heads. We were supposed to ponder. We prayed. We were all doing this. We were having our peyote meeting. In the west the sun thundered and made terrible noises. I was hearing this sound. Oh, the sky was very black! I had my head bowed, but this is what I saw. The sky was terribly black. The storm clouds came whirling.[16]

One measures the distance between this clear, candid, and ecstatic recollection and the simulation of repetitive speech in Gertrude Stein.

After the dark clouds Mountain Wolf Woman felt all around her the violence of tearing winds, saw fleeing women, and thought: So they do not know that the only refuge is in Christ. Then behold, Christ appears, and she feels compelled to stand up and imitate him by praying. She dares to get up: "I asked for a good life, thanking God who gave me life. This I did. And as the drum was beating, my body shook in time to the beat. I was unaware of it. I was just contented. I never knew such pleasure as this."

The followers of the peyote cult and those faithful to tradition were at odds. Mountain Wolf Woman does not throw light on this dispute between different forms of worship, but ethnologists have recorded the statements of an initiate of ancestral knowledge. According to this source, the infernal forces of the earth have always been kept in bounds by rites, and now they might become unleashed.

Even though a participant in the peyote cult, Mountain Wolf Woman still felt under the sway of tradition. It was her custom to take clothes and food to an old relative (Lurie observes that in this veneration for the holy old people is mixed a fear of their vaguely vampirelike magic), and one day she gives him a stove and in return receives the Indian "medicines." The old man's son is a staunch adherent of the peyote cult and for this reason cannot inherit them, so Mountain Wolf Woman is extremely welcome.

What you are saying is very good, granddaughter. I like that. A long time ago when you were a little girl this was meant to occur. Way back then you were working for it. When mother used to give medicines to the white people you used to help her by being her interpreter. Since that time these medicines were going to be yours. You have been working for them since long ago. You have been working for this. Today it has come about.

At this point a light floods the entire story: it was not a mere string of events but a destiny with a hidden design, and sudden depth is added to the two-dimensional everyday flatness. When she persists in the traditional scalp dance, shaking the head of hair of a German who died in the Second World War, and abides by the ceremony's strict rules (most people, when they are tired, go to sleep in the cars parked outside the sacred enclosure), she alone is rewarded with a vision: she sees the fair young man who was scalped, and tells him that his power has been absorbed by the tribe. This is the kind of vision sought for by the warlike ritual.

∴

In 1919 a Crow warrior, Two Leggings, also told the story of his life,[17] which is entirely dominated by the slow gathering of various elements that would compose his medicine bundle. "Each item in the medicine bundle is a concrete and quasi-sacramental symbol of the most significant points of intersection, points where the dynamic of nature, of culture, of inspiration, of individual passion and interest all clash and render flashes of meaning," Thomas Merton wrote.[18] However, the encounter between Merton and Indian mysticism was not a happy one; the close connection between Two Leggings' career as a warrior and a hunter eludes him, perhaps because Merton did not keep in mind the equally close nexus of these activities in the mysticism of the more energetic Western saints (and Puritan diarists). The protagonist in both *Two Leggings* and *Crash-ing Thunder* simulates spiritual experiences, but the misfortunes he then incurs persuade him to search for a medicine bundle of authentic fetishes. Two Leggings described how the imposition of Western culture snuffed out contacts with a world of spiritual presences.

But white life is a gamut of sufferings for the Indian; in *Sundown* (1934) the half-breed John Joseph Mathews told the story of the failure of an assimilated, educated, and rich Osage.

In 1938 Leo W. Simmons met Don C. Talayesva, a Hopi who agreed to be interviewed in the way common to sociological inquiries. The book that began to emerge gradually became tinged by the affection that sprang up between the two men and is the story of a life confided to a close and dear friend. Yet even this warm relation could not dispel the secrecy enveloping the occult ceremonies in which Talayesva had partici-pated (although his information on Hopi rituals is among the most detailed and extensive).

The autobiography was finished in 1941 and appeared the following year with the title *Sun Chief.*[19] In its frankness it includes frightful, disgusting details, and even though the contemporary reader may be inured to naturalistic crudities, it often makes the blood run cold.

Talayesva tells the story of his childhood and adolescence in the village of Oraibi up until his none too fierce initiation when he reaches puberty. In the ceremonial chamber decorated with symbolic designs, during an inexplicable pantomime, he undergoes the ritual beatings at the hands of masked men. The next day the creatures he thought to be supernatural prove to be his relatives or people he knows. From that moment on, he becomes more serious and anxious to learn about gods and spirits.

> . . . I felt ready at last to listen to my elders and to live right. Whenever my father talked to me I kept my ears open, looked straight into his eyes, and said "Owi" (Yes). One of the first rules was to rise earlier, run to the east edge of the mesa, and pray to the Sun god to make me strong and brave and wise. My father also instructed me to go to the foothills and run for exercise, and to bathe in the spring, even in winter.

But initiation at puberty is only the first step. After this, true religious life begins, and the many initiatory possibilities of the secret fraternities open up, each possibility in keeping with a certain personal vocation, with its distinct ritual, its teachings and the special powers that derive from them; finally, there is the progression of stages that the novice cannot possibly imagine in advance. The adolescent has already caught allusions to the supernatural possibilities of clairvoyance, communion with certain animal spirits, and therapy, and he has also had experiences of the other world in the context of everyday events. The two orders of reality are equally vivid, and much of the book's fascination comes from their fusion in the story.

The government had begun to insist that Indian children attend the public schools; the young boy gradually learns English and adopts the white man's ways.

I could name all the states in the Union with their capitals, repeat the names of all the books in the Bible, quote a hundred verses of Scripture, sing more than two dozen Christian hymns and patriotic songs, debate, shout football yells, swing my partners in square dances, bake bread, sew well enough to make a pair of trousers, and tell "dirty" Dutchman stories by the hour.

This rigmarole straight out of Jarry's *Ubu Roi* sums up the abject kind of civilization imposed with bureaucratic cruelty on the young Hopis so that, by imitating the whites, they might become "like whites themselves . . . and act as crazy as chickens with their heads chopped off."

A sudden illness is the prelude to his spiritual return to indigenous civilization. He lies half alive in a hospital bed, when a figure in sacred clothing appears before him in the space till now occupied by nurses and doctors.

Then I saw a tall human being standing by my bed in Katcina costume. He was well dressed in a dancing kilt and a sash, was barefoot, and wore long black hair hanging down his back. He had a soft prayer feather (*nakwakwosi*) in his hair and carried a blue one in his left hand—blue being the color which signifies the west and the home of the dead. He wore beads and looked wonderful as he watched me. When the nurses brought food, he said, "My son, you had better eat. Your time is up. You shall travel to the place where the dead live and see what it is like." I saw the door swing slowly back and forth on its hinges and stop just a little open. A cold numbness crept up my body; my eyes closed; and I knew I was dying.

The strange human being said, "Now, my boy, you are to learn a lesson. I have been guarding you all your life, but you have been careless. You shall travel to the House of the Dead and learn that life is important. The path is already made for you. You had better hurry; and perhaps you will get back before they bury your body. I am your Guardian Spirit (*dumalaitaka*). I will wait here and watch over your body; but I shall also protect you on your journey."

The pain disappeared and I felt well and strong. I arose from my bed and started to walk, when something lifted me and pushed me along through the air, causing me to move through the door. . . . I was swept along northeast-ward by a gust of wind.

The journey into the other world is supposed to teach him caution and attentiveness to the supernatural, certainly not the white man's moralism. After having got past a group of benevolent clowns, he sees the inferno into which the miserable "Two-Hearts," malign beings who cause mis-chief, are sent.

On his return his soul re-enters the numb, cold body that the nurses are watching apprehensively. His guardian has warned him, so now he must be alert: ". . . I shall hold you lightly, as between two fingers, and if you disobey me I will drop you."

Talayesva becomes a pure Hopi again. His vision works in a mysterious way. One day he goes on a trip to gather salt from some distant beds and realizes that he is traveling the same road as on his death journey. But the vision also lights up the past like a beacon: Talayesva now understands that it was his Guardian Spirit who had stopped him one day when he raised a stone to kill a snake.

Talayesva's Hopi life is a sequence of work, dances, flirtations with girls, supernatural apparitions strikingly similar to those of the Homeric gods, complicated ceremonies, pilgrimages, and many sacred pranks. Among the Hopis, too, the pranks of certain initiates conceal a thought that resembles that of the Sioux *heyoka,* who foster humility and achieve negation of the ego by making themselves deliberately ridiculous with clownish tremblings and sighs, performing everything backward after the "thunderbird" has been revealed to them. Talayesva maintains the secret of the ceremonial mysteries, yet he makes us share in an intellectual as much as an aesthetic exaltation through the profusion of symbols dis-played during certain dances in lavishly decorated, sacred places. But Talayesva's clownish character is paired with some repulsive traits, such as his continuous, trivial erotic adventures (the Hopi religion exalts purity as a magical force).

The struggle against witchcraft crops up again and again throughout the book. Talayesva himself, four of whose children died one after the other, is accused by his neighbors of being a "Two-Heart," a sorcerer who feeds off the lives of others in order to prolong his own. Gossip being a great evil, "Two-Hearts must promote it . . . to peddle gossip is like playing checkers with an evil spirit. You win occasionally but you are more often trapped at your own game," Talayesva tells his wife Irene.

A dispute with a friend who had spread the calumny is described as follows:

He exclaimed: "I met you on the road to your sheep camp and caught you crying. I took your side then and helped you free your mind of evil thoughts. Why are you against me now?" I told him that he had no right to call me a Two-Heart, that I had never attended a secret meeting of the underworld people, that I had not caused the death of my children, and that I had no power to defend myself. I reminded him that I had caught him crying in the field and that he had fled like a coward. . . . Nathaniel threatened to strike me. . . . I was daring him to kill an innocent man and, expecting a blow, I raised my arm. In fact, I almost struck the Two-Heart; but my Guardian Spirit checked my fist before it fell and flashed a message to my mind to take the first blow like a man. I think Nathaniel read my mind by magic, for instead of striking me, he bowed his head and had no more to say. I had him cornered; the people cheered me, and a few spat at Nathaniel.

It is a wholly interior encounter, a hand-to-hand struggle between thoughts that from time to time manifest themselves in sudden gestures.

To understand this part of the autobiography one must remember the concept of black magic held by the Indians of the Southwest. Among the Mohaves it is said that in the sixth month of conception fetuses begin to dream. Future normal men dream of their birth, while future sorcerers dream of ways of not being born. Indeed, they detest life; they would like to die while being born and drag their mothers along with them, so they place themselves crosswise in the womb.

Those who are strong in evil die in accordance with their desire; the others are thrust into the world unwillingly, where they will be both cowardly and stoical. They will learn how to cast their enchantments like a blob of spit on their victims; they will sequester them with their invisible double, and as a result the victims will dream of them. Why are they so implacable with these chosen creatures? An impulse of love binds them to them, and trouble will be in store if they cannot possess them magically, if they do not succeed in killing them and then possessing them in their obscene dreams.

But the most profound desire in the depths of the sorcerer's soul is to be killed. Only on this condition will he be master after death of the souls he has bewitched. And in fact once the beloved creature has died, the sorcerer offers himself to his executioner: longing for death, he provokes him.[20] Is not this the pattern of the Redeemer's life turned upside down? And the archetype of every tyrant's life?

Another tribe greatly feared by the Hopis because of the great number of witches among them is the Navajos, among whom Clyde Kluckhohn studied the initiation rites of their black magic societies.[21] The initiation is attained by murdering a member of one's family, after which one is taught to prepare a poison made from macerated babies' corpses—preferably twins—a poison that looks like pollen. The witches often work together, one witch weaving the spell while the other offers to cure the sick person or recommends a witch to lift the enchantment. The adepts meet at night to call down curses, contrive plots, fornicate with dead women, and eat human flesh. They sit in a circle, naked except for masks and covered with jewels, a basketful of human flesh in front of each one. One witch will often force all the rest to do his will, and each witch is assisted by a wretched being—a "helper."

Generally, all those who disregard a taboo are suspected of black magic; hence the atmosphere of suspicion which Bandelier and Talayesva have described—suspicion that is then rekindled by the use of sorcery for sexual purposes, or to obtain good luck in gambling, trade, or hunting.

For good as well as evil, an enormously rich inwardness determines the decisive events that take place in the "Hopi way." Its religious teaching is summed up in the words that Talayesva's Guardian Spirit pronounced during an admonitory dream: " 'Alas, you are getting off the Sun Trail again. You are now a middle-aged man and ought to know better, for nothing good can come from evil thoughts, arguments, and worry. Your Sun God, who is chief of all other gods, is getting weary at the way you worry over these things.' " The village chief repeats: ". . . You must drive out your bad thoughts. Just say, 'Get away, evil spirits,' and then pull yourself out of their hands like a free man."

∴

Though undistinguished as a writer, John G. Neihardt served as the channel for a rich variety of Indian experience; his writings are characterized by a profound knowledge of the Indian. Born in Illinois, he spent most of his life in Bancroft, Nebraska, and established close relations with the Omahas. He caught fire at the thought of the modern "epic of the Aryan race," the discovery and exploration of the American West, and tried to become its romantic bard in his *Cycle of the West,* a cycle of heroic songs, among them *The Song of the Indian Wars,* published in 1925. Like Sandoz, Neihardt told the story of the battles fought by Sitting Bull and Crazy Horse ("The wizard eyes, the haggard face and thin/ Transfigured by a burning from within/ Despite the sweat-streaked paint and battle grime!"). But the attempt at writing an epic racist poem failed because of the unintended humor of its pantingly fierce tone, while the determination to believe in the myth of race ("The driving breed, the takers of the world/ The makers and the bringers of the law") stiffened into clumsy magniloquence.

Yet once freed of the impediment of poorly mastered metrics, the wish to approach the defeated magnanimously was better expressed in his book of short stories, *Indian Tales and Others* (1926). Neihardt tried to reproduce the rhythms of Indian speech, which almost never is successful. "The Singer of the Ache" has a beginning which is intended to be incantatory and reminds one of Maeterlinck's "lunar" prose:

Now this is the story of one who walked not with his people but with a dream.
To you I tell it, O White Brother, yet it is not for you, unless you also have followed the long trail of hunger and thirst—the trail that leads to no lodge upon the high places or the low places, by flowing streams or where the sand wastes lie.

The narrator is torn from his childhood games by his parents:

So they sent him at nightfall to the hill of dreams—as is the custom of our people.
Wahoo! the bitter hill of dreams!
And he of the many names went up into the hill of dreams and dreamed. And in through the mists that strange winds blow over the hills of sleep burst a white light, as though the moon had grown so big that all the sky was filled from rim to rim, leaving no place for sun and stars. And upon the surface of the white light floated a face, an awful face—whiter than the light upon which it floated; and so beautiful to see that he of the many happy names ached through all his limbs, and cried out and woke.

The vision is considered inauspicious, and the young man must return to the hills. But he has the selfsame vision of a moon face flashing out a pale flame, which does not symbolize any known destiny, either that of a warrior, a hunter, or a saint.

The young man becomes a poet and, like Baudelaire's albatross, cannot adapt himself to everyday life. But the mimetic care of the opening is wasted; romantic fantasizing takes over.

Even in those places where Neihardt is rather felicitous, his attempt to "narrate at white heat" often becomes a parody of itself, and the visionary Indian atmosphere that he is sometimes on the point of bringing to life encounters the stumbling block of his inability to distinguish between vision and dream.

So, too, in another Indian short story, "The Look in the Face," the attention to impalpable magical events, to the power of the glance, is drenched in a sentimentality that derives from white commercial literature, not from the austere indigenous world. In the same way, "The White Wakunda" tries to produce a religious shiver by telling essentially the same story as "The Singer of the Ache," though with another ending: a boy has a different vision from the usual ones and therefore a unique destiny. He follows the track of his dream, returns to his tribe to proclaim Christ's message of love, and as a result is beaten to death. Much the same thing can be said of the other stories: Christianity reduced to the ethic of benevolence is the narrator's point of view, from which he observes the fascinating, fantastic, but for him inferior world of the Indian. Neihardt is never freed from the paralysis of romantic, humanitarian ideology, even by his knowledge of all aspects of Indian life and his sympathy for it.

Thus some scenes that are extraordinarily faithful to Indian reality stand out in the forced and commonplace context. For example, the ceremony of the pipe in "Vylin": "As they passed the pipe about the circle, there were no words; for in the silence the good spirits may speak . . ."; and the old man's thoughts: "Who can bury a bad thing deeper than the spirits see?" Yet what is missing is the one thing that would transcend the limitations of entertainment literature with all that is catchily superficial patchwork in it: the abandonment of the point of view of "civilization." Neihardt could not reach it by himself. In middle age, however, he was singularly fortunate. He encountered a sublime religious figure, Black Elk, and from the conversations he had with him a book was born, *Black Elk Speaks.*[22]

But Neihardt himself was not transformed by the encounter; he was merely a means, similar to a medium who, after having served alien powers, returns to his narrow, cramped world, a world whose ideology is precisely that of a Carl Sandburg.

At eighty-five, Neihardt, with the progressivist frigidity of an Andrew Jackson or a Theodore Roosevelt, was to speak in 1966 of the Indian collapse to an interviewer from a Phoenix newspaper:

It was an old culture being destroyed by a new culture; that's the epic period for you every time. But what we did to the Indians was not peculiar in history. You always find when a great mass of human beings are moving they are utterly without morals and pity. They are to be compared with flood, fire and wind. You can't sentimentalize about it because you're dealing with an unhuman power—the stream of history. It's a pity when somebody falls by the wayside, but if we were God and could see everything we might feel differently about it.[23]

∴

The beginning of *Black Elk Speaks* is memorable:

My friend, I am going to tell you the story of my life, as you wish; and if it were only the story of my life I think I would not tell it; for what is one man that he should make much of his winters, even when they bend him like a heavy snow? . . . It is the story of all life that is holy and is good to tell, and of us two-leggeds sharing in it with the four-leggeds and the wings of the air and all green things. . . .

This religious lyricism is concretized in ritual, the ceremonial of the pipe that Black Elk explains:

These four ribbons hanging here on the stem are the four quarters of the universe. The black one is for the west where the thunder beings live to send us rain; the white one for the north, whence comes the great white cleansing wind; the red one for the east, whence springs the light and where the morning star lives to give men wisdom; the yellow for the south whence come the summer and the power to grow.

But these four spirits are only one Spirit after all, and this eagle feather here is for that One, which is like a father, and also it is for the thoughts of men that should rise high as eagles do.

Black Elk reveals that in his tribe, too, a holy man had prophesied that the four-leggeds were going back into the earth and that "a strange race had woven a spider's web all around the Lakotas"; in a vision he saw the horrid houses of the future on barren land, and died of sorrow because of it. So no one had any illusions when the white men came.

Since his boyhood Black Elk has heard the whispers of supernatural voices. At nine he is already a warrior, and now events come thick and fast. He hears someone calling him, but as he leaves the tepee his thighs begin to hurt: his whole body becomes swollen, and he drags himself around painfully.

A few days later he is lying in the tepee, looking up into the sky, when he is summoned again. "I could see out through the opening, and there two men were coming from the clouds, head-first like arrows slanting down, and I knew they were the same that I had seen before. Each now carried a long spear, and from the points of these a jagged lightning flashed."

They reach the ground and urge him to hurry: his grandfathers are calling him. "Then they turned and left the ground like arrows slanting upward from the bow." The pain in his legs disappears. He comes out of the tepee, and a fast-flying cloud carries him off: "Then there was nothing but the air and the swiftness of the little cloud that bore me and those two men still leading up to where white clouds were piled like mountains on a wide blue plain, and in them thunder beings lived and leaped and flashed."

Suddenly he finds himself on a plain surrounded by mountains and has visions of dancing horses, then of animals of every kind, and finally there appears before him a tepee in which his ancestors are seated at a meeting.

The oldest spoke. . . . "Your Grandfathers all over the world are having a council, and they have called you here to teach you." His voice was very kind, but I shook all over with fear now, for I knew that these were not old men, but the Powers of the World. And the first was the Power of the West; the second, of the North; the third, of the East; the fourth, of the South; the fifth, of the Sky; the sixth, of the Earth.

The old man of the West tells him that he will be taken to the center of the universe; then he gives him a wooden cup full of water and in the water was the sky—the power to create—and then a bow—the power to destroy. Then he points to himself and says, "Look close at him who is your spirit now, for you are his body and his name is Eagle Wing Stretches."

After having spoken, the old man is transformed into an emaciated, sickly horse. The old man of the North gives him a herb that cures the horse. The third old man gives him a pipe and becomes a goose; the fourth old man, the old man of the South, gives him a stick and becomes an elk; the fifth, the Spirit of the Sky, changes into an eagle; the sixth, the Spirit of the Earth, is very old but gradually grows young, "and when he had become a boy, I knew that he was myself with all the years that would be mine at last."

Other frightful and sublime events that follow transport him to the center of the earth and the very source of the Apocalypse, and from this succession of images Black Elk learns figuratively of his future as a succorer and nourisher of his people. When he awakes he is still swollen, but he feels well again; for twelve days he has lain there like a dead man. To the medicine man's eyes, he is filled with luminosity.

The events of ordinary life take him away from the contemplation of what he has seen, but when the thunder rumbles in the sky, or on other sublime occasions, he is exalted by a joyous memory.

Although considerably less impressive, the childhood experiences described by Jonathan Edwards in his *Personal Narrative* are quite similar: that sense of "inward sweet delight," that "calm, sweet abstraction of soul from all the concerns of this world; and sometimes a kind of vision, or fixed ideas and imaginations, of being alone in the mountains, or some solitary wilderness, far from all mankind, sweetly conversing with Christ, and wrapt and swallowed up in God."

Black Elk gradually recovered elements of his vision in life. Thus, "that evening just before sunset, a big thunder cloud came up from the west, and just before the wind struck, there were clouds of split-tail swallows flying all around above us. It was like a part of my vision, and it made me feel queer."

The chief of the tribe, Crazy Horse, is powerful because he can remember the vision he had at the time when he gained access to the world of archetypes, on the watershed between the divine and the human:

. . . Crazy Horse dreamed and went into the world where there is nothing but the spirits of all things. That is the real world that is behind this one, and everything we see here is something like a shadow from that world. He was on his horse in that world, and the horse and himself on it and the trees and the grass and the stones and everything were made of spirit. . . .

The secret of Crazy Horse's power lies in this vision—"he has only to think of that world to be in it again, so that he could go through anything and not be hurt." In the village, he would go about without noticing people. He is to lead the tribe in victorious battles against the whites, later to be related to Neihardt in a kind of chorus by Black Elk and other old friends of his. The epic that Neihardt had vainly tried for by looking at events from the side of the conquerors develops page by page now that he sees events through the eyes of the Indians. Crazy Horse is trapped and treacherously killed, his murderers being helped by a close friend: the archetypal fate of a savior of the people.

Black Elk is fifteen. Part of his revelation has been confirmed, but he dare not manifest it or declare himself; he feels that its power is growing, since he can foresee dangers and warns his people each time their enemies are about to surprise them. (During a flight to safety ". . . a thunder cloud came from the west behind us, and I knew it was coming to protect us. I could hear the thunder beings crying 'Hey hey!' to me. The cloud stood over us and did not rain much, but it was full of lightning and of voices.") But also a great fear began to grow within him

("I was so afraid of being afraid. . . .") The medicine man in whom he confides exclaims, "You must do your duty and perform this vision for your people upon earth. You must have the horse dance first for the people to see. Then the fear will leave you; but if you do not do this, something very bad will happen to you."

So, eight years after he has had the vision, it is staged for the tribe. On the tepees they paint the beings and objects he has seen, he teaches the songs he has heard (in the sky the thunder accompanies them, as though encouraging them to continue), each person takes a part, and even horses of various kinds have been gathered to represent the four cardinal points of the compass.

The representation begins, with alternating *tableaux vivants* and songs, and then behold! Black Elk is seized by ecstasy amid the neighing of the horses:

And as they sang, a strange thing happened. My bay pricked up his ears and raised his tail and pawed the earth, neighing long and loud to where the sun goes down. And the four black horses raised their voices, neighing long and loud, and the whites and the sorrels and the buckskins did the same; and all the other horses in the village neighed, and even those out grazing in the valley and on the hill slopes raised their heads and neighed together. Then suddenly, as I sat there looking at the cloud, I saw my vision yonder once again—the tepee built of cloud and sewed with lightning, the flaming rainbow door and, underneath, the Six Grandfathers sitting, and all the horses thronging in their quarters; and also there was I myself upon my bay before the tepee. I looked about me and could see that what we then were doing was like a shadow cast upon the earth from yonder vision in the heavens, so bright it was and clear. I knew the real was yonder and the darkened dream of it was here.

After the dance they all feel better, "Even the horses seemed to be healthier and happier. . . ."

The following spring Black Elk goes off by himself to invoke the supernatural powers with weeping, lamentations, and prayers for understanding. Thinking of all the dead, he cries very hard, hoping that his crying might kill him and bring him "in the outer world where nothing is ever in despair." The new vision comes to him as a cloud of butterflies, swarming around him with "a whimpering, pitiful noise, and it reveals the future to him in images, like a new chapter of the Apocalypse."

On his return, Black Elk tells his vision to the old men, and they ask him to perform it before the people, with the *heyokas*, or sacred fools, who do everything wrong or backward in order to make people laugh. (". . . it is planned that the people shall be made to feel jolly and happy first, so that it may be easier for the power to come to them"—because truth comes into the world with two faces, one sad, the other laughing; for each person the face that is opposite to the state in which he happens to be in is better.) So the thirty *heyokas,* one for each day of a moon, perform their clownish dances during the sacrifice of the dog. They are strangely dressed and painted and make people laugh, yet each detail in their getup speaks with sacred eloquence. They are painted red with black stripes that signify lightning, while the right sides of their heads are shaved so that when they look to the south the bare sides of their heads are turned toward the west in sign of humility before the powers of thunder. At the conclusion of the ceremony everybody feels much better. "They were better able now to see the greenness of the world, the wideness of the sacred day, the colors of the earth, and to set these in their minds."

∴

After the victory over Custer, Black Elk reluctantly agrees to live with his people in a repulsively square log cabin on the reservation. What power can be obtained in a square? The sacred form is a circle, as is shown by the sky and the earth, the wind that whirls about, the birds' nests, and the seasons of the year. Living in these square boxes, the power is gone, and it is very difficult to develop oneself, whereas in the old days boys were men at puberty. Black Elk concludes in his quiet, powerful voice: "Well, it is as it is. We are prisoners of war while we are waiting here. But there is another world."

He continues to be guided by his visions. He tells how by following clues—a bird's flight, a landscape similar to the one that appeared during his vision—he discovered the healing herb pointed out to him by the supernatural beings, and how in fact the next day he was summoned to cure a sick boy.

He begins by smoking and beating the drum:

You know, when the power of the west comes to the two-leggeds, it comes with a rumbling, and when it has passed, everything lifts up its head and is glad and there is greenness. . . . Also, the voice of the drum is an offering to the Spirit of the world. Its sound arouses the mind and makes men feel the mystery and power of things.

Probably the translation dilutes the meaning of the original words, that is, the particular rhythm and essence of things which the drum reproduces (in shamanistic cures the drum follows the heartbeat as it throbs in the patient, and gradually modifies it to make him healthy).

The second therapeutic act is to walk around the sick person from left to right. Black Elk cannot reveal all the reasons for this, but he indicates that life comes from the south, and the old walk toward the north, while the east is the source of light and of knowledge. In the end, one returns to a second childhood. "The more you think about this, the more meaning you will see in it."

Then begins the ceremony that revives and imitates the forms of the vision. Black Elk beats the drum until he feels the power flowing through him from the feet up, and then he invents the details of the procedure.

The time of desolation comes; the whites have exterminated the last of the bison herds. Since part of his vision is still obscure and because he hopes to learn from the whites some secrets that might somehow help his people, Black Elk agrees to join Buffalo Bill's circus. Far from his own country, he feels like a man who has never had a vision, as if he were dead. Traveling about Europe, he discovers that there is no feeling of solidarity among the white men. One day, while dining with some friends in Paris, he smiles and falls off his chair; for three days he is in a coma, and the doctors give him up for dead.

He returns in spirit to his native country. On his return in flesh and blood he will ascertain that everything is just as he had seen it during his ecstatic state in Paris.

Destiny brings him close to the extraordinary Provençal poet Folco de Baroncelli, though their paths never cross, but other Indian warriors in Buffalo Bill's show welcome the Provençal as a peer in Toulouse. De Baroncelli had developed a theory of the "red race," in which gypsies and redskins are assimilated with each other. He had even conceived the project of an alliance between the descendants of the Cathars and the Sioux resistance for the purpose of a joint fight against "progress." The outgrowth of these ideas are the Indian poems in de Baroncelli's book *Bled de luno;* here the "Indian brothers" are saluted as the victims, like the Provençals, of the *tuaire d'ideau*—murderers of the ideal, who are the force behind "material progress."

∴

Knowledge of the Dogon metaphysic reached the Western world because an old, blind priest decided to summon Marcel Griaule and communicated to him the heretofore well-guarded secrets in his keeping.

This encounter gave birth to a masterpiece, *Dieu d'eau,* and a school of white exegetes of the spiritual patrimony of the blacks: Germaine Dieterlen, Geneviève Calame-Griaule, Jean Servier, Jean Rouch, and Dominique Zahan. Knowledge of these teachings, whose complexity comes close to surpassing even our own medieval theological structures, did away with European prejudices concerning African spirituality.

Something analogous happened when Black Elk confided to Neihardt the secrets of the esoteric Sioux tradition, a tradition then on the point of total eclipse. Black Elk had wanted to make the tree of life flourish again in his people, but his hopes were dashed.

With tears running, O Great Spirit, Great Spirit, my Grandfather—with running tears I must say now that the tree has never bloomed. A pitiful old man, you see me here, and I have fallen away and have done nothing. Here at the center of the world, where you took me when I was young and taught me; here, old, I stand, and the tree is withered, Grandfather, my Grandfather!

Again, and maybe the last time on this earth, I recall the great vision you sent me. It may be that some little root of the sacred tree still lives. Nourish it then, that it may leaf and bloom and fill with singing birds. Hear me, not for myself, but for my people; I am old. Hear me that they may once more go back into the sacred hoop and find the good red road, the shielding tree!

Neihardt would have remained the regional storyteller of Nebraska and one of the last provincial versifiers if the encounter with Black Elk had not given him the chance to write a memorable book. In its wake, also in search of the holy Indian, came a young student of ancestral knowledge, Joseph Epes Brown, author of an essay on Chinese magical mirrors, who describes how

it was not until 1948, after many months of travel, that I was able to find him living with his family in a little canvas wall tent in a migrant potato-picking camp in Nebraska. I well remember him as he sat on an old sheepskin hide, ill and pitiful, with his almost totally blind eyes staring beyond that which surrounded him. . . . We smoked in silence until finally, with a soft and kindly voice, he spoke in Lakota. Translated by his son, he surprised me by saying that he had anticipated my coming, was glad that I was there beside him, and asked if I would remain with him, for there was much that he would like to tell me before, as he said, "he would pass from this world of darkness into the other real world of light." I therefore returned with him to his log cabin on the reservation, living with him and his generous family for almost a year. . . . Every day he talked for several hours until a veil of silence fell in which one could sense that he was so absorbed within the realities of which he was speaking that words no longer had meaning.[24]

Thus Brown transcribed Black Elk's fundamental work: *The Origin of the Sacred Pipe*.[25] Frithjof Schuon then followed in the footsteps of his predecessors and talked with Black Elk's son, with Last Bull, the last custodian of sacred arrows among the Cheyennes, and others. In his preface to the French translation of the work he provided the commentary to a literary genre evolved from the work of the highly unusual white apprentices to the last indigenous wise men.

The reaction to the new spirit that can be felt in Joseph Epes Brown's work was inept or malicious. In *The American Anthropologist*, in 1954, G. W. Hewes denied that it could be compared in terms of ethnological rigor to La Flesche's recordings of Osage myths or Michelson's texts and translations of Fox ceremonial. However, Black Elk's "ethnographic" knowledge might be considered adequate. A. N. Chamberlin reviewed the book in the San Francisco *Chronicle* and wondered whether Brown had been completely objective; he questioned "how much of his [Brown's] own beliefs mixed unconsciously with those of Black Elk." In other words, to comprehend and to love would constitute an obstacle to objectivity.

Yet the significance of the pipe as a metaphysical expression had never before been so perfectly understood. It was not understood by the Jesuits, who were the first to see the messengers of the sacred pipe appear in Canadian villages, while Clark Wissler, an authoritative interpreter and anthropologist, confessed that "we of this generation and time [do not] understand it either."[26]

∴

The particular identification of every part of the body with the parts of the pipe was first discussed by La Flesche in 1920,[27] but it was Brown who understood the spiritual process of the ritual.

The filled pipe is . . . "Totality," so that when the fire of the Great Spirit is added a divine sacrifice is enacted in which the universe and man are reabsorbed within the Principle, and become what in reality they are. In mingling his life-breath with the tobacco and fire through the straight stem of concentration, the man who smokes assists at the sacrifice of his own self, or ego, and is thus aided in realizing the Divine Presence at his own center. . . . In smoking the pipe together each man is aided in remembering his own center, which is now understood to be the same center of every man, and of the Universe itself.[28]

This victory over the *moi haïssable* comes before a qualitative leap that permits one to escape from the world of forms and images in order to draw upon the world of archetypes (with Jonathan Edwards one can say: "from types to antitypes"), to which Black Elk had alluded several times in Neihardt's book. One seems to hear again the voice of Jonathan Edwards, who in *Images and Shadows of Divine Things* teaches that all visible things subsist only with the purpose of invoking the truth in hieroglyphic form. The spring thaw exists so that one may recall the necessity of contrition, seeing the mud of fallen nature before gaining the joy of the sun; the snake fascinates the squirrel, which yields while pretending to flee, so that one will recall the hypocrisy of the sinner tempted by evil, and so on with each of nature's spectacles. Black Elk taught the same reversal in the daily relationship of reality, the same primacy of the idea over contingent appearances.

And among all the images or shadows of divine things, the Indian, as Black Elk explained to Neihardt, chooses the circle. This is the basic image with which the ceremony of the pipe connects:

. . . The Indian, after the manner of our compass, not only organized the plane of the earth with respect to the radical four of the cardinal points, but . . . he also subdivided the Above and the Below into zones and latitudes. . . . the redman's projection of his universe . . . is a circumscribing sphere with axis and equator, longitudes and latitudes, and . . . the ritual of the pipe is schematically a recognition of the points from which the great lines of the sphere are generated.[29]

If circularity was the perfect form for the Indian, Schuon observes,

all the static forms of existence are in this way determined by a concentric material or mental archetype: centered on its qualitative and totemic "I," almost impersonal, the Indian tends to independence and therefore indifference in respect to the external world: he encircles himself with silence as though inside a magic circle and this silence is sacred because it transmits celestial influences. From this silence the Indian draws his spiritual strength; his customary prayer is silent, it does not require thought, but rather an awareness of the Spirit, and this awareness is as immediate and informal as the sky above him. Hence the indifference of the nomadic Indian to space and visible, stable structures: he shuns fixed dwellings, made of stone, and even shuns writing, which would condense, petrify, the silent flow of the Spirit. European civilization, in both its dynamic and its static forms, is anchored in space and extends quantitatively over it, whereas the Indian of America has his pivot outside of space itself, in nonlocalized principles.[30]

Just as Black Elk disclosed the genesis of Indian drama and liturgy, another chief, Hosteen Klah, a Navajo, transmitted certain secrets of sacred painting and many myths. His biography, written by Frank J. Newcomb, who lived for a long time with the tribe, has scant literary value and the tribe's misfortunes never really touch us; this is also true of the stories of suffering that the victims seem almost afraid to tell. The book, however, becomes exultant when it speaks of the ceremonial preparations surrounding ritual painting; the painting of Byzantine icons called for similar circumspection. The Navajo priests, as B. H. Haile informs us, set to work only after having contemplated the stars that corresponded to the chosen theme and chanted corresponding hymns.*

Sand painting for ceremonial purposes is a collective rite directed by the medicine man:

Klah opened a sack of pollen and blessed all of the sand that would be used that day; then someone handed him a long cord, which was held across the background sand, first from east to west then from north to south. This, snapped into the sand to make crossed lines, located the center. Klah took black sand to make a small black lake in this center which he bordered with white to represent foam, yellow for pollen, blue for summer rain, and red for sunlight. He then returned to his place and the five painters continued the design. Four black logs pointed in the four directions, while the four sacred plants, corn, beans, squash, and tobacco, were laid in the quadrants. At the east stood Hastje-altai, the teacher; at the west stood Hastje-hogan, the god of reproduction; on the north and on the south were the Bighones-kidi, the seed gatherers, bearers, and guards. A rainbow arc was painted to protect three sides, but the eastern side was open, with no guardian symbols.[31]

After a benediction, the painting becomes an altar and can cure a sick man, to whom, having been blessed with pollen and touched by fetishes, songs are chanted. Finally, the medicine man presses his wet hands on the head of the painted figures and dries them on the patient's head. He does the same on the shoulders and other parts of the painted, exalted bodies, transferring their sacramental virtues to the sick man's body. Each illness requires entirely different figures.

∴

Still close to the world of tradition is the painting of Monroe Tsa Toke, a Kiowan who drew a series of emblems of the peyote cult that hover

* B. H. Haile, *Starlore Among the Navaho.* The constellation *Corvus* stands for a man with feet set wide apart; a part of Scorpion represents the originator of witchcraft. This is the type of vision granted to assiduous contemplators of the stars and the thirty-six Navajo constellations.

midway between real and visionary life. His comments are akin to poetry.[32] The scene is described with simplicity:

They all take puffs of cigarettes and utter prayers to the Unknown and this is the seal of relationship between the "greats" and the "humans." . . . One is . . . the Earth God, sometimes known as mother. . . . The second is . . . Spirit God—sometimes Sun God. The third is "In Between God;" this is the god who joins the Earth and Spirit Gods and is between them, is also known as "messenger god." The winds and birds are part of this "In Between God" and help join the Earth and Spirit. When the prayers begin the messenger gods begin to weave back and forth. They begin to lay designs, the prayers are designs. Out of the prayers new designs become visible. . . . The beauty of the day in the East becomes apparent. The inspiration rises, although often it is seen through a veil, such as an object or a song.

One of these designs represent a "Song Bird." It comes to life as one contemplates a fan made of the scissor tails of swallows:

My conception of this bird is graceful in flight, who knows the different winds of the air, as it glides so beautifully through the air. Under the sensation of peyote, I gather an idea of two birds gliding across with the most beautiful feathers flying over the fireplace, disappearing in the distance. Then I notice that the bird is reflected in the fire as if the bird lay in the fire. The wood that is parched out of fire turns into feathers. Then I found that the birds are known to be singers. The rhythms as he glides and sings through his flight are some of the most beautiful in song.

Toke records the soul's progress from reality to clusters of light and color and from these to sheer rhythmic, divine essences.

The Kiowa N. Scott Momaday is the author of lyrics or paintings in prose rather than real novels. He often gives us lessons in Indian attentiveness: on how the ability to meditate in a relaxed yet disciplined manner upon the qualities of objects permits one to grasp their symbolism. Thus, concerning the eagles in *House Made of Dawn* he explains:

They are sacred, and one of them, a huge female, old and burnished, is kept alive in a cage in the town. Even so, deprived of the sky, the eagle soars in man's imagination; there is divine malice in the wild eyes, and unmerciful intent. The eagle ranges far and wide over the land, farther than any other creature, and all things there are related simply by having existence in the perfect vision of a bird.

These—and the innumerable meaner creatures, the lizard and the frog, the insect and the worm—have tenure in the land. The other, latecoming things— the beasts of burden and of trade, the horse and the sheep, the dog and the cat—these have an alien and inferior aspect, a poverty of vision and instinct, by which they are estranged from the wild land, and made tentative. They are born and die upon the land, but then they are gone away from it as if they had never been. Their dust is borne away in the wind, and their cries have no echo in the rain and the river, the commotion of wings, the return of boughs bent by the passing of dark shapes in the dawn and dusk.[33]

Here is another lesson in Indian attentiveness:

. . . stopping once to drink from the river, he turned around and saw the valley below, a great pool of the sunlit sky, the red and purple hills; and here and upward from the height to the top of the continent the air was distilled to the essence of summer and noon, and nothing lay between the object and the eye.

He began almost to be at peace, as if he had drunk a little of warm, sweet wine, for a time no longer centered upon himself. He was alone, and he wanted to make a song out of the colored canyon, the way the women of Torreón made songs upon their looms out of colored yarn, but he had not got the right words together. It would have been a creation song; he would have sung lowly of the first world, of fire and flood, and of the emergence of dawn from the hills. And had he brought food to eat along the way, he would have wanted it to be a crust of oven bread, heavy and moist, pitted with cinders and ash, or a blue cornmeal cake full of grit and sweet smoke.

Chapter XII

———•◦•———

Notes on the Future

Leaving one of the highways that cut across New Mexico to follow a wagon road winding among deserted expanses of plain and the infrequent cultivated fields, one ends up in one of the surviving Quere Indian villages. The adobe houses, squat and elegant, with their projecting roof beams, cluster around a plaza; entering the maze of streets at a certain time of the year, one hears a chorus of voices, now guttural, now roaring. Women emerge from the houses with their children and hasten to the plaza, carrying dishes of many-colored foods. They have a secretive look, and their rapid strides make their green and scarlet capes sway.

Suddenly the plaza opens out, vast, flooded with sunlight; the grim, imperious chant of the dancers lined up in its center reverberates like a series of blows striking against the dry earth. The brownish circle of the houses is broken by the vivid colors of the knots of women who watch motionlessly, standing erect on the terraces, their capes shaken by the hot, aromatic wind.

The dancers are in a long line, their lustrous skins glistening in the sun, covered by bright green leaves, beating time, their ankles ringing with bells, waving feathers, symbols of the prayers ascending to the sky. The dance is not marked by emphatic, sweeping movements; on the contrary, it is made up entirely of minimal gestures, like the Japanese Noh dance, and the impression is one of immense, withheld strength, the same as that of the harsh chant. This strength, on the verge of overflowing, together with subtle discretion, commands an unyielding attentiveness, by means of which one slowly penetrates beyond the apparent monotony. The scene remains unchanged throughout the entire morning, under the rays of the sun. Then the line of dancers goes to the houses, where the women have prepared the sacred meal.

Some of the dances and their songs have been explained in long commentaries that dispel the mystery of the repetitions with their too simple or too enigmatic outward appearance. As for the symbols concealed in the costumes, one knows at least some of their meanings. But the hypnosis of the sun, the deep-chested, rhythmic beat of the voices, the limpid light of desert and mesa, the incenselike perfumes of plants given off in the heat, the taste of the food—all form a vibrant setting that covers the invisible truth of which the chant speaks. It is a truth more ancient but not in disharmony with what is proclaimed by the Spanish churches in the village, also built of adobe, painted a bright white and with projecting beams, having forms very similar to certain Romanesque structures found in Sardinia, and often adorned with gay folk frescoes.

The Pueblos have never agreed to make a violent separation between their ancient truths and the truths brought to them by the sixteenth-century Franciscans; they have, conversely, been able to enrich the new faith. Where indeed could one find anything like the exquisite small church of Chimayo? It is a sanctuary made of adobe, its altarpiece of a provincial, touching charm; the features of Christian saints are modeled on the masks of native spirits. A small room hidden behind the altar is dominated by a figure of the Christ child; the naked earth of the floor has miraculous properties. A person who has eaten it or rubbed himself with a paste made of it may be able to leave behind in the sacristy the prostheses and crutches on which he dragged himself here. The railings are hung with the evidences of cures. An album is there for visitors' devout comments; on the last pages female hands have traced, either in the noble Renaissance Spanish that is still spoken here or in English, supplications for the village's young men in danger in Vietnam.

Thus the alchemy of differing devotions has reproduced in this rustic sanctuary the practice recalled by Paracelsus and ancient medical treatises—that is, eating the earth of certain privileged places (in Europe it is called "sealed earth").

Anyone who travels up from Santa Fe, proceeding along a fertile river valley to the tableland, comes upon the most famous and ancient village, Taos. Leaving graceful Spanish Taos behind, one goes down a country road, and here is the native Taos, unchanged perhaps since the sixteenth century. Here again are the square houses, one built on top of another, with terraces that lead from one to the next, and giving somewhat the impression of a fortress, like certain Tibetan monasteries. And here, too, is the small maze of streets, and then finally the very wide plaza. If one stops here at the center, one senses a felicity full of peace and awareness, the same feeling that can be experienced standing at the meeting of the *cardo* and the *decummanus* at Paestum or in what remains of any city built in accordance with an ancient sacred plan. Just as at Paestum the mystical center of the town is the *mundus,* that is, a subterranean building which does not coincide with the geometric center of the two main streets, so the builders of Taos also made sure that in the plan of their town there was a place dedicated to the contemplation of cosmic harmony. The *mundus* of Taos is called a kiva. Projecting out of the ground are the superstructures with stairs that give access from above to the interior: symbol of the world's axes. Only men versed in the holy ceremonies are permitted to enter the kiva, in which sacred objects are kept.

Standing in the plaza one feels a singular joy, which comes not only from the beauty of the purple mountains that form a crown around the circle of houses but also from feeling oneself part of a geometry of perfect proportions, answering to the very norms that uphold our bodies and order our thoughts. The line that joins noon to sunset is marked by the brook that goes sparkling through the village. On the axis that unites east to west the public road leads into the plaza, passing by the church. Originally, to contemplate meant to establish exactly the orientation of a site.

But the central point of the most profound religious thoughts of the people of Taos is not symbolized by any place in their village; in fact, it is hidden behind the ridges of the nearby mountains, beyond the pastures where the horses are freely grazing. There is a bowl in the mountains covered with conifers, and at its center lies the sacred Blue Lake. When, on the appointed day the people of Taos in procession descend in concentric circles toward the lake, it is said that the fish run in dense schools on the surface of its water.

When I asked the significance of the lake they asked me where I came from, and I told them I was an Italian. They explained: "The lake is for us what Rome is for you. The pilgrimage we make to it is what Easter is for you."

Taos elects a chief, who at the moment of his designation ceases to remember English and speaks only Tewa and so, majestic in his cape, together with his interpreter, like Moses with Aaron, represents his people in Washington.

Thus one is forced to return to the world of everyday politics, where the Indians with whom I spoke move with great adroitness. It would, I believe, be very difficult to make use of their sufferings for ends that are not theirs. They are capable of rejecting those who, having accepted the crude modern and progressivist civilization, now try to exploit their Indian ancestry as political material. But how deep and terrible those sufferings were, and still are. The most conscientious element in American politics is beginning to regret the harm done to the Indians, and the present government recognizes that the chief demands of the tribes are justified and promises its support. But there are still people who have the temerity to press the Indians to "evolve" so that they may become as perturbed and distressed as the inhabitants of the big industrial cities. It is a relief to read *The Sentinel*, the bulletin of the National Congress of American Indians, and to see that a new kind of manifesto is now being published in Washington: society, it warns, must ineluctably return to concerning itself with the earth as man's home and not, as before, as an economic jungle. Gradually, as society becomes more humanized, it will be obliged to adopt certain features of Indian sociality. The Indian tribes will emerge as the only force capable of facing the social problem. From now on, Indians must consider their reservations as homelands, not to be sold, rented, or exploited at the whim of some bureaucrats and sacrificed without reason.

Indian land must be dedicated to the people's spiritual needs, and only the Indians—or at any rate those faithful to the tradition, who resist the threat of being transformed into the interchangeable parts of the production process, transformed from actors in sublime rites into the spectators of movie or television screens, from explorers of the divine into superstitious believers in progress—they alone in America have kept intact a living idea of spiritual needs. The deadening environment of concrete, asphalt, and steel has not yet atrophied their senses, nor has Enlightenment barbarism destroyed their religious strength. Can so subtle a reality find a political defense?

The new Indians demonstrate a political awareness that will make it quite difficult to exploit them for other people's adventures. Like religious men in general, they are averse to that surrogate for faith, Utopia, and so they do not offer a support for political deception.

Mad Bear, the Tuscarora chief, in 1958 went to visit Castro, with the idea of obtaining Cuban support for admission of an American tribal organization to the United Nations. Yet his action was carefully circumscribed; an Indian certainly does not believe that he has anything to learn from modern ideologies.

The Indian is well aware of the dangers of being used by what he uses, and so he has abstained from formulating in the modern fashion a charter or manifesto to express his sense of justified grievance that is now characteristic of a growing number of tribes. He has left this task to a white man,

Stan Steiner, without giving him a mandate and without furnishing him with any form of recognition. In his manifesto in book form, *The New Indians,* Steiner has compiled a series of quotations from "new Indians." He captures the feeling of the young Indian college graduates as it found expression at a meeting held in the cathedral of St. Francis at Santa Fe in 1954. The graduates, who had assimilated the modern catchwords, did not, however, deny their tradition but looked instead to the old men of the tribes for guidance and support. For once, scientistic and progressivist magic had been defeated by young people almost inevitably destined to be its docile victims (like the young horses in Vergil's *Georgics:* "while the minds of the young are tractable and they are in the pliable age").

Since then, other similar congresses have been held; they have brought to the fore what Steiner calls the "academic aborigines," such as Clyde Warrior, an Indian of the Makah tribe. He has worked in research groups at universities, has furnished his credentials as an academic scholar fulfilling all the customary quasi-ritual requirements, providing meticulous bibliographies, and publishing "contributions" in scholarly journals. With all this—a thing rare in the West, where academics tend to be hypnotized by this kind of work—he has been able to disregard the fetish of "scientific rigor," recognizing the superiority of indigenous mystical life that his colleagues in anthropology regard as something to be pinned down like a dead butterfly, within the frame of their materialistically and economically oriented hypotheses.

In the magazine edited by native college graduates, *ABC: American Before Columbus,* he wrote with wrath and contempt of the "religious operators," of the teachers with closed minds, of the pseudosocial sociologists who knowingly provoke the cultural genocide of Indian youth, and the bureaucrats who try to pass laws and regulations that would result in further "progress."

The long-standing lie of material progress nauseates not only this young Indian but also the finished products of progressivist delirium. On a wall in Greenwich Village there appeared this one word written in block letters: PROGRASS (the "grass" referring, of course, to marijuana). But Warrior—and with him the new Indian in general—refuses to be confused with "radicals" of a Western stamp; indeed, if we are looking for a formula, his is a revolution with an archaic imprint. But any sort of definition would be deceptive. Those who insist on affixing political labels to the Indians, he says, do not understand that since they reject the values of a society they cannot be judged according to them. They are not radicals. They do not propose to revolutionize society. If society would leave them in peace, they would cease to be concerned with it.

What will happen on the not so distant day when the feeling of "closeness to Indian values" becomes an effective political force? In fact, attempts are now being made to constitute a rather compact electoral front. The Indians are beginning to register as voters in ever greater numbers. The Navaho *Times* in particular supports this use of the ballot box, which has helped the Apaches and Sioux to acquire weight on the sensitive scales of local politics.

One might suspect that all the talk about spiritual and mystical values among Indians of the young generation is, as it often was in the recent European past, an empty noise. And yet to be convinced of the persisting life of the spirit, of the "intellect of love" among them, it is enough to leaf through a modest little book mimeographed by the State School for Indians at Santa Fe, where the students are trained in the appreciation of their old traditions. Titled *The Writer's Reader,*[1] it publishes the students' papers. The quality of this poetry strikes one as being superior to that of the poems generally published in literary reviews or by the large publishing houses.

A girl poet of the Susquamish tribe, Agnes Pratt, writes this poem on pride:

> Ebullient sun,
> Ego taught and sure.
> Much I have learned,
> Teach me more.
> Life is a spring,
> And hope is tiny bits of quartz,
> Shining up through watery pools,
> Pricking sun and me with rays of promise.

And this poem titled "Rebel":

> Rebel, living your young life in shorthand
> You're cryptic quick jerks, leaps, and running.
> Where are you running to, Rebel?
> Rebel, deaf to the whole of the ballad,
> You're singing but half of the story.
> Rebel, why do you ask me to listen?

Alonzo Lopez, a young boy from the Papago tribe of Arizona, writes about a subtle cosmogony, using homespun images:

I see a star.
Yet it is day.
The hands of my mother
Make it grow.
It is a black star
Set against a white sky.
How gentle that star,
Now that she weaves
Devils' claws
Together to make
A basket.

And in his second language he summarizes the ancient teachings:

I was directed by my grandfather
To the East
So I might have the power of the bear;
To the South,
So I might have the courage of the eagle;
To the West,
So I might have the wisdom of the owl;
To the North,
So I might have the craftiness of the fox;
To the Earth
So I might receive her fruit.
To the Sky
So I might lead a life of innocence.

The Nez Percé Phil George also puts into English verse the ancestral teachings on the sacred symbolism of the lodges where steam baths are taken:

OLD MAN, THE SWEAT LODGE

"This small lodge is now alive,
The womb of our mother, Earth.
The blackness in which we sit,
The ignorance of our impure minds,
These burning stones are
The coming of a new life."
Near my heart I place his words.

Naked, like an infant at birth, I crouch,
Cuddled upon fresh straw and boughs.
Confessing, I recall all evil deeds.
For each sin I sprinkle water on fire-hot stones;

Their hissing is a special song and I know
The place from which Earth's seeds grow is alive.

Old Man, the Sweat Lodge heals the sick;
Brings good fortune to one deserving.
Sacred steam rises—vapor fills my very being—
My pores slime out their dross.
After chanting prayers to the Great Spirit,
I lift a blanket to the East;
Through this door dawns wisdom.

Cleansed, I dive into icy waters.
Pure, I rinse away unworthy yesterday.
"My son, walk straight in this new life.
Youth I help to retain in you.
Return soon. Visit an old one.
Now, think clean, feel clean, be happy."

I thank you, Old Man, the Sweat Lodge.

The Choctaw Marie Jacob re-creates the enchantments of tribal life
with the grace of a Japanese poet:

RIVAL OF VOICES

Silent, forewarning moonlight
Drifted in between the trees.
A light breeze stirred

I hastened toward a dimly outlined shack,
Wan, pale moonlight hid behind musty velvet cloaks
Of darkness. Murky mud squashed beneath my feet,
Clinging damp-wood odors rose.
I heard and listened, startled!
Rasping whispers from my childhood broke.
"Remember, little one, good and evil dwell in the wind.
Heed black forms. Beware! Shadowy powers,
Cunning spirits in blind guises
Spring alive when touched by the moon.
Remember, evil surrounds you.
Spirit casts spells to harm.
'Come'—they call, and the circle widens to absorb and
Gather in all evil, enclosing you."

Why did I not heed the words of the wise one
And stay in the light in the midst of the good?
And good? I wondered . . . Is the good alive?

Which will overcome . . . Nothing.
Only the whistling wind answered, by thrusting itself
Into my coat and tousling my hair—
Suddenly my father's voice boomed in my pounding pulse:
"No fear, little one, for in calmness did I once
Dare the shape of evil and rid of thoughts
The eerie moon cast upon him.
The shape turned real and became a friend.
Remember, when Evil controls, we are living forms
Dropped in the dark depth of silent pools,
And we ripple and flow where he wants us to."

These are the first fruits of young people who tomorrow may well be the creators of a new, extraordinary Indian literature in the English language, and—poetry always being a presage of the future—we find in these early verses the promise of fresh life suffusing the ancient tradition. To find in pages of such modest appearance so much ground for expectation is truly astonishing. And how could one be prepared for the inner experience revealed by a young Indian Chippewa girl, Julie Wilson?

I traveled to the west
Riding on a coyote's lonely cry.
I saw blackberry shadows turn into death before me.
I stumbled and fell in with the souls that lay in
This rotting pit.
Everything I touched turned to dust.
I accepted blackness and wondered
How long a million years would last
Far off in this blackness I spied a white minute form
This I fed and nourished with my body, giving it my entire self.
Carrying me to the east, I was grateful, until finding I could not
Detach myself from it, for this was I, going with myself.

On the white side, all the indications point to a renewal of reverence. In the 1968 issue of the *New Directions Annual*,[2] Allen Katzman writes of his "Comanche Cantos" that Indians dance to encircle the rotating earth, not to sink into it:

They dance and the earth turns. The earth
is dancing.
They encircle her, her speed, her roundness.

The earth turns. The earth
is turning.
Those who are not dancing will die.

They will set their lives according to
the sun and moon:

Their face is their face. Their hands hold
the moon aloft
They are child to the tree when the moon
lies in its branches.
Their eyes are untouched, a kind
of bird.

And he understands that

The Indian rides alone upon the
flat caress of the sun.
He has somewhere to go beyond
the fringe of dreaming.

Notes

CHAPTER I

1. New York, 1960, p. 728.
2. *The Advancement of Learning* and *New Atlantis* (Oxford, 1956), p. 273.
3. *Essays*, ed. W. H. Rouse (London, n.d.), p. 200.
4. *Ibid.*, p. 85.
5. *The Advancement of Learning*, p. 228.
6. See H. Fairchild, *The Noble Savage: A Study in Romantic Naturalism* (New York, 1961), p. 22.
7. *Lollardy and the Reformation in England*, vol. I (London, 1908), p. 4.
8. H. R. Trevor-Roper, *Archbishop Laud* (London, 1965), p. 56.
9. As Gilbert Chinard observes in *L'Exotisme Américain dans la Littérature Française au XVI Siècle* (Paris, 1911).
10. On Spenser as Bruno's opponent: S. Evans, "A Lost Poem by Edmund Spenser," *Macmillan's Magazine*, 1880; "Spenser as a Philosophic Poet," *Edinburgh Review*, January, 1885, and January, 1905.
11. Wilcomb E. Washburn, "The Moral and Legal Justification for Dispossessing the Indians," in *Seventeenth-Century America: Essays in Colonial History*, ed. James M. Smith (Chapel Hill, N.C., 1967), p. 24.
12. See D. Masson, *Drummond of Hawthornden* (London, 1873), p. 139.
13. Edward Arber, *The First Three English Books on America* (London, 1885), p. xxvii.
14. W. Cunningham, *The Cosmographical Glasse*, cited by Lewis Hanke in *Aristotle and the American Indians* (London, 1959), p. 99.
15. Until 1565 the Dominican Victoria had upheld *jus commercii* as the title of conquest of the Spaniards in America; since the natives do not have the sense of property it will be necessary to make them subjects in order to be able to exercise that right.
16. Perry Miller, "The Religious Impulse in the Founding of Virginia: Religion and Society in the Early Literature," *William and Mary Quarterly*, III, 5

(1948), pp. 492–522. The ideal contact with Thomas More's fantasies is captured very well by Franca Rossi in "Le prime relazioni inglesi sulla Virginia," *Studi Americani*, vol. XI (Rome, 1965), p. 35.

17. Hakluyt Society, *Works* (London, 1849), p. 82.
18. *A Relation of the Colony of the Lord Baron of Baltimore in Maryland*, trans. N. C. Brooks (Baltimore, 1847), p. 24.
19. Daniel G. Brinton, *Myths of the New World* (New York, 1968).
20. See *Works* (Birmingham, 1884).
21. George Alsop, *A Character of the Province of Maryland* (New York, 1869), p. 73. On the political sagacity and complexity of the Powhatan confederacy: Nancy Lurie in *Indian Cultural Adjustment to European Civilization in Seventeenth-Century America* (Williamsburg, 1959).
22. Peter Forse, *Tracts and Other Papers, relating Principally to the Origin, Settlement, and Progress of the Colonies in North America*, vol. II (New York, 1947), p. 40.

CHAPTER II

1. *The Works of James F. Cooper. The Wept of Wish-ton-Wish* (New York and London, n.d.), p. 4.
2. Cited in Cyclone Covey, *American Pilgrimage* (New York, 1961), p. 21, together with other testimony to this Puritan desire to die to the world.
3. *Address Before the Society for the Promotion of Collegiate and Theological Education* (New York, 1855), cited by Walter R. Agard in "Classics on the Midwest Frontier," in W. D. Wyman and C. B. Kroeber, *The Frontier in Perspective* (Madison, Wis., 1957).
4. *William Byrd's Histories of the Dividing Line Betwixt Virginia and North Carolina*, ed. W. K. Boyd (Raleigh, 1929).
5. Elémire Zolla, "Lo Stile di Thomas Hooker" [The Style of Thomas Hooker], *Studi Americani*, vol. XI (Rome, 1965).
6. Reprinted in *Massachusetts Historical Society Collection*, 1st ser., vol. I, pp. 125–39.
7. Cited in Charles Francis Adams, *Three Episodes of Massachusetts History*, I (Boston–New York, 1903), p. 128.
8. In his *History of Plymouth Plantation, 1606–1646*, in *Original Narratives of Early American History* (New York, 1908), p. 47.
9. *Magnalia Christi Americana*, I, II, 6.
10. This is how it is regarded by Charles Francis Adams in his *Three Episodes of Massachusetts History*, pp. 28–29. Puritan historiography in its relations with the Indians is examined in every detail in the book by G. Spini, *Autobiografia della giovane America* [Autobiography of Young America] (Turin, 1968).
11. *Winthrop's Journal* (New York, 1908), vol. II, p. 18.

12. See Douglas Edward Leach, *Flintlock and Tomahawk* (New York, 1958), p. 192.
13. Richard S. Dunn, "Seventeenth-Century English Historians of America," in *Seventeenth-Century America: Essays in Colonial History*, ed. James M. Smith (Chapel Hill, N.C., 1967), pp. 195–225.
14. *Truth Held Forth and Maintained* (New York, 1695) and *New England Persecutors Mauled with Their Own Weapons* (New York, 1697).
15. *Narratives of the Indian Wars* (New York, 1913), pp. 278–79.
16. *Remarkable Providences* (London, 1890), p. 255.
17. In *American History Told by Contemporaries*, ed. A. B. Hart, vol. I (New York, 1897), pp. 458–60.

CHAPTER III

1. Truman Nelson, "The Puritans of Massachusetts: From Egypt to the Promised Land," *Judaism*, Spring, 1967.
2. Collected by J. Paul Hunter, "Friday as a Convert: Defoe and the Accounts of Indian Missionaries," *The Review of English Studies*, XIV, 55 (August, 1964).
3. See Thomas Shepard, *The Clear Sun-shine of the Gospel Breaking Forth upon the Indians in New England*, 1648 (reprinted in *Massachusetts Historical Society Collections*, 3rd ser., IV, 1834).
4. Convers Francis, *Life of John Eliot, the Apostle to the Indians* (New York, 1849), p. 67.
5. See Vernon L. Parrington, *American Dreams: A Study of American Utopias* (New York, 1964).
6. "An Account . . . of the Christian Indians," in Transactions and Collections of the American Antiquarian Society, vol. II (Cambridge, Mass., 1836).
7. J. Edwards, *The Life and Diary of David Brainerd* (Chicago, n.d.), p. 64.
8. *Ibid.*, p. 331.
9. Elémire Zolla, *Le Origini del Trascendentalismo* [The Origins of Transcendentalism] (Rome, 1963), pp. 27–28.
10. William B. O. Peabody, *Life of David Brainerd* (New York, 1856).
11. Alfred O. Aldridge, *Jonathan Edwards* (New York, 1964), pp. 43 ff.
12. Perry Miller, in his biography of Jonathan Edwards (Cleveland–New York, 1963), attempts to make a connection between his experience during his years at Stockbridge and the work on the nature of the will written in that period, but his evidence is very vague.
13. *Bonifacius* (Cambridge, Mass., 1966), p. 155.
14. H. P. Lovecraft, *At the Mountains of Madness* (Sauk City, Wis., 1964), p. 101.

15. *Wonder-Working Providence of Sions Saviour* (New York, 1910), p. 263.
16. *Ibid.,* p. 168.
17. In *Narratives of the Indian Wars* (London, 1675; New York, 1913), p. 44.
18. *Magnalia,* VII, XVIII.
19. Montague Summers, *The Geography of Witchcraft* (Evanston–New York, 1954), pp. 346 *et seq.*
20. See my preface to the Italian edition of *Septimius Felton* (Vicenza, 1966).
21. F. J. Turner, *The Frontier in American History* (New York, 1920), p. 44.
22. *The Return of the Vanishing American* (New York, 1968), p. 98.
23. See *America Begins,* ed. R. M. Dorson (New York, 1950), pp. 218–43, 286–89, 309–11.
24. Partly reprinted in R. M. Dorson, *America Rebels* (New York, 1953).

CHAPTER IV

1. Perry Miller, *Jonathan Edwards* (Cleveland–New York, 1963), pp. 255 ff.
2. Antonello Gerbi, *La disputa del nuovo mondo* [The Controversy in the New World] (Naples, 1956), p. 5.
3. That seventeenth-century ideologies revolving around a return to nature are progressivist despite their regressive fantasies is the thesis of Louis Whitney in *Primitivism and the Idea of Progress* (Baltimore, 1924).
4. William E. Alderman, "Shaftesbury and English Speculation," *Publications of the Modern Language Association,* 1928, p. 191.
5. See Raymond D. Havens, "Simplicity, a Changing Concept," *Journal of the History of Ideas,* January, 1953. C. S. Lewis traces the general history of the word in *Studies in Words* (Cambridge, 1967).
6. Republished in 1931 (Baltimore–Paris–Oxford) under the editorship of G. Chinard.
7. *Ibid.,* p. 3.
8. *Othello,* I. iii.
9. Letter to Lord Percival, March, 1723, cited by A. C. Frazer in *The Works of George Berkeley* (Oxford, 1901), vol. IV, p. 343.
10. *Ibid.,* p. 349.
11. *Ibid.,* p. 359.
12. *Ibid.,* p. 358.
13. *Ibid.,* p. 404.
14. See William B. O. Peabody's life of Oglethorpe in Jared Sparks's *Library of American Biography,* Series II, vol. II (Boston, 1844).
15. In *Narratives of Early Carolina,* ed. A. S. Salley (New York, 1911), pp. 284–85.
16. London, 1714 (rev. ed., Richmond, 1952).
17. Rev. ed., Chapel Hill, N.C., 1947.
18. Robert Beverley, *The History and Present State of Virginia,* p. 205.

19. *John and William Bartram's America,* ed. Helen G. Cruickshank (New York, 1961), p. 33.
20. N. Bryllion Fagin, *William Bartram* (Baltimore, 1933).
21. *The Papers of Benjamin Franklin,* vol. IV (New Haven, 1961), p. 148.
22. Fairchild remarks that in a later work, in 1801, *Voyage dans le Haute Pennsylvanie et dans l'Etat de New York,* Crèvecoeur, unmoved now by these charms, denounced as extravagances the praises of the woodland state, perhaps annoyed by the underhanded use made of his work by the Jacobins.
23. *The Papers of Benjamin Franklin,* vol. IV, p. 121.
24. *History of the Five Indian Nations,* London, 1727 (rev. ed., New York, 1902).
25. *The Savages of America* (Baltimore, 1965), p. 181.
26. Rush E. Welter, "The Idea of Progress in America," *Journal of the History of Ideas,* June, 1955.
27. "Address to the Agricultural Society of Albemarle," in *Letters and Other Writings,* vol. III (Philadelphia, 1865), p. 64.
28. *Poems of Philip Freneau,* vol. I (Princeton, 1902), p. 281.
29. Freneau also wrote prose essays on the subject of the Indians, and R. N. Colombo in "La Prosa di Philip Freneau" [The Prose of Philip Freneau], *Studi Americani,* vol. XIII, 1967, has supplied a good survey of this work, noting the appearance of Puritan themes, as in the condemnation of science.
30. Letter of June 28, 1812, in *The Works of John Adams,* vol. X (Boston, 1850–1856), pp. 18–20.
31. *The Yemassee,* ed. A. Cowie (New York, 1937), p. 22.
32. *Ibid.,* p. 48.
33. *Ibid.,* pp. 93–95.
34. *Ibid.,* p. 276.
35. On the Indian in Simms's work see F. C. Gozzini, "W. G. Simms e 'The Yemassee,'" *Studi Americani,* vol. XIII, 1967.
36. See Alphonso Whetmore, "Biography of Blackbird," in *America Is West,* ed. John T. Flanagan (Minneapolis, 1945), p. 53.

CHAPTER V

1. Boston, 1790. The author signs herself "Philenia, a Lady of Boston."
2. W. L. Schramm, "*Hiawatha* and Its Predecessors," *Philological Quarterly,* XI, 4 (October, 1932), p. 326.
3. Leslie Fiedler, *Love and Death in the American Novel* (New York, 1960), p. 189.
4. Arthur Ekirch, *The Idea of Progress in America, 1815–1860* (Chicago, 1952).

5. James Fenimore Cooper, *The Redskins, or Indians and Injuns*, Mohawk Edition (New York, n.d.), p. 788.
6. *Travels in the Great Western Prairies* (Poughkeepsie, 1841), cited in Henry Nash Smith, *Virgin Land* (New York, 1950), pp. 77–78.
7. New York, 1820.
8. *Illustrations of the Manners, Customs and Conditions of the North American Indians*, 9th ed. (London, 1857), vol. II, p. 225.

CHAPTER VI

1. Walter Scott, *Letters on Demonology and Witchcraft*, 1830, p. 84, citing Patrick Walker, *Biographia Presbyteriana*, II, p. 23.
2. E. D. Andrews, *The People Called Shakers* (New York, 1953), p. 89.
3. Perry Miller, *Roger Williams* (Indianapolis–New York, 1953).
4. Providence, 1936, pp. A2 ff.
5. Cited in Albert C. Applegarth, *Quakers in Pennsylvania*, in Johns Hopkins University Studies in Historical and Political Science, 10th ser., VII–IX (August–September, 1892).
6. George Bancroft, *History of the United States*, vol. II (Boston, 1873), pp. 338, 377–380.
7. In *American History Told by Contemporaries*, ed. A. B. Hart (New York, 1897), vol. I. p. 558.
8. "Positive Information from Pennsylvania," in *Narratives of Early Pennsylvania, New West Jersey and Delaware* (New York, 1912).
9. *Ibid.*
10. *Account of the History, Manners, and Customs of the Indian Nations, Who Once Inhabited Pennsylvania and the Neighboring States* (Philadelphia, 1819).
11. Edwin Cady, *John Woolman* (New York, 1965), p. 36.
12. *Jonathan Dickinson's Journal or God's Protecting Providence* (New Haven, 1961), p. 13.
13. *Ibid.*, p. 38.
14. Thomas C. Battey, *The Life and Adventures of a Quaker Among the Indians* (Norman, Okla., 1968), pp. 63–64.
15. *Ibid.*, p. 175.
16. *Ibid.*, p. 182.
17. George Bancroft, *A History of the United States*, vol. III (Boston, 1873), pp. 256–57.
18. *Ibid.*, p. 265.
19. *Ibid.*, p. 291.
20. *Ibid.*, p. 300.
21. *Ibid.*, p. 302.

22. *The Complete Poetical Works of John Greenleaf Whittier* (Boston–New York, 1894).

23. See Claude Lévi-Strauss, *Structural Anthropology* (New York, 1963), pp. 202 ff.

24. Albert Keiser, "Thoreau's Manuscripts on the Indians," *Journal of English and Germanic Philology*, XXVII, pp. 183–99.

25. Reginald L. Cook, *Passage to Walden* (New York, 1966), p. 90.

26. *Journal* (Boston, 1906), p. 294.

27. New York, 1893, vol. I, p. 4.

28. *Ibid.*, vol. II, p. 172.

29. *Crumbling Idols* (Gainesville, Fla., 1952), p. 190.

30. Owen J. Reamer, "Hamlin Garland and the Indians," *New Mexico Quarterly*, XXXIV, 3 (Autumn, 1964), p. 259.

31. *Ibid.*, pp. 260–61.

32. *Booklover's Magazine*, II, 1903.

33. *Prairie Folks* (Chicago, 1895), p. 194.

CHAPTER VII

1. In *Legends of the West* (1832) and *Sketches of History, Life, and Manners in the West* (1834).

2. Anonymous author in the *North American Review*, July, 1828, cited in Warren S. Walker, *Leatherstocking and the Critics* (Chicago, 1965), p. 14.

3. *The Works of Edgar Allan Poe*, vol. V (New York, 1908). Published anonymously in *Burton's Gentleman's Magazine*, January–June, 1840.

4. F. J. Turner, *The Frontier in American History*, (New York, 1920).

5. Robert Bird, *Nick of the Woods* (London, 1856), p. 102.

6. Cited by W. R. Agard in "Classics on the Midwest Frontier," in W. D. Wyman and C. B. Kroeber, *The Frontier in Perspective* (Madison, Wis., 1957), pp. 177–78.

7. In Lloyd McFarling, *Exploring the Northern Plains, 1804–1876* (Caldwell, Ind., 1955).

8. *Life, Letters and Travels of Father Pierre-Jean de Smet, 1801–1873*, ed. H. M. Chittenden and A. T. Richardson (New York, 1905).

9. Stanley Vestal, *Sitting Bull* (Norman, Okla., 1957), p. 109.

10. *Audubon's America*, ed. Donald C. Peattie (Boston, 1940), p. 293.

11. *Ibid.*, pp. 282, 295.

12. "At Concord," *Works of Ralph W. Emerson*, Centenary Edition, vol. XI.

13. *Life of Henry Wadsworth Longfellow*, ed. Samuel Longfellow (Boston, 1886), vol. II, p. 266.

14. Francis Parkman, *The California and Oregon Trail* (New York, 1849), pp. 324 f.

15. *Ibid.*, Preface to 1872 edition (Boston, 1895), pp. ix, x.

16. *Ibid.*, Preface to 1895 edition (Boston, 1902), pp. ix, x.

17. *Ibid.*, 1895 edition, pp. 310–11.

18. Boston, 1880, LXXX, LXXXVIII. George Henry Loskiel (1740–1814), bishop of the Moravian Church, published in 1789 *Geschichte der Mission der evangelischen Brueder unter den Indianern in Nordamerika;* English version, 1794. Samuel Jarvis, the Episcopal minister (1786–1851), presented his doctrine in *A Discourse on the Religion of the Indian Tribes of North America* (1820), which is cited at the beginning of Chapter IX: "The Literature of Reverence."

19. Francis Parkman, *The Jesuits in North America* (Boston, 1899), p. 418.

20. In *Literary Reviews and Essays by Henry James,* ed. A. Mordell (New York, 1957).

21. *In Defense of Harriet Shelley and Other Essays* (New York–London, 1918), p. 264.

22. *The Works of William Ellery Channing* (Boston, 1892), pp. 856, 672.

23. Sydney J. Krause, "Cooper's Literary Offences: Mark Twain in Wonderland," *New England Quarterly,* September, 1965.

24. Elizabeth Madox Roberts, *The Great Meadow* (New York, 1930), pp. 24, 105–6.

25. *Saratoga* by Eliza Cushing and *Hobomok* by Lydia Maria Child, both published in 1824, begin the series.

26. Robert Rogers wrote the first of these in 1766, *Ponteach, or the Savages of America,* which speaks out against the frauds and thefts suffered by the Indians. In 1808 *The Indian Princess; or La Belle Sauvage,* by J. N. Barker appeared, and thirty-five other plays were written over the century.

27. Nicholas J. Karolides, *The Pioneer in the American Novel, 1900–1950* (Norman, Okla., 1967). Also Henry N. Smith, *Virgin Land: The American West as Symbol and Myth* (Cambridge., Mass., 1950).

28. See the two passages in Robert Taft's *Artists and Illustrators of the Old West, 1850–1900* (New York, 1953), p. 66, and Lloyd McFarling, *Exploring the Northern Plains, 1804–1876,* p. 374.

CHAPTER VIII

1. "The Ethnological Significance of Esoteric Doctrines," *Science,* n.s., vol. XVI, p. 902, included in *Race, Language and Culture* (New York, 1940).

2. *Ibid.,* p. 323.

3. *Algic Researches,* vol. I (New York, 1839), p. 10.

4. *Historical and Statistical Information Respecting the History, Conditions, and Prospects of the Indian Tribes of the United States* (Philadelphia, 1851), Part I pp. 327 ff.

5. *Algic Researches,* vol. II, p. 80.

6. Henry R. Schoolcraft, *The Myth of Hiawatha and Other Oral Legends, Mythological and Allegoric of the North American Indians* (Philadelphia, 1856), p. xvii.

7. Daniel G. Brinton, *The Iroquois Book of Rites,* Library of Aboriginal American Literature (New York, 1882–1890), pp. 37–38.

8. *Ibid.,* p. 189.

9. *Ibid.,* p. 190.

10. Henry R. Schoolcraft, *Algic Researches,* vol. II, pp. 50–51.

11. In *The Knickerbocker Gallery* (New York, 1855), p. 376.

12. Elémire Zolla, "Le Fonti e la Struttura di 'Clarel'" [The Sources and Structure of *Clarel*], *Studi Americani,* X, 1964. Schoolcraft has already written in *Algic Researches:* "Medical magic spread the charms of its delusions over the semi-barbaric tribes who, at a very early epoch, spread from the Arabian Gulf to the Mediterranean."

13. Schoolcraft, *Historical and Statistical Information Respecting the Indian Tribes of the United States.*

14. Schoolcraft, *The Indian Tribes of the United States* (Philadelphia, 1884), p. 185.

15. Roy H. Pearce, *The Savages of America* (Baltimore, 1965), p. 130.

16. Lewis H. Morgan, *Houses and House-Life of the American Aborigines* (Washington, 1881).

17. See Elémire Zolla, "La Città Perfetta" [The Perfect City] in *L'Approdo Letterario* (Turin, 1967).

18. *The Unpublished Letters of Adolph F. Bandelier* (New York, 1942), p. 3.

19. New York, 1890. All quotations are from the New York, 1971, reprint.

20. Charles F. Lummis testifies to this in his note, "In Memory," in the 1971 (New York) edition of *The Delight Makers.*

CHAPTER IX

1. Samuel Farmar Jarvis, *A Discourse on the Religion of the Indian Tribes of North America,* in *Collections of the New York Historical Society,* 1st ser., vol. 3, p. 1.

2. *Ibid.,* p. 190.

3. *A Traveler in Indian Territory, Journal of Ethan Allen Hitchcock,* ed. Grant Foreman (Cedar Rapids, 1930).

4. Margery Silver, Preface to *Etruscan Magic and Occult Remedies* (New York, 1963), p. xxviii.

5. Charles G. Leland, *The Algonquin Legends of New England* (Boston and New York, 1884), pp. 2–3. Prior to this collection, only a few legends had been published, edited by S. T. Rand, in *The Dominion Monthly,* 1871.

6. *Ibid.,* pp. 338 f.

7. *Ibid.,* p. 339.

8. *Ibid.*, p. 350.

9. *Ibid.*, p. 376.

10. Minnie Myrtle, *The Iroquois, or The Bright Side of Indian Character* (New York, 1855), p. 47.

11. Stanley Vestal, *Sitting Bull: Champion of the Sioux* (Norman, Okla., 1957), p. 256.

12. James Mooney, "The Ghost-Dance Religion and the Sioux Outbreak of 1890," Fourteenth Annual Report, Bureau of American Ethnology, Washington, D.C., 1896.

13. Harriet Converse, *Myths and Legends of the New York Iroquois* (New York, 1962).

14. B. H. Haile, *Starlore Among the Navaho* (Santa Fe, 1947). The Navajo taught that in ancient times the sky was in perfect order and that later it was disrupted by the coyote, the "trickster."

15. Converse, *Myths and Legends*, p. 53.

16. John G. Bourke, "The Medicine Man of the Apache," Ninth Annual Report, Bureau of American Ethnology, Washington, D.C., 1892.

17. G. B. Grinnell, *Where Buffalo Ran* (New Haven, 1920).

18. G. B. Grinnell, *Pawnee, Blackfoot and Cheyenne* (New York, 1961), pp. 25–26.

19. William G. Simms, *The Yemassee* (New York, 1937), p. 16.

20. G. B. Grinnell, "The Boy Who Was Sacrificed," *Pawnee Hero Stories and Folk Tales* (Lincoln, Neb., 1961), pp. 161 f.

21. G. B. Grinnell, "The Ghost Bride," *Pawnee Hero Stories*, p. 193.

22. G. B. Grinnell, *Blackfoot Lodge Tales* (Lincoln, Neb., 1962), pp. 93 ff.

23. Walter McClintock, *Old North Trail* (Lincoln, Neb., 1968), p. 32.

24. "Bullying the Moqui," Prescott, Ariz., 1968, p. 32.

25. *The Bridge* (New York, 1970).

26. T. M. Pearce, *Mary Hunter Austin* (New Haven, 1965), pp. 52–53.

27. Mary Austin, *The Land of Little Rain* (Boston, 1903).

28. "The Basket Maker," *The Land of Little Rain*, pp. 163–79.

29. Henry J. Forman, "On a Letter from Mary Austin," *New Mexico Quarterly*, XXX, 4 (Winter, 1961–62).

30. "Non-English Writing," in *Cambridge History of American Literature*, IV (New York, 1921), p. 615.

31. *The Arrow Maker* (Boston, 1915), Preface.

32. *The American Rhythm* (Boston, 1930).

33. *Chippewa Music*, Bureau of American Ethnology, Bulletin No. 45, Washington, D.C., passim.

34. *Teton Sioux Music*, Bureau of American Ethnology, Bulletin No. 61, Washington, D.C., p. 352.

35. Mary Austin, in *The Path on the Rainbow: An Anthology of Songs and*

Chants from the Indians of North America (New York, 1918), pp. 223–24, 222–23.

36. Dorothy Brett, *Lawrence and Brett: A Friendship* (New York, 1938), p. 83.

37. *The Winged Serpent: An Anthology of American Indian Prose and Poetry,* ed. Margot Astrov (New York, 1946), p. 3.

38. Eda Lou Walton, *Dawn Boy: Blackfoot and Navajo Songs* (New York, 1926), p. 72.

39. W. B. Yeats, *Ideas of Good and Evil* (New York, 1957), pp. 247–48.

40. *The Path on the Rainbow* (New York, 1918), p. xvi.

41. Willa Cather, *Death Comes for the Archbishop* (New York, 1964), p. 234.

CHAPTER X

1. "Waiyautitsa of Zuni," *The Scientific Monthly,* November, 1919.

2. Norman, Okla., 1945, p. 46. Alice Marriott also wrote a book, *Maria, the Potter of San Ildefonso,* about the Pueblo Indians.

3. Theodora Kroeber, *Ishi in Two Worlds* (Berkeley, Calif., 1964), p. 177.

4. Laura Thompson and Alice Joseph, *The Hopi Way,* with a foreword by John Collier, Commissioner of Indian Affairs, New York. First published in 1944 by the United States Indian Service; reissued 1965. See also John Collier, *Patterns and Ceremonials of the Indians of the Southwest* (New York, 1949), p. 63.

5. New York, 1929. It received the Pulitzer Prize for 1929. In 1942 La Farge edited the symposium, *The Changing Indian.*

6. Frank Waters, *The Man Who Killed the Deer* (Toronto, 1942), p. 133.

7. *Ibid.,* p. 150.

8. *Ibid.,* p. 252.

9. Leslie Fiedler, *The Return of the Vanishing American* (New York, 1968), pp. 170–71.

10. "Two Views of Nature: White and Indian," *South Dakota Review,* May, 1964.

11. "The Novels of William Eastlake," *New Mexico Quarterly,* Summer, 1964.

12. *Three by Eastlake* (New York, 1970), p. 3.

13. *Crazy Horse* (Lincoln, Neb.), 1961.

14. *Ibid.,* p. 230.

15. Among them, "La psychologie religieuse des Achumawi," *Anthropos,* 1929.

16. *Witch Doctor* (New York, 1959), reprinted as *Shaman* (New York, 1972), p. 16.

17. *Ibid.,* p. 39.

18. *Ibid.,* p. 57.

19. *Dance Back the Buffalo* (New York, 1959), p. 273.

20. *Ibid.,* p. 77.

21. New York, 1963.

22. *When the Legends Die,* p. 18.
23. Richard Lancaster, *Piegan* (New York, 1966), p. 119.
24. New York, 1964.
25. Thomas Berger, *Little Big Man,* p. 44.
26. New York, 1951.

CHAPTER XI

1. Lawrence C. Wroth, "The Indian Treaty as Literature," *Yale Review,* July, 1928.
2. Walter J. Meserve, Jr., "English Works of Seventeenth-Century Indians," *American Quarterly,* Fall, 1956.
3. *Walam Olum or Red Score: The Migration Legend of the Lenni Lenape or Delaware Indians* (Indianapolis, 1954).
4. See Ake V. Strom, "Red Indian Elements in Early Mormonism," *Temenos, Studies in Comparative Religion,* vol. V, Helsinki, 1969.
5. *Geronimo's Story of His Life,* ed. S. M. Barrett (New York, 1906).
6. Charles Alexander Eastman (Ohiyesa), *The Soul of the Indian, An Interpretation* (Boston–New York, 1911).
7. New edition (Lincoln, Neb., 1962), pp. 11–13.
8. *Wooden Leg: A Warrior Who Fought Custer,* interpreted by Thomas B. Marquis (Lincoln, Neb., 1957), pp. 123, 130, 137.
9. *University of California Publications in American Archaeology and Ethnology,* vol. 33, no. 5 (1934), pp. 423–38.
10. *Memoirs of the American Anthropological Association,* No. 46 (1936), Suppl. vol. 38, no. 2, pt. 2, Menasha, Wis.
11. *Son of Old Man Hat,* transcribed by Walter Dyk (Lincoln, Neb., 1967), p. ix.
12. Alice C. Fletcher, "The Hako: A Pawnee Ceremony," Bureau of American Ethnology, Twenty-second Annual Report, Part 2 (1904).
13. Mary Austin, *The American Rhythm* (Boston, 1930), p. 174.
14. *The Story of the Red Indian* (New York, 1944), prologue; and *The Winnebago Indians,* Bureau of American Ethnology, Twenty-seventh Annual Report (1905–06).
15. Radin first published it in part in the *Journal of American Folklore* (1913), then in more extended versions in the sixteenth volume of the *University of California Publications in American Archaeology and Ethnology* under the title *The Autobiography of an American Indian;* and finally there appeared the last and popular version—*Crashing Thunder, The Autobiography of an American Indian* (New York, 1926).
16. Nancy O. Lurie, *Mountain Wolf Woman, Sister of Crashing Thunder: The Autobiography of a Winnebago Indian* (Ann Arbor, Mich., 1961), p. 41.

17. Peter Nabokov, *Two Leggings: The Making of a Crow Warrior* (New York, 1967).

18. "War and Vision: The Autobiography of a Crow Indian," *The Catholic Worker*, December, 1967, p. 4.

19. *Sun Chief: The Autobiography of a Hopi Indian*, ed. Leo W. Simmons (New Haven, 1942).

20. Georges Devereux, "L'envoûtement chez les Indiens Mohave," *Journal de la Société des Américanistes*, vol. XXIX (Paris, 1937), p. 2.

21. *Navaho Witchcraft* (Boston, 1962).

22. John G. Neihardt, *Black Elk Speaks* (Lincoln, Neb., 1961).

23. *Arizona Republic*, August 28, 1966.

24. Joseph Epes Brown, *The Sacred Pipe: The Spiritual Legacy of the American Indian*, Pendle Hill Pamphlet No. 135 (Lebanon, Pa., 1964), pp. 10–11.

25. *The Sacred Pipe: Black Elk's Account of the Seven Rites of the Oglala Sioux*, recorded and edited by Joseph Epes Brown (Norman, Okla., 1953). The persistence of Black Elk's teachings is proved by the activities of the esoteric Black Elk Kituhwa Society, whose rites of purification (Inipi) were described in the Indian newspaper *Many Smokes* (Second Quarter, 1967).

26. *Indians of the United States* (New York, 1966), p. 59.

27. "The Symbolic Man of the Osage Tribe," *Art and Archaeology*, vol. IX, no. 2, pp. 68–72. The information provided by Henry R. Schoolcraft in *Historical and Statistical Information Respecting the . . . Indian Tribes of the United States* merely skims the surface.

28. Brown, *The Sacred Pipe: The Spiritual Legacy of the American Indian*, p. 25.

29. Hartley Burr Alexander, *The World's Rim* (Lincoln, Neb., 1953), p. 10.

30. Preface to the French edition of *The Sacred Pipe. Hekaka Sapa; Les Rites Secrets des Indiens Sioux* (Paris, 1953).

31. Frank Johnson Newcomb, *Hosteen Klah: Navaho Medicine Man and Sand Painter* (Norman, Okla., 1964), p. 122.

32. *The Peyote Ritual: Visions and Descriptions of Monroe Tsa Toke* (San Francisco, 1957), pp. 7–8, 33.

33. N. Scott Momaday, *House Made of Dawn* (New York, 1966), p. 57.

CHAPTER XII

1. *The Writers' Reader, Creative Writing Classes, 1962–1966*, Institute of Indian Arts, Santa Fe.

2. New York, 1968.

Index